EUROPEAN STUDIES ON CHRISTIAN ORIGINS

Published under
LIBRARY OF NEW TESTAMENT STUDIES
426

Formerly the Journal for the Study of the New Testament Supplement series

THE FOURTH GOSPEL
IN FIRST-CENTURY MEDIA CULTURE

Edited by

ANTHONY LE DONNE
TOM THATCHER

t&t clark

Published by T&T Clark International
A Continuum Imprint
The Tower Building, 11 York Road, London SE1 7NX
80 Maiden Lane, Suite 704, New York, NY 10038

www.continuumbooks.com

British Library Cataloguing-in-Publication Data
A catalogue record for this book is available from the British Library

ISBN: HB: 978-0-567-46468-2

Typeset by Free Range Book Design & Production Ltd
Printed and bound in Great Britain

CONTENTS

CONTRIBUTORS   vii

1   Introducing Media Culture to Johannine Studies: Orality,
Performance and Memory
Anthony Le Donne and Tom Thatcher   1

Part I: John and Oral Culture

2   Seeing, Hearing, Declaring, Writing: Media Dynamics in
the Letters of John
Jeffrey E. Brickle   11

3   The Riddle of the Baptist and the Genesis of the Prologue:
John 1.1-18 in Oral/Aural Media Culture
Tom Thatcher   29

4   A Performance of the Text: The Adulteress's Entrance
into John's Gospel
Chris Keith   49

Part II: John as Oral Performance

5   John's Memory Theatre: A Study of Composition in
Performance
Tom Thatcher   73

6   The Medium and Message of John: Audience Address and
Audience Identity in the Fourth Gospel
Thomas E. Boomershine   92

7   Jesus Retold as the World's Light in Johannine Oral
Prophecy
Antoinette Wire   121

8   Scripture *Talks* because Jesus *Talks*: The Narrative
Rhetoric of Persuading and Creativity in John's Use
of Scripture
Michael Labahn   133

Contents

Part III: John in the Medium of Memory

9   John's Gospel and the Oral Gospel Tradition
      James D. G. Dunn   157

10   Memory, Commemoration and History in John 2.19-22:
      A Critique and Application of Social Memory
      Anthony Le Donne   186

11   Abraham as a Figure of Memory in John 8.31-59
      Catrin H. Williams   205

Part IV: Reflections and Directions

12   What Difference Does the Medium Make?
      Barry Schwartz   225

13   Introducing Media Culture to Johannine Studies:
      Orality, Performance and Memory
      Gail R. O'Day   239

BIBLIOGRAPHY   251

INDEX   279

CONTRIBUTORS

Tom Boomershine was formerly Professor of Christianity and Communication at United Theological Seminary (USA). The founder of the Network of Biblical Storytellers, and of the Bible in Ancient and Modern Media Section in the Society of Biblical Literature, Tom has long been a leading figure in the study of ancient and modern media culture. He is the author of a wide range of articles on the Gospels as narrative and digital biblical hermeneutics, and also of *Story Journey: An Invitation to the Gospel as Storytelling* (Abingdon 1988). He is currently completing a media commentary on Mark's passion narrative.

Jeffrey E. Brickle (PhD, Concordia Seminary, St Louis) is Associate Professor of Biblical Studies at Urshan Graduate School of Theology in Florissant, Missouri. His research focuses on the confluence of ancient media culture with Johannine literature. He recently completed his doctoral dissertation, entitled 'Aural Design and Coherence in the Prologue of First John'.

James D. G. Dunn, MA, BD, PhD, DD, FBA, is Emeritus Lightfoot Professor of Divinity at Durham University, where he taught from 1982 to 2003. He is now retired to Chichester in West Sussex. His recent publications include *Theology of Paul the Apostle* (Eerdmans 1998), *Christianity in the Making: Vol. 1, Jesus Remembered* (Eerdmans 2003), *Vol. 2, Beginning from Jerusalem* (Eerdmans 2009), *The New Perspective on Paul* (revised; Eerdmans 2008), *New Testament Theology: An Introduction* (Abingdon 2009), *The Living Word* (second edition; Fortress 2009), and *Did the First Christians Worship Jesus? The New Testament Evidence* (SPCK/WJK 2010).

Chris Keith (PhD, University of Edinburgh) is Assistant Professor of New Testament and Christian Origins at Lincoln Christian University (Lincoln, IL). He is the author of *The Pericope Adulterae, the Gospel of John, and the Literacy of Jesus* (Brill 2009), a winner of the 2010 John Templeton Award for Theological Promise, and *Jesus' Literacy: Scribal Culture and the Teacher from Galilee* (T&T Clark, forthcoming).

Michael Labahn is '*Privatdozent*' at the Martin-Luther-University of Halle-Wittenberg, Germany, and a scientific researcher at postdoctoral level in a DFG (*Deutsche Forschungsgemeinschaft*) project of the Kirchliche Hochschule, Wuppertal, Germany. He is the author and editor of numerous books and articles in German and English, including *Jesus als Lebensspender* (1999), *Offenbarung in Zeichen und Wort* (2000), *Der Gekommene als Wiederkommender. Die Logienquelle als erzählte Geschichte* (ABG 32; Leipzig: Evangelische Verlagsanstalt 2010), and *Repetitions and Variations in the Fourth Gospel* (with Gilbert van Belle and Petrus Maritz, 2009). He currently serves as editor of the ESCO series and is a member of the LNTS series editorial board. His research focuses on the Fourth Gospel and the Sayings Gospel, and he is currently preparing a commentary on the Apocalypse of John.

Anthony Le Donne (PhD, Durham University) is Assistant Professor of New Testament and Second Temple Judaism at Lincoln Christian University, Lincoln, Illinois. He is the author of *The Historiographical Jesus: Memory, Typology, and the Son of David* (Baylor University Press 2009) and *Historical Jesus: What Can We Know and How Can We Know It?* (Eerdmans 2010). Together with Jacob Neusner and Bruce Chilton he is co-editing *Soundings in The Religion of Jesus* (Fortress, forthcoming in 2012). His home on the web is anthonyledonne.com.

Gail R. O'Day is Dean and Professor of New Testament and Preaching at the Wake Forest University School of Divinity. She has written the commentary on the Gospel of John in *The New Interpreter's Bible* and is editor or co-editor of several volumes, including the *Oxford Access Bible* and the *Theological Bible Commentary*. She was editor of *JBL* from 1999 to 2006, and is currently General Editor of the SBL book series *Early Christianity and its Literature*.

Barry Schwartz, Professor Emeritus of Sociology at the University of Georgia, has addressed collective memory issues through his work on American presidents (*Abraham Lincoln in the Post-Heroic Era*, 2008) and on comparative studies involving the United States, Germany and modern Israel, as well as Japan, Korea and China (*Northeast Asia's Difficult Past*, 2010). He is presently at work on the third part of a trilogy of books on Abraham Lincoln in American memory.

Tom Thatcher is Professor of Biblical Studies at Cincinnati Christian University. He has authored or edited numerous books and articles on the Johannine Literature and early Christian media culture, including *Memory, Tradition, and Text* (with Alan Kirk; SBL 2005), *Why John Wrote a Gospel* (WJK 2006), and *Jesus, the Voice, and the Text* (Baylor University Press 2008). A co-founder and former chair of the 'Mapping

Memory' research group in the Society of Biblical Literature, Tom now serves on the programme committee of the SBL's Bible in Ancient and Modern Media section.

Catrin Williams is a senior lecturer in the School of Theology at the University of Wales, Trinity Saint David. She is the author of numerous works on the Johannine Literature and the Jewish context of early Christianity, including *I Am He* (Mohr Siebeck 2000). Catrin is a member of the steering committee for the John, Jesus, and History Group in the Society of Biblical Literature, and she recently organized and convened the conference 'John's Gospel and Intimations of Apocalyptic' at the University of Wales, Bangor. Her current research interests include the memorial dynamics of early Christ tradition, and the reception of the book of Isaiah in late Second Temple Judaism.

Antoinette Clark Wire is Professor Emerita at San Francisco Theological Seminary and the Graduate Theological Union in Berkeley, California. She is author of *Holy Lives, Holy Deaths: A Close Hearing of Early Jewish Storytellers* (SBL Press 2002). Her book *The Case for Mark Composed in Performance* will be available this autumn from Cascade Books, Wipf and Stock Press.

Chapter 1

INTRODUCING MEDIA CULTURE TO JOHANNINE STUDIES:
ORALITY, PERFORMANCE AND MEMORY

Anthony Le Donne and Tom Thatcher

This book seeks to introduce Johannine specialists to the potential value of
ancient media studies and to illustrate ways in which the Fourth Gospel and
the Johannine Epistles might be reconsidered from ancient media perspectives.
In recent decades, major currents in Johannine scholarship have followed
four well-worn channels of research: the Fourth Gospel's historical value (or
lack thereof); the sources of the Johannine tradition and possible relationships between that tradition and the Synoptic trajectory; the compositional
development of the text, particularly the relationship between the Gospel's
composition-history and the history of the Johannine community; and the
potential inherent in reading the Gospel as a self-contained narrative whole.
While each of these paths has provided unique and valuable insights, all have
tended to neglect the media culture in which the Johannine Christians lived
and in which Johannine literature was produced. This lacuna is particularly
notable for two reasons: first, because scholarship on the Synoptic Gospels
has been significantly informed by media issues for at least the past 25 years;
secondly, because all four of the major interpretive trends noted above are
largely dependent on implicit assumptions about the ways that Johannine
Christians remembered Jesus and communicated their ideas about him orally
and in writing. The essays in the present volume, both individually and taken
collectively, proceed from the assumption that *the Johannine Literature was
a product of first-century media culture and, in turn, significantly contributed
to early Christian memory and identity*. This book will thus illustrate the
interpretive potential of media criticism for understanding the Gospel of John
and the Johannine Epistles.

   The term 'ancient media culture' is shorthand for several overlapping
sets of interests related to the cognitive and communications environment(s)
of antiquity. Studies of the Bible's media culture are generally concerned
with three sets of interlocking issues: the nature of *ancient oral cultures*; the
dynamics of *ancient oral performance*; and the workings of *memory*. As a
corollary, the intersection of these three concerns has led to an increasing
interest in aurality, particularly in the active dimensions of *hearing* oral

art/texts/traditions performed and in the hermeneutical implications of the relationship between a composer and a live listening audience. A brief overview of the types of concerns carried by each of these three streams will contextualize the more focused essays to follow in this volume.

Oral Culture

The texts of the New Testament emerged from a society that was largely illiterate yet keenly invested in the memorization and rehearsal of significant textual traditions (see Hezser 2001: 496; Thatcher 2006: 37–49). Indeed, in the New Testament period even written texts were oral in nature, as documents were generally written by dictation to an amanuensis and then recited aloud to groups in public readings.[1] This means that ancient Jesus traditions and other early Christian communications were created and re-created in a media culture quite different from that of the modern Western world.[2] Rather than describing the traditioning process in terms of 'transmitting', 'writing', 'revising' and/or 'copying' fixed texts, oral-traditional culture is better characterized as a complex matrix of communicative influences upon multiple trajectories of recollections of the past – recollections of both the actual past and of past discussions/commemorations of those events. These communicative patterns are critical not only for understanding how people in oral cultures communicate, but also for developing adequate models of cognitive processes and identity formation in traditional societies, including those of the ancient Mediterranean world.

Oral historians are primarily interested in how societies remember people, events, myths and other cultural dialectics in the absence of, or alongside, written documentation. Indeed, in most pre-modern and/or largely illiterate societies, orality is the default venue for the passing on of tradition and the creation of collective identity. Moreover, since 'history proper' is normally written and disseminated by the educated, the politically dominant and the social elite, oral history often provides a window into the perspectives of the oppressed and the marginalized. Perhaps for this very reason, until very recently literate historians and biblical scholars tended to treat oral history as inferior to formal historiography, emphasizing the perceived unreliability of collective memory and oral traditioning processes. As children of von

---

1   As Richard Horsley notes, 'In an environment in which communication was mainly oral, oral forms, techniques, and style carried over in the production of manuscripts' (2006: x).

2   See Chris Keith's essay in the present book for a nuanced approach to the interaction between oral and written tradition (cf. Gamble 2000: 646; Parker 1997: 179, 205). But inasmuch as most scholars still operate with a literary model of transmission, it remains helpful to emphasize the important differences between a primarily oral culture and highly literate Western societies.

Ranke (i.e., historical positivism) born into the Gutenberg galaxy, biblical scholars in the modern period have tended to believe that written books are capable of preserving facts in ways that oral histories cannot. Today, however, historians do not automatically grant a higher degree of factuality to written texts, nor do they extol factuality as the highest virtue of historiography. Conversely, there is now a greater recognition of the balance between stability and variability achieved within oral cultures, and of the fact that oral recollections tend to move toward fixed and durable forms as the core of a tradition stabilizes (Bowman and Woolf 1994; Harris 1989; Lord 1968; Ong 1982; Vansina 1985; Watchel 1996). As a result of these trends, recent schools of thought have narrowed the perceived gap between written text and spoken word, and oral history has emerged as a respectable sub-field within university history departments.

While Johannine scholars have largely overlooked their implications, increasing awareness of the dynamics of oral culture has begun to significantly impact studies of the Synoptic problem, the communities behind the biblical texts, historical Jesus research, the rhetorical/compositional structure of the Pauline letters, and the manuscript history of the New Testament. The pioneering works of Birger Gerhardsson (1961) and Werner Kelber (1983) reframed Synoptic studies in terms of contemporary research in orality, making significant strides beyond the overly linear conception of the interfaces between oral and written texts that had limited the earlier work of Dibelius, Bultmann and other form critics.[3] Parallel to the continued work of Kelber, a number of recent studies of the Jesus tradition have reconceptualized the object of their inquiry by taking oral culture seriously (see, for example, Byrskog 1994, 2002; Dunn 2003; Foley 1988; Harvey 1998; Mournet 2005). Serious attention to orality has also undermined overly-literary explanations of the Synoptic problem. James Dunn (2003) and Terence Mournet (2005) have argued that the variances in Jesus tradition manifested from Gospel to Gospel show remarkable affinity to the variances that folklorists expect from traditional oral compositions. Rather than viewing the Synoptic problem in terms of the various Evangelists gathering and editing literary sources in a unidirectional way, students of orality suggest a complex of intersecting influences that shift around a stable core of tradition. Serious attention to orality also has the capacity to undermine one of the chief presuppositions of textual criticism: the quest to reconstruct 'the original manuscripts'. If a story has been given life within an oral culture, there simply is no 'original' text to be reconstructed, but rather an ongoing, multi-generational interaction between tellers and audiences with scribes acting as tradents in the traditioning process. In an oral context, a story can be told with varying

---

3   The groundbreaking work of Joanna Dewey (1989) and Paul Achtemeier (1990) should also be mentioned here.

details according to the occasion of the telling and still be recognized as the 'same' story.

The essays in Part I of this volume explore various interfaces between the Fourth Gospel and its oral media culture. *Jeffrey Brickle* discusses the nature of, and impetus for, letter-writing in the ancient world by focusing on 1 John. Adopting Thatcher's (2005; 2006) thesis that, for the Johannine community, the written word held a symbolic authority that oral communication did not, Brickle contends that 1 John was written to wield a unifying power in the face of a possible church split. Because each faction in the debate had equal access to the Johannine oral tradition (as mediated by the Holy Spirit), 1 John was written to quell attempts to misconstrue the memory upon which Johannine Christians based their collective identity. Brickle also discusses the interplay between oration for writing and writing for oration in the Johannine context. He argues that the Johannine Letters invoked formative memories to confront the Johannine community's present identity crisis.

Tom Thatcher's essay revisits the question of the composition-history of the Fourth Gospel's prologue (John 1.1-18). Thatcher challenges the consensus view that the prologue is a traditional hymn that was contaminated by the interpolation of details about John the Baptist. Oral performers and aural audiences would not think in terms of interruptions of, or interpolations into, an original text; rather, they would have heard alternate performances of familiar material as distinct texts with particular meanings. Further, the specific compositional dynamics of the prologue suggest that the material on the Baptist is not an interpolation; rather, John 1.1-18 is better understood as an interpretive expansion of the traditional saying attributed to John the Baptist at 1.15. Thus, when viewed in the context of its oral media environment, the prologue emerges as a highly unified textual unit that was likely composed from traditional material at the same time as the Gospel narrative that it now introduces.

Finally, *Chris Keith*'s essay sheds new light on the issue of Jesus's literacy and the impetus for the textual placement of John 7.53–8.11. While most explain the insertion (or deletion) of the story of the Adulterous Woman in terms of the pericope's ideological content, Keith suggests that this story was added to the Fourth Gospel as a unique witness to Jesus's literacy and, hence, of his academic credentials as a biblical interpreter. Keith further undermines the central presupposition of textual criticism by suggesting that there never was an 'original form' of the Gospel of John. Clearly, the fact that early manuscripts were capable of absorbing this non-Johannine (possibly oral) traditional story suggests that ancient readers had different conceptions of the boundaries of the 'Johannine' tradition and of the physical text of the Fourth Gospel than do many modern scholars. Finally, Keith explores the implications of his discussion by challenging the assumption that written tradition existed in a 'static' mode while oral tradition existed in a 'performance' mode. In his view, even written texts such as the Gospel of John were capable of adapting to the performance needs of their audiences.

Oral Performance

Oral performance criticism emphasizes the cultural prevalence and compositional impact of public recitations and audience responses. Depending on the venue and the relationship between teller and audience, an ancient oral performance could involve demonstrative interaction that substantially impacted the shape of the spoken text. Thus, oral performances can and will vary in content, gesture, metre, volume and tone based on the immediate presence and response of the aural audience. A simple request for clarification, stated verbally or merely in the form of facial expression and body language, might create a long parenthetical digression or clarification of details absent from other tellings but true to the core of the composition. Importantly, while individual tellings or public readings may vary widely, the framework of an oral composition will most often remain intact so that it may be recognized as the 'same' text that has been composed on previous occasions in other settings. Recognition of these dynamics of oral performance – which would be typical of the social contexts in which the New Testament documents were produced – has led ancient media specialists to emphasize the notion of 'multiple originals': every performance context that includes a teller and an audience is a unique social interaction that produces a unique text. In short, the oral performer or orally performing text (a text written to be read aloud to a listening audience) must conform to the expectations, demands, presuppositions, prejudices, attitudes and direct interactions of a live audience. Obviously, this communications environment differs quite significantly from that of modern authors whose readers are never present at the moment of composition. With respect to the Jesus tradition, scholars now imagine varying contexts of performance and varying degrees of audience participation (see Dewey 1992; Gamble 1995; Hearon 2006; Shiner 2003; Upton 2006).

The essays in Part II of this volume explore the implications of oral performance dynamics for the interpretation of the Fourth Gospel. *Tom Thatcher*'s article provides a comprehensive paradigm for understanding Johannine compositional techniques. Appealing to a wide range of ancient rhetorical theories on the interface between memory and live performance, Thatcher suggests that the Fourth Evangelist utilized a 'memory theatre' model of composition. While ancient texts were composed and performed orally, rhetoricians and storytellers typically used visual memory strategies to organize and recite information. Following this approach, John narrated stories about Jesus through techniques of visualization that shaped both the content and structure of his presentation.

Tom Boomershine's essay describes the Fourth Gospel as an evangelistic tool aimed at the conversion of non-Christian Jews. Taking cues from first-century performance culture, Boomershine suggests that audiences of oral recitations of the Gospel would have slipped naturally into the role of Jesus's dialogue partners during the presentation of his speeches. These dialogue partners include sympathetic characters such as the disciples, Nicodemus and

Peter, but also, and perhaps most often, 'Jews' who reject Jesus's claims. Thus, in public recitations of the text, both Jewish and Christian audiences would have heard Jesus's words to unbelieving Jewish characters as a direct address to themselves, and would have been encouraged to reflect on the adequacy of their own understanding of Christ. This being the case, Boomershine argues that the Fourth Gospel was written and performed primarily for Jewish audiences who were undecided on Jesus's identity, and thus at a time before the Johannine community had left the synagogue. Obviously, this approach not only departs from traditional media models that picture the Fourth Evangelist writing silently for private readers, but also significantly challenges the long-standing consensus that the Gospel of John was written for believing Christians and expresses a hostile attitude toward Jewish people.

Antoinette Wire's essay challenges traditional developmental approaches to the composition of the Fourth Gospel on the basis of oral media dynamics. Her discussion of prophetic speech takes seriously John's notable emphasis on the memorial work of the Holy Spirit. Wire suggests that John's famous 'I am' sayings are best understood as the product of the prophetic spirit, as Jesus's traditional words were re-narrated as first-person declarations before live audiences in order to harness the rhetorical impact of Christ's authoritative presence. This being the case, the problem of the historical value of the Fourth Gospel must be re-envisioned in terms of the evolving reality of the ongoing presence of Jesus in the life of the Johannine community. Wire's analysis of John 9, a chapter that has functioned as the *crux interpretum* of the Johannine literature for four decades now, illustrates the implications of this compositional model as a case study.

Finally, *Michael Labahn's* essay argues that the Fourth Gospel portrays the Jewish Scriptures as both a written authority and a speaking character. While the Johannine Jesus uses persuasive speech to claim undisputed authority for himself as an interpreter of the Jewish Bible, the Scriptures themselves would speak directly to the audience when recited in oral performance. Building on these observations, Labahn describes the Gospel's relationship to Jewish Scripture in terms of the hermeneutical process of 'oral enactment', a dynamic model that moves beyond long-standing debates about the precise sources and accuracy of John's 'citations' of the Bible. Viewed in terms of oral performance, the Scriptures that appear in the Fourth Gospel should not be understood as embedded chunks culled from earlier documents, but rather as a dynamic form of divine communication that continues to testify on Jesus's behalf alongside the voices of other characters that function as 'witnesses'.

Memory as Medium

Building on the seminal work of French sociologist Maurice Halbwachs (1925; 1941), social memory theorists argue that memory is not a passive retrieval of stored information, but rather a fluid and creative process that conforms the realities of the actual past to the needs of the present. Past and present must be linked simply because memory is formative for a group's collective identity and sense of continuity with earlier generations. This being the case, memory is never perceived outside of social frameworks; rather, it is always spurred and constrained by social contexts (see J. Assmann 1992; 1995; 2000; Connerton 1989; Fentress and Wickham 1992; Hutton 1993; Namer 1987; Nora 1989; Schwartz 1982; 2000; E. Zerubavel 2003; Y. Zerubavel 1995).[4]

Social memory theorists think of 'memory' not as the content of recollections, but rather as a dynamic *dialogue* that is continually reconfigured by the immediate social frameworks in which speech about the past is localized. Because events are inherently subject to multiple interpretations, impressions of the actual past require constant redefinition to remain intelligible and relevant. One of the more significant cross-cultural strategies of redefinition involves narrativization, the process of organizing and structuring recollections in the form of stories with linear sequences. Beginnings, settings, climaxes and conclusions are (often subconsciously) imposed upon memories in order to arrange pertinent details. The more important an event is to a person or a society, the more quickly it will be localized in familiar narrative frameworks that follow archetypal patterns which will be recognizable to most members of the group. As a result, narrative presentations of the past are typically stamped with the values and power relations that drive a group's patterns of socialization and domination. While some theorists have emphasized this point to challenge the historical value of collective memories, most contend that the actual past and earlier forms of commemoration constrain new representations. Further, popular memory and formal historiography serve similar social functions, and both depend on active interpretive frameworks and social constraints to remain intelligible. Ultimately, then, social memory theorists are less concerned with the content of collective memory and its potential historical value than with the ways that specific artifacts of memory (such as the Johannine writings) reflect the structure, values and identity of the groups that produced them.

The essays in Part III of this volume illustrate differing approaches to the interface between memory, tradition and text in the Johannine context. *James Dunn*'s study surveys prominent parallels between the Synoptic Gospels and the Gospel of John, and attempts to explain the tortured relationship between these books in terms of ancient media culture. Extending the conclu-

---

4   Even when memories are employed in isolation, social frameworks spur and constrain them. As Michael Schudson notes, 'even where memories are located idiosyncratically in individual minds, they remain social and cultural in that (a) they operate through the supra-individual cultural construction of language; (b) they generally come into play in response to social stimulation, rehearsal, or social cues, ... and (c) there are socially structured patterns of recall' (Schudson 1995: 347; see also Thatcher 2006: 54–60).

sions of his magisterial series *Christianity in the Making*, Dunn argues that apparent tensions between John and the Synoptics are actually typical of the variability and stability observable in variant collective memories of Jesus' historical impact. In Dunn's estimation, the Gospel of John lies close to the outer limit of how memories could be creatively altered while still remaining faithful to the core of a common tradition. *Anthony Le Donne*'s article attempts to reconceptualize conventional understandings of 'Jesus tradition' by describing the interfaces between history, tradition and text in terms of collective memory dynamics. Le Donne's article takes important strides by emphasizing the relationship between personal memories of Jesus and commemorations of him in texts such as the Fourth Gospel. Using the 'temple saying' in John 2 as a test case, Le Donne shows how Jesus's words could be retained yet reinterpreted when moving through successive group memory frameworks on their way to inclusion in the written text of the Fourth Gospel. *Catrin Williams* explores the Fourth Gospel's strategic appeals to Abraham in terms of combative speech and group interaction. Drawing on a variety of social memory and social identity theories, Williams analyses ways that the Fourth Evangelist selects, contests, appeals to and reconfigures Jewish memories of Abraham in the light of Johannine belief in Jesus. Thus, Abraham is reshaped to serve as a witness to Jesus's role as the exclusive mediator of salvation.

Taken together, the essays in Part III illustrate the multiple facets of social memory studies as applicable to the Fourth Gospel: Dunn examines what Aleida Assmann would call 'communicative' memory (1999: 64), the matrix of oral contexts from which memories emerge in the first two generations of a new group; Williams examines what Assmann calls 'cultural' memory, the reshaping of significant figures and events from the past for purposes of identity construction; Le Donne explores the relationship between commemorative texts like the Fourth Gospel and early and widespread memories of the historical Jesus.

Following these focused case studies, Part IV of this volume features reflective responses from experts on media studies and the Johannine Literature. *Barry Schwartz*, widely recognized as a leading authority on the interfaces between memory, history and popular culture, reflects on the Johannine literature's potential contribution to broader understandings of media culture. *Gail O'Day*, widely respected for her expertise in biblical studies generally and the Johannine literature specifically, reflects on the implications of media studies for future research on the Fourth Gospel and 1, 2 and 3 John. Their willingness to tackle such a vast array of topics outside their own disciplines speaks to the generous characters and intellectual versatility of these respondents. Hopefully, this dialogue will stimulate further fruitful discussion for both disciplines.

PART I

JOHN AND ORAL CULTURE

Chapter 2

SEEING, HEARING, DECLARING, WRITING: MEDIA DYNAMICS
IN THE LETTERS OF JOHN

Jeffrey E. Brickle

More than mere adjuncts to the Fourth Gospel, the Letters of John serve as important documents in their own right. As products of first-century media culture, these discourses reflect decisions to utilize particular media forms in particular ways. Fittingly, the Prologue of 1 John indicates that the reality of 'that which was from the beginning' had been apprehended through the senses, then conveyed and received through various media agencies, including both oral (μαρτυροῦμεν, 'we are bearing witness'; ἀπαγγέλλομεν, 'we are declaring') and written (γράφομεν, 'we are writing') discourse. From a media perspective, the status of the Letters as written literature can be misleading, for from start to finish – from pre-compositional debate to dramatic performances before audiences – these documents engage a wide variety of communicative forms. This essay explores the interactive elements constitutive of the media world of the Letters, ranging from textuality to orality/aurality, performance and memory, and also offers ways in which these elements might be exploited in an effort to better appreciate the Letters' media dynamics.

Conceived in a Media Crisis

Patristic evidence suggests that the Letters of John originated in Asia Minor (Brown 1982: 100–3; Trebilco 2008: 241–71). It is conceivable that one of the congregations in Ephesus, where the author of the Letters may have resided, served as a mother church with some jurisdiction over a circle of satellite churches located in the surrounding region (Brown 1982: 32, 101–2; Thatcher 2005b: 419). While the precise situation underlying the Letters is impossible to reconstruct with certainty, formulation or adoption of a preliminary working model is necessary to account for their form and content (Kruse 2000: 1–2).

Raymond Brown's influential hypothesis (1982: 69–71) posits that within the community interpretations arose that distorted the original Johannine teachings reflected in the Fourth Gospel, eventually leading to schism. In Brown's view (1982: 86–100), 1 John imitated the Gospel in terms of genre, structure, style and argumentation in an attempt to respond to and correct deviant understandings of the Gospel that denied Jesus's coming in the flesh (1 John 4.1-3). Brown's hypothesis has been criticized at various stages, not least for an exegesis largely dependent on a mirror reading in which Brown surmises the opponents' views on the basis of the author's antithetical statements (Lieu 1991: 5–6; Childs 1985: 482–5).

Whether or not one supports Brown's polemical reconstruction, it would seem clear from an examination of the Letters, especially 1–2 John, that disagreements within the community had arisen over opposing views on Christology and ethics, precipitating a crisis of verbal discourse – a virtual war of words. At some point before the Letters were recorded, sharp debate between the parties ultimately led to rupture, with one side pulling out of the community (1 John 2.18-19). Seeking inroads in which to prey upon vulnerable members still loyal to the 'original' Johannine tradition, these secessionists likely employed persuasive rhetoric in order to reassert influence among their former associates (1 John 2.26). Fittingly, while frequent references to forms of γράφω ('to write') within the Letters attest to their inscribed nature (1 John 1.4, 2.1, etc.), numerous terms scattered throughout also denote verbal interaction (e.g., ἀγγελία/ἀναγγέλλω and ἀπαγγέλλω, 'message'/'to declare'; ἀρνέομαι, 'to deny'; διδαχή/διδάσκω, 'teaching'/'to teach'; λόγος/λαλέω and λέγω, 'word'/'to speak'; μαρτυρία/μαρτυρέω, 'witness'/'to bear witness'; ὁμολογέω, 'to confess'; and ψεύστης/ψεῦδος/ ψευδοπροφήτης/ψεύδομαι, 'liar'/'lie'/'false prophet'/'to lie'). The conflict between the parties had spilled over into writing.

Why Did John Write *Letters?*

If a modest attempt to establish a tentative, pre-compositional situation behind the Letters suggests that they originated in a media crisis entailing oral speech, what prompted the writing of the Letters? On one level, the answer to this type of question has often been sought as if it was merely an historical issue: *why* did John write letters? (See Thatcher 2006: 1–9). Working at the problem from this angle, scholarship has chiefly been engaged in an effort to undercover the underlying historical purpose(s) for the Letters. Brown (1979), for example, has attempted to respond to the question at length by imaginatively recreating the history of the Johannine Community and demonstrating how the various writings of John may have fitted into this reconstructed account.

I prefer, however, to approach the problem from a media angle by taking up the focused question that Tom Thatcher (2006: 1–9) has recently posed of the Fourth Gospel (Why did John *write* a Gospel?) and apply it to John's Letters (Why did John *write* letters?). Reframing our question slightly, why did John elect not to continue responding to the crisis at hand solely via an oral medium but choose rather to enlist the aid of another form of technology – writing? We will first consider Thatcher's approach to the question as it pertains to the writing of John's Gospel, before applying it to the writing of the Letters.

Basing his approach to the Fourth Gospel largely on modern theories of social memory, especially the seminal work of Maurice Halbwachs – who argued that memory is not a neutral construct but one shaped by and within communities (Thatcher 2005a: 86–8; 2006: xiii–xiv, 56) – as well as the distinctly Johannine understanding of the nature of memory (Thatcher 2005a: 82–5; 2006: 23–36), Thatcher posits an important distinction between the consensus view of writing as archive, as opposed to writing as rhetoric. In the former model, a Gospel functions essentially as a 'sacred filing cabinet' used for the deposit and retrieval of 'raw recollections' (Thatcher 2006: 23; 2005a: 80–82). Under the latter model, given the Holy Spirit's critical role in the Johannine memory system as preserver of the content and proper interpretation of tradition, writing was rendered unnecessary for the mechanical storage and recall of memories. Liberated from its role as a surrogate for cognitive memory and bestowed with special prestige by society, writing could thus be exploited for its rhetorical or symbolic value (Thatcher 2005a: 85–6; 2006: 37–49). For Thatcher (2006: 38), then, a history book retained a 'special aura' or 'halo of authority' absent from mere oral histories.

Placed within the *Sitz im Leben* of a struggle between Johannine loyalists and antichrists over conflicting interpretations of Jesus, Thatcher's approach envisions a rhetorical employment of writing as a means by which the former group of 'dogmatists' could attempt to counteract the counter-memory spawned by the latter group of 'mystics'. Given the fluid nature of living, with oral memories rendering basic data vulnerable to interpretive reconfiguring, the mystics could quite freely expand and reorder the traditional database (Thatcher 2006: 122). Given that these mystics, as former members of John's community, based their teachings on the same database and pneumatic memory framework as John did (Thatcher 2006: 74), John could not attack these shared resources directly. Rather, he harnessed the power of a written Gospel, which allowed him to uphold a Spirit-driven memory of Jesus 'while confining that memory to the boundaries of traditional Christological creeds' (Thatcher 2006: 102).

We are immediately confronted with two problems when we attempt to consider the purpose behind the Letters of John in light of Thatcher's hypothesis. First, the author explicitly tells his recipients several times the various reasons why he wrote 1 John (1.4: to cultivate joy; 2.1: to prevent sin; etc.). Focusing exclusively on these passages, though, somewhat sidesteps the specific media-related question at hand: why did John *write* rather than continue to engage solely in *oral* discourse? In 1 John, the concentration of passages dealing with writing may indicate, however, that the recipients, who perhaps were located in close proximity to John, had been wondering why John wrote when he could have continued to impart his message orally.

Secondly, unlike the Fourth Gospel, the Letters are clearly not historical narratives and thus would not have functioned in precisely the same way. In his study, Thatcher explicitly treats the Gospel, rather than letter, genre from a media angle. While 2 and 3 John reflect nearly model Greco-Roman letters (Lieu 1986: 37–51), the genre of 1 John has remained controversial due to its lack of an epistolary framework (Brown 1982: 86–92). For example, David Aune (1987: 218) classifies 1 John as 'a deliberative homily' (cf. Culpepper 1998: 251) whereas Rudolph Schnackenburg (1992: 4; cf. Watson 1993: 118–23) denies that it is a homily.

At any rate, if Thatcher's overall assumptions about why John *wrote* a Gospel are correct, I wish to propose that John's Letters, like the Fourth Gospel, were also written as a tactic to exploit the rhetorical power of writing but without the full-fledged authority inherent in a work of history. In this regard, Thatcher's minority opinion (2006: 64–7) that the Letters may have preceded the Gospel appears compelling, although the specific order of composition is not critical. Oral discourse had failed to quell the secessionist onslaught and the Christians loyal to John remained understandably uneasy about the threat that they posed. In my view, then, the Letters of John, provisionally standing in for John's pending *Parousia* (2 John 12; 3 John 10, 14), paved the way for the eventual composition of John's capstone project – his magnum opus – the Fourth Gospel. Under this paradigm, the Letters, on the continuum from oral discourse to written text, represent a midway point before John resorted to a written Gospel as the ultimate countermeasure.

1 John, which comprised a kind of first written response to the secessionist menace, functioned as anti-viral software designed to thwart the antagonists' attempts to reconfigure the traditional database. 1 John tried to achieve this goal in part by reaffirming who the bona fide system managers were who had authorization to access and interpret the data, and by identifying the illegitimate hackers who sought to expand the information in the database. To draw on another metaphor, 1 John acted as the physician's initial attempt to treat the patient by radiating the spreading cancer.

On the other hand, 2 John – a parenthetic letter (Watson 1989a: 107–8) – was likely sent to an outlying house church in an effort to instruct the recipients on how to brace themselves for the imminent secessionist invasion. While it is not entirely clear whether 2 John was sent in lieu of John's physical presence (I consider this issue further below) – and hence as a stopgap to substitute for his inability to instruct them orally – we can surmise that as a written document 2 John also presented a rhetorically powerful statement. It may be that the 'media crisis' that preceded the writing of 1 John had yet to reach the setting of the 'elect lady' and that 2 John is this house church's first notice of and exposure to John's oral debate with the secessionists. It is possible that the process of responding to the immediate situation at hand with 1 John prompted the author to send out 2 John as well.

As for 3 John (an epideictic letter; Watson 1989b: 484–5), nowhere is the main antagonist, Diotrephes, explicitly identified as a secessionist or the problem of false teachers ever mentioned (Thomas 1995: 70; Lieu 2008: 12–14; contra Thatcher 2006: 92, 99, 122). It is thus not entirely clear whether Diotrephes was, to use Thatcher's terms, a 'dogmatist' who was essentially pro-traditionalist or a 'mystic' who sided with the secessionists. 3 John 9–11 indicates that Diotrephes' loyalty towards the author was in serious question and so we might refer to him as a 'counter-dogmatist' or 'alternative-dogmatist' for refusing to cooperate with the authorized system manager (John) and his 'support reps', such as Demetrius (3 John 12). Evidently, verbal discourse preceded the composition and sending of this letter, for John had heard of and rejoiced over reports of Gaius' stand for truth (3 John 3-4) and hospitality (3 John 5-6), as well as favourable testimonies concerning Demetrius (3 John 12). These were networks John certainly hoped to reinforce. On the other hand, according to 3 John 10 he learned of Diotrephes' abusive verbiage that had been directed at him (λόγοις πονηροῖς φλυαρῶν ἡμᾶς, 'slandering us with wicked words') and he countered by a written rhetorical threat of a personal confrontation (ἐὰν ἔλθω, ὑπομνήσω αὐτοῦ τὰ ἔργα ἃ ποιεῖ, 'if I come, I will recall his deeds which he is doing').

Before moving on, two specific passages that relate directly to media concerns should be considered. At the close of the two shorter letters (2 John 12; 3 John 13-14), John registered his preference to engage his recipients through direct oral communication (στόμα πρὸς στόμα λαλῆσαι, 'to speak [literally] mouth to mouth') – at least in the handling of the situations addressed by these letters. It appears, then, at least on the surface, John *reluctantly* settled on the alternative to speaking: pen, ink and paper. Brown (1979: 693–95, 749), however, whose interpretation is open to debate, dismisses the face value of John's expressed wish to personally visit his recipients as an artificial, conventional way to bring these documents to a close. Significantly, Margaret Mitchell (1992) has argued that Paul employed writing and envoys not merely as substitutes for his personal presence, but in some cases as preferred, more effective means to deal with problems in the churches. If the latter principle applies to John's letters, the power of writing and sending letters was harnessed as the favoured method *under the circumstances* to represent John's presence, since speech was normally the favoured method for conveying teaching (Malherbe 1986: 68). Whether or not John routinely preferred oral communication over writing, as many ancients did (Witherington 2007), he elected to respond to the issues at hand via writing.

While Thatcher's overall approach to the purpose underlying the Fourth Gospel's writing is intriguing, well-argued and quite helpful, I find one aspect problematic: his insistence that since most of the first-century population was illiterate (Thatcher rightly cites William Harris' 1989 landmark study), those unable to read would have had little knowledge of the contents of this document (Thatcher 2006: 39–43, 158–9; 2005a: 96–7). Thatcher goes as far as stating that 'most people in John's culture could not read, a fact that would make it *impossible for them even to discuss the actual contents of John's Gospel*, much less to challenge its claims' (2006: 153; emphasis is mine).

It is almost certain, however, that many, even most, illiterate persons would have had access to texts, not in the same manner as a modern reader, but through the surrogacy of a skilled reader-performer – the lector – a role I will discuss in more detail below. This fact would have rendered the lack of literacy largely a non-issue. Far more than venerated artifacts accessible only to a privileged few trained to read them, texts maintained ongoing lives among communities through the agency of lectorial performance (Gamble 1995: 204–5). During such performances, texts were highly visible since they were often read from directly (as in a first-century synagogue: Luke 4.16-20) or held in the lector's left hand when recited from memory (Shiner 2003: 18; Shiell 2004: 40–1, 48–9). Particularly within the intimate context of a Christian house church, the lector may have been immediately accessible to the audience to explain issues arising from the text's content (Richards 2004: 202). The likelihood exists that through exposure to repeated performances of a text, an illiterate person could have become familiar enough with a text to have memorized it. To his credit, Thatcher (2005a: 81) is aware of ancient oral performances, but in my estimation fails to adequately factor this aspect of first-century media culture into his overall analysis (see Kelber 1997: xxi–xxiv, who addresses this shortcoming in his own, previous scholarship).

How Did John Write Letters?

From a media angle, how did John compose these letters? The primary method of composition in antiquity was by dictation to a scribe (Achtemeier 1990: 12–15; Gamble 1995: 204; Harvey 1998: xv), although some authors wrote in their own hand. Even in the latter case, authors tended to dictate as they wrote (Gamble 1995: 204). People who were illiterate required the services of a scribe, and even the highly literate generally preferred to relinquish such duties to a scribe, who was often a slave (Keener 1993: 449; Campbell 2001: 33). The employment of a scribe or amanuensis other than the author is uncertain in the case of John's letters, as none is formally credited (cf. Romans 16.22; 1 Peter 5.12). Furthermore, the single occurrence in 1 John 1.4 of the first person plural for the act of writing (γράφομεν, 'we are writing') does not imply the presence of a secretary or joint authorship, but indicates an appeal to testimony beyond that of the author alone (Brown 1982: 172; Painter 2002: 137–8; contra Bauckham 2006: 370–5).

John probably worked through the substance and structure of his letters in his own memory before dictating them to a scribe (Horsley 2005: 61; Shiner

2006: 153–4). The dictated oral texts may have been captured initially in a form of shorthand Greek (Richards 2004: 67–74) and written on tablets, which served as rough drafts (Richards 2004: 55–7). The texts were likely reworked and at some point in the process converted to *scriptio continua* (a writing convention devoid of space between words, paragraph divisions and punctuation), perhaps when finally committed to parchment or papyrus (Richards 2004: 48–9).

The fact that John wrote letters – letters which may have undergone revisions before being sent – does not eradicate their oral nature, however, for the overall process suggests that from birth by dictation to subsequent delivery before an audience these letters retained a spoken essence. As Harry Gamble (1995: 204) affirms, 'in the composition of a text the oral was converted to the written' and subsequently 'in reading aloud the written was converted into the oral'. Given a text's method of production and later functioning, writing served in large measure as a script to preserve an oral event for later oral re-enactment (Stanford 1967: 3; Shiner 2003: 14; Witherington 2007: 28). Thus, textuality functioned first 'as a representation of speech' (Shiner 2009: 49) or 'the symbol for the spoken word' (Lenz 1989: 4), and then 'as an aid to oral presentation' (Dewey 1994: 45). John Foley (2005: 233) has well pointed out that 'at its very best a textual reproduction – with the palpable reality of the performance flattened onto a page and reduced to an artifact – is a script for reperformance, a libretto to be enacted and reenacted, a prompt for an emergent reality'.

A Multi-Media Event

The practice of silently scanning texts has largely dominated the landscape of modern, Western reading. Paul Saenger (1997) argues that the advent of silent reading in the late Middle Ages corresponded roughly with the introduction of word separation by Irish scribes during the seventh and eighth centuries, although the technology did not arrive on the European continent until the late tenth century. Although ancient reading was commonly conducted aloud (Balogh 1926; Hendrickson 1929–30; Graham 1987: 30–5; Achtemeier 1990: 15–17; Gamble 1995: 203–5; Winger 2003), evidence suggests (contra Saenger) that silent reading occurred more frequently in antiquity than has often been maintained (Clark 1930–1; Slusser 1992; Gilliard 1993; Gavrilov 1997; Burnyeat 1997; Johnson 2001; Shiner 2003: 14). Evidence for the existence of silent reading in the ancient world does not, however, eradicate the necessarily dominant role played by audible reading in service to a mostly illiterate public, and it seems that even the literate aristocracy generally preferred to be read aloud to by their household servants. Furthermore, even silent reading likely involved the phenomenon of *parole intérieure*, the sounding out of the words in the reader's mind (Hendrickson 1929–30: 194).

Reading was typically carried out through the agency of a skilled lector (Starr 1991; Shiell 2004: 104–7), who in essence 'became the mouthpiece to allow an audience to "read" a text for themselves' (Shiell 2004: 4). The lector stood in for, and hence represented, the voice and persona of the author. In some cases the scribe, the envoy and the lector were the same individual. The lector attempted to re-enact the original (compositional or dictated) performance of the text, bringing the inscribed words to life for the audience through gesticulations, facial expressions and vocal inflections (Shiell 2004: 201). As Richard Ward (1994: 95) has suggested, 'oral performance is a means of transforming silent texts into sounds and movement through the mediums of speech and gesture'.

The oral, performative nature of ancient reading, therefore, shows that we are dealing with texts that are inherently multi-dimensional. As 1 John, for instance, was first read or recited aloud to its recipients, its text was experienced aurally and visually by means of the voice, body and character of the lector, through the ears and eyes of the audience. In addition, the total atmosphere, including the make-up and emotional disposition(s) of the gathered audience as well as the setting's backdrop of sights, sounds and smells, rendered the ancient reading experience a multi-media event. As Holly Hearon (2006: 11) has observed, texts 'must be understood in terms of the interaction between a performer and an audience and the tangled web of discourse and experience that binds them together in a particular place and time'.

Could it be that by silently scanning John's letters, we have missed important dynamics of the ancient reading experience that the audiences would have taken for granted? In much the same way that conventional wisdom has perpetuated the myth that Greco-Roman statues were 'plain old white' when in fact they were brightly painted (Reed 2007: 34), many modern readers, silently beholding the Letters of John as bare, cold sculptures of stone, have failed to fully appreciate their rich, living tapestry of sounds and colours. We will now consider in more detail these various aspects of the ancient media experience of oral reading.

Can You Hear the Text?

As we have discussed, one dimension of the multi-media reality of ancient reading entails the imposing presence of sound. Sound is extremely important to biblical interpretation, because 'thinking about the Bible as an oral document leads to a different set of questions that are acoustemological rather than epistemological' (Webb 2004: 199). Regrettably, the oral nature of the ancient world has largely been neglected by contemporary biblical research (Kelber 2002: 59). David Rhoads, in a pun derived from the title of a classic monograph by Hans Frei, bemoans 'the eclipse of biblical orality'. Harry Gamble (1995: 204) and Rosalind Thomas (1992: 117–23) recommend that if we are to experience texts as they were in antiquity, we must read them aloud, since ancient authors composed for the ear. Whitney Shiner (2003: 16) concurs, noting that 'as a result of the dictation process, the author composes with an awareness of the aural effect, and writers often 'wrote' by speaking in a manner that would approximate the intended oral delivery'.

During the performance of an ancient text, a variety of sound patterns in turn assaulted and provoked, soothed and delighted audiences. William Stanford (1943; 1967: 51–6) describes the differing euphonic impact of various letters of the Greek alphabet as assessed by Dionysius of Halicarnassus in his *On Literary Composition*. Some letters or letter combinations were considered harsh, others pleasant. Composers sought to employ the right blend of phonic ingredients to achieve the desired aesthetic effect. In a composition some correlation may have existed between the perceived pleasantness and roughness of the discourse or scene being depicted, and the relative smoothness or harshness of the sound patterning of the corresponding lines (Packard 1974). A preliminary analysis conducted by the author of this essay utilizing David Packard's harshness formula shows a significantly higher harshness factor for 1 John 2.18, in which John addresses the unpleasant departure of the secessionists, as opposed to the opening verse of the letter, designed to immediately gain the recipient's receptivity.

Hearers interpreted and reacted to texts as they were read aloud, and were largely guided through this process by their perception of unfolding sound patterns. Thus, in the absence of visual markers, an array of auditory signals helped to facilitate movement and structure (Achtemeier 1990: 17–19; Dewey 1992), a phenomenon Van Dyke Parunak (1981) refers to as 'oral typesetting'. Such signals often crossed, resulting in a 'plethora of backward and forward echoes' (Dewey 1989: 29; cf. Malbon 1993). In other words, complex overlapping or interlacing acoustic patterns together knit 'an interwoven tapestry' (Dewey 1991).

Not all scholars agree as to what precisely constitutes an aural pattern, or how to analyse such a pattern. Bernard Scott and Margaret Lee (formerly Margaret Dean), however, have carried out valuable research in the area of orality/aurality, being among the first scholars to pioneer an actual methodology of aural analysis (Scott and Dean 1993; Dean 1996), which they refer to as 'sound mapping'. In her doctoral dissertation (Lee 2005: 127), Lee contends that sound analysis must be carried out before more traditional forms of exegesis. She discusses the complex interplay in Hellenistic Greek writings of aural repetition and variation at the level of phonemes and syllables, cola and periods, and applies these dynamics to the Sermon on the Mount. I will draw in part from Scott and Lee's insights in my brief analysis that follows below.

Although scholars have considered the role of orality/aurality in a variety of New Testament writings, including the Gospels and Acts (e.g., Bartholomew

1987; Dewey 1989; 1991; 1992; 2001; Bryan 1993; Kelber 1997; Knowles 2004; Borgman 2006; Gilfillan Upton 2006), the Pauline Letters (Kelber 1997; Winger 1997; Harvey 1998; Davis 1999), and the Apocalypse (Barr 1986), relatively little interest has been directed to the aural nature of the Letters of John. While some have noticed that 1 John exhibits aural characteristics (e.g., Perkins 1979; Neufeld 1994), Russ Dudrey (2003a: 236) is one of the first scholars to draw attention to these elements, noting that 1 John 'furnishes a specific case of a biblical document consciously written to be read aloud to an audience – a document of "oral literature" full of identifiable oral and auditory features'. He notes (2003a) the presence of an array of auditory features, such as aphorisms, balanced structures (including comparisons, parallelisms, chiastic structures and binary oppositions), verbal jingles, repeated use of the coordinating conjunction καί ('and'), repetition, and fixed language patterns.

Dudrey extends his research on the auditory features of 1 John by investigating the role of sound ingrained in the document's macrostructure. Determining 1 John's overarching organization has long been considered problematic. For example, Raymond Brown (1982: 117–268) claims that it has 'no discernibly regular pattern', David Rensberger (2006: 279) likewise asserts that it 'does not have a clear outline or pattern of development', and Gary Burge (1997: 597) maintains that 'discovering a recognizable pattern or structure of thought … has proven impossible'. Alan Brooke (1912: xxxii) suggests that the quest be relinquished altogether.

Dudrey insists, however, that scholars have pursued the issue in entirely the wrong way, for the macrostructure of 1 John must be sought through an auditory rather than literary paradigm: 'Analyzing 1 John by literary criteria yields confusing results at best, but analyzing it by oral and auditory criteria frees the letter to function by its native rules.' Dudrey maintains that 1 John is framed by 'topical cycles of auditory material', comprising the topics of Christology and theology, holy living and brotherly love. The topics are not organized by 'linear logic, but in spirals of interwoven material, whose seams are stitched together by oral and auditory cues that John could expect his hearers to pick up'. Dudrey's observations are clearly important, yet could benefit from further development.

While this is not the place to offer a full-blown analysis of the dynamics involved in 1 John's auditory matrix, I do wish to comment on the role the Prologue's sounds play in the initial unfolding of John's message. The following brief analysis represents some highlights on aural patterning from two of my presented papers and my doctoral dissertation entitled 'Aural Design and Coherence in the Prologue of First John'. The Prologue, consisting of a complex passage that has earned the possible distinction of being 'the most complicated Greek in the Johannine corpus' (Brown 1982: 152), serves as the piece's auditory prelude or foyer, providing a palette of sound colours for the artist's brush as he moves on to paint the composition's body and conclusion.

The opening of the Prologue with its 'initial aural formula' (see Scott and Dean 1993: 679 and 708), ὃ ἦν ἀπ' ἀρχῆς ('That which was from the beginning'), begins to establish a principal sound pattern, elements of which recur throughout the Prologue and beyond. Examples of these recurring 'sound bites' include the relative pronoun ὃ and the elided preposition ἀπ', the latter of which forms an alliteration with some of the words which immediately follow (ἀρχῆς ... ἀκηκόαμεν, 'beginning ... we have heard') and anticipates the prefixed preposition of the compound first main verb (ἀπαγγέλλομεν, 'we are declaring') in v. 3. The phrase ἀπ' ἀρχῆς ('from the beginning') arguably plays a key role in the letter (2.7, 13, 14, 24; 3.8, 11; cf. 2 John 5, 6).

The overall syntactical organization of the Prologue, which may be mapped out as a simple ABC/A'B'C' configuration, is supported and enhanced by the strategic use of sound patterning. This patterning serves to mark the Prologue's aural foreground and background as well as drive its progressive, unfolding discourse forward, building auditory suspense. Each of the two main sections consists of a direct object (A/A'), main verb (B/B'), and purpose clause (C/C'). Section 1 (vv. 1-3) features an extended, amplified direct object and purpose clause, each incorporating a parenthetical digression showcasing the themes of ζωή ('life') and κοινωνία ('fellowship'), respectively. Section 2 (v. 4), on the other hand, is considerably abridged, with its abbreviated length in comparison to that of Section 1 reflective of Dionysius of Halicarnassus' concern for variety in beautiful composition (Caragounis 2006: 411). Three key sound patterns, ὃ ('which'), καί ('and'), and the vowel-μεν verbal termination ('we'), occur in the Prologue, often in conjunction with one another: ὃ ... vowel-μεν and καὶ ... vowel-μεν.

Margaret Lee (Dean 1998: 86) notes that sound not only supports a text's rhetorical structure, but also helps lend it its persuasive force. Given the brief analysis above, how does 1 John's overall aural patterning function? How does its form relate to its content? In short, 1 John's aural patterning agrees with its primary message, even though sound and semantics can intentionally be set at odds (Lee 2005: 109–12). Through the integration of sound patterning with syntactical structure, the author highlights the centrality of the direct object (summarized as ὃ), and in part by the repeated soundings of the vowel-μεν pattern (signifying 'we') establishes the authority and ethos that he and his associates share, closely linking the direct object with the witnesses/transmitters of the tradition (ὃ ... vowel-μεν). Significantly, little is said specifically in the Prologue concerning the profile of the recipients ('you'), other than that the tradition had been transmitted to them. Their anticipated κοινωνία 'with the Father and with his Son, Jesus Christ' (1.3) was contingent upon (implied by ἵνα, 'in order that') fellowship with the tradition bearers, with a more detailed elucidation of the requirements for κοινωνία reserved for the body of the letter (e.g., 1.6-7).

Unfortunately, the aural and literary qualities of 1 John have not always been appreciated. The grammatical integrity and coherence of the Prologue, for example, have often been denigrated, as the following appraisals (based primarily on a silent reading paradigm) suggest: a 'grammatical tangle' (Dodd 1946: 3); 'grammatical impossibilities' and 'undeniable crudity of expression' (Houlden 1973: 45); a 'morass', 'scramble' and 'befuddling array of language' with its 'Greek border[ing] on incongruence' (Kysar 1986: 30, 34); 'confused' (Strecker 1996: 8); 'nearly impossible grammar' (Rensberger 1997: 45); and 'nearly impenetrable' to the modern reader (Black 1998: 382).

Admittedly, the Prologue presents difficulties, including its extended length and parenthetical interruptions, postponement of its main verb, and alternation of its verb tenses (Brown 1982: 153), not to mention a host of ambiguities (Anderson 1992: 8–19). The problems surrounding the Prologue's complexity are not insurmountable, however, and its design becomes more evident when it is read aloud as it was intended. I would even suggest that some of the alleged difficulties may have actually contributed to the aural effect John desired. In short, we must learn to read 1 John, along with all ancient literature, 'with our ears as well as our eyes' (Yaghjian 1996: 207).

Can You See the Text?

While the theme of the dramatic nature of the Johannine Writings is not new (Brant 2004; Smalley 2005), relatively few studies have acknowledged this aspect of the Letters of John. Ironically, however, the opening words of 1 John, reflecting 'the abundant sensuality of the apostolic encounter with the Word', show that its dynamic sensory language is germane to the theatre arts (M. Harris 1990: 2). While many ancients were unable to visually decipher a written text for themselves, a text achieved visible form through its delivery. In other words, audiences 'read' the lector's performance. Our modern, literate society, by contrast, is awash with visible texts, for 'we live in a world of visible words' (Small 1997: 3).

Hand gestures were an important component of oral delivery. As an 'inseparable accompaniment of any spoken language' (K. Thomas 1991: 6), gestures functioned as a sort of second text. Thus, a Roman orator while speaking was in effect 'simultaneously communicating in two languages, one verbal and one nonverbal' (Aldrete 1999: 6). The study of gesticulation, itself an important element of ancient delivery and hence of rhetorical training (Graf 1992: 37), is critical to any consideration of ancient media culture. In many contexts, body language is more important than the words that are spoken (K. Thomas 1991: 6). While certain universal gestures have retained the same general meaning over time and across cultures, body language tends to evolve. If we are to adequately interpret communication from the past, we must become students of gestural delivery (K. Thomas 1991: 10).

Through a consideration of discussions in rhetorical handbooks and references in other literary sources as well as depictions of oratory in paintings,
sculptures, coins, and the like, scholars have attempted to reconstruct ancient
gesturing and its accompanying postures (Shiell 2004: 34–7). Gregory
Aldrete (1999: 3–43), for example, has assembled a repertoire, illustrated
with helpful sketches, of ancient Roman oratory gestures and body motions.
We do not have space in this essay to adequately explore this approach
further, but future studies could attempt to plot out or 'gesture map' an
imaginative performance matrix for the Letters of John. By correlating the
texts of the letters with known gesturing language, we might come closer to
resurrecting their ancient performances.

Such a performance matrix could also furnish clues which might help
solve grammatical and semantic ambiguities in the Letters of John. It is
likely that a number of puzzling and awkward features inherent in the text
of 1 John might be resolved if we could have been present at one of its
ancient presentations and 'read' the lector's body language. Interestingly,
Alan Boegehold (1999: 8) notes that many instances of conundrums in
ancient Greek texts, including baffling word meanings, ellipses, or irregular
constructions, are best explained not through textual emendation but by the
addition of an expected nod or hand gesture. The application of gesture to
thorny passages can inform both semantics and grammar, since gesture can
'complete the sense where canonical philology falls short' and serve 'as a way
of undoing certain knots grammar does not untie' (Boegehold 1999: 6, 10).
For instance, the dangling relative clause ὃ ἦν ἀπ' ἀρχῆς ('That which was
from the beginning') which begins 1 John lacks a grammatical antecedent
(Baugh 1999: 2), yet its original oral reading might have been accompanied
by a clarifying gesture.

Another element that can augment our understanding of the Letters of
John is to consider the symbolic value of the surroundings within which
the original performances were held. Aldrete (1999: 18–19) points out
that performance environments, such as buildings or spaces, served as rich
sources for symbols that the orator could refer to in verbal or non-verbal
ways (1999: 24). He notes (1999: xix) that 'because of the richly symbolic
landscape in which most speeches were delivered, by using pointing motions
an orator could draw on this environment to enhance or supplement his
words'. Along similar lines, Barbara Burrell's recent study (2009) suggests
powerful ways in which an analysis attuned to environmental factors, such
as the arrangement of buildings, streets, and décor encircling inscriptions,
can impact our understanding of ancient reading dynamics.

In the case of the Letters of John, private residences, likely owned by
wealthy members of the respective congregations, probably functioned as the
original 'theatres' in which lectorial performances were held. As the lectors
recited, they may have gestured periodically towards their surroundings,
including structures or objects in the homes, to add emphasis or to offer
clarification. Framework, such as doorways, floors, columns, windows and

ceilings, as well as furniture and décor, including tables, chairs, paintings, mosaics and sculptures, could have served as ready object lessons. In this regard, a close study of the design and furnishings of the terrace houses excavated in Ephesus (Trebilco 2008: 34, n. 151; Murphy-O'Connor 2008: 192–7) could provide archaeological models for the type of settings the letters were read in, keeping in mind that overtly pagan objects, such as representations of mythological figures, may have been removed by Christians from their gathering places. Examples of the symbolic exploitation of a performance site might include 1 John 5.21, where the lector, in cautioning the audience to avoid idols, may have gestured towards a statue located outside (for two differing interpretations of idols in this passage, see Griffith 2002: 206 and Bultmann 1973: 90–1), or 2 John 10, in which the lector may have pointed to the door of the house where the audience was gathered as he admonished them not to receive any false teachers into their house church.

Can You Remember the Text?

Memory, a technique of ancient rhetoric that enabled orators to recall and deliver lengthy speeches (Yates 1966: 2), was highly revered in antiquity (Byrskog 2002: 160–1), and even integrated into the educational system (Carruthers 2008: 8). The memory served as the 'principal faculty for intellectual and moral formation' (Kirk 2008: 219) and as the 'main textual reservoir' of ancient 'literary life' (Jaffee 2001: 18). Like many other ancient compositions, the Letters of John were written to be memorable, a trait beneficial to both speaker and hearer (Dewey 2001: 241).

It is probable that the original lectors knew well the text of John's Letters before they read them aloud (see Carr 2005: 4), and that they likely recited them by heart (Horsley 2005: 61). This left their eyes and hands unencumbered, thus freeing them to gesticulate (Shiner 2003: 103–4) and make solid eye-contact with the audience. A memorable compositional design and style aided a lector's efforts to commit the text to memory, helped render the reading event itself an unforgettable occasion for the audience, and supported the audience's long-term recall of the text's structure and wording. It was especially critical that the lector could remember a document's structure, 'since an ancient rhetor who lost control of the structure of his argument proved himself to be a second-rate rhetor, thereby undermining the effectiveness of his own argument' (Longenecker 2005: 6).

The framework of John's Letters facilitated their memorization (J. Thomas 1998: 380). Shiner (2003: 114–17) has suggested that relatively short sections predicated on triplet episodes and the use of chiasms contribute to the memorable nature of Mark's Gospel. John's penchant in his letters for moderately brief segments, typically structured internally by groupings of three (e.g., 1 John 2.12-14; 15-17), as well as the employment of triplet word repetitions, likewise indicate techniques that support the memory. Through a compositional strategy that integrated key themes, strong imagery and the persuasive use of sound – the prime ingredients for effectively transmitting traditions in an oral culture (Rubin 1995) – John rendered his letters memorable.

Various mnemonic techniques were employed among Greeks and Romans (Small 1997: 81–116), some of which have parallels with the visual, tactile and aural methods employed by modern musicians (Marvuglio 2007). We cannot be certain what approach(es) the Johannine lectors used to memorize the Letters. Shiner (2006: 152–3) notes that speeches were committed to memory either word-for-word or in essence. One could memorize a written speech through repeated oral readings or resort to an artificial memory technique involving, for example, image association. With this latter method, images that corresponded to portions of the text were mentally placed into various locations in a background, such as a building or landscape, which had been committed to memory beforehand. Then the person memorizing the speech would mentally revisit the locations in order, retrieving the associated images (Shiner 2006: 153).

Given their brevity as well as the gravity of the matters they addressed, as stated above the Letters of John were likely memorized verbatim. The lectors may have relied on image association in this process. This method was utilized to memorize each word of a speech, or merely the outline (Shiner 2006: 153). Various key terms, representative of sections in 1 John, seem to inherently conjure up strong images (e.g. κόσμος, 'world', for the section 2.15-17; ἀντίχριστος, 'antichrist', for 2.18-27), and may have worked particularly well for remembering the text's structure. In the Prologue of 1 John, anatomical associations are implicitly or explicitly made by the text (e.g., the ear for ἀκηκόαμεν, 'we have heard'; eyes for ἑωράκαμεν, 'we have seen' and ἐθεασάμεθα, 'we have beheld'; and hands for ἐψηλάφησαν, 'they have handled'). By imaging human anatomy while memorizing this passage, the lector would have encountered an intrinsic mnemonic aid that naturally facilitated properly-ordered recall.

Memory plays an important role in the Letters of John not only as an aesthetic component, aiding in its composition, delivery and subsequent recall, but as an integral part of John's message itself. Drawing on the past, John calls his recipients (1 John 1.1-3) to fellowship (κοινωνία) with him and his associates through participation in the experience of the 'word of life' (τοῦ λόγου τῆς ζωῆς), whose manifestation was firmly anchored in John's memory. John bears witness (μαρτυροῦμεν) to his remembrances of that 'from the beginning' (ἀπ᾿ ἀρχῆς), an important phrase which also appears in Luke's Prologue and suggests eyewitness presence at the events themselves (Bauckham 2006: 119; cf. Dunn 2003: 178).

Later in the letter, as his recipients heard John referring to *their* original reception of the message 'from the beginning' (1 John 2.7, 24; 3.11; cf. 2

John 6), these references would have triggered recollections of their past experience. John was urging them to cultivate their remembered past (1 John 2.24) and relate it to the present crisis, knowing that the inspiration behind the secessionists' discourse and behaviour stemmed ultimately from an altogether different beginning (1 John 3.8) than that which John was remembering.

Have You Responded to the Letters?

In recent decades, reader-response criticism has heightened awareness of the key role that audiences play in the communicative process (Tompkins 1980). The Greco-Roman audience was, of course, no less a vital player in the ancient reading process. Far from fulfilling a passive role, those to whom the Letters of John were sent served as active participants in the reading event.

It is highly improbable that the Letters of John were originally recited in a monotone voice, with no show of emotion on the part of the lectors or the recipients. Had they been, their effectiveness would be in doubt, for as Shiner (2003: 57) has observed, 'The success of verbal art was often judged by the way it affected the emotions of the listeners.' Rather, John's Letters were likely spoken in a highly animated fashion. Even though philosophical groups such as the Stoics sought to suppress the so-called passions (though see Sorabji 2000), studies attest to a wide range of emotional expression in ancient culture (Fortenbaugh 2002; Knuuttila 2004; Konstan 2006). Pathos was an integral component of ancient rhetorical theory (Kennedy 1984: 15; Welborn 2001) and emotional expression was considered part and parcel of both delivery and audience response.

As noted above in the section, 'Can You See the Text?', an array of gestures was available to the ancient lector and these were exploited to elicit specific emotional responses from audiences. As Aldrete (1999: 6) has observed, 'certain gestures were associated with various emotions so that as an orator spoke, his body offered a separate and continuous commentary on what emotions the words were intended to provoke'. These gestures could portray emotions such as 'surprise, indignation, entreaty, anger, adoration, reproach, grief, insistence or emphasis, and aversion' (Shiell 2004: 62). Fittingly, references to emotions or passions like these appear fairly frequently in the Letters of John (e.g., forms of ἀγάπη/ἀγαπάω/ἀγαπητός, 'love'/'to love'/'beloved'; μισέω, 'to hate'; ἐπιθυμία, 'lust'; φόβος/φοβέω, 'fear'/'to fear', and χαρά/χαίρω, 'joy'/'to rejoice').

Perhaps one of the reasons that 1 John follows no patently logical structure is that its rhetoric was not aimed chiefly at the intellect but towards the heart. Arguably, the primary function of all of John's letters was to procure responses from the audiences by appealing to their emotions. Any attempt at accurately reconstructing these responses rests largely, of course, on imaginative conjecture.

One document that stems from the same general milieu and era, and addresses a Hellenistic audience not unlike the recipients of John's letters, is the Acts of the Apostles. Numerous speeches and a few embedded letters are included in Acts. In several cases the audience's reaction to a declamation is described (e.g., Acts 2.37, 'pieced in the heart'; 4.2, 'being disturbed'). Perhaps most important for our purpose is the account of the Jerusalem Council, which attempted to settle a heated dispute between the apostles and a Judaizing faction over the ongoing role of the law in relation to Gentile converts to Christianity (15.1-21). The meeting resulted in a letter being dispatched to Syria and Cilicia (15:22-30) in which the recipients who heard it read aloud (15.31) 'rejoiced for the encouragement' (ἐχάρησαν ἐπὶ τῇ παρακλήσει) and were also edified through the prophetic ministry of Judas and Silas (Acts 15.32).

While clearly the situations described in Acts 15 and 1 John are markedly different in many ways, Luke's account of the response to the reading of the letter stemming from the Jerusalem Council may offer some indication of how the recipients of 1 John may have reacted. In both situations, it is evident that debate had been intense and tensions were running high. Like those who had encountered the adamant claims of the Judaizers (Acts 15.1, 5), John's constituents probably felt intimidated, troubled and confused in their confrontations with the secessionists (Marshall 1997: 4).

While not denying that a dire threat remained, John attempted to defuse the volatile situation by offering a degree of resolution through a sense of hope (1 John 3.3), joy (1.4), victory (4.4; 5.4), and guidance (4.1-3), and attempting to achieve solidarity with his recipients (1.3). The ending of 1 John (5.13-21), with its emphasis on confidence (παρρησία) in prayer and knowledge (Smalley 1984: 293), reflected in a cadence of first-person plural verbs of knowing (οἴδαμεν), likely instilled renewed assurance among the Johannine Christians. It is reasonable to surmise, therefore, that these people experienced emotional release or catharsis (Shiner 2003: 58), 'rejoiced for the encouragement' (Acts 15.30) the letter provided, and expressed their reaffirmed unity with the author through his designated envoy.

The Curtain Closes

The study of ancient media culture has the potential to transform the way we think about and experience texts, especially when the totality of media expression is considered. Regrettably, though, the dynamic manner in which such media avenues as textuality, orality/aurality, memory and performance operated in antiquity has been largely shrouded by modern, Western sensibilities. Our literary biases and dependence on electronic and digital communication and information storage tend to obscure our perception and consciousness of first-century media culture. Fortunately, over the course of the last few decades a number of scholars have chosen to pursue the path of ancient media studies and apply the resulting insights to various biblical documents. Despite these advances, however, many texts await further exploration of their multi-media character, including probing their written nature, aural profiles and memory dynamics, and reconstruction of their original performances. For the Johannine corpus as well as other early Christian literature, the study of ancient media culture promises innovative means to explore texts in ways that enhance conventional modes of exegesis.

Chapter 3

THE RIDDLE OF THE BAPTIST AND THE GENESIS OF THE PROLOGUE: JOHN 1.1-18 IN ORAL/AURAL MEDIA CULTURE

Tom Thatcher

> The Prologue
> is not a jig-saw puzzle
> but one piece of solid theological writing.
> The evangelist wrote it all...
>
> (Barrett 1971: 27)

> Still, it would be strange indeed
>   if the verses
>   so commonly regarded as secondary insertions
>   were the pivots or central verses
> of the entire prologue!
>
> (Culpepper 1980: 6)

This paper will seek to answer to the question, 'How might a more acute sensitivity to ancient media culture impact understandings of the composition-history of the Prologue to the Gospel of John?' Analysis of this passage has generally proceeded from the assumption that John 1.1-18 is a fragment or reworking of an ancient 'hymn' – originally composed in honour of Wisdom, John the Baptist, or Jesus Christ – that would have been familiar to John's first audiences from their liturgical experience. This conclusion is based both on the content of the unit and, perhaps more particularly, on its style and structure. Following this line of reasoning, scholars have attempted to reconstruct this primitive hymn in search of clues to the Fourth Evangelist's own theological interests and tendencies. Through close source-critical analysis, one may distinguish the text of the hymn from John's revisions and interpolations, a process that promises to expose major themes that may be present elsewhere in the Gospel, and to offer a glimpse into the devotional life of the Johannine Christians.

But while source-critical approaches to John 1.1-18 have produced interesting readings both of this text specifically and of Johannine theology generally, I will argue here that they are based on an essential misconception of the media dynamics of early Christian culture. Further and more narrowly, these approaches reflect a failure to account for the actual compositional dynamics of the passage itself. In my view, John 1.1-18 should *not* be understood as the reworking of a hymn, but rather as an original composition and as the Evangelist's poetic expansion of a traditional saying associated with John the Baptist. Because a version of this traditional saying may now be found at John 1.15 ('the one coming behind me [John the Baptist] became ahead of me because he was before me'), this verse may be regarded as the genesis of the Prologue.

To defend this thesis, I will first briefly survey source-critical research on John 1.1-18, focusing on approaches that view the Prologue as a primitive hymn that has been absorbed into the text of the Fourth Gospel. I will then place these approaches in dialogue with Werner Kelber's research on the problem of the 'original form' of an oral text. As will be seen, Kelber's theory substantially problematizes attempts to reconstruct any text that may underlie John 1, and in fact would suggest that the very notion of an 'original' hymn is misguided. Having cleared this ground, I will proceed to show that the Prologue evidences a high level of compositional unity. I will propose that this literary unity is a product of the fact that the Prologue was composed through the expansion of a traditional oral unit, which may now be found on the lips of John the Baptist at John 1.15. By all appearances, John 1.1-18 seems to have been orally composed as an organic element of the larger narrative that it introduces.

The Problem of the Prologue: The Quest for the Hymn

The Fourth Gospel's opening verses, often referred to as 'the Prologue' (John 1.1-18), immediately reveal several of the major themes and interests of the book. These themes include Christ's pre-existence, Christ's revelatory work as the 'light' who brings 'life', Jesus's rejection by 'his own' (the majority of Jews), and the notion that believers are, like Jesus, 'born of God' (see Carson 1991: 111; O'Grady 2007). As a result, John, unlike Mark, does not lead the reader through a gradually deeper revelation of Jesus's identity that is fully manifest only at the empty tomb. Rather, in the Fourth Gospel Jesus's identity and mission are clear from the very beginning of the narrative, and the reader is warned that their own identity is defined by acceptance or rejection of John's claims (John 1.10-13). John 1.1-18 thus provides a comprehensive overview of the complex relationships between Christ, believers, and the world.

Yet while John 1.1-18 is well integrated into the Fourth Gospel's symbolic world, most commentators have concluded that the Prologue is based upon, or perhaps even directly quotes, an earlier Jewish or Christian hymn. According to this proposal, John cited the hymn because it was familiar to his first audiences and modified this text to fit his immediate literary purposes, primarily by adding new material that disrupted its poetic structure. Scholars who take this approach seek to reconstruct this hymn and identify its major movements and themes. Once these have been isolated, one can speculate on the exegetical and theological significance of the ways that John has filtered this material into his Jesus story. To survey this line of research, it will be helpful first to look at the evidence that might suggest that John 1.1-18 is based on a hymn, and then at possible reconstructions of this earlier liturgical text.

Several pieces of evidence, some internal to the Fourth Gospel and others drawn from the broader milieu of primitive Christianity, have led scholars to conclude that the Prologue is based on an early Christian – or, at least, Christianized – hymn. First and most significantly, the Greek text of John 1.1-18 is characterized by what appears to be a poetic style. To take but two notable examples, portions of verses 1-5 and 9-11 are often cited as instances of *sorites*, 'a remarkable chainlike sequence of terms in which the last word of one strophe becomes the first word of the next' (Smith 1999: 5–6).[1] Following this pattern, lines are connected through the repetition of significant words that emphasize and expand key concepts and motifs, creating a strong sense of flow through the movement of the argument. This structural feature of the Prologue is so prominent that it is observable even in a literal English translation (all translations mine throughout).

The poetic structure of the Prologue is also particularly evident in the various chiasms that appear throughout the passage, both on a micro-level (within and between individual lines) and on a macro-level (in the larger conceptual movement of the whole).[2] The former phenomenon is conveniently illustrated by the opening verses of the Fourth Gospel.

A. Ἐν ἀρχῇ (the beginning)
   B. ἦν ὁ λόγος καὶ ὁ λόγος (the Word)
      C. ἦν πρὸς τὸν θεόν καὶ θεὸς (God)
   B. ἦν ὁ λόγος οὗτος ἦν (the Word)
A. ἐν ἀρχῇ πρὸς τὸν θεόν (the beginning)

---

1   Alan Culpepper, like other scholars who have compared the Prologue to the poetic structure of Hebrew verse, describes this literary pattern as 'a beautiful example of stair-step parallelism' in which 'the second term in each line becomes the first term in the next' (1998: 112; 1980: 8–9; see also Boismard 1957: 76–7; Brown 1966/1970: 1.19).

2   Significant attempts to identify and outline chiasm(s) within the Prologue (and sometimes within the larger narrative of the Fourth Gospel as well) include Lund 1931 (which focuses on the outline of the primitive hymn and treats vv. 6-8, 15 as interpolations); Boismard 1957 (which incorporates the material on the Baptist into the chiasm without stating a definitive conclusion on the authorship of these lines; see 24–7, 5876–81, esp. 80); Feuillet 1968, whose outline balances each element of the Prologue in such a way that the text does not have a central crux; Culpepper 1980; Staley 1986 (which highlights the literary, rather than theological, relationship between the Prologue and the remainder of the Gospel and also incorporates the Baptist material into the chiasm; see 245–6, 249); Ellis 1999. Notably, these studies are not agreed on which, if any, lines in the Prologue function as the conceptual crux of the passage.

Table 1: *Sorites* in John 1.1-5, 9-11[3]		
1.1	Ἐν ἀρχῇ ἦν ὁ λόγος καὶ ὁ λόγος ἦν πρὸς τὸν θεόν καὶ θεὸς ἦν ὁ λόγος	In the beginning was the **Word**, and the **Word** was with **God**, and **God** was the **Word**.
1.2	οὗτος ἦν ἐν ἀρχῇ πρὸς τὸν θεόν	**This one** (the Word) was in the beginning with **God**.
1.3	πάντα δι᾽ αὐτοῦ ἐγένετο καὶ χωρὶς αὐτοῦ ἐγένετο οὐδὲ ἕν	All things through **him** became, and without **him** became not one thing.
1.4	ὃ γέγονεν ἐν αὐτῷ ζωὴ ἦν καὶ ἡ ζωὴ ἦν τὸ φῶς τῶν ἀνθρώπων	What has become in him was **life**, and the **life** was the **light** of humanity.
1.5	καὶ τὸ φῶς ἐν τῇ σκοτίᾳ φαίνει καὶ ἡ σκοτία αὐτὸ οὐ κατέλαβεν	And the **light** shines in the **dark- ness**, and the **darkness** did not overcome it.
1.9	ἦν τὸ φῶς τὸ ἀληθινόν ὃ φωτίζει πάντα ἄνθρωπον ἐρχόμενον εἰς τὸν κόσμον	It was the true **light** Which **lights** all people by coming into the **world**.
1.10	ἐν τῷ κόσμῳ ἦν καὶ ὁ κόσμος δι᾽ αὐτοῦ ἐγένετο καὶ ὁ κόσμος αὐτὸν οὐκ ἔγνω	In the **world** he was, And **the world** became through him And **the world** did not know him.
1.11	εἰς τὰ ἴδια ἦλθεν καὶ οἱ ἴδιοι αὐτὸν οὐ παρέλαβον	To **his own** he came And **his own** did not receive him.

3   The division of the Greek text in Table 1 reflects an attempt to highlight the apparent parallelism, with the assumptions that καὶ is generally used to indicate the beginning of a new line and that οὗτος in v. 2 takes the immediately preceding ὁ λόγος as its antecedent ('God was the Word. This Word was in the beginning with God.'). This approach also supports the Nestle–Aland text, which inserts a break after the words οὐδὲ ἕν in v. 3, thus suggesting that ὃ γέγονεν begins a new sentence: '...without him became not one thing. What became in him was...'. As a side-note, the *sorites* pattern may also suggest that δι᾽ αὐτοῦ ('through him') in v. 3 takes τὸν θεόν as its antecedent ('All things became through God, and without God became not one thing') rather than ὁ λόγος, in which case vv. 2-4 would be a general summary of Jewish views of creation rather than a specifically Christian claim that the Word created all things.

Extending this observation, Alan Culpepper has argued that John 1.1-18 is a complex conceptual chiasm which revolves around the claim at 1.12 that those who accept Christ become God's children (see Culpepper 1980: 9–17; 1998: 116).

> A. The Word with God (1.1-2)
> > B. What came through the Word (1.3)
> > > C. What was received from the Word (1.4-5)
> > > > D. John the Baptist announces the Word (1.6-8)
> > > > > E. The Word enters the world (1.9-10)
> > > > > > F. The Word and his own people (1.11)
> > > > > > > G. The Word is accepted (1.12a)
> > > > > > > > H. The Word's gift to those who accepted him (1.12b)
> > > > > > > G. The Word is accepted (1.12c)
> > > > > > F. The Word and his own people (1.13)
> > > > > E. The Word enters the world (1.14)
> > > > D. John the Baptist announces the Word (1.15)
> > > C. What was received from the Word (1.16)
> > B. What came through the Word (1.17)
> A. The Word with God (1.18)[4]

Alongside stylistic elements that might be typical of oral poetry, such as parallelism and chiasm, many scholars have noted that the conceptual content of John 1.1-18 seems similar to other New Testament passages that are usually identified as hymns. Like the Prologue, these liturgical fragments typically emphasize Christ's divine nature and describe his descent from heaven, revelatory career on earth, and exaltation after resurrection. Notable examples include Romans 1.3-4, Philippians 2.6-11, Colossians 1.15-20, 1 Timothy 3.16 and 1 Peter 3.18-22, all of which seem to follow a common outline with individual variations reflecting the respective literary contexts in which the hymns appear.[5]

---

4   As is the case with any attempt to identify chiastic patterns in biblical texts, there is no consensus on the correct way to outline John 1.1-18. Since most studies of chiasm are grounded in the premise that 'the central idea or message is almost always found in the ... central section of the chiastic pattern', these alternate outlines generally produce very different readings of the Prologue and its main emphases (quote Ellis 1999: 274; on the Prologue specifically see Culpepper 1980: 14).

5   Of course, the absence of one or several of the typical thematic elements may simply indicate that a biblical author has cited only the relevant portion of a longer composition. In my view, a specific passage need not evidence every thematic element of the genre in order to be classified as a 'hymn'.

Table 2: The Prologue and Other New Testament 'Hymns'	
Theme	Citation
Christ's divinity and pre-existence	**John 1.1-2, 15**; Phil. 2.6; Col. 1.15
Christ's role in the creation and sustenance of the universe	**John 1.3-4**; Col. 1.16-17
Christ's incarnation	**John 1.5, 9-10, 14, 18**; Phil. 2.7; Col. 1.19; 1 Tim. 3.16
Christ's sacrificial death by crucifixion	Phil. 2.7-8; Col. 1.20; 1 Pet. 3.18
Christ's resurrection and exaltation	Rom. 1.4; Phil. 2.9-10; Col. 1.18; 1 Tim. 3.16;[6] 1 Pet. 3.18-22

As Table 2 indicates, John's Prologue is somewhat notable for its lack of reference to the death and exaltation of Jesus.[7] This anomaly may be readily explained, however, by the fact that the Evangelist has adapted the hymn to function as the introduction to a Gospel narrative that culminates in a sustained account of Jesus's death and several detailed resurrection appearances. The original hymn may have included references to these events which the Evangelist deleted, or perhaps he simply overlooked them to emphasize the incarnation of the eternal Word in Jesus.

Moving beyond the biblical text, the notion that John 1.1-18 includes citations of a Christological song is consistent with extra-biblical evidence which suggests that hymns were a regular feature of early Christian worship. Two of the most significant sources, Pliny the Younger and Eusebius, may

6   The logic of the sequence of events described in 1 Timothy 3.16 is difficult to determine. The table here reflects Luke Timothy Johnson's suggestion that 'the last four verses [of the hymn] do not represent a chronological sequence, but four *aspects* of Christ's being 'made righteous by spirit', that is, four aspects of his resurrection and exaltation (Johnson 2001: 236). Following this reading, 1 Timothy 3.16 focuses on the incarnation and vindication/exaltation of Christ.

7   Or may allude to Christ's resurrection/exaltation in a veiled way. See here Barrett 1971: 26–7, who argues that the testimony of the Baptist at John 1.15 refers to Christ's glorification, with primary emphasis on the notion that Christ 'became ahead' of John. It should be stressed, however, that Barrett believes that the Prologue is the Evangelist's original composition and that vv. 6-8, 15 are organically related to the remainder of the passage. As such, he does not attribute the exaltation theme to a primitive hymn.

be briefly mentioned here. In a famous letter to the Emperor Trajan written some time between 111 and 113 CE, Pliny, governor of Pontus/Bithynia in Asia Minor, asks for advice on how to deal with those accused of involvement in the Christ cult. During interrogation under torture, Christians confessed that 'they had met regularly before dawn on a fixed day to chant verses alternately among themselves in honour of Christ as if to a god [*carmenque Christo quasi deo dicere*]' (Pliny, *Letters* 10.96.7). While it is impossible to reconstruct an early Christian liturgy from Pliny's description, his combination of the terms *carmen* and *dico* seems to suggest, as indicated by the Loeb edition translation cited above, that church gatherings included group recitation of Christological confessions in the form of chants or songs.[8] Considerably later than Pliny but within the Christian community, Eusebius, writing in the 320s, seems to assume that the singing of psalms and hymns had been a feature of Christian worship since the earliest times: 'All the Psalms and hymns which were written by faithful Christians from the beginning sing of the Christ as the Logos of God and treat him as God' (*Eccl. Hist.* 5.28.5–6; see also 10.3.3–4; 10.4.5–6). Notably, Eusebius' summary here includes several key Johannine terms and themes: 'from the beginning' (ἀπ᾽ ἀρχῆς; 1 John 1.1; 2.7, 13-14, 24; 3.11; 2 John 5-6), 'Christ as God' (John 1.1; 8:58; 10:30, 38; 14:9-10; 17:21-3), and 'Christ as the Logos of God' (τὸν λόγον τοῦ θεου John 1.1, 14). These allusions may suggest that Eusebius himself, and perhaps several generations of Christians before him, understood John 1.1-18 and 1 John 1.1-3 to be early hymns. At the very least, Eusebius assumes that Christological songs/chants had been in use since the early days of the church.

It seems entirely reasonable, then, to suggest that John 1.1-18 was adapted from a pre-existing hymn. The Apostle Paul urges believers to encourage one another by singing 'psalms, hymns, and spiritual songs' (ψαλμός/ὕμνος/ᾠδή; Eph 5:19; Col 3:16), apparently in community gatherings, and evidence from both the New Testament and extra-biblical sources indicates that the early Christians sometimes sang or chanted confessional statements together. Scholars who associate John 1.1-18 with this hymnic tradition have highlighted a number of features of the Greek text that seem typical of ancient poetry, including the repetition of words and sounds, possible chiastic structures, and various forms of parallelism. Aside from such stylistic evidence, several key themes in the Prologue may be found in other NT texts that are typically identified as liturgical fragments. Following this train of thought, John 1.1-18 may be viewed as an early Christian song that John

---

8   Noting that Pliny was governor of the Roman district of Bithynia, Raymond Brown finds it 'interesting that these references to hymns [in Pliny and Eusebius] have some connection with Asia Minor; thus, the conjecture that the original of the Prologue was a hymn of the Johannine church at Ephesus has a claim to likelihood' (1966/1970: 1.20).

adapted to introduce his story of Jesus, similar to the way modern preachers might quote a hymn or poem in the course of a sermon.[9]

Since ancient Christian hymns, like modern worship songs, would theoretically be composed, transmitted and performed orally in community gatherings, and since John 1.1-18 clearly reflects numerous features that would be typical of an oral style of composition, the passage would seem ripe for analysis in terms of ancient media dynamics. In fact, however, much modern research on the Prologue has been driven by the source-critical premise that the meaning of this text lies in the differences between the original source document and the Evangelist's adaptations of it. In order to identify these adaptations, of course, it is first necessary to reconstruct the *Grundschrift* that the Evangelist has incorporated into his Gospel. Once the specific contours of this earlier text have been defined, one may proceed to speculate on its theological emphases and possible origins. How, then, can one determine which verses and lines in John 1.1-18 were original to the hymn, and which were added by the Evangelist in adapting the hymn to the larger narrative?

Answers to the above question generally reflect a widespread belief that the Prologue does not flow quite as smoothly as it might. Most notably, vv. 6-8 appear to break the poetic rhythm of the opening lines, with the resumption of the parallelism pattern at v. 9. Indeed, as Culpepper observes, 'in contrast to most of the rest of the prologue, these verses [vv. 6-8, 15] are written in relatively flat prose style' (1980: 13). This break in structure coincides with a sudden change in topic, from the creation of 'all things' through the influence of the Word to the testimony of John the Baptist. Further, one may readily observe, even from a literal English translation, that John 1.9 is an instance of *Wiederaufnahme*, a 'repetitive resumptive' pattern. M. E. Boismard, who highlighted this device as a feature of Johannine style, explains that 'when a redactor wishes to insert a gloss of average length into an already existing text, he is often compelled to resume … expressions used before the gloss in the primitive story in order to be able to renew the thread of the story' (1977: 235; translation mine). In this case, the word φῶς/'light' – which serves as both the subject and the main verb of the primary clause in v. 5 (τὸ φῶς ἐν τῇ σκοτίᾳ φαίνει; 'the light shines in the darkness') – reappears prominently in v. 9 immediately after the digression on the witness of the Baptist ('it was the true light, which lights all people'). A similar thematic disruption is evident at v. 15, where the Baptist suddenly reappears to offer an oblique 'testimony' in the middle of a discussion of the revelation of God's grace through Christ. Here again, *Wiederaufnahme* may be detected: v. 14 closes with the assertion that the Word, as the 'only-born' (μονογενής) of God, is 'full of grace and truth' (πλήρης χάριτος καὶ ἀληθείας); after the intrusion of the Baptist, v. 16

---

9   Ben Witherington has compared John 1.1-18 to the hymns of homage to the emperor that preceded some Roman dramas, seeing them as closer to the Fourth Evangelist's own milieu (1995: 5, 47).

immediately resumes this theme by noting that 'from his [the Word's] fullness we all have received grace against grace' (ὅτι ἐκ τοῦ πληρώματος αὐτοῦ ἡμεῖς πάντες ἐλάβομεν καὶ χάριν ἀντὶ χάριτος). It appears, then, that the Prologue would read more smoothly if vv. 6-8, 15 were removed, suggesting that these lines may be interpolations into an earlier composition.

Building on these observations, one can readily imagine that the Fourth Gospel, like Mark, originally opened with an account of the testimony of John the Baptist. Following this scenario, the Evangelist or a later redactor merged several of the opening lines about the Baptist into the text of the Prologue in the process of adding the hymn to the Gospel narrative (see Boismard 1957: 24–5). The reverse scenario is also reasonable: perhaps John's Gospel originally opened with the Logos hymn, which was later modified by the insertion of material that would clarify, for apologetic purposes, the Baptist's inferiority to Christ. In either case, the poetic and conceptual structure of the hymn was disrupted in the process of combining it with the prose narrative, leaving the textual evidence that now facilitates the reconstruction of the primitive liturgical unit.

Building on the thesis that the Baptist material is intrusive, a number of scholars have suggested that other lines and verses in the Prologue also should be viewed as interpolations into the earlier composition. To take but one notable example for purposes of illustration, Rudolf Schnackenburg's influential commentary offers a detailed reconstruction of the primitive hymn that underlies John 1.1-18. In Schnackenburg's view, John adapted a liturgical song that had been written by Christian 'converts from Hellenistic Judaism', adding lines that 'expounded it [the terminology of the hymn] more strictly in terms of the Incarnation and of the reception of the Logos among men (belief and unbelief)' (Schnackenburg 1982: 1.231, 1.227). Applying this criterion – that Jewish Christian Wisdom themes may be differentiated from John's incarnational Christology – Schnackenburg suggested that the primitive hymn included only portions of verses 1, 3, 4, 9-11, 14 and 16. Verses 2, 5, 6-8, 12-13, 15 and 17-18 were added by John to emphasize the work of the historical Jesus and the world's response to his revelation. Schnackenburg proceeded to divide the reconstructed Logos hymn into four distinct stanzas (see discussion 1982: 1.226–32).

In Schnackenburg's view, the Evangelist's own theological interest in the incarnation of the Word explains the interpolation of the disruptive material on the Baptist at John 1.6-8. 'The introduction of John the Baptist here [vv. 6-8], in narrative style, already suggests the time of the historical coming of Christ, the Incarnation of the Logos, which is then resoundingly proclaimed in v. 14.' The same principle explains John's insertion of the phrase 'coming into the world' at v. 9, of the summary of the world's rejection of Jesus's message at vv. 12-13, of the phrase 'we beheld his glory' at v. 14, and of the concluding assertion at vv. 17-18 that grace and truth were revealed through the ministry of the historical Jesus (Schnackenburg 1982: 1.227). While Schnackenburg admits that the details of his reconstruction may be off at minor points, he assures his readers that precision is not essential as 'long as one admits in principle that an independent Logos-hymn has been transformed into the introduction to the Gospel' (1982: 1.227).[10]

The Prologue and the Problem of the Primitive

All attempts to analyse John 1.1-18 in terms of the differences between the hymn on which this passage is based and the Evangelist's revisions and adaptations of that hymn are predicated on two significant assumptions. First, source-critical approaches obviously assume that such a hymn existed in the first place and, further, that Johannine Christians used songs or chants of this kind in their community gatherings. I do not think it possible to prove or disprove the latter claim, and for the sake of argument I will essentially grant the former. In other words, for the purposes of this essay it makes no difference whether a Logos hymn existed, and I will basically assume that it did. As will be seen, the more significant question is exactly what it would mean to say that 'a Logos hymn existed' in the media culture in which the Fourth Gospel was produced and published. Secondly, source-critical approaches to the Prologue further assume that it is possible to disentangle two distinct texts – the primitive Logos hymn and the larger narrative in which it is now embedded – that have been fused in the Evangelist's composition. As noted earlier, this disentangling almost always involves the subtraction of the material on John the Baptist in vv. 6-8, 15, and often of other 'alien' lines and phrases as well. If these foundational premises were found to be cracked, much of the past century of research on the Prologue would require significant revision.

In the remainder of this essay, I will argue that source-critical approaches to John 1.1-18 are questionable in light of (a) recent research on the media dynamics of early Christian literature, and (b) the actual data from the text of the Fourth Gospel itself. To begin with the least difficult premise, this section will argue that attempts to isolate and reconstruct the 'original' version of a primitive Logos hymn are grounded in an essential misconception of the nature of oral texts. After establishing this point, I will proceed to highlight elements of John 1.1-18 which suggest that the Prologue was composed orally as an extension of the testimony of John the Baptist that now appears in v. 15. Whether or not the author of John 1 was aware of a Logos hymn, the current text of the Prologue should be viewed as a unified oral composition and as an integral element of the larger narrative that it introduces.

---

10   Schnackenburg's reconstructed Logos hymn differs substantially from other hymns cited in the New Testament in its emphasis on 'the rejection of the Redeemer by the world', a theme that is attested nowhere else. Schnackenburg resolves this problem by noting that John's Logos hymn is clearly obligated to Jewish Wisdom speculation, which frequently suggests that divine Wisdom descended among men but was rejected by most (1982: 1.228; see Witherington 1995: 49–53).

As noted above, attempts to reconstruct a primitive Logos hymn from John 1.1-18 are predicated on the assumption that it would, in fact, be possible to dislodge the lines of this primitive song from the current text of the Fourth Gospel. These approaches further assume that it would be possible to identify and remove alien interpolations so as to reconstruct the original contours and content of the hymn. Finally, since any such hymn would have been performed and transmitted orally in the community gatherings of Johannine Christians, these studies essentially assume that an oral text can be isolated within, and precisely reconstructed from, a written document such as the Gospel of John. These premises, though foundational to form-critical study of the Gospels, have been convincingly rejected in a series of significant books and essays by Werner Kelber, who asserts that references to 'the original' version of an oral text are misguided. While many aspects of Kelber's argument are relevant to the present study, in view of space limitations I will focus here on his theory of 'equiprimordiality' in oral communication environments.[11]

In Kelber's view, every oral text is a free-standing composition with a distinct identity and meaning. This is the case because oral words, unlike printed words, are events in time rather than objects in space. As such, the meanings of spoken words are specific to situations, while the meanings of written words transcend the circumstances of any individual reading (see Kelber 1983: 109–10). Speakers select terms that they hope will communicate certain ideas to a particular audience in a particular way, and they adjust their modes of delivery in response to the audience's immediate feedback. Through this process, both the shape and meaning of oral discourse grow organically within the dialogue context. Kelber refers to the social setting in which words are exchanged as a 'biosphere in which speaker and hearers live … an invisible nexus of references and identities' (Kelber 1995: 159). In any act of oral communication, the social biosphere functions as a human intertext, creating the referential field from which the discourse derives its value – these words mean what they mean because they are connected to these people at this particular moment in time (Kelber 1990: 77–8). Because oral words are shaped by the dynamics of their social contexts, and because every social context is a unique historical event, no two oral texts can ever be entirely identical.

Following Kelber's biosphere model, even if the same actors exchange the same words in the same place on different occasions, the respective utterances will differ at least in terms of the time that has passed between them.

---

11   While Kelber has offered several insightful readings of the Fourth Gospel, including sustained remarks on the Logos terminology of the Prologue, his comments have focused on the hermeneutics of orality and print rather than on the specific compositional dynamics of John 1. See here Kelber 1990; 1996. In my view, the current study is a complement to, and a logical extension of, Kelber's research.

Thus, if a certain grandmother were to tell the story 'Little Red Riding Hood' to a group of children on four consecutive days, these renderings would doubtless evidence a similar structure and include many of the same words. An observer could readily recognize the obvious similarities between these texts, and could identify each as a rendering of the same fairy tale. Yet each telling would be distinct from the others to the extent that it emerged at a unique moment in time and in the context of a unique interaction between this speaker and her audience. Similarly, and perhaps more material to the present study, a devoted fan of a particular musical artist might see three live performances of a certain song on consecutive nights. While the fan would immediately recognize the song in question after a few measures had been played, each performance would differ slightly due to the specific circumstances of each individual concert.

Kelber refers to this event-quality of oral texts and other live compositions as 'equiprimordiality'. In the examples just cited, the principle of equiprimordiality would suggest that 'each rendition [of Red Riding Hood and the song] was an original version, and in fact *the original version*' (Kelber 1995: 151; see also 2002: 64; 2005: 237). There would be no point in comparing grandmother's four accounts in order to determine which one most likely reflects the 'true' or 'original' version of Red Riding Hood. Each is, in a real sense, an original composition, and each would reflect the dynamics of the interaction between grandmother and her young audience on the specific day the story was told. Similarly, no true fan would insist that any one of the three live musical performances was the 'original', even though they might prefer the version they heard at one particular concert over other versions. Of course, if grandmother were to publish a book on Red Riding Hood, complete with pictures and an edited text, one might meaningfully refer to 'variations' on this 'original' – perhaps, for example, if she were to change some of the words or add details while reading the book to her grandchildren. Similarly, the musician's fan might note that he or she was playing their favourite song in a way that did not exactly resemble the version recorded in the studio for radio play. But this would simply demonstrate the extent to which the notion of the 'original text' is a consequence of mass media technologies like print, radio and film. The children cannot complain that grandma has 'skipped a page' when there are, in fact, no pages to be skipped.

While Kelber's theory of equiprimordiality is based on a disarmingly simple observation about the nature of oral speech, it carries dramatic implications for any attempt to reconstruct the 'original' version of an oral text. Indeed, the very 'notion of "the original form" is a phantom of the literary – not to say typographic – imagination and incompatible with oral hermeneutics' (Kelber 2005: 231). This being the case, as Kelber has often pointed out in his critiques of form and source criticism, any quest to locate the 'original' version of an oral story or saying is doomed from the start, simply because there is no 'original' to reconstruct. Applied to problems in Christian origins, the very notion of the 'original' version of a unit of oral tradition would have been puzzling to the early Christians and the authors of the Gospels. 'When the charismatic speaker pronounced a saying at one place and subsequently chose to deliver it elsewhere, neither he nor his hearers could have understood this other rendition as a secondhand version of the first one ... [or] would have thought of differentiating between the primary, original wording and its secondary, derivative version' (Kelber 2005: 238).[12] Rather, in an oral communication environment, the audience would understand that each utterance is an original composition, even if the basic formula or storyline was familiar, and therefore would not be particularly disturbed by minor variations in wording, emphasis or detail (see Kelber 1983: 30; 1990: 74). This being the case, it is futile to compare written sources in hopes of reconstructing the 'original' version of an oral text, and in fact any effort to do so reflects a typographic mentality that would be uncharacteristic of early Christianity.

Applying Kelber's observations on the nature of oral communication to the problem at hand, it appears that at least one of the foundational assumptions of source-critical research on the Prologue is seriously flawed. Specifically, it would be impossible to reconstruct the 'original' version of the Logos hymn underlying John 1.1-18, simply because no such original version existed. Manifestly, when we speak of a 'primitive Christian hymn', we are not talking about the sort of fixed, copyrighted texts that appear in modern songbooks or on PowerPoint slides. Even if primitive hymnals existed, most Johannine Christians would not have been able to read them, and would have learned the lyrics to various liturgical songs in the same way that Christians today learn the lyrics to songs on the radio: by listening to them and singing them over and over again. Each performance of a hymn would thus be equiprimordial, a unique and distinct communication event reflecting the circumstances of a specific occasion.

Further, if each performance or citation of an oral liturgical unit 'was equiprimordial with every other one', it is essentially inaccurate to suggest that John 'interpolated' alien lines into an early Christian hymn (quote Kelber 1990: 74). It would be more correct to say that the content of early hymns was always fluid, subject to the memory of the performer(s) and to the particular point that the performer(s) wished to make at any given moment. If, then, John quoted portions of a familiar hymn and added lines about John the Baptist, it seems unlikely that he (or his first audiences) would view these lines as violations of the integrity of the original. At most, they might simply note to themselves that John was singing the song a different way on this particular occasion.

---

12   The term 'charismatic speaker' here refers specifically to Jesus, an itinerant teacher who published his message through numerous recompositions of the same material in different locations. The above quote, however, summarizes Kelber's understanding of the nature of all texts and traditions in oral communication environments.

Of course, one might argue that John 1.1-18, even if a free-standing composition in its own right, may be regarded as 'traditional' in the general sense that this text had been previously performed on numerous occasions by Johannine Christians. Further, because songs and chants typically evidence a poetic structure, one might expect repeat performances of a Logos hymn to resemble one another more closely than, say, consecutive retellings of the story of the Bethesda healing (John 5). In other words, even if John is not quoting a fixed text, his first audiences may have recognized that he was re-performing a familiar song and adapting it to his narrative. Granted this possibility, it would remain essentially impossible to reconstruct earlier versions of this hymn by subtracting specific lines and phrases from the current text of the Fourth Gospel. Certainly, it would be impossible to do this with the level of certainty that would be needed to support a redaction-critical reading, which would require a strict differentiation between material original to the hymn and the Evangelist's own revisions and adaptations. In a communication environment that does not recognize 'originals', interpolations are simply a form of virtuosity.

The Riddle of the Baptist as the Core of the Prologue

As noted earlier, the Prologue to the Fourth Gospel evidences a number of stylistic features that might be typical of hymns, chants and other orally-composed texts. These features include various forms of parallelism, chiasm, and other literary devices that facilitate the division of John 1.1-18 into verbal and conceptual lines and stanzas. Building on this evidence, scholars have proposed that the Prologue is based on an earlier hymn and have attempted to reconstruct this primitive song by removing extraneous lines and phrases. Almost all of these reconstructions assume that the material on John the Baptist in vv. 6-8, 15 has been interpolated by the Evangelist or a later redactor, a hypothesis that explains the apparent verbal and thematic breaks in the flow of the passage as well as the presence of *Wiederaufnahme*. In terms of the interests of the present volume, no less an authority than Rudolf Bultmann made the astute suggestion that the first audiences of the Fourth Gospel would have recognized these lines as interpolations, for 'in oral recitation the [Evangelist's] "comments" would be distinguishable by the tone of the speaker' (1971: 16 n. 3).

In my view, despite the limitations noted in the preceding section of this paper, source-critical studies of John 1.1-18 have set an important precedent for future research by giving sustained attention to the oral-compositional dynamics of a critical passage in the Fourth Gospel, one that introduces the key theological themes of the book and that lays the foundation for the irony that characterizes John's narrative style.

However, despite their careful attention to poetic patterns and liturgical units, source-critical approaches have overlooked two aspects of the Prologue that would have been immediately obvious to first-century audiences who experienced John's Gospel through public readings in community gatherings – with their ears rather than their eyes. First, despite the apparent thematic breaks, the overall movement of John 1.1-18 is highly unified by the repetition of key terms and phrases, which is to say, through the repetition of notable sounds. Secondly, and building on the first point, the material on John the Baptist in vv. 6-8, 15 is thoroughly integrated into the structure of the narrative as it stands. For listening audiences, the most striking feature of John 1.1-18 would surely be the monotonous repetition of sounds that draw attention to the key characters and events under consideration. In my view, these listeners would not sense that the material on the Baptist was an interpolation into an earlier text, or at least would view the current composition as a unified whole even if some lines sounded less familiar than others.

In the remainder of this essay, I will briefly unpack the two asser-tions outlined above – that the compositional unity of the Prologue is evident in the repetition of key words/sounds, and that the verses on John the Baptist are highly integrated into the text as it stands – before proceeding to suggest that John 1.15 is not an alien interpolation into an earlier text but rather a traditional oral unit from which the remainder of the Prologue has been generated. Specifically, the evidence suggests that John 1.1-18 was composed by expanding the terms/sounds in the riddle of the Baptist at 1.15, which was likely a traditional confes-sional saying used by the Johannine churches. Thus, far from being a secondary intrusion, John 1.15 is the core of the Prologue.

On the first point above, from the perspective of oral performance – which is to say, from the perspective of a largely illiterate first-century audience that would experience the Gospel of John only through public readings – the flow of the Prologue is much stronger than is typically suggested. A quick look at the Greek text of John 1.1-18 reveals that three key verbs – ἦν ('was'), γίνομαι/ἐγένετο ('became'; NRSV: 'came into being'), and ἐρχόμαι/ἦλθεν ('come/came') – recur in various forms throughout the passage, even in those verses that are typically regarded as interpolations. While these words are certainly less glamorous than 'life' or 'grace', I call them 'key' terms simply because the text is saturated with them: ἦν occurs eleven times (vv. 1 [x3], 2, 4 [x2], 8, 9, 10, 15 [x2]), forms of γίνομαι appear nine times (vv. 3 [x3], 6, 10, 12, 14, 15, 17), and forms of ἐρχόμαι appear four times (vv. 7, 9, 11, 15). If an average reader could vocalize the 252 words of the Greek text of John 1.1-18 before a church gathering in, say, four minutes, the audience – for whom any sense of 'poetic structure' would be a matter of sounds rather than of lines on a page – would hear some form of the words 'was', 'become' or 'come' every ten to twelve seconds, giving them a strong sense of the overall unity of the verbal structure of the passage.[13]

Alongside the recurrent use of the three verbs ἦν, γίνομαι/ἐγένετο, and ἔρχόμαι/ἦλθεν, the aural continuity of the Prologue is enhanced by the repetition of other key terms/sounds. The noun λόγος is used four times (vv. 1, 14), three in the first verse alone, and forms of the pronoun αὐτός ('him') are used twelve times to keep the listener's ear focused on the Word as the primary subject of the discourse (vv. 3 [x2], 4, 5, 10 [x2], 11, 12 [x2], 14, 15, 16). Again following the four-minute performance model, listening audiences would be reminded once every fifteen seconds that they are hearing a story about the Word that came into the world and became flesh. The close connection between the Word and God is stressed by the repetition of the noun θεός eight times throughout the passage (vv. 1 [x2], 2, 6, 12, 13, 18 [x2]). The revelatory aspect of the Word's advent is emphasized by the use of noun and verb forms of the word 'light', φῶς/φαίνω/φωτίζω, which appear eight times in an even distribution through the first nine verses (vv. 4, 5 [x2], 7, 8 [x2], 9 [x2]). Other key terms are repeated in specific movements of the composition: μαρτυρέω/μαρτυρία ('witness/testify') is used three times in vv. 7-8 and once again in v. 15 to define the scope of the Baptist's work; κόσμος ('world') is used four times in vv. 9-10 to name the venue of the Word's revelatory mission; χάρις ('grace') is used three times in vv. 16-17 to contrast the giving of the Law through Moses with the genesis of grace in the incarnation. Whether John 1.1-18 is based on an earlier hymn or is the Evangelist's original spontaneous composition – and as noted earlier, even if the former is true the current text should be viewed as the latter – its most notable stylistic feature is the repetition of key words/sounds both within and across its various conceptual movements.

Secondly, alongside the overall repetition of words/sounds, the compositional unity of the Prologue is enhanced by the fact that the material on John the Baptist in vv. 6-8, 15 is highly integrated into the present text. This is evident not only from the presence of key terms within the lines that discuss

13   Of course, I do not presume that the 252 words in the Nestle–Aland text necessarily represent the version of the Prologue that would have been used in the Johannine churches, nor that a public 'reading' of the Fourth Gospel would involve the verbatim rendering of each and every word on the page and only of the words on the page. I think it likely that the written text of the Fourth Gospel would function, if ever used at all, as a memory prompt for spontaneous oral performances of the traditional material that it contains. For purposes of the present discussion, however, I would assume that the specific performance of the Prologue now preserved in the manuscript tradition would reflect the typical Johannine idiom, and therefore would evidence a relatively typical rate of occurrence for these three verbs and other important terms. Put another way: I would assume that the current text of John 1.1-18 is a typical summary of many oral performances of this material, each of which would be equiprimordial but all of which would likely reflect a similar idiom.

the Baptist, but also from the fact that the language of 1.15 is closely tied to the grammatical structure of the lines that immediately follow John's testimony.

On the first point noted above, several of the most significant words/ sounds that unify the Prologue appear in vv. 6-8, 15, giving these lines a strong acoustic mooring in the larger composition. Thus, ἦν appears in v. 8 and twice again in v. 15; ἐγένετο appears in vv. 6 and 15; ἦλθεν appears in v. 7 and seems to be implied again in v. 8 (ἀλλ᾿ ἵνα μαρτυρήσῃ περὶ τοῦ φωτός [ἦλθεν]), while ἐρχόμαι appears in v. 15; the pronoun αὐτός is used in reference to the λόγος in v. 15; θεός is used in v. 6; forms of φῶς/φαίνω/ φωτίζω appear in v. 7 and twice in v. 8. In view of this repetitive sound structure, *if* John's first audiences were already familiar with a community hymn on which the Prologue may have been based – 'familiar' meaning that they had heard and chanted this song in the past, not that they had ever seen it in print; indeed, it is unlikely that such a thing ever existed in print, if it existed at all – they could only be impressed by John's ability to integrate his new content so cleanly into the soundscape of the traditional unit.

Table 3: Unifying Words/Sounds in the Prologue's Material on the Baptist (vv. 6-8, 15)				
Word	Times used in vv. 1-5	Times used in vv. 9-14	Times used in vv. 16-18	Times used in vv. 6-8, 15 (Baptist material)
ἦν	6	2	0	3
γίνομαι	2	3	1	2
ἐρχόμαι	0	2	0	2
λόγος/ αὐτός	7	7	1	1
θεός	3	2	2	1
φῶς/φαίνω/φωτίζω	3	2	0	3

Aside from this repetition of sounds, the grammatical structure of John 1.15-17 suggests that these verses represent a continuous flow of thought, a fact that weighs against any evidence that the testimony of the Baptist in v. 15 is an alien interpolation. Verse 15 is structurally linked to vv. 16 and 17 by the double repetition of ὅτι ('because'), creating a balanced climactic structure that moves from the Baptist's testimony about Christ, to the revelation of God's grace through Christ's advent, to Christ's superiority over Moses as the giver of 'grace and truth'. The climactic pattern is enhanced by the use of the verb ἐγένετο at the end of v. 17, which creates an *inclusio* by closing the aural parenthesis opened by γέγονεν in the Baptist's testimony at v. 15.

Table 4: The Structural Unity of John 1.15-17	
Ἰωάννης μαρτυρεῖ περὶ αὐτοῦ καὶ κέκραγεν λέγων οὗτος ἦν ὃν εἶπον	John testifies about him and has cried out, saying, 'This was the one about whom I said,
ὁ ὀπίσω μου ἐρχόμενος ἔμπροσθέν μου γέγονεν ὅτι πρῶτός μου ἦν	"The one coming behind me *became* ahead of me *because* he was before me."'
ὅτι ἐκ τοῦ πληρώματος αὐτοῦ ἡμεῖς πάντες ἐλάβομεν καὶ χάριν ἀντὶ χάριτος	*Because* from his fullness we all received grace against grace.
ὅτι ὁ νόμος διὰ Μωϋσέως ἐδόθη ἡ χάρις καὶ ἡ ἀλήθεια διὰ Ἰησοῦ Χριστοῦ ἐγένετο	*Because* the Law was given through Moses, [but] grace and truth *became* through Jesus Christ.

Of course, this is not to say that John 1.15-18 are a single sentence, or even that all three statements should be understood as comments by the Baptist. It appears that the Evangelist has carefully balanced three distinct sentences, at least one of which is spoken by the Baptist, through the repetition of the connecting term ὅτι. If the Baptist is still speaking in v. 16 – and whether he is or is not would perhaps be obvious to listening audiences, assuming that public readers of the text might use different voices to represent the narrator and various characters – his comments would represent an admission that even his own prophetic gift emerged from the overflowing 'fullness' of Christ. In any case, if the Evangelist added v. 15 to a pre-existing hymn, he has carefully worked the interpolation into the structure of the original text.

Moving beyond the above observations, further reflection on the overall movement of the Prologue reveals that John 1.15 is not only well integrated into the larger unit, but also in fact appears to be its acoustic epicentre. As noted earlier, aural audiences of John 1.1-18 were doubtless struck by the repetition of the verbs ἦν ('was'), γίνομαι/ἐγένετο ('become/became') and ἐρχόμαι/ἦλθεν ('come/came'), which together represent some ten per cent of the total number of words in the composition. These three terms appear together in the same sentence only once, at 1.15. There, John the Baptist 'testifies' that 'the one coming (ἐρχόμενος) behind me became (γέγονεν) ahead of me because he was (ἦν) before me'. Two other words in this same sentence, αὐτοῦ and οὗτος, remind the reader that John is speaking of the incarnate Logos mentioned in v. 14 (see Staley 1986: 247). At the very least, the saying at John 1.15 appears to be the acoustic fulcrum of the Prologue's soundscape, the point where the primary unifying terms converge.

Of course, one could readily argue that John 1.15 consciously reflects the terminology of the earlier hymn into which it has been inserted. In other words, the Evangelist, in composing the testimony of John the Baptist, may have imitated the language of the song in an attempt to maintain the integrity of the poetic structure of the original. In my view, however, this conclusion is insufficient on two grounds. First, as noted earlier, Kelber and others have argued convincingly that the notion of 'originals' and 'interpolations' is essentially unhelpful for understanding early Christian compositions. Building on this premise, if the Evangelist did, in fact, compose v. 15 in the course of quoting a familiar song it seems unlikely that he would understand this as an 'interpolation'. Rather, the current text of John 1.1-18 should be viewed as a new and distinct composition in its own right.

Secondly, and more narrowly, John 1.15 appears to be a traditional sayings unit that takes the form of a common speech genre, the riddle. At first glance, the Baptist's testimony is nonsensical: manifestly, it would be impossible for someone who 'was before' and 'became ahead' of John to be 'coming behind him', especially if the terms ὀπίσω and ἔμπροσθέν are taken in their normal sense as referring to spatial relationships ('behind' and 'in front of'). The calculated ambiguity of the Baptist's comment suggests that John has uttered a riddle, a saying that intentionally points the listener/reader to multiple possible referents and asks them to identify the correct one (see discussion in Thatcher 2000: 109–78; 2006: xiv–xvii, 3–30). Of course, members of the Johannine community, like modern Christian readers, would readily understand that the solution to this puzzle lies in the Evangelist's understanding of the unique relationship between the Baptist and Jesus: Christ 'came behind' the Baptist in the sense that his ministry began after John's, but 'became ahead' of John in the sense that John was simply a 'witness' while Jesus was the revealer of God's grace and truth. Jesus was able to fulfil this superior ministry because he, as the Word become flesh, existed 'before' the Baptist. Since this understanding of Christ's identity was likely common knowledge in Johannine circles, the riddle of the Baptist could function as a short, memorable summary of core theological values and was perhaps used as a confessional statement.

At the very least, then, if John 1.15 seems to break the poetic rhythm of the Prologue, it does so not because it is a literary interpolation into an existing text, but rather because it takes the form of an oral genre (the riddle) that would not necessarily evidence the same poetic structure as another oral genre (the hymn).

Applying all these observations to the problem at hand, it seems that John (the Evangelist) composed the Prologue by reading Christ's ministry through major events from Genesis and Exodus and organizing his comments on the grid of the three verbs contained in the 'Riddle of the Baptist'. In my view, this proposal – that John 1.1-18 is essentially an expansion of the riddle at v.

15, which I view as a traditional sayings unit – makes the most sense of the available data with the least amount of speculation, with the added bonus of compatibility with the media culture in which the Fourth Gospel was written. The individual lines in the Prologue should therefore be interpreted as parts of a larger organic whole; put another way, I see no real value in distinguishing between the 'original' lines and 'interpolations', and do not believe that John has 'added' anything to a pre-existing hymn that can be reconstructed from John 1.1-18. John has, rather, used a familiar confessional statement that took the form of a riddle to compose a remarkable introduction to his narrative. Viewed in this light, the material about John the Baptist at 1.6-8, 15 is an essential – in fact, the essential – structural element of the passage, not an afterthought or a polemical aside.

Chapter 4

A PERFORMANCE OF THE TEXT: THE ADULTERESS'S ENTRANCE INTO JOHN'S GOSPEL

Chris Keith

> Society at large was characterized by a lively synergism of the oral and the written. Modern theoretical models of a fundamental disjunction between the oral and literate modes (whether social, linguistic, cognitive, or hermeneutical) fail to illuminate either their manifest coexistence or their fluid interaction in the Greco-Roman period.
>
> (Gamble 2000: 646)

> As text the gospel exhibits a virtually limitless ability to attract and absorb materials.
>
> (Kelber 1983: 105)

The following essay will present the relevance of the phenomenon of the insertion of the *Pericope Adulterae* (John 7.53–8.11; hereafter PA) into the Gospel of John (hereafter John) for three overlapping issues in textual criticism, orality/textuality studies and social/cultural memory studies:[1] (1) the search for an 'original' text; (2) the dichotomy of fluid oral tradition versus fixed written tradition; and (3) the alleged disjunctive transition from oral Jesus tradition to written Jesus tradition.

---

1   For a recent introduction to orality/textuality in NT studies, see Hearon (2006). For introductions to social/cultural memory studies, see Zelizer (1995); Kirk (2005); and J. Assmann (2006b: 1–30). For integrations of the two, see Kirk and Thatcher, eds (2005); Horsley, Draper and Foley, eds (2006). The overlapping nature of many questions in these disciplines with questions in textual criticism has not yet been given the attention it deserves. 'Social memory' often refers to the work of Maurice Halbwachs while 'cultural memory' refers to the work of Jan and Aleida Assmann (see Kirk [2005: 2–6]). J. Assmann distinguishes their work from Halbwachs in J. Assmann (2006b: 8–9), with the essential factor being the transmission of group memories beyond interpersonal interaction or a single generation enabled by writing (20–21).

Despite overwhelming scholarly neglect in this regard, PA's significance for early Christian media culture lies in the fact that it is the only certain instance of an intact gospel tradition (i.e. a full, independent story) being absorbed into a canonical Gospel once that Gospel has already reached an authoritative status in the early Church.[2] A caveat is needed at the outset, however – by necessity this is an exercise in inductive reasoning and thus it is unclear how relevant my conclusions will be for broader theories on the Jesus tradition as a whole (whatever one may consider that to be). Nevertheless, it is best to proceed from the available evidence to theoretical models, and so I will venture some comments on the implications of PA for current theories of gospel transmission. I begin with introductory remarks on the insertion of PA into John.

The Attentive Interpolation of PA into the Gospel of John

PA's entrance into the stream of Johannine tradition is a complex and multi-faceted issue, not least because PA occurs in at least 12 different manuscript locations in John and Luke's Gospel.[3] Nevertheless, in previous work I have argued in detail that PA's traditional location in the canonical Gospels, John 7.53–8.11, is the location at which an attentive interpolator first placed PA in (what would become) canonical tradition (Keith 2009: 119–40).[4] I have furthermore argued that the interpolator chose this location not randomly, but quite purposefully and based on his careful reading of the narrative of John, especially John 7 (Keith 2009: 141–202). The interpolator's insertion of PA as a form of commentary on John 7 is foundational for the following argument, and so I will summarize some of my previous conclusions briefly here.

2   Scholars frequently cite PA alongside the 'long ending' of Mark as the longest of New Testament interpolations. Technically, however, the two are different phenomena, insofar as Mark 16:9-20 is clearly dependent upon other gospel traditions (see Kelhoffer 1999: 123–56) whereas PA is independent. Some may object that John 21 is also an independent addition, but John's original circulation without chapter 21 is far from certain. The discovery of a fourth-century Coptic manuscript that ends at John 20.31 raises the intriguing possibility, but, as a singular, late, versional witness, does not prove it (see Schenke 2006: 893–904, especially the appropriately cautious statements regarding a Greek original on p. 902). By contrast, there is ample manuscript and patristic evidence that the Gospel of John circulated both with and without PA (see Keith 2009: 123–35). The closest parallel to PA is the insertion of the parable of the man working on the Sabbath at Luke 6.1-11 in Codex Bezae (D), but this story did not become ingrained into the full manuscript tradition to the degree that PA did, as it appears only in this manuscript.

3   For full presentation of the locations, see Keith (2009: 120–1); see also Parker (1997: 96); Robinson (2000: 41–2).

4   The critical evidence is that John 7.53–8.11 is the only known location for PA in canonical tradition until late ninth-/tenth-century manuscripts that include it elsewhere. See further Keith (2009: 122–33).

In assessing why the interpolator inserted PA, scholars should base their theories not on what PA adds to the (canonical) image of Jesus, but on what PA adds *that would otherwise be absent*. That is, one should focus not on what is attested elsewhere (such as Jesus's treatment of women, his treatment of a sexual sinner, or his stance on the Mosaic Law) but instead on what is otherwise unattested, namely the claim in John 8.6, 8 that Jesus could write. In this light, it appears that PA's interpolator was a careful reader of the narrative into which he placed this independent Jesus tradition. For, in John 7.15, 'the Jews' question Jesus's knowledge of letters, i.e., his literacy.[5] Additionally, the Jewish leadership of 7.49 sees knowledge of the Law as the difference between themselves and the gullible crowd that acknowledges Jesus as prophet/messiah. They chastise Nicodemus in 7.52 when he defends Jesus because, based on his ability to search the law – an ability the crowd would not have had – he should know better about the prospect of a Galilean prophet. Indeed, Nicodemus's apparent non-consultation of the law leads them to question whether he too is an uneducated Galilean (like the Jesus of 7.15). In John 7, literacy and knowledge of the law are tightly wound with Jesus's identity as a teacher/prophet/messiah and the crowd's, as well as the Jewish leadership's, ability to identify him properly. Critical to note, then, is that when the interpolator inserted PA after John 7.52, his augmentation of the Johannine Jesus demonstrated the falsity of the Jewish leadership's assumptions regarding Jesus's literacy (7.15) and therefore the ability of a Galilean to consult the law (7.52).

This, however, is not the end of the interpolator's engagement with the issues of John 7. The interpolator describes Jesus's writing in John 8.6 with καταγράφω, and then uses γραφω for Jesus's second act of writing in John 8.8. Between these two acts of literacy is Jesus's 'interpretation'[6] of Moses' required punishment for a crime that was forbidden by the seventh commandment of the Decalogue. These facts are important because the only place in the LXX where καταγράφω and γράφω are used in parallel with the complex verb preceding the simple verb is Exodus 32.15, where they are employed to describe the first stone tablets of the Decalogue as written on both sides.[7] Both sides of the tablets that contained the core of the Torah are surrounded by writing from the finger of God (Exodus 31.18); both sides

---

5   To my knowledge, the first scholar to suggest that a scribe inserted PA as a response to John 7.15 is Goodspeed (1942: 70; 1945: 104, 108).

6   Quotation marks are provided here because, despite the request of the scribes and the Pharisees in John 8.5, Jesus does not actually offer a statement on the required punishment of the adulteress (i.e., an interpretation), but rather shifts the grounds of the discussion to the requirements of the executioners.

7   καταγράφω and γράφω also parallel each other in 2 Chronicles 20.34 and 1 Maccabees 14.18, 26 (ET 14.18, 27). Neither of these parallel usages share the Mosaic themes that Exodus 32.15 and John 8.6, 8 share.

of Jesus's pronouncement in John 8.7 are surrounded by writing from the finger of Jesus (John 8.6b); and the same rare language is used to describe them both.

Thus, in response to the crowd's and the Jewish leadership's argument against each other and amongst themselves over Jesus's identity as a prophet/ messiah, and against the Jewish leadership's assumption that they alone truly 'know' the Mosaic Law, the interpolator inserts a story where Jesus is asked to judge a sinner who has broken a Decalogue commandment and thus is asked to oppose Moses (John 8.5). In doing so, the interpolator claims that Jesus's identity parallels neither a prophet's, nor a messiah's, nor even the identity of Moses himself. Rather, Jesus's identity parallels Yahweh the divine author of the Decalogue.[8]

In light of this evidence, it is hardly the case that 'the scribes who considered [PA] too important to be lost were not at all sure where to place it' (Gench 2004: 142).[9] To the contrary, PA's insertion at John 7.53–8.11 was purposeful, and in this light a sophisticated form of Gospel commentary, an interaction with the text by a careful reader (or readers) of John. I will return to this issue shortly, but first I will address PA's relevance for the search for an 'original text'.

'The Best Manuscripts' and the Limits of Johannine Tradition

Numerous scholars cast aside or qualify PA's relevance for their various studies by noting that 'the earliest and best manuscripts' of John do not include PA. In fact, this rejoinder is so frequent that it is not necessary or possible to cite all of its occurrences here. That the earliest manuscripts of John omit PA is demonstrably true. However, stating that the 'best' manuscripts omit PA is a qualitative assessment, implying the manuscripts' relevance for a particular task. Thus, one must ask, 'The "best" manuscripts *for what?*' Behind the common rejoinder regarding the 'earliest and best' manuscripts is the assumption that the right and proper goal of NT textual criticism is the reconstruction of an 'original text'.[10] The 'best' manuscripts

---

8   Jesus's claim of non-judgement in John 8.15 may have further solidified the appropriateness of John 7.53–8.11 as a narrative location for PA (since Jesus enacts non-judgement in 8.11).

9   Gench says this in light of PA's numerous manuscript locations and similar comments are made by Burge (1984: 144) and Rius-Camps (2007: 382). See, however, above footnote 4.

10   Consider the oft-quoted definition of textual criticism by Greenlee: 'Textual criticism is the study of copies of any written work of which the autograph (the original) is unknown, with the purpose of ascertaining the original text' (1995: 1). Similarly, Vaganay and Amphoux: 'By "textual criticism" is meant any methodical and objective study which aims to retrieve the original form of a text or at least the form closest to the original' (1991: 1; Heimerdinger, trans.).

are those that help scholars establish an original version of John; PA clearly was not in those manuscripts, and thus PA's importance is often neutered. Even those scholars who feel obliged to cover PA in their commentaries note the passage's lack of Johannine authenticity. As one example of many, Beasley-Murray begins his discussion of PA: 'It is universally agreed by textual critics of the Greek NT that this passage was not part of the Fourth Gospel in its *original form*' (Beasley-Murray 1999: 143; emphasis added).[11]

As is well known, however, orality specialists have strongly questioned the idea of an 'original form' of Jesus tradition, with Kelber even referring to it as 'a phantom of the literate imagination' (Kelber 1983: 59, also xv, 45–6, 51, 191; similarly Dunn 2003a: 96–8, 123[12]). Likewise, more recent text-critical scholarship has begun to treat the idea of an 'original text' as an academic unicorn by calling its search into question (most prominently, Petersen 1994; Parker 1997; Epp 1999; Epp 2007: esp. 279–81). PA is a specific example of the problematic idea of an 'original text', a problem that believers in 'a single authoritative text … generally ignore' (Parker 1997: 95–102 [quotation 95]; Schröter 2006: 113–4).

The problem PA poses for the idea of an 'original text' derives from the fact that myriads of Christians throughout history have read versions of John with PA included, and most with no knowledge that it is not in the oldest manuscripts. For those individuals, PA is a generative 'authentic' element of John; i.e., as 'Johannine' as the rest of the Fourth Gospel (likewise Schröter 2006: 114). Although statements such as 'Only *one* reading can be original' may make sense in the context of a tree-shaped scholarly reconstruction of a textual tradition that emerges from a single point, they are unhelpful when considering the texts' impact(s) on Christian readers (quotation Aland and Aland 1989: 280; emphasis original). As Epp observes, 'Variant texts were for some Christians at some time and place the "original" text; it would be a denial of history to ignore them under any circumstances' (1966: 13).[13] Additionally, the fact that PA was absent in some manuscripts of John appears not to have been a problem for its overall authoritative status in some parts of the ancient church. This is the case with Jerome and Augustine, who both demonstrate knowledge of John's omission of PA in

---

11   Beasley-Murray, and others, are mistaken when they claim 'universal' agreement of PA's Johannine inauthenticity. See further the survey in Keith (2008: 379–84).

12   Note that the page numbers reflect the reprint of Dunn's 2003 article ('Altering the Default Setting: Re-envisaging the Early Transmission of the Jesus Tradition') as an appendix in his 2005 book, *A New Perspective on Jesus: What the Quest for the Historical Jesus Missed*.

13   Cf. also Parker (1997: 102) regarding PA specifically: 'We may make the decision that it is not a part of the canonical Gospels; we may even decide that it is not an account of an incident in the life of Jesus. But, however we read the Gospels or think about the historical Jesus, this story will have influenced our views, and we cannot read or think as we would had it never existed.'

some manuscripts (*Pelag.* 2.17; *Incompt. nupt.* 2.7, respectively) but also both cite PA as fully authoritative scripture, with Jerome even including it in his Vulgate.

Furthermore, the act of inserting PA into a manuscript of John suggests that, at least for some scribes, the limits of 'Johannine' tradition were not quite as rigid as they are for modern scholars. This is not to claim that Christian scribes of various historical periods were unaware that PA was not strictly 'Johannine'. They clearly were, as evidenced by the obelisks and other textual markers in numerous manuscripts (Aland 1964: 43; Metzger 1975: 189; Parker 1997: 96; Epp 2002: 509–10).[14] The scribe of MS 565 (ninth century CE) even notes that he omitted PA although his exemplar included it (Schilling 1955: 92; Parker 1997: 96). However, the act of inserting PA into John reveals that the interpolator thought differently than the scribe of MS 565. The interpolator read John, also read and/or heard PA, deemed PA capable of functioning within and contributing to that Gospel, and eventually placed it between John 7 and 8. Based on this act, one must assume that his answer to the question 'Is PA Johannine?' would be in the affirmative, or at least, 'It is now'.

The Text in Performance Mode

If the interpolator inserted PA specifically at John 7.53–8.11 as a result of his reading of John 7 and the rest of the Johannine Gospel, however, this raises an important issue for scholars of orality/textuality. PA's insertion questions what has become known as 'The Great Divide' and the resultant antithesis of oral and written tradition, suggesting that textual tradition, like oral tradition, could and did function in 'performance mode'. As the most prominent proponents of the significance of orality for conceptions of the transmission of the Jesus tradition, the inevitable dialogue partners for this section are Werner Kelber and James D. G. Dunn.

'The Great Divide'
Many current assumptions regarding the textualization of the oral Jesus tradition rest upon a contested-yet-stubborn dichotomy between oral tradition as 'free' or 'fluid' and written tradition as 'fixed' or 'stable'.[15] In the

---

14   Aland (1967: 43) counts 195 miniscules from the ninth to the eighteenth centuries CE that express doubt about PA's belonging to (*Zugehörigkeit*) the text. On scribal confusion over PA's textual status, see further Keith (2009: 133–5). Robinson (2000: 46) and van Lopik (1995: 290) suggest that the asterisks and obeli are not text-critical markers but rather part of the 'lectionary equipment' (van Lopik).

15   The dichotomy persists despite studies that have argued against it, such as Gamble (1995: 28–32); Hurtado (1997); Carr (2006); cf. Achtemeier (1990); Horsley (2003: 34).

introduction to the 1997 edition of his landmark *The Oral and the Written Gospel*, Kelber claims that his study is not responsible for this notion, which has become known as 'The Great Divide' between orality and textuality (Kelber 1997: xxi–xxii). He even insists (correctly) that 'the Great Divide separating orality from textuality as two distinct domains is not true to the facts pertaining to tradition and Gospel text' (xxii).[16] Despite this insistence, however, one can easily amass citations from his much-read study that lend themselves to just this sort of interpretation. Kelber often speaks of the 'frozen' or 'fixed' nature of texuality and the concomitant 'still' or 'static' life – or death – that it brings to oral tradition (62, 63, 91, 94, 158, 217; cf. 194, 203). He further references the 'written regimentation of textualization' (146) associated with the move 'from oral fluidity to textual stability' (211), and thus thoroughly juxtaposes fixed textuality with 'the fluid medium of orality' (202) and 'free-floating oral speech' (209). That is, for Kelber, it is a situation of 'orality *versus* textuality' (32; emphasis added).

The Relevance of PA for 'The Great Divide'

The primary purpose of the present study is not to provide a full refutation of Kelber on this issue. This is unnecessary because others have already offered such a critique,[17] and because this simple schema does not adequately reflect Kelber's full, and certainly not his most recent, thoughts regarding Christian scribality.[18] Rather, the primary purpose is to ask what relevance PA's unique example has for such theories. And the evidence of PA is still relevant for at least two reasons. The first reason is the lingering prevalence of this distinction in scholarly discussions. Note the prominence of the dichotomy in the following statement of Thatcher on why the author of John textualized

---

16   Kelber continues, 'I do not myself use the term *the Great Divide*, nor was it part of our vocabulary in the late seventies and early eighties when the book was written' (1997: xxi; emphasis original). Note, however, that in a discussion of the move from oral Q to written Mark, Kelber cites Tödt's observation of 'something like a gulf' separating Q from Mark' and claims it is 'comparable only to the other great divide, that between the epistles and the gospels' (1983: 203).

17   See, for example, Halverson (1994: 180–95); Hurtado (1997: 91–106); Dunn (2003b: 199–204).

18   Consider the quotation from *The Oral and the Written Gospel* at the beginning of this essay regarding the ability of texts to absorb new material. In contrast to an inherent stability of textual tradition, in a 2005 study, he claims, 'The scribalization of tradition is ... by no means a guarantor of continuity and stability' (2005: 229). Likewise, in a 2007 paper he presented at the University of Glasgow (and which he kindly made available to me), he notes, 'The fuller textual evidence with regard to biblical texts ... points to variability as being symptomatic for the behaviour of textual traditions ... Textual pluriformity is a way, and perhaps **the** way, of textual life at that time' (2007: 4; emphasis original). In both personal conversation and the response session to a version of this essay presented at the 2007 SBL, Kelber acknowledged that he has moved closer to a view of early Christian scribality such as the one argued for here.

his tradition: 'It appears that John wished to capitalize on the rhetorical value of writing by converting the *fluid*, charismatic memory of Jesus to a *fixed* history book, a move that would at once preserve his unique vision of Jesus, *freeze* that vision in a *perpetually nonnegotiable medium*' (Thatcher 2005a: 94; emphases added; see also Bauckham 1998: 29). As another example, one may cite a recent *status quaestionis* essay by Hearon. She uses Kelber's theories as a platform but also backs away from a full juxtaposition of the oral and written media by taking account of the performance dynamic of written texts. Hearon notes carefully that 'although both [oral and written] texts would be performed, written texts are 'fixed' in a way that oral texts are not' (Hearon 2006: 11). That is, Hearon here technically claims not that written texts are 'fixed' and oral texts are not, but rather that there is a difference in the manner of their respective 'fixedness'. Nevertheless, even on the same page, Hearon cannot avoid speaking of 'fixed, written texts and … unstable, oral texts' (Hearon 2006: 11).[19] It seems this dichotomy is so much a part of the scholarly apparatus that even discussions of its limitations inevitably must employ it.

The second reason PA's evidence is relevant to the issue of 'fixed' written tradition versus 'fluid' oral tradition is that scholars consistently describe PA as an example of 'fluid' or 'free-floating' tradition, often specifying it as oral tradition (*inter alia*, see Jenkinson 1925: 31; Taylor 1953: 84; Brown 1966: 332; Burge 1984: 144, 145; Minear 1991: 23; Ross 1992: 153–6; Parker 1997: 101). In his important study that argues against seeing texts as 'fixed', Parker cites PA as oral tradition that was placed in a book 'for safe keeping' (1997: 101) and therefore as evidence that 'the oral tradition is thus not something which ended at some point in the second or third or fourth century' (1997: 102). Not all scholars agree that PA definitely was oral tradition prior to its insertion into John, however. Several see the connective phrase in John 7.53–8.1 as evidence of a previous *textual* location for PA prior to its inclusion in John (Becker 1963: 176, Morris 1971: 885, Lindars 1972: 308, von Campenhausen 1977: 164, Rius-Camps 2007: 380).

PA's media status prior to its inclusion in John is a complicated issue that has not received a full treatment. While no explicit statement is made, it seems that scholarly conviction that PA was oral tradition prior to its insertion is based on the idea that it 'free-floated' into John and, if this is the case, here one again sees the underlying dichotomy that views fluidity as a characteristic of oral tradition in contrast to written tradition.[20] This study will make no

---

19   Note, however, that Hearon observes, 'Just how large the divide is between the two may be debated' (11). Kelber too allowed that in certain instances 'the lines of orality and textuality were indeed blurred … The medium situation of the synoptic transmission was thus a complex one, and we shall never know its full actuality, let alone the precise shadings and degrees of interplay between the two media' (1983: 23).

20   This is not a suggestion in favour of viewing PA as textual tradition prior to its inclusion into John, however. An attentive interpolator could have written John 7.53–8.1

attempt to offer a full treatment of this issue, however. This lack of an attempt to resolve PA's media status prior to insertion is primarily because the criteria one might use for such a decision are based on assumptions regarding the respective natures of orality and textuality that this study seeks to undermine (such as the inherent fixity of texts or the disassociation of performance from texts). That is, the main thrust of the current argument is that PA's insertion into John reveals not that PA was oral or written tradition, but that both forms of tradition could and did function – in some respects – in the same manner. And the manner in which the John functioned when it absorbed PA is best described as 'performance'.

Normally, scholars reserve describing the Jesus tradition as functioning in 'performance mode' for discussions of oral tradition. The description itself highlights the 'live' environment as a storyteller performs the tradition for an audience. The audience contributes to the shape of the performance because the performer reacts to their reception of the story: 'Narrators narrate what audiences call for or will tolerate' (Ong 2002: 66; see also Kelber 1983: 109). Thus, at the heart of the performance of oral tradition is the mutual engagement of both performer and audience (see further Vansina 1985: 34). Dunn's studies especially have insisted on the significance of the 'performance' aspect of oral tradition for scholarly conceptions of the Jesus tradition (Dunn 2003a: 89–101; Dunn 2005a: 43, 46–53; Dunn 2005b: 52–3; see Hearon 2006: 10–11). Among other things, he has helpfully reminded NT scholars of the oral characteristic of 'variation within the same' (Dunn 2003a: 99[21]) and sees this concept as one reason for insisting, 'Oral tradition is characteristically ... a combination of *fixity* and *flexibility*, of *stability* and *diversity*' (2003a: 98; emphasis original).

Especially pertinent for the situation of PA, though, is that, as Hearon notes, Dunn's view is that 'the relationships among the Gospels rest in performance *rather than in written texts*' (Hearon 2006: 10; emphasis added). That is, he associates 'performance' with orality *in contrast* to textuality, which may reflect the latent assumptions of the alleged 'Great Divide' between orality and textuality. For example, Dunn claims, 'Most obvious – or should be most obvious – [is that] an *oral performance* is *not* like reading a literary text ... A written text can be revised, or edited, and so on. But none of that is possible with an oral tradition. An oral performance is evanescent. It is an event' (Dunn 2003a: 94; emphases original, slightly restated in Dunn 2005a: 46). He thus insists on 'the flexibility of oral performance' (2005b: 69) and views Gospel texts as 'frozen performances' (2005b: 57; also 2003a: 120).[22]

---

in order to make the insertion smooth. Thus, 7.53–8.1 is not clear evidence of a prior textual location.

21   Dunn here cites Kelber (1983: 54) and Havelock (1963: 92, 147, 184).

22   Perhaps revealing just how stubborn the dichotomy between fluid orality and fixed textuality is, note that Dunn continues to use the metaphor of frozen texts in 2005

Dunn's commitment to the intrinsic connection between orality and performance leads him to describe texts as functioning in oral performance mode, even in places where he acknowledges literary acts of transmission. For example, he speaks of the manner in which the Evangelists were 'writing the story in oral mode' (Dunn 2003b: 214). That is, according to Dunn, Matthew and Luke (as authors) could have *written* or even *copied* Mark (2003b: 218) – acts that are, if nothing else, textual – in oral mode. They 'produced their written text in the manner and with the freedom of an oral performance (in oral mode)' (Dunn 2005b: 50; similarly, 2003a: 110; 2003b: 212, 214, 218, 220, 221, 237, 254; 2005b: 53, 59). The key point here is that, in cases where texts evince the characteristics he associates with orality, Dunn does not reconsider his understanding of 'textual mode' but rather maintains the connection between orality and performance by claiming that the text functions *as if it were* oral tradition.[23]

That there are differences in the dynamics of oral performance and the acts of reading and writing is unquestioned, with the live environment of oral performance[24] and the relatively more fixed nature of texts being examples. But it is the hesitance to see texts as performing – and thus textual tradition as functioning in a performance mode – that the particular example of PA's insertion calls into question.[25] More succinctly, Dunn claims that a written text, in contrast to an oral performance, can be 'revised, or edited, and so on' (2003a: 94), and I suggest that it is in these very operations that one can see the complex interaction between performer (i.e., author), tradition and audience (i.e., reader or implied reader) typically associated with oral performance. First, though, a brief excursus is necessary regarding the

---

even though he acknowledged two years earlier that after the oral Jesus tradition was written, 'the written text was still fluid, still living tradition' (Dunn 2003b: 250; citing Parker [1997]).

23   Bauckham follows Dunn: 'Many differences, especially in narrative, will be due to the variability normal *in oral performance* ... Matthew and Luke varied their Markan written source in the same kinds of ways they would have done *had they been performing oral tradition*' (Bauckham 2006: 286; emphases added).

24   Note however that the live reading of texts to an audience complicates this example (see Achtemeier 1990; and especially Johnson 2001: 593–627). Both Kelber (1983: 169, 197, cf. 218) and Dunn (2003a: 94; 2005a: 47–8) discuss the fact that many ancient texts were intended to be read and view it as 'second' or 'secondary orality' ('orality derived from texts' [Kelber 1983: 197]) instead of an essential feature of textuality. (On this terminology, see below footnote 27.) Elsewhere Dunn acknowledges that reading a text was 'like a performance' while criticizing Kelber (Dunn 2003b: 201, 204, cf. 249–50).

25   Regarding the examples he cites as texts functioning in oral mode, Dunn also observes correctly, 'The material can then count in part at least as a good illustration of the way tradition, including tradition already in writing, would be used in an oral society' (2005b: 59). Given statements such as this, I am perhaps splitting hairs. However, the present argument is that these texts are not functioning in 'oral mode' based on the fact that they are performance, but that textual mode itself entails performance.

scholarly assumption that oral performance stands primarily *in contrast* to textuality.

Oral Performance versus Textuality

As noted just previously, I do not question that there are numerous distinctions between oral performance and textuality. However, scholarly insistence on the differences between oral tradition and written tradition has obscured the numerous ways in which oral tradition and written tradition were transmitted similarly in the ancient world (likewise Carr 2005: 6–7). The lack of attention to the similarities between orality and textuality derives from two common but questionable refrains in discussions of the nature of oral tradition: (1) Palestine was an oral culture; and (2) this oral culture is nearly incomprehensible to modern scholars. Though he is by no means alone, Dunn again provides exemplary statements:

> 'We are, therefore, in no fit state to appreciate how a *non-literary* culture, an *oral* culture, functions' (Dunn 2003a: 83; emphases original).

> 'All this means that we have little or no idea what it would have been like to live in an *oral* culture. But first-century Palestine certainly was an oral rather than a literary culture' (Dunn 2005a: 36; emphasis original).

Such statements are questionable not because they fail to reflect historical reality; they are questionable because they only partially reflect historical reality, and therefore lead to a confusion of categories. It is true that first-century Palestine was an oral culture in the sense that most individuals were illiterate, but Dunn overstretches the evidence when he claims it was 'non-literary' and oral 'rather than' literary. For, 'Jewish society of the first century was both textual and oral' (Beaton 2005: 119), and, even more important, one cannot equate the lack of personal access to texts and/or ability to read them ('literacy') with lack of knowledge of them or their effects. First-century illiterates knew textuality and its impacts. As Millard observes, 'The Roman land tax needed surveyors to measure fields and estimate yields and clerks to record the taxes due, so even the most remote peasant farmers would know that the black marks on papyrus rolls or the scratches on wax tablets spelled out their fate' (Millard 2001: 170; similarly Bagnall 1995: 13, 15; Thatcher 2006: 43). Beyond this, the vast majority of observant Jews recognized the life-defining significance of the Torah scroll even though they could not read it themselves.[26] Similarly, the majority of early Christians would have recognized that the papyrus (or, later, codex) that the reader held in his hand contained the story of Jesus or an epistle of Paul that offered statements about who they are or should be. Illiterate individuals had multiple avenues

---

26 See below on the role of identity in both oral and written transmission.

for participating in literate culture, and thus one must recognize that early Christianity's 'oral culture' was one that was simultaneously inundated with texts, not something close to Ong's 'primary orality', which is 'that of persons totally unfamiliar with writing' (Ong 2002: 6).[27] In short, the Jesus tradition emerged in a culture that was not oral *rather than* textual, but oral *and* textual.[28]

Dunn's claim that early Christianity was an oral culture 'rather than' a textual culture is therefore clearly an overstatement. However, it should likely be taken as rhetoric in service of a particular point that he is impressing upon his reader, namely that the early Christian environment is very different from the context of the modern scholar and one must recognize the tremendous distance between the two worlds before proceeding with other questions. He claims,

> My point is rather to bring home the danger of *envisaging* the process of tradition transmission in too exclusively literary terms and to suggest that it will be necessary for us deliberately to alter our print-determined default setting when we try to envisage the early transmission of the Jesus tradition. (2003a: 93; emphasis original)

---

27   NT scholars' usage of Ong's categories of 'primary orality' and 'secondary orality' creates some nomenclature confusion with regard to describing early Christian textual practices. For Ong, the former category refers to cultures 'untouched by literacy' whose tradition is thus 'purely oral' (1983: 6, 11, respectively). In contrast, the latter category refers to oral culture in the context of modern scholars, 'a new orality [that] is sustained by telephone, radio, television, and other electronic devices that depend for their existence and functioning on writing and print' (1983: 11, see also 3, 133–5), i.e., a 'residual orality' (157). Early Christianity was neither of these, however, as its constituents were mostly illiterate, but part of a culture in which textuality was rampant, and, as Ong acknowledges, 'It takes only a moderate degree of literacy to make a tremendous difference in thought processes' (2002: 50). For Kelber (for example), 'secondary orality' refers to 'orality derived from texts' (1983: 197), by which he refers to ancient contexts such as the public reading of Paul's epistles or the gospels – a socio-historical literary context that falls into neither of Ong's categories (see further 217–8). In a footnote, he refers to electronically mediated orality (Ong's 'secondary orality') as 'tertiary orality' (226 n. 118). Further, Schröter (2006: 112–3) uses 'secondary orality' to refer to situations such as the quotation of apocryphal Jesus traditions in *1* and *2 Clement* alongside other Jesus traditions that appear to be located in a gospel text. Quite another phenomenon is revealed in *1 Clement* in the various locations where the author claims that a text contains a particular statement 'somewhere' (που – 15.2, 21.2, 26.2, 28.2; ὅπου – 23.3). This situation appears to be neither strict orality nor strict textuality, but rather the memory of a text. More clarity is needed in the scholarly apparatus here, for Ong's 'primary orality', Ong's 'secondary orality' (Kelber's 'tertiary orality'), the public reading of a text, Schröter's 'secondary orality' (citation of a 'free' Jesus tradition alongside a known written Jesus tradition), and scribal access to a text via memory are all interrelated yet distinct phenomena with their own sets of media dynamics.

28   I take up the concept of 'illiteracy' and the oral-yet-textual nature of Palestinian society more fully in Keith (2009: 53–94).

This is a much-needed reminder for biblical critics, but the manner in which both Dunn and Kelber have carried it out perhaps creates unnecessary confusion in an already complex nexus of ideas. Note in this quotation from Dunn that the two options are either our 'print-determined' culture or the ancient culture. He focuses again on the difference between the modern and ancient context when he says, 'We are all children of Gutenberg and Caxton. We belong to cultures shaped by the book' (2003a: 82). Likewise, Kelber refers to the 'oral state of mind' (1983: 23), 'oral mentality' (204), and the 'oral lifeworld' (91, 152, 163) that is perplexing for modern minds attuned to 'typography': 'If to the modern typographical consciousness the epistemological flavor of Paul's discourse on the fall inclines toward the pessimistic, one must remember that the apostle approaches the Law in the fashion of an oral traditionalist' (1983: 164, cf. 166). Here again, the juxtaposition involves the ancient – *oral* – mind and the modern one that struggles with ancient transmission processes due to its text-dependence.

As noted above, however, there was likely no such thing as a purely 'oral mind' in first-century Judaism or early Christianity, as even illiterates were aware of writing and its effects. Further, while it is true that we are children of Gutenberg, it is also true that texts and textuality existed long before Gutenberg. Individuals arranged their lives around sacred texts that were read to them, died with land contracts they could not read,[29] and travelled long distances with their families to answer the order of a census that would had to have been translated[30] long before the typography of moveable print. Second Temple Judaism *also* was 'shaped by the book' or, at least, the scroll. Thus, the proper contrast is not between our typographical mindset and the ancient oral mindset, but rather between our oral-written matrix and their oral-written matrix;[31] between our appropriation of texts and their appropriation of texts.[32]

I now return to PA as one example of ancients' appropriation of texts, an example that demonstrates how textual tradition performed in the hands of an interpolating scribe.

The Performance Dynamics of PA's Insertion
Clearly, I am not the first to argue that, in contrast to an inherent fixity, the written Jesus tradition of the early Church is 'free' or 'living'. Parker's

---

29   The Babatha cache (dated to the Bar Kochba revolt) was found with skeletons in a cave, one of which presumably was Babatha herself. Interestingly, and despite the clear importance of these documents given that Babatha literally took them with her to her death, several reveal that Babatha was not even literate enough to sign her name (e.g., *P. Yadin* 15.35–6, 16.35, 22.34). For texts, see Lewis et al., eds (1989).

30   See comments of Millard (2001: 37) on Luke 2.1.

31   I borrow the phrase 'oral-written matrix' from Carr (2005).

32   Similarly, Hurtado (1997: 97).

1997 *The Living Text of the Gospels* is one prominent example, and, more recently, Schröter observes poignantly:

> As the reception of the Jesus tradition in the second century shows, neither the compass nor the wording of the traditions traced to Jesus or to 'the gospel' was firmly fixed … We may conclude from this that there was no fundamental difference in the first centuries of Christianity between oral and written tradition. Instead, in both spheres we observe the analogous process of a free, living tradition that adapted its concrete form to the understanding of the content in each case. (Schröter 2006: 120–1)

However, and even though both Parker and Schröter discuss PA (Parker 1997: 95–102; Schröter 2006: 113–114), the precise manner in which one can understand PA's insertion as a performance has been overlooked. Critical to understanding the performance nature of this textual variant (and many others as well)[33] is the aforementioned performance model of interaction between storyteller and audience. Under this model, every performance is unique ('original') because the storyteller is affected by the audience's reception of the tradition, altering the story in slight ways to reflect the expectations/reactions of the audience. The end product – the tradition/performance itself – is thus the product of both performer and audience. And, again, the slight alterations to a known story produce the concept of 'variation within the same' that 'makes it possible for the community both to acknowledge its tradition and to delight in the freshness of the individual performance' (Dunn 2003a: 99).

This dialectical 'give and take' between performer and audience that scholars claim is so characteristic of oral performance is evident also in the interpolator's insertion of PA, a thoroughly textual act. Technically, PA's insertion reveals two textual performances. First, the interpolator's insertion of PA *at John 7.53–8.11* displays his role as the audience of John's author. The choice of John 7.53–8.11, based on his reading of John 7 and the rest of the Johannine narrative, is a form of commentary on John insofar as the interpolator's decision that PA can and should contribute to the narrative at that point assumes prior decisions on the part of the interpolator regarding the narrative and meaning of John. Here, then, the text of John, from the hand of its author/storyteller, performs and elicits a response from its audience, the interpolator. The insertion of PA at that location is evidence of the reader's interaction with the tradition.

Second, the interpolator's *insertion* of PA at John 7.53–8.11 displays his role as author/storyteller who has creative control over the tradition, augmenting it for the purposes of his own audience. He knows his audience,

---

33   One can also view the textual variants that Ehrman (1993) and Kannaday (2004) discuss as textual performance, insofar as the textual variants witness to an interaction between the author, text and reader.

the readers/hearers of the text he has altered, will recognize John as a familiar story, and practises something like 'variation within the same' by adding PA and creating a fresh performance of the Johannine narrative in light of his own social context. I have elsewhere argued for particular socio-historical conditions that prompted his insertion (i.e., the needs in his audience to which he is responding).[34] But the key point at present is that the act of insertion is a performance of the tradition reflecting both the interpolator (storyteller/author) and his reader/audience. Without a social context, he would not be able to form opinions on how, or even if, the text should change.

Interpolation and the Extended Situation

The role of the interpolator as both a reader and performer of John, entrenched in his own social context, contradicts the idea that 'oral language is bound up with' a social context while 'written language assumes a posture of aloofness from' a social context (Kelber 1983: 109). It also contradicts the idea that a 'writer works in a state of separation from audiences, and hearers or readers are excluded from the process of composition' (Kelber 1983: 92, see also 115). It is true that the complex interactions between the author of John (performer), John (tradition), the interpolator (audience/performer), and PA (tradition) lack the live environment of a storyteller standing before his audience. However, this fact does not mean that PA's insertion should not be considered a (textual) performance, as lack of physical presence is not a total lack of presence. In his discussion of Paul, Kelber claims that the Law *as text* 'circumscribes a medium world that is tighter and more sealed off from life than spoken words whose acoustic field is both fluid and open' (1983: 155). But PA's insertion demonstrates the exact opposite – in the hands of the interpolator, John is open and fluid and connected to the life of the community.

Indeed, the interpolator's insertion of PA is a prime example of what J. Assmann describes as the 'extended situation' (*zerdehnte Situation*)[35] that written texts enable. In an extended situation, 'speaker and hearer, encoder and decoder are no longer co-present within the spatial and temporal limits of human voice' (J. Assmann 2006a: 75). Whereas Kelber claims that the foundational difference between orality and textuality is the lack of the live environment in the latter, J. Assmann instead asserts that the primary difference between the two media is this broader social context(s)

---

34   See Keith (2009: 203–56). I propose there that the interpolator wished to attribute grapho-literacy to the authoritative fourfold image of Jesus in light of, especially, pagan criticisms of Christian illiteracy in the second and third century CE.

35   J. Assmann translates 'zerdehnte Situation' as 'extended situation' in J. Assmann (2006a: 75). The English translator of his *Religion und kulturelles Gedächtnis* translates it as 'expanded context' (J. Assmann 2006b: e.g., 100).

of communication (J. Assmann 2006a: 74; 2006b: 105; see similar observations by Alexander 1998: 90–1).[36] This difference is not one of kind, but one of participants, as the text stretches the hermeneutical interaction from a situation where both audience and author share the same socio-historical context to one where each can arrive at the text as a touchstone between their different socio-historical contexts.

> The immediate situation is replaced with the extended situation unfolding in at least two and, in the case of literature, virtually infinite concrete situations that may stretch in time as long as the text is preserved and the conditions for its readability and understandability are assured. (J. Assmann 2006a: 75; see also 2006b: 103)

The above understanding of PA's insertion highlights the extended situations between John's author and the interpolator as reader, as well as the extended situation between the interpolator as author and his (implied) reader(s). Thus, PA's insertion by the interpolator is a snapshot of the 'extended situation' at work in two 'concrete situation[s]', and shows that author and audience still interact in the transmission of textual tradition.

In summary then, the interaction of Jesus tradition that PA's insertion into John displays is highly relevant for scholarly discussions of oral and written tradition, especially the so-called 'Great Divide'. An unfortunate by-product of correct scholarly efforts to demonstrate the significant differences between the two media has been the oversight of similarities. One important similarity that PA's insertion reveals is that texts could and did function in 'performance mode'. In at least this example, textual variance is textual performance.

The Disruption of Textualization?

PA's demonstration of similarities between orality and textuality may have broader implications for scholarly conceptions of the move from the oral Jesus tradition to the written Jesus tradition. The final section of this essay will thus move tentatively from the unique example in PA of how two different Jesus traditions interacted (and display the extended situation of textuality) to consider continuous aspects of the transition from oral tradition to written tradition.

One of the foundational arguments of Kelber's *Oral and Written Gospel* is that the move from the oral Jesus stories to the written Jesus stories

---

36   Responding to Kelber (1983: 19), J. Assmann says, 'This is quite true: the non-distinction between signifier and signified is typical of the oral situation. However, writing does not automatically bring about an awareness of the distinction, nor is this awareness restricted to writing' (2006a: 74). See also J. Assmann (2006b: 105).

was disruptive to the tradition. His concern was to counter the idea that something in or about oral tradition itself inevitably led to the process of textualization (Kelber 1983: 90), the idea of an 'unbroken continuity of oral and written contextuality' (195). According to Kelber, the move from orality to textuality was not inevitable, one point upon a logical trajectory, but rather cataclysmic, 'a transmutation more than mere transmission, which results in a veritable upheaval of hermeneutical, cognitive realities' (Kelber 1983: 91). In short, it was 'a disruption of the oral synthesis' (92) and throughout his study Kelber describes the move from orality to textuality as 'disorientation', 'disruptive', 'destructive' and 'disjunctive' (*inter alia*, 1983: 91, 92, 94, 169, 172, 207). In further research, he continues to describe the move to textuality as 'deviating from or even rupturing' orality (Kelber 2005: 229).

Kelber is entirely correct to argue that scholars should resist conceiving of the move from orality to textuality as sensible, logical and inevitable. Given that the vast majority of early Christians did not need a text in order to encounter the story of Jesus, the textualization of those narratives is indeed as significant as Kelber has consistently argued that it is. Is it necessarily a *disruptive* process, however? Or, perhaps a better question to ask is: Does *disruption* as a descriptor encapsulate all the aspects of that move? Others have expressed similar reservations regarding Kelber's model,[37] and I here join them by suggesting that the move from oral Jesus tradition to written tradition can be conceptualized as continuous in at least two ways: (1) the extension of the interaction between author, tradition and audience; and (2) the role of both forms of tradition as markers of social identity.

The Continuity of the Extended Situation
According to J. Assmann's model of the 'extended situation' that textual transmission provides, the move from orality to textuality involves not a break of the previous hermeneutical situation but rather a broadening of it. True enough, elsewhere J. Assmann conceives of the move to textuality as a breakage (*Bruch*) of cultural memory, insofar as it enables the ability to forget and thus threatens continuity (1992: 101; 2006b: 118). But one must note that this concept refers technically to a break in the storage form of the tradition, because it creates the possibility for the identity-informing rituals and festivals associated with oral tradition to fall out of practice (2006b: 118). That is, writing can create a break in tradition, not transmission.[38] For, according to J. Assmann, what writing threatens to end in the form of ritual it more than compensates for in the form of communication. Textuality

---

37   See especially the criticism of Gamble (1995: 29–30) and Dunn (2003b: 202–4).
38   On the communicative nature of the extended situation: 'The concept of the expanded context does not apply to the *storage*, but to the *communication* of a message' (J. Assmann 2006b: 105; emphases original).

enables the tradition to do across cultural gaps of space and time what it was already doing in the live environment of orality:

> The extension of the situation of communication past the limits of direct interaction, as well as the creation of a hyper-situation extending over several millennia, is an achievement of memory ... To reconnect with the meaning of written cultural texts, you do not have to wait for the next performance, you just have to read them. (2006a: 77)

The interaction between author and reader, performer and audience, is not disrupted, but quite literally extended in order to include more potential readers. Thus, he observes that writing enables a 'perpetuation' or 'growth' of memory (2006b: 20, 21) that 'can forge links at a spatio-temporal distance between speaker and listener' (104). As the above argument has detailed, PA's insertion is evidence of this similarity between the oral and written Jesus tradition. The textualized tradition of John allows the interpolator not only to interact with the author of John as a reader, but also with his own audience as an author, and the resultant version of John (with PA included) bears the marks of this/these extended situation(s). In this sense, then, one can view the move from oral Jesus tradition to written text as one of continuity and advancement, a furthering of dynamics in oral performance rather than a disruption.

The Continuity of Group Identity
The extension of the author/audience interaction by textuality is not the only manner in which one can conceptualize the move from oral to written tradition in terms of continuity. Perhaps an underappreciated aspect of Kelber's initial proposal is his insistence on the role of social identity as the key for understanding the transmission of the oral Jesus tradition. Prefiguring current usage of social memory theory in New Testament studies for similar purposes (see essays in Kirk and Thatcher 2005), Kelber observes:

> Remembrance and transmission depended on the ability to articulate a message in such a way that it found an echo in people's hearts and minds. Primarily those sayings, miracle stories, parables, and apophthegmatic stories will have had a chance of survival that could become a focus of identification for speakers and hearers alike ... In short, oral transmission is controlled by the law of *social identification* rather than by the technique of verbatim memorization. (Kelber 1983: 24; emphasis original)

With this statement, Kelber brings to the fore of the 'traditioning' process the common identity shared by performer and audience, and the tradition itself as an expression of that identity. Dunn too views social identity and community formation as a crucial aspect of the transmission of oral tradition (2003b: 215, 224, 226, 228, 230, 238, 242, 244, 254).

Increasingly, however, scholars from various disciplines are recognizing that social identity is as critical to textual practices as it is to oral practices. NT text critic Bart Ehrman demonstrates that many early Christian manuscripts of NT texts bear the marks of their social contexts as scribes of one community asserted their theological commitments over another community (Ehrman 1997). Wayne Kannaday too has pursued the socio-historical contexts behind several NT textual variants (Kannaday 2004).

In an illuminating article, papyrologist William A. Johnson perceptively emphasizes that the reading of texts in antiquity was an intricately social process and a reflection of identity (Johnson 2001: 593–627, esp. 602–3). Similar to the present argument that the interaction between author and audience is not restricted strictly to oral performance, Johnson notes: 'Whether based on an actual group (such as a class), or an imaginary group (intellectuals, lovers of poetry), the reader's conception of "who s/he is", that is, to what reading community s/he thinks to belong, is an important, and determinative, part of the reading event' (Johnson 2001: 602). He further claims, 'Reading is, to be sure, the individual's construction of meaning, but it is never wholly interior; rather, sociocultural influences always inform the meaning that the reader seeks to construct' (603).

J. Assmann, already discussed, shows in his cultural memory studies not only that the decoration of material artifacts reflects group identity (2006a: 69–70) but also that some texts also do so in their capacity as 'cultural texts', which 'form the cement or connective backbone of a society that ensures its identity and coherence through the sequence of generations' (2006a: 78).[39] He observes, 'By the transmission of cultural texts, a society or culture reproduces itself in its "cultural identity" through the generations' (2006a: 76). One may here cite Christian adoption of the codex as a distinctively Christian book form as a conflation of both types of identity expression.[40] Christian codices were both cultural texts and decorated material artifacts with a recognizable physical form. Transmission of Christian texts via codices thus doubly reflected Christian identity. Relatedly, the transmission of cultural texts in order to maintain/construct group identity is at the core of Carr's model for the rise of Jewish scriptures (Carr 2005). He refers to such texts as 'long-duration texts' and the process of learning them as 'education-enculturation'. Importantly, he observes an overlap of media in their transmission: 'Both writing and oral performance fed into the process of indoctrination/education/enculturation' (Carr 2005: 5).

---

39   Similarly, 'Cultural texts lay claim to an overall social authority; they define the identity and cohesiveness of a society' (J. Assmann 2006b: 104).

40   For the most recent assessments of early Christian adoption of the codex, see Gamble (1995: 49–66); Hurtado (2006: 43–93); Snyder (2000: 212–4); Millard (2001: 60–83); Stanton (2004: 165–91).

Furthermore, J. Assmann's concept of 'cultural texts' strongly resembles Zerubavel's 'master commemorative narrative', which 'refers[s] to a broader view of history, a basic 'story line' that is culturally constructed and provides the group members with a general notion of their shared past' (1995: 6). A master commemorative narrative is thus what any average person would know about the past of his or her people group without necessarily being conscious that he or she knows it. It represents the history of the group as it exists on the popular level, as opposed to what is sought by critical historians. Indeed, a master commemorative narrative is the *only* history for cultures that lack historiographical consciousness. The success of an emerging distinct group to build upon and claim a previous group identity (e.g., the one from which it emerged) as its own depends upon that group's ability to intertwine the defining narrative(s) of their own historical events (i.e., their commemorative narratives) with an extant master commemorative narrative.[41] In terms of the early Christian context, this process is obvious as authors graft the story of Jesus and the early church into the master commemorative narrative of the Hebrew Scriptures, and thus claim the Jewish identity represented by those texts as their own.[42] Equally, however, the process is revealed by the physical insertion of PA as a commemorative narrative into the (master) commemorative narrative of John and, likely, the fourfold Gospel.

Importantly, both oral narratives of Jesus's life and written ones could function as cultural texts, as (master) commemorative narratives.[43] Both reflected group identity and were transmitted for that purpose. The move from oral tradition to written tradition would therefore not have disrupted the tradition's function as marker of group identity, but rather hardened or solidified it into a physical presence capable of being shown and seen. In the form of a manuscript, an early Christian community could carry the narrative of its founding figure into any social context and did not have to wait on a performer to enact it.

Therefore, in addition to and interrelated with the ability of a text to extend the oral hermeneutical situation between author and reader (performer and audience), the tradition's group identity function would also

---

41   Zerubavel's work is a case study of how the Zionist Jews selectively emphasized some events from the Jewish master commemorative narrative and de-emphasized others in order to assert their own unique Jewish identity.

42   I have pursued one example of this phenomenon in terms of social/cultural memory in Keith 2006.

43   For J. Assmann, the significant difference between written cultural texts and, e.g., ritual cultural texts is in the manner in which cultures retrieve the tradition: 'If the text is available in written form, then the form of that retrieval can be more or less arbitrary. However, if it is available only in the form of a memory store, then it can be reintroduced into the communicative process only with the aid of fixed social agreements and guarantees' (2006b: 106).

have remained continuous in the transition from orality to textuality. These two cases suggest that the adjective 'disruptive' and its synonyms are not entirely appropriate for the Jesus tradition's transition from the oral medium to the written one.

Summary and Conclusions

This essay has surveyed the relevance of the insertion of PA into John (at John 7.53–8.11) by an attentive interpolator for three overlapping issues in textual criticism, orality/textuality, and cultural memory: (1) the search for an original text; (2) the dichotomy of orality and textuality; and (3) the alleged disruptive nature of textuality. With regard to the first issue, PA's insertion – and acceptance – demonstrates the limited use of the concept of an 'original text' when considering how early Christians used their texts. With regard to the second issue, PA's insertion shows that texts could and did function in performance mode, and that this is an important similarity between oral and written media. With regard to the third issue, PA's insertion (insofar as it is a 'snapshot' of the interaction of two different Jesus traditions) suggests that the move from oral Jesus tradition to written Jesus tradition was characterized by continuity in some respects.

To conclude, then, this study has introduced PA as primary evidence for the interaction of Jesus traditions in early Christianity. In the process, it has also observed that certain aspects of the disciplines of textual criticism, media studies and memory studies overlap to a high degree.

Part II

John as Oral Performance

Chapter 5

JOHN'S MEMORY THEATRE:
A STUDY OF COMPOSITION IN PERFORMANCE[1]

Tom Thatcher

> The huge repository of the memory, with its secret and unimagi-
> nable caverns, welcomes and keeps all these things, to be
> recalled and brought out for use when needed; and as all of
> them have their particular ways into it, so all are put back again
> in their proper places ... [I]n this wide land I am made free ...
> to run and fly to and fro, to penetrate as deeply as I can, to col-
> lide with no boundary anywhere.
>
> Augustine *Confessions* 10.8, 17[2]

> Indeed it is not without good reason that memory has been
> called the treasure-house (*thesaurus*) of eloquence.
>
> Quintillian *Institutio Oratoria* 11.2.1[3]

> At first, his disciples did not know these things. But when Jesus
> was glorified, then they remembered that these things had been
> written about him and that they did these things to him. There
> are also many other things that Jesus did; should they each be
> written down, I don't think the world could hold the books that
> had been written.
>
> John 12.16; 21.25[4]

Over the past 50 years, multiple currents have run through the study of the
Gospel of John. One major branch of Johannine studies has focused on the

---

1   This paper originally appeared in *Catholic Biblical Quarterly* 69 (2007): 487–504.
The editors extend their gratitude for permission to reprint it here.
2   Cited from Augustine 1997, trans. Maria Boulding.
3   All citations of Quintillian's *Institutio Oratoria* are from the Loeb edition
(2001).
4   All citations of the Gospel of John are my (Thatcher's) translation.

discovery of the Fourth Gospel's sources, including possible relationships between John and the Synoptics.[5] Another stream, fed by J. Louis Martyn's groundbreaking work on the history of the Johannine community, has pursued the course of the Fourth Gospel's developmental history, attempting to identify layers of revision in the current text and appealing to the historical circumstances that prompted these revisions as interpretive keys.[6] A third current, bubbling up from Alan Culpepper's *Anatomy of the Fourth Gospel* but now overflowing that basin, has cut its way into the Fourth Gospel's narrative technique, exploring the nooks and crannies that the text leaves open for multiple readings.[7] Obviously, these varying approaches have produced very different interpretations of the Johannine literature, each with its own unique insights into the complexities of the Fourth Gospel's peculiar presentation and theology. At the same time, however, these streams of interpretation converge in a common interest in the Fourth Evangelist's compositional technique, the way that John went about writing his book about Jesus and the impact of his compositional method on the resultant style, structure and content of the text.[8] Regardless of the sources John used (oral or written), the number of revisions the text had already undergone before he went to work, the literary and rhetorical patterns he chose to follow, and the ideological biases that he imprinted on his narrative, what was John actually doing at the moment when the Fourth Gospel was put to paper? Every reading of the Gospel of John is predicated to some degree on an answer to this question.

In view of the fact that some theory of the Fourth Evangelist's compositional technique underlies almost every reading of the Fourth Gospel today, it is striking to note that almost no attempts have been made to describe the way that John and other Johannine Christians went about telling stories about Jesus. Even those scholars who have been most interested in the precise

---

5   For milestone source-critical studies of the Fourth Gospel, see Bultmann 1971; Fortna 1970; Smith 1984b. On the relationship between John and the Synoptics, see Barrett 1974: 228–33; Neirynck 1977; Brodie 1993; Anderson 1996, who argues here and elsewhere that John and Mark reflect parallel and mutually influential, yet ultimately independent, trajectories of tradition.

6   For a sampling of major studies driven by the developmental approach, see Brown 1979; Painter 1993. A similar approach, with emphasis on the reinterpretation of earlier material at each stage of revision and expansion, is advocated by Jean Zumstein; see his collected essays in Zumstein 2004.

7   Milestone narrative-critical studies of the Fourth Gospel include Wead 1970; Culpepper 1983. For a sampling of post-structural and reader-oriented approaches, see Segovia 1996.

8   The name 'John' is used throughout this study in reference to that individual who was primarily responsible for the production of the Fourth Gospel as it exists today, including the addition of Chapter 21. In my view, this individual was an associate of the 'Beloved Disciple' who appears in the Fourth Gospel. The pronoun 'he' is used of this author in agreement with the gender of the name 'John'.

moment when John wrote his book – source-critical theorists, who view John as a redactor of existing materials, possibly including the Synoptics; and developmental theorists, who imagine John revising a cherished community text – have generally not attempted to explain what was happening in the room when John's story about Jesus was committed to paper. This lack of reflection is particularly notable when viewed against the fact that scholars in other camps of New Testament studies have been discussing the inter-pretative and theological implications of first-century media culture for quite some time. Following the precedent of Werner Kelber's *The Oral and the Written Gospel* and Paul Achtemeier's milestone essay '*Omne verbum sonat*', a growing number of scholars have pursued the implications of contemporary approaches to orality, textuality and memory for the inter-pretation of biblical texts (Kelber 1983; Achtemeier 1990). This research is driven by a sharp awareness that the NT documents were composed in a world where orality was the dominant mode of communication and the vast majority of people could not read.[9] But while an enhanced sensitivity to the complex interfaces between speech and writing has deeply impacted studies of the Synoptics and the historical Jesus, Johannine scholars have shown remarkably little interest in John's method for developing and presenting Jesus material within the broader media culture of his day. Of course, almost all scholars would recognize that John, unlike some medieval scribes and all modern novelists and historians, did not write his book in silence and alone. But what precise activity on John's part led to the production of the text of the Fourth Gospel?

The present study will offer a preliminary answer to the question, 'How did John write his book about Jesus?' What compositional strategies did John utilize in developing gospel stories, and what impact has this had on the nature of the text of the Gospel of John that we read and study today? Evidence from the Fourth Gospel and contemporary sources suggests that the most likely answer to this question lies in the direction of ancient memory techniques. Following this model, John 'wrote' stories about Jesus through a process of interior visualization, placing Jesus and other characters in specific scenarios and describing the words and interactions that he observed between them. Such an approach can readily explain a number of the Fourth Gospel's peculiar literary features.

---

9   On ancient literacy rates, see Harris 1989; Hezser 2001: 496. Harris concludes that 'the classical world, even at its most advanced, was so lacking in the characteristics which produce extensive literacy that we must suppose that the majority of people [above 90 per cent] were always illiterate' (Harris 1989: 13, 22).

Visual Memory, Oral Performance: The Ancient Art of Talking About Pictures

In 1532 CE, Giulio Camillo (1480–1544), formerly a professor in the university at Bologna, captured the attention of Venice with the unveiling of a remarkable invention. Vigilius Zuichemus, in a letter to his friend Erasmus, described it as 'a certain Amphitheatre, a work of wonderful skill, in which whoever is admitted as spectator will be able to discourse on any subject' (Yates 1966: 130–1). While the precise architectural details of the structure are vague, Vigilius's later reports indicate that Camillo had indeed built a sort of 'Memory Theatre', a wooden booth at least large enough to admit two adults. Once inside the compartment, visitors stood in the position of the actors and looked out upon an audience of carefully arranged images that summarized, according to Camillo, all the knowledge contained in Cicero's voluminous writings (excerpts from which were stored in boxes behind, or drawers beneath, the pictures). 'He [Camillo] pretends that all things that the human mind can conceive and which we cannot see with the corporeal eye, after being collected together by diligent meditation may be expressed by certain corporeal signs in such a way that the beholder may at once perceive with his eyes everything that is otherwise hidden in the depths of the human mind' (Yates 1966: 132, 144). These provocative pictures, in other words, functioned as an index of all knowledge of the natural, celestial and divine worlds, and through concentrated reflection upon them one could attain the wisdom of the ancients.

If Camillo's memory theatre seems novel to modern readers, it was in many respects typical of ancient, medieval and Renaissance understandings of the art of memory. Camillo's theatre was not a place for watching performances, but rather a way of composing oral texts through techniques of visualization. His 'theatre' was, in fact, a complex system for arranging symbolic images; 'memory' was not the recall of personal experiences or facts, but rather the capacity to regenerate old knowledge (historical, cultural, artistic, scientific) through intense reflection on archetypal symbols and themes. While the Hermetic-Cabalistic aspects of Camillo's theatre may have confounded some of his more rational contemporaries, the widespread popular interest in his project may be explained by the fact that it was based on a theory of memory that was already two thousand years old. Camillo could easily justify his efforts by appealing to the familiar writings of Plato, Aristotle, Cicero and Quintillian, classical authors whose works had achieved an almost canonical status. While these ancient authorities did not build memory theatres per se, they clearly asserted that memory is a visual phenomenon, and they developed complex artificial memory systems based on places and images to support the needs of rhetorical performance. As will be seen, Camillo's memory theatre was a logical extension of the ancient notion that controlled recall involves the ordering of provocative pictures in familiar spaces.

Picturing the Past

The available evidence suggests that many Greco-Roman philosophers and
rhetors, although immersed in an oral world of speeches and debate, viewed
memory primarily as a visual phenomenon. Plato, despite his well-known
suspicion toward the written word (see esp. *Phdr.* 274–5), popularized the
notion that memory is a form of mental writing, in which schematic images
of things and ideas are imprinted on the mind for later review. Specifically,
'memory may be rightly defined as the preservation of perception', a process
by which the senses and feelings 'write words in our souls' (*Phlb.* 34A,
35A–D, 39A).[10] In a famous passage of *Theaetetus* that influenced the later
Latin rhetorical theorists, Socrates compares the acquisition of memory
to a block of wax and asserts that 'whenever we wish to
remember anything we see or hear or think of in our minds, we hold this
wax under the perceptions and thoughts and imprint them upon it, just as we
make impressions from seal rings; and whatever is imprinted we remember
and know as long as its image lasts, but whatever is rubbed out or cannot
be imprinted we forget and do not know' (191D, 193C).[11] Plato's friend
Critias appeals to this principle to support his claim that he can recall all the
details of the Atlantis legend, even though he learned the story when he was
only ten years old, because his grandfather was 'eager to tell me [the tale],
since I kept questioning him repeatedly, so that the story is stamped firmly
on my mind like the encaustic designs of an indelible painting' (ὥστε οἷον
ἐγκαύματα ἀνεκπλύτου γραφῆς ἔμμονά μοι γέγονε; *Ti.* 26C).[12]

Like his illustrious teacher, Aristotle also argued that memory is a visual
phenomenon. Aristotle's minor treatise *On Memory* is predicated on the
premise, more fully developed in *De Anima*, that 'it is not possible to think
without an image'; consequently, 'memory, even the memory of objects of
thought, is not without an image (φάντασμα)' (*On Memory* 449^{b}30–1;
450^{b}20–451^{a}1; cf. *De An.* 431^{a}14–19; 432^{a}5–9).[13] Aristotle also follows
Plato in comparing memory to an imprint (τύπος) and a signet ring (οἱ

---

10   All citations of Plato's *Philebus* are from the Loeb edition (1925), trans. Harold
North Fowler.

11   All citations of Plato's *Theaetetus* are from the Loeb edition (1952), trans. Harold
North Fowler. While Cicero and the author of *Ad Herennium* adopted Plato's 'wax tablet'
model, Plotinus (d. 270 CE), a prominent Platonist, vigorously opposed it on the grounds
that it implies an inadequate view of the soul. 'We do not assert that the impression of
the sense-object enters the soul and stamps it, nor do we say that memory exists because
the impression remains' (*Ennead* 4.6.1; cited from the Loeb edition [1984], trans. A. H.
Armstrong).

12   All citations of Plato's *Timaeus* are from the Loeb edition (1961), trans. R. G.
Bury.

13   Aristotle proceeds to describe memory images as copies of the mental images
formed by the original sensory impression (*On Memory* 451^{a}14–17). All citations of
Aristotle's *On Memory and Recollection* are from Sorabji 1972.

σφραγιζόμενοι τοῖς δακτυλίοις), analogies that conveniently explain why some people have better memories than others (*On Memory* 450^{a}25–31).[14] Aristotle's commitment to visual models of memory is particularly evident in his insistence that individual acts of recall involve two mental images at once. Because 'memory' is distinguished from other cognitive capacities by its retrospective orientation, the remembrancer must bring together an image of the thing or idea being remembered and a second image representing the perceived duration of time that has passed since the event(s) occurred (*On Memory* 452^{b}23–453^{a}3). Following this logic, in order to 'remember' an idea that I had yesterday (rather than simply coming to the same conclusion a second time), I must evoke a mental image representing the idea itself and a second image representing 'yesterday'.[15] Memory is thus distinguished from other mental operations by historical consciousness.[16]

The lasting influence of Plato and Aristotle's theory of visual memory is evident from its re-emergence in prominent Latin writings of the first centuries BCE and CE. Cicero's mnemotechnique, developed as an aid to rhetorical performance, was grounded on a Platonic theory of memory that prioritized interior visualization. After noting that 'the most complete pictures are formed in our minds of the things that have been conveyed to them and imprinted on them by the senses', Cicero proceeds to assert that 'the keenest of all our senses is the sense of sight'. This being the case, 'perceptions perceived by the ears or by reflection can be most easily retained in the

---

14   For Aristotle, the notion of 'mental writing' is tied to a biological theory of memory, whereby sensory impressions are stored in the body and 'recollection is a search in something bodily for an image'. Deliberate attempts to recall information initiate a sequence of physiological processes that locate and retrieve the relevant impressions. Following this logic, Aristotle links memory capacity to age and body type (*On Memory* 450^{a}32–450^{b}11; 453^{a}31–453^{b}6). A physiological approach can also explain why we often recall things several minutes or hours after we have given up our attempts to remember them. 'Just as it is no longer in people's power to stop something when they throw it, so also he who is recollecting and hunting moves a bodily thing in which the affection resides … [O]nce moved, the fluid is not easily stopped until what is sought returns and the movement takes a straight course' (*On Memory* 453^{a}14–25).

15   Aristotle's discussion of the memory's perception of relative time is somewhat obscure. See the oft-cited solution proposed by J. I. Beare and G. R. T. Ross 1931 (see translation of 3.452^b–453a and notes); also Sorabji 1972: 18–21.

16   For Aristotle, memory is distinguished from other mental operations primarily by its retrospective posture. '[M]emory is not perception or conception, but a state or affection connected with one of these, when time has elapsed … [P]erception is of the present, prediction of the future, and memory of the past' (*On Memory* 449^{b}24–9). Cicero embraces a similar model in *De Inventione* (c. 80s BCE) when discussing the three divisions of wisdom: 'memory, intelligence, and foresight'. 'Memory (*memoria*) is the faculty by which the mind recalls that which has happened (*repetit illa quae fuerunt*). Intelligence (*intellegentia*) is the faculty by which it [the mind] ascertains what is. Foresight (*providentia*) is the faculty by which it is seen that something is going to occur before it does' (2.160; all citations of *De Inventione* are from the Loeb edition [1960], trans. H. M. Hubbell).

mind if they are also conveyed to our minds by the mediation of the eyes'; the mind therefore automatically assigns 'a sort of outline and image and shape' even to abstract ideas and concepts in order to foster their retention (*De Or.* 2.357).[17] In a similar vein, Quintillian's discussion of the art of memory is founded on the premise that 'the most important factor in Memory is mental concentration, a sharp eye, as it were, never diverted from the object of its gaze' (*Inst.* 11.2.11). Extending this logic, Cicero follows Plato and Aristotle in describing memory as 'the twin sister of written script' (*gemina litteraturae*; *Part. or.* 26).[18]

Overall, the available evidence suggests that Greco-Roman models of memory focused on the development, retention and mental manipulation of images, and that Greek philosophers and Latin rhetors occasionally even compared the works of memory to characters inscribed on wax or paper. Mary Carruthers has therefore asserted that 'the metaphor of memory as a written surface is so ancient and so persistent in all Western cultures that it must ... be seen as a governing model or "cognitive archetype"' (Carruthers 1990: 16). While Plato and Cicero lived in a predominantly oral world, their inner space was filled with pictures and writing.

Placing the Past

Ancient mnemotechnique, and models of composition based on such techniques, were based on strategies for arranging and ordering mental images in ways that would facilitate recall in oral performance. Aristotle's advice on preparation for dialectical debate illustrates this approach. In Aristotle's view, memorial images can be arranged in the mind in sequences and sets of associations, making it possible to recall one item by its similarity or proximity to another item in the imaginary rubric (*On Memory* 451^{b}18–452^{b}6). He therefore advocates the technique of 'midpoints', an indexing strategy whereby the remembrancer places memory images in a linear sequence and then recollects the needed information by moving forward or backward from any specific point in the series. Thus, for example, one might assign the numerals 1, 2, 3, 4, 5 to the five points of an argument; when attempting to recall points 2 or 4, the remembrancer would begin at the midpoint of the series, point 3, and then move left or right from that location to the desired data (*On Memory* 452^{a}17–24).[19] Such strategies are critical to successful debate because, in Aristotle's words, 'whatever has some order, as things in

17   All citations of Cicero's *De Oratore* are from the Loeb edition (1959), trans. E. W. Sutton and H. Rackham.

18   All citations of Cicero's *De Partitione Oratoria* are from the Loeb edition, trans. H. Rackham.

19   See discussion in Sorabji 1972: 31–4, who argues that Aristotle's argument is best understood 'if we assume that the recollecting is being done through some [organizational] system of images'.

mathematics do, is easily remembered. Other things are remembered badly and with difficulty' (*On Memory* 451^{b}29–452^{a}3; see also 452^{a}12–16).

While Aristotle's *On Memory* describes a linear sequencing technique based on numbers or letters of the alphabet, the Latin rhetorical theorists were more heavily influenced by a three-dimensional ordering strategy attributed to Simonides of Ceos (550s–460s BCE).[20] Simonides was (in)famous in the ancient world as the first lyric poet to work on commission, for the invention of the Greek letters H, Ω, Θ, and Ψ, and also for calling 'painting silent poetry and poetry painting that speaks', thus making oral composition analogous to the visual arts.[21] His most lasting influence, however, originated in a legendary escape from death. On one occasion, Simonides was at a large banquet, and after performing an ode to his host he was called to the door for an urgent message. As he spoke to the messengers outside, the building suddenly collapsed behind him, killing all those in attendance. The weight of the stones crushed many of the corpses beyond recognition, and the friends and family of the deceased appealed to the lucky bard to identify the remains. Simonides discovered that he could name the mangled corpses by visualizing the banquet table at the moment before the disaster and noting the position of each guest. This remarkable experience led him to conclude that 'the best aid to clearness of memory consists in orderly arrangement', specifically arrangements based on familiar physical locations (see Cicero *De or.* 2.355; Quintillian *Inst.* 11.2.11–16).[22]

---

20   While *On Memory* focuses on linear sequencing and 'midpoint' techniques, Aristotle also seems to have advocated, or at least been aware of, a 'place system' of artificial memory. In Book 8 of his *Topica*, Aristotle urges students to come well prepared for dialectical debates, with a firm grasp of 'arguments dealing with questions of frequent occurrence and especially primary propositions', 'a good supply of definitions', and an awareness of 'the categories into which the other arguments most often fall' (163^{b}18–24; cited here from the Loeb edition [1960], trans. E. S. Forster). One's memory of such principles is critical because, 'just as to a trained memory the mere reference to *the places in which they occur* causes the things themselves to be remembered, so the above rules will make a man a better reasoner, because he sees the premises defined and numbered' (*Top.* 163^{b}28–32; emphasis added). While the precise meaning of Aristotle's reference to the 'places' (τόποι) which 'cause things to be remembered' (ποιοῦσιν αὐτὰ μνημονεύειν) is debated, the quote above seems to refer to memory theatre techniques of spatial visualization. See also *De Anima* 427^{b}18–22, which indicates that Aristotle was at least aware of place systems of artificial memory, even if he did not promote them himself.

21   See the biographical notes gathered in *Lyra Graeca* (LCL), 2.249–53, 2.258–59, 2.266–67. While Simonides' works are no longer extant, a number of ancient allusions suggest that he posited a general correlation between sound/speech and images/writing. The medieval Byzantine scholar Michael Psellus (ca. 1018–1078 CE) summarizes Simonides' approach in the maxim ὁ λόγος τῶν πραγμάτων εἰκών ἐστι ('the word is the icon of things'; cited from *Lyra Graeca* 2.258, trans. J. Edmonds).

22   In Yates's view, Quintillian's discussion suggests that the Simonides legend 'formed the normal introduction to the section on artificial memory' in Greek treatises on rhetoric (Yates 1966: 27).

Simonides proceeded to develop a memory system based on the interior visualization of two types of pictures, which the Latin rhetors would later call *loci* and *imagines*. According to the anonymous author of *Ad Herennium* (80s BCE), an 'image' is 'a figure, mark, or portrait of the object we wish to remember' (3.29); *imagines*, then, are symbolic visual representations of the individual facts and ideas that one needs to recall when delivering a speech.[23] *Loci* are mental snapshots of real or invented places, such as the rooms of a house or a familiar street.[24] Rhetors and philosophers could prepare for a speech or debate by arranging memorial images representing the relevant facts and arguments in a fixed *locus*; at the moment of delivery, one would simply review the symbolic images in the order in which they appear on the imagined schema and discuss the points associated with each.[25] For example, in preparing a long speech, one might attach each of the major points to a mental image of a piece of furniture, and then situate each of the respective pieces of furniture in the rooms of a familiar villa. In performance, the rhetor would simply walk through the house in his mind's eye and discuss the points associated with the objects he encountered in each room. Such a technique would facilitate accurate recollection of the individual points of the speech and would also ensure that the facts and arguments are presented in the

23   Obviously, symbolic images can help us remember things only if we can first remember the images themselves. One should therefore take care to fill the *loci* of memory with images of things that are 'base, dishonourable, extraordinary, great, unbelievable, or laughable ... striking and novel' (*Ad Herennium* 3.35–7). Because people have differing ideas about what is striking or exotic – or even about which things resemble other things or concepts – *Ad_Herennium* refuses to offer a standardized set of memory images; each orator should develop and utilize images that are personally memorable and provocative (3.38–9). All citations of *Ad_Herennium* are from the Loeb edition (1954), trans. Harry Caplan. While the author of *Ad Herennium* is unknown, the treatise was attributed to Cicero through the Middle Ages and therefore enjoyed widespread influence (see Yates 1966: 5–6; Caplan 1954: vii–ix).

24   *Ad Herennium* advocates the development of a stock repertoire of memorable *loci* that could function as structural outlines for any number of speeches by the insertion of different image sets. 'We shall need to study with special care the backgrounds we have adopted so that they may cling lastingly in our memory, for the images, like letters, are effaced when we make no use of them, but the backgrounds, like wax tablets, should abide.' Once the system of *loci* is firmly established, one can simply replace old images with new ones each time a new speech is delivered, the same way that one might erase letters from a chalkboard between lectures. The author therefore describes a number of techniques for developing and ordering a personal repertoire of memory *loci* (3.31–2).

25   In Cicero's words, 'persons desiring to train this faculty [memory] must select localities and form mental images of the facts they wish to remember and store those images in the localities, with the result that the arrangement of the localities will preserve the order of the facts, and the images of the facts will designate the facts themselves' (Cicero, *De Or.* 2.355). Similarly, Quintillian advises that performance memory 'needs (1) Sites, which may be invented or taken from reality, (2) Images or Symbols, which we must of course invent' (*Inst.*11.2.21).

proper order.[26] Cicero assures his students that this method will enable them to easily recall the facts of the case, the outline of the arguments, points of style in delivery, and precedents from other settlements (*De or.* 2.355).

Aside from its utility, Simonides' mnemotechnique appealed to the Latin rhetors because it was readily compatible with the Platonic/Aristotelian theory of visual memory. In Cicero's view, remembering is a form of mental writing, analogous to notes for a speech: 'we shall employ the localities and images respectively as a wax writing tablet and the letters written on it' (*De or.* 2.351–354).[27] *Ad Herennium* extends this metaphor to characterize recall as a form of literacy: 'the backgrounds [*loci*] are very much like wax tablets or papyrus, the images like the letters, the arrangement and disposition of the images like the script, and the delivery is like reading' (3.30). The same logic applies in situations where the orator wishes to recite a memorized passage verbatim: Quintillian advises those who take this approach to visualize the words on the page and then simply read the remembered text to the audience (*Inst.* 11.2.32). Overall, ancient rhetorical theorists seem to have viewed Simonides' mnemotechnique as a natural extension of the theory that memory is a visual art.

Quintillian's *Institutio Oratoria* – written some time in the mid-to-first century CE – illustrates the extent to which place systems of memory had come to dominate theories of rhetorical performance in the New Testament period. In one respect, Quintillian departs from other ancient theorists in his strong preference for the mental discipline of rote memorization – in *Ad Herennium*'s terms, for 'word memory' over 'subject memory' (*Inst.* 11.2.32–5, 40–2). 'If Memory supports me, and time has not been lacking, I should prefer not to let a single syllable escape me' – i.e., in an ideal world, Quintillian would write and then memorize every word in the speech before he arrives at court (11.2.45).[28] Quintillian also highlights the limitations of a

26   'This done, when they have to retrieve the memory, they begin to go over these Sites from the beginning, calling in whatever they deposited with each of them, as the images remind them' (Quintillian *Inst.* 11.2.20). For a popular modern system for the use of visual images to memorize things and words, see Lorayne 1957; Farber 1991 esp. 81–96.

27   Elsewhere: 'Just as script consists of marks indicating letters and of the material on which those marks were imprinted, so the structure of memory, like a wax tablet, employs "topics" (*locis*), and in these stores images (*imagines*) which correspond to the letters in written script' (Cicero, *De Part. Or.* 26).

28   Specifically, Quintillian seems to feel that the rhetor should compose and essentially memorize portions of a speech, then use memory sites and images as prompts for the recitation of this memorized information. 'By [memory] Images I mean the aids we use to mark what we have to learn by heart; as Cicero says, we use the Sites as our wax tablet, the Symbols as our letters' (*Inst.* 11.2.20–42, quote 21). The author of *Ad Herennium* also extols the virtues of rote memorization, but primarily because this discipline improves one's skill in developing and manipulating artificial *imagines* and *loci* (3.39–40).

place system approach, noting for example that some aspects of a prepared speech, such as conjunctions and transitions, do not naturally associate themselves with visual images, and that imaging techniques cannot ensure the exact reproduction of important strings of words (11.2.24–5). These aspects of Quintillian's model reflect his concern with accuracy and precision in recall, a desire to repeat prepared material verbatim whenever possible. But at the same time, he realizes that rote memorization and verbatim repetition are not always possible, or even appropriate. Public debate requires more than simple recitation of facts and prepared remarks; the rhetor must also be able to recall, rearrange and respond to the points of the opponent's speech (11.2.2, 11). Further, rote recitation is generally less impressive than spontaneous composition, and may even arouse the audience's suspicion. 'Memory also gives a reputation for quickness of wit, so that we are believed to have made the speech up on the spot, instead of bringing it ready made from home; and this impression is very valuable both to the orator and the Cause, because the judge admires more, and fears less, things which he does not suspect of having been prepared in advance to outwit him' (11.2.47).[29] Finally, life is busy, and we do not always have time to memorize prepared remarks; in such cases, it is 'far safer to secure a good grasp of the facts themselves and to leave ourselves free to speak as we will' (11.2.48). In view of these and other practical considerations, Quintillian's discussion of mnemotechnique wavers between the ideal of a memorized text and the reality of spontaneous oral composition based on place systems.

How, then, should modern scholars – who live in a world where political speeches, sermons and academic papers are typically written and then recited verbatim to literate audiences – conceptualize the mnemotechnique of a disciple of Simonides, Cicero or, in the first century CE, Quintillian? Ancient rhetors and philosophers would prepare for public performance by outlining, perhaps in writing, the relevant facts of the case and the most effective style and sequence of presentation. They would then associate the major points, significant facts and possibly also short memorized passages with provocative mental images. These images were situated against a familiar backdrop, perhaps a physical location like one's house or the local gymnasium, or within some larger visualized scheme that was equally easy to recall, such as Metrodorus of Scepsis's outline based on the 12 signs of the zodiac (early first century BCE; see Quintillian *Inst.* 11.2.22). During the public performance of the discourse, the orator would mentally perambulate his memory theatre, noting the items he encountered in each compartment and discussing the points attached to these items. The images in the theatre would thus preserve the content of the speech, while the physical structure

---

29   Hence, if one has written the speech in verse or rhythmical prose it must be presented in non-rhythmical style, and one must occasionally pretend to be searching for words (Quintillian, *Inst.* 11.2.47).

of the theatre itself would ensure that the points were discussed in the proper order.[30]

In summary, four aspects of the classical theory of memory are relevant to the question of the Fourth Evangelist's compositional model.

- *First*, in the New Testament era, mnemotechnique was a performance art, the property of public speakers and directly associated with problems of composition in performance. The artificial memory systems of Cicero, *Ad Herennium* and Quintillian were all designed to generate lengthy, well-ordered oral texts.
- *Secondly*, while mnemotechnique was a branch of ancient rhetoric and thereby a key element of oral composition, the authors surveyed above conceptualize memory as a visual, rather than an auditory, phenomenon.[31] In John's media culture, lengthy oral texts were often – the extant evidence would suggest normally – produced by evoking and describing mental images.
- *Thirdly*, ancient mnemotechnique served oral performance by ordering provocative images in ways that would facilitate spontaneous composition. Place systems provided orators with a stack of mental note cards or, perhaps more accurately, a series of mental snapshots. Each picture represents one moment in a larger story or argument, prompting the remembrancer to evoke the host of data associated with this particular scene. Following this model, 'oral composition' means 'discussing a sequence of images as they move across the imagination's field of vision'.
- *Fourthly*, and perhaps most significantly here, it is everywhere clear that Cicero, Quintillian and the anonymous author of *Ad Herennium* see nothing novel in the methods they prescribe. Rather, these rhetors seem to assume that their readers will agree that memory is a visual phenomenon and that place system techniques are a logical (and, indeed, typical) way of delivering public speeches.[32]

---

30   See Yates: 'We have to think of the ancient orator as moving in imagination through his memory building *whilst* he is making his speech, drawing from the memorised places the images he has placed on them' (1966: 3; emphasis in original).

31   Yates concludes that ancient mnemotechnique depended 'on faculties of intense visual memorisation' (1966: 4). Plotinus even conceptualizes sound and speech in visual terms, and portrays listening as a form of reading: 'the [acoustic] impression is in the air, and is a sort of articulated stroke, like letters written on the air by the maker of the sound; but the power and the substance of the soul does something like reading the impressions written on the air when they come near and reach the point at which they can be seen' (*Enn.* 4.6).

32   In this connection, Yates notes that any interpretation of *Ad Herennium*'s theory of memory is complicated by the fact that the author 'is not setting out to explain to

Jesus at the Theatre: John's Visual Memory

In two key passages in the Fourth Gospel, John pauses to note that the disciples 'remembered' something that Jesus did and/or said. At John 2.22, after Jesus has challenged 'the Jews' in the temple courts to 'tear down this temple, and in three days I will raise it' (2.19), the narrator breaks in to clarify (for the reader, not the bewildered Jews) that 'Jesus said this concerning the "temple" of his body. Then, when he was raised from the dead, his disciples remembered (ἐμνήσθησαν) that he said this, and they believed the Scripture and the word that Jesus spoke.' A similar aside appears at John 12.16, where the narrator interrupts the Triumphal Entry to reveal that 'the disciples did not know these things at first, but when Jesus was glorified, and then they remembered (ἐμνήσθησαν) that these things were written about him and that they did these things to him'. In the Farewell Address (Jesus's lengthy discourse in the upper room on the night of his arrest), John characterizes these memories of Jesus as a gift of the Holy Spirit, who will 'teach' the disciples 'all things' and 'remind you of everything that I [Jesus] said to you' (ὑπομνήσει ὑμᾶς πάντα ἃ εἶπον ὑμῖν; John 14.26, see 16.13). In all these instances, John uses the verb 'remember/remind' (μνημονεύω/ὑπομιμνήσκω) to describe the disciples' subsequent recollections of, and presumably their stories about, Jesus's remarkable deeds and words.

From the perspective of modern Western readers – who are inclined to agree with Aristotle that 'memory' is a physiological process whereby we pull lingering impressions out of our brains 'like checked baggage from storage' – John 2.22 and 12.16 fit nicely with other passages in the Fourth Gospel which claim that John's story is based on the 'witness' of an associate of the historical Jesus (quote Lowenthal 1985: 252; see *On Memory* 450ᵃ32–450ᵇ11, 453ᵃ14–25, 453ᵃ31–453ᵇ6). At 19.35, after noting that 'water and blood' flowed from Jesus's body when the soldiers pierced his side, John insists that 'the one who saw has testified (ὁ ἑωρακὼς μεμαρτύρηκεν), and his testimony is true'. The juxtaposition of the verbs 'saw' and 'testified' would logically imply that some person who observed Jesus's death later recalled and discussed that experience,

people who know nothing about it what the artificial memory was. He is addressing his rhetoric students as they congregated around him circa 86–82 BC, and *they* knew what he was talking about; for *them* he needed only to rattle off the "rules" which they would know how to apply' (Yates 1966: 6; emphasis in original). In a similar vein, Quintillian's *Institutio* – produced at the same moment in history when Christians were telling stories about Jesus to Greek audiences and Matthew, Mark, Luke and John were writing Gospels – clearly presupposes that the reader is already aware of the basic details of the Simonides legend, and seems more concerned with correcting misunderstandings and abuses of Simonides' technique than with explaining how to use it (see 11.2.11–22).

and that John is claiming that his account is based on this person's recollections.[33] A similar statement appears in the closing verses of the book, where the reader is assured that the preceding narrative is based on information provided by the mysterious Beloved Disciple, a close friend of Jesus who, again, 'testifies about these things' (ὁ μαρτυρῶν περὶ τούτων; 21.24). Taken alongside John 2.22 and 12.16, these verses would suggest that the Beloved Disciple saw Jesus do, and heard him say, certain things; on some later occasion(s), this person recollected these pieces of information and told stories about his experiences; John's book, based on the 'testimony' of this person, is essentially a written report of these memories.

Following the above reading of John's statements on 'memory' and 'witness', John 2.22 and 12.16 are problematic on several counts. First, if John is simply indicating the source of his information, these verses are redundant. Since John claims that his entire narrative is based on the Beloved Disciple's testimony about Jesus (see esp. 21.24), it seems obvious that everything in his Gospel must be someone's 'memory' of something that Jesus did. It is therefore unnecessary to state that the disciples 'remembered' that Jesus said certain things in the temple on one occasion – if nobody 'remembered that he said this', John presumably would not be able to tell the story in the first place. Second, one must also wonder why John feels compelled to stress that his accounts of the Temple Incident and the Triumphal Entry are based on the disciples' memories of Jesus, when he does not make a similar claim for other events that seem more immediately relevant to his theological interests. Finally, and much more substantially, it is clear from these passages that John uses the word 'memory' in a very nuanced way, one that does not coincide with modern definitions of that term. A closer reading of John 2.22 and 12.16 reveals that the disciples' memories of Jesus were influenced by their post-resurrection faith and subsequent messianic interpretations of the Hebrew Bible, an admission that would seem to compromise the integrity of their testimony. On a number of fronts, then, the words 'memory' and 'witness' clearly do not merge in John's mind at the same point where they intersect in modern understandings.

But if the Fourth Gospel's unusual perspective on 'memory' and 'testimony' seems perplexing to modern readers, a first-century audience would likely understand these terms as indications of John's compositional technique. Specifically, when John says that the disciples 'remembered these things', his first audiences would understand that Jesus's followers later visualized their experiences with him; when John says that the Beloved Disciple 'testified'

---

33   The preceding context suggests that 'the one who saw these things' must be the Beloved Disciple, who is standing with Jesus's mother and several other women at the foot of the cross (John 19: 25–7; see Brown 1970: 2.936–7). Some scholars even suggest that the author is here revealing himself to be the Beloved Disciple; see Carson 1991: 625–7; Köstenberger 2004: 553.

about Jesus's words and deeds, his audience would assume that this disciple sometimes told stories by reflecting on memorial images. Viewed from the perspective of ancient mnemotechnique, John 21.24 – οὗτός ἐστιν ὁ μαθητὴς ὁ μαρτυρῶν περὶ τούτων καὶ ὁ γράψς ταῦτα ('This is the disciple who testifies about these things and who wrote them') – would simply indicate that Johannine Christians followed the typical rhetorical practice of composing, and sometimes writing down, stories about Jesus through strategies of visual memory.

Following this model, a Johannine Christian (like the Beloved Disciple or the Fourth Evangelist) would narrate Jesus's signs and sayings by visualizing a place and occasion, locating images of Jesus and other actors against this backdrop, and then describing the interactions that he imagined between them. John could, for example, visualize the temple courts (the buildings, the money tables, the noise and smell of the animals); picture Jesus, the crowd, the disciples and the Jews in that context; and then describe what these people did and said in that place. The account at John 2.13-20 would thus be the written version of a running commentary on what John (or the person whose words he was dictating) saw in his mind's eye. Through this means, the testimony of the Beloved Disciple would be preserved and recreated in new performance contexts through the power of ocular imagination.[34]

Many of the Fourth Gospel's peculiar literary features are consistent with a memory theatre approach to composition. Three of the more obvious will be briefly noted here: (1) the high level of detail in John's narration of Jesus's 'signs'; (2) the problem of blended voices in John 3; and (3) the peculiar 'purpose statements' at John 20.30-1 and 21.25.

Seeing Signs

Aside from the fact that they generally do not enjoy multiple attestation, John's narratives of Jesus's mighty deeds are notable for their remarkable level of detail. For example, John's 'water to wine' story (2.1-11) – the first of Jesus's 'signs' – evidences a well-developed plot with substantial staging, a large cast of characters, and elements of irony and suspense. Jesus is at a wedding in Cana of Galilee on 'the third day' (2.1); the host has run out of wine for the feast; Mary attempts to take charge of the situation but fails to secure Jesus's aid; after refusing her appeal, Jesus suddenly changes his mind and tells the servants to fill six large purification jars, each of which holds 'two or three μετρήτοι' (= c. 75–115 litres) with water; Jesus turns

---

34   See the similar discussion of A. Dewey (2001), who focuses on the implications of John's mnemotechnique for evaluations of the Fourth Gospel's historicity. Of course, John's first-century audiences might also have understand the terms 'witness' and 'memory' as claims to historical reminiscence. The implications of John's references to 'witness' and 'memory' for considerations of the Fourth Gospel's historicity are beyond the scope of this study.

the water into wine without even approaching the jars; some servants take the wine to the head waiter; the head waiter compliments the befuddled groom on the quality of his wine. Thus, in only eleven verses, John names six different characters (counting 'the servants' and 'the disciples' each as a single character), indicates the location and date of the event, describes critical stage props, identifies the unusual dilemma that Jesus must resolve (the strange lack of wine at a wedding banquet), introduces subplots (Mary's interactions with the servants; the tension between Jesus and his mother; the private discussion between the symposiarch and the bewildered groom), and provides, as necessary, relevant information on cultural backgrounds (2.6).

A similar level of detail characterizes the Bethesda healing at John 5.1-9. This episode is particularly notable for its large number of framing devices: Jesus meets a man, who has been lame for precisely 38 years, in Jerusalem, at a 'Feast of the Jews', beside a pool near the Sheep Gate that is called 'Bethesda' in Aramaic; the pool is surrounded by five porticoes, in which reside a large number of blind, lame or otherwise disabled persons; these sick people run to the pool for healing whenever the surface of the water is stirred; the encounter takes place on a Sabbath during 'a Feast of the Jews' (5.1, 9) – the reader almost needs a map and calendar to follow the action. The level of incidental detail evident in the first Cana miracle and the Bethesda story are entirely typical of John's presentation of all of Jesus's signs.

John's preference for detailed miracle stories with multiple character inter-actions, fixed locations and dates, and complex plots may or may not offer insights on his theological interests or the historical value of his narrative, but it certainly reflects his compositional technique. In narrating Jesus's deeds, John situates images of the characters involved against snapshots of the scene of the action and then tells the audience what he sees in his mind's eye. Thus, at the moment of composition, John (or the person whose words he is recording) envisions the pool at Bethesda, places images of Jesus and the lame man against that vivid backdrop, and proceeds to describe what these people do in this place. Bethesda thus functions as one of the *loci* in John's memory theatre, a stage for his *imagines agentes*; John could visit this theatre to observe and discuss Jesus's healing of the lame man on any occasion when he might want to tell this story. As a result of this technique, John's narra-tives of Jesus's miracles are characterized by a large number of references to things, people and details that happen to catch his mind's eye. Perhaps John's preference for the term 'signs' reflects not only his Christology, but also the visual techniques through which he himself has experienced and narrated Jesus's mighty deeds.

Blending Voices

A memory theatre model may also explain, as an alternative to the conclu-sions of source criticism and developmental approaches, the occasional blending of voices in the Fourth Gospel's dialogues. In some instances, the voice of a character in John's story (normally Jesus) blends with that of the narrator to such an extent that it is impossible to determine who is speaking. The most notable instances of this phenomenon occur in John 3. As Carson notes, at 3.15-21 and 3.31-6 'the words of the speaker (Jesus and John the Baptist respectively) are succeeded by the explanatory reflections of the Evangelist. Because the ancient texts did not use quotation marks or other orthographical equivalents, the exact point of transition is disputed' (Carson 1991: 203–4). The first ten verses of John 3 clearly recount a conversation between Jesus and a leading Jew named Nicodemus, yet commentators almost unanimously agree that the narrator is addressing the reader directly by v. 21.[35] Similarly, John 3.27-30 describes a conversation between John the Baptist and his disciples, yet most commentators argue that the Fourth Evangelist has broken into the Baptist's monologue without warning to deliver vv. 31-6 himself.[36]

While problems of this sort are typically listed among the Fourth Gospel's 'aporias' and hence as evidence of redaction or revision, the preceding discussion would suggest that the blending of voices in John 3 is the natural result of a compositional technique based on what might be called 'dual vocalization' or, more specifically here, 'dual visualization'.[37] When presenting Jesus's speeches in live performance (or when writing a book by dictation), the oral composer always speaks in two voices to two audiences at once: as Jesus to other characters in the story, and as himself to his own audience/reader. In terms of the present discussion, as John tells the story of Nicodemus, he must visualize Jesus's audience (Nicodemus) and speak to that audience in the first person on Jesus's behalf. At the same time, however, John is always aware of the presence of his own audience, who hear Jesus's words to Nicodemus as bystanders. Thus, in oral narrations of gospel material, John speaks both to the audience that he envisions in his narrative (characters in the story) and to the actual, real-world audience that is visually present before him (Johannine Christians) at the same time. At John 3.16 and 31, these two images have merged in John's imagination, blurring the line between the past and present audiences and allowing John to shift from memory to commentary. In the first portion of Chapter 3, John is clearly speaking to Nicodemus on Jesus's behalf as his own audience listens on the sidelines; at some point, John's eye shifts from Nicodemus to his own

35   While Carson locates a break after 3.15, Schnackenburg argues that 'verses 13-21 [of John 3] do not form part of the Gospel narrative, but come from a kerygmatic exposition of the evangelist' in which they originally followed 3.31-6 (1987: 1.361). For an alternate view, see Brown (1966/1970: 1.149), who asserts that Jesus is speaking up through v. 21 with no direct intrusion by the narrator.

36   Barrett, however, argues that the Baptist is still speaking at 3.31-6 (1978: 219, 224).

37   For readings that view the break at John 3.31-6 as evidence of redaction or revision, see Brown 1966/70: 1.159–60; Bultmann 1971: 131–2. On dual vocalization, see Thatcher 2000: 173–4.

audience, Johannine Christians, to whom he offers his interpretation of these events. Similarly, at 3.27-30 John envisions and narrates a discussion between the Baptist and his disciples while John's own audience listens in; at v. 31, John turns his gaze away from the characters in the story to exhort his own audience directly. In general, a memory theatre approach would tend to view the Fourth Gospel's individual signs and speeches, and perhaps the larger narrative, as unified compositions, and would treat the Fourth Gospel's aporias as logical accidents of the movement of John's mind's eye.

Filling the World with Pictures
The Fourth Gospel is notorious for its dual endings. The narrative seems to conclude with a direct appeal to the reader at 20.30-1, but this altar call is immediately followed by a lengthy resurrection story that focuses on the fates of Peter and the Beloved Disciple. After this interlude, John 21.24-5 reasserts the verity of the Beloved Disciple's testimony about Jesus. Many Johannine scholars have concluded that Chapter 21 was a later addition to John's text, which originally ended at 20.31. Following this reading, John 21.24-5 should be viewed as an unknown editor's attempt to wrap up the revised narrative by returning to the theme of John's closing remarks.

For purposes of the present study, however, the editorial history of the Fourth Gospel is less significant than a remarkable admission that appears in both endings of the story. Immediately after Christ's blessing upon 'those who have not seen me [i.e., those who were not associates of the historical Jesus] and believed', John suddenly tells his audience that 'Jesus did many more signs in the presence of his disciples that are not written in this book' (20.30). This statement is repeated with emphasis at 21.25, where the author boasts that 'should they [Jesus's deeds] all be written down, I do not think the world could hold the books that had been written'. The casual tone of these comments is particularly striking when compared to Luke's purpose statement, which appears at the beginning of his Gospel (Luke 1.1-4). The Prologue to Luke–Acts acknowledges that other accounts of Jesus's life, based on the testimony of eyewitnesses (αὐτόπται), are already in existence. Luke, however, has carefully reviewed these texts against his own field notes, and is now prepared to preserve in writing a definitive version of Jesus's life and teachings, so that Theophilus may 'know the certainty' of what he has been taught. John, by contrast, makes no promises: his book explicitly seeks to lead the reader to faith, and it may or may not include the most important events of Jesus's career. The second ending at 21.25 goes further, warning the audience that the Fourth Gospel does not even begin to exhaust what might be said about its main character. Viewed positively, both of the Fourth Gospel's endings assure the reader that much more information can be provided on demand.

John's confident claim(s) that he could provide an almost endless stream of stories about Jesus follows the logic of ancient mnemotechnique. Practitioners of the ancient art of visual memory regularly asserted that their methods could support almost unlimited spontaneous composition. As a wise man once told Themistocles, the workings of visual memory 'would enable him to remember anything' in the sense that the skilled remembrancer could compose texts on a wide variety of events and subjects (Cicero *De or.* 2.299). Quintillian also notes the almost unlimited potential of visual techniques: memory does not 'simply string a few words together, but continues unimpaired almost infinitely; even in the longest pleadings the patience of the audience flags sooner than the speaker's trusty memory' (*Inst.* 11.2.8–9). The length of the oral performance could be extended indefinitely simply by expanding the number and arrangement of the archetypal images which provoked memory texts – more images, more locations and more scenes would support more and more words. As proof of this point, the Elder Pliny – a contemporary of the Fourth Evangelist, whose son was one of Quintillian's students – describes a number of remarkable feats of memory and claims that Simonides' place system, as perfected by Metrodorus, made it possible for 'anything heard to be repeated in identical words' (*NH* 7.89).[38] Guided by the logic of ocular imagination, John does not exaggerate when he says that he could fill the whole world with books about Jesus.

---

38   Cited from the Loeb edition (1947), trans. H. Rackham.

Chapter 6

THE MEDIUM AND MESSAGE OF JOHN:
AUDIENCE ADDRESS AND AUDIENCE IDENTITY IN THE FOURTH
GOSPEL

Thomas E. Boomershine

The message and meaning of the Gospel of John in its original historical context was shaped by the medium of the Gospel as much as by its form and content. Until very recently, the unquestioned picture of the medium of John in Johannine scholarship has been that it was a written document composed for reading by individual readers. A further dimension of this picture has been that John's readers read in silence as contemporary readers do. This assumption about the original medium of the Gospel has been associated with methodological practices in contemporary scholarly investigations of John's Gospel. In silent reading, the entire text is available for synchronic examination by the eyes in space as well as for diachronic reading in time. Reading in silence reduces or eliminates movement in a straight temporal progression through the text. It also contributes to the possibility that the reader will become an analyst rather than a participant in the author's story. While a reader of the Fourth Gospel *can* get caught up in the story and keep moving in the direction established by the narrator, it is easy to disrupt involvement in the story for reflection and for retracing steps to answer questions.

A primary consequence of individual reading by readers for centuries has been an abandonment of the story as an experience in favour of a search for the ideas implicit in the story. One of the enduring results of reading the Fourth Gospel in this way is that Jews have come to represent disbelief and have been seen as the objects of Johannine polemic.

Recent research about the communication world of antiquity has shown that this picture of the medium of the Fourth Gospel is improbable. The evidence from documents in the ancient world indicates that documents were written for performances to audiences and were rarely read in silence by individuals. In modern terms, ancient writers were more like composers than authors or writers. The implica-

tions of this realization for our understanding of the Fourth Gospel and
for exegetical methodology have only begun to be explored.[1]

The purpose of this article is to sketch the outlines of an answer to the
question implicit in this recognition: what can we discern about the message
and meaning of the Gospel of John if it was experienced as a story told or
read by a storyteller/performer to audiences rather than read in silence by
individual readers? What difference would this reconception and recovery
of the original medium of John make in our understanding of its original
message and meaning? The focus of this article will be the structure
of audience address in the speeches of Jesus and the storyteller's direct
comments to the audience. When the Gospel was performed, the performers
of the story addressed their audiences in more than half of the story *as Jesus*
speaking to specific groups that are identified in the story. The audience as
a result was addressed *as those groups* to whom Jesus, embodied by the
storyteller, is speaking: e.g., the Jews (6.41), Jews who believed in him (8.31),
Pharisees (9.40), the disciples (13-16). Thus, throughout the story, the storyteller was continually speaking to the audience as Jesus, and the audience
was continually being addressed by the storyteller/Jesus as one or another of
various groups of Jews.

This claim may strike the reader of this article as strange. We are accus-
tomed to reading the Evangelist's story with the assumption that the audience
was composed of believers who were *listening in*, as Jesus, with whom
they identified, addressed various non-believers, with whom they did not
identify. Indeed, John's story can be read, both silently and aloud, to generate
this experience. The thesis of this article is that the Fourth Gospel and its
audience is perceived in a radically different way if the document is experienced and analysed as a story told to audiences rather than as a document
read by readers. Even to consider this new thesis, however, the researcher
has to both experience and present John's story in its original oral medium.[2]
She or he must also be willing to explore the possibilities and capabilities
of this medium for producing experiences of the Fourth Gospel excluded
by the tradition of silent reading that has been the unexamined tradition of
biblical scholarship.

The thesis here is that, when the Fourth Gospel was told to audiences, the
Johannine storyteller always addressed the audiences of the Fourth Gospel
as Jews. Furthermore, there was a clear structure to the addresses to the

---

1   Richard A. Horsley notes that modern methods of study assume, incorrectly, a
reader reading in silence: 'we can no longer project the assumptions and typical approaches of literary study that assume a writer at a desk and an individual reader'. He further
comments, 'established Gospel studies in particular and New Testament studies in general
are ill-equipped to understand orally performed narratives' (2006: 166).

2   See Rhoads (2006: 173–80) for the transformative impact of performance on the
perception of biblical texts.

audience that moved from the performer, speaking as both him/herself and as Jesus, first addressing the audience as Jews who are interested in and drawn to Jesus (chapters 1 to 4), then as Jews who are torn between wanting to kill him and believing in him (chapters 5 to 12), and as Jews who are his beloved disciples (chapters 13 to 16). This character of audience address in turn indicates the probability that the actual historical audiences of the Gospel were predominantly Jewish. At least, the audience is always addressed *as if* they are Jews. The impact of the story was to engage the audience in a dynamic and passionate interaction with Jesus as a character who directly addressed them throughout the story. The message implicit in the Gospel was to appeal to Jewish listeners to move through the conflicts of engagement with Jesus to belief in Jesus as the Messiah. When heard as addressed to first-century Jewish audiences, the Fourth Gospel presented Jesus as engaged in passionate interaction with other Jews as the fulfilment of the prophetic traditions of Israel, specifically a prophet like Moses, and as the King of the Jews who gave his life for the nation.

The Fourth Gospel and its Readers in the Work of J. Louis Martyn

The refinements in our understanding of the Fourth Gospel that may develop from a more precise definition of the Gospel's medium will be sharpened by entering into dialogue with a highly influential picture of John in recent scholarship. In his engaging conversational manner, J. Louis Martyn has invited us all into an exploration of the Gospel of John in its late-first-century context. Martyn proposes that the Gospel was conceived and experienced as a 'two-level drama'. In this drama the characters from the original story, such as the blind man in John 9, represent both the original persons who interacted with Jesus and persons in John's context. As readers of the Gospel read, they perceived in the drama going on in Jesus's life a similar drama taking place in their own lives. As Martyn writes,

> In the two level drama of John 9 the man born blind plays not only the part of a Jew in Jerusalem healed by Jesus of Nazareth but also the part of Jews known to John who have become members of the separated church because of their messianic faith and because of the awesome Benediction. (Martyn 1979: 62)

The 'benediction' to which Martyn refers is the Benediction against Heretics, the *Birkath ha-Minim*, which in Martyn's view was published by the Jamnia academy about 85 CE. This prayer was reformulated as part of the required 18 benedictions or prayers that were a fixed element in the order of worship in the synagogues. The reformulated 12th benediction contained this prayer: 'Let the Nazarenes [Christians] and the Minim [Heretics] be destroyed in a moment and let them be blotted out of the Book of Life and not be inscribed together with the righteous' (Martyn 1979: 58). Since all members of synagogues were required to lead the prayers periodically, if a member of the synagogue either refused or stumbled in the reading of this prayer, he would be detected as a heretic and expelled from the synagogue. The story in John 9 of the blind man who is expelled from the synagogue (John 9.34) thus reflects the experience of John's Jewish Christian community.

Martyn identifies in the two-level drama of the Gospel major elements of the Johannine Christian community's life and thought. The community is a predominantly Jewish community of Diaspora Jews in a Hellenistic city, perhaps Alexandria, which shares a common belief in Jesus as the Messiah. Many have been or will soon be expelled from the synagogue and, therefore, from Judaism and the Jewish community. The community is in steady dialogue with other Jews who are observing the law as it is being interpreted by the Academy at Jamnia that has replaced the Sanhedrin as the governing body of Judaism in the aftermath of the Jewish war (66–70 CE). This highly polarized dialogue is reflected in the dialogues of Jesus with the Pharisees and other Jews in the Gospel. The Gospel also reflects the ongoing disputes within the community about the various dimensions of the community's theology, such as the identity and appropriate names of Jesus.

Martyn's interpretation, which accords with that of Raymond Brown with whom he was in conversation,[3] has generated much lively discussion and critique in subsequent years.[4] The lasting contribution of Martyn's study is the recognition of the interplay in the Gospel's stories between the events and stories of Jesus's life in their original context of the 30s of the first century, and the experience of religious communities in the 90s of that same century. He has shown the ways in which John's story weaves together elements from the experience of his time with the stories of Jesus's time.[5]

Martyn also shares the common scholarly understanding of the medium of the Gospel in the mid-twentieth century. He writes regularly about John's

3   For a critical discussion of Martyn's position, see Burton L. Visotzky 2005: 91–4.

4   For a succinct review of this subsequent discussion, see Burton L. Visotzky 2005: 95–6. The chief criticisms are a 'vast overestimation of the power and importance of the Yavnaen rabbis in the late first century', and 'the growing consensus that the explicitly anti-Christian portion of the *Birkat HaMinim* was most probably added to the prayer only in the fourth century'. See also Becker and Reed 2007: 4–5.

5   For a minimalist view of the role of the later community's experience in the shaping of the Fourth Evangelist's narrative, see Adele Reinhartz, 'John and Judaism: A response to Burton Visotsky' (Donahue 2005: 111): 'There is in fact nothing explicit and, I would argue, nothing at all in the Gospel to support the assumption that the Gospel encodes the community's experience or the methodological approach of reading the community's history out of the Gospel. This is not to discount the possibility that the Gospel was written in a way that would resonate with the experience of the first readers.'

'readers' and what they perceived.[6] And his conceiving of them as readers is critical to his understanding of the way in which the Gospel impacted them. It is important for the purpose of this article to acknowledge that the issue of John's medium is not directly addressed in Martyn's book, nor were questions about John's medium being asked at the time of the study. However, the presupposition that the audience for the Gospel consisted of readers has clearly shaped the picture of the meaning of the Gospel of John that emerges from this study. In effect, Martyn proposes that the Evangelist's audience read his Gospel as a kind of historical allegory in which all of the major characters in the stories of Jesus stand for persons and groups in their own context. The Pharisees represent the rabbis of Jamnia and the Pharisaic authorities or Gerousia in John's city. Nicodemus represents secrets Christians who may be members of the Gerousia and who are afraid to confess their messianic belief. The blind man in John 9 represents Jewish Christians who have confessed Jesus as Messiah and have been expelled from the synagogue. And the Jews represent those who have rejected messianic belief in John's context.[7] Instead of being swept along by John's story, caught up into the action and the experience of the characters as they engage and listen to Jesus, in the presence of the text the readers slow down and reflect on the way in which Jesus and the characters he engages represent people in the drama of their own experience. Rather than being drawn by the narrator into sharing the experience of the various characters, the readers equate many of the characters in the story of Jesus with people in their own world who are other than, and often in opposition to, the readers.

In reading John's story of the blind man, for example, John's late-first-century reader read it as an event in the life of Jesus some six or seven decades earlier in which she or he recognized the conflicts between Jewish Christian believers and the supporters of the Jamnia academy in his own local synagogue who were using the newly rephrased Benediction against the Heretics to detect and expel secret believers in Jesus as the Messiah.

There is a further critical dimension to Martyn's understanding of the Fourth Gospel. Martyn sees the primary readers of John's Gospel as having been the members of his church. While it is not out of the question that non-believers could have read the Gospel (opponents of the early Christians, like Celsus, read Christian literature in order to attack it), Martyn agrees with the majority of Johannine scholars who explicitly reject the possibility that

---

6   The most extensive discussion of John's readers occurs in Martyn's discussion of the Hebrew term *Messiah* and its translation, *Christos* (Martyn 1979: 92–4). Other references to the reader occur throughout the book (e.g., Martyn 1979: 18, 69, 72, 83, 87, 89, 134, 137, 146).

7   See Raymond Brown (1979: 25–91) for an elaboration of this reading of John as a reflection of specific groups in John's historical context.

the Fourth Gospel was intended for readers other than believing Christians.[8] Martyn, however, in his exposition of the story of the first disciples – Andrew, Simon Peter, Philip and Nathaniel – does also propose that there are non-Christian readers on John's horizon to whom the announcement is that *Jesus* is the Messiah:

> Here we see that John is acquainted with non-Christian readers who already have conceptions of the Messiah. With *these* readers the task is not to awaken expectations of the Messiah, but rather – with certain qualifications – to announce that *Jesus* is the long-awaited Messiah. That is to say, 1.35-51 is not primarily designed to tell the reader that 'Jesus is *Messiah*'; in the first instance it is composed for readers who already have (at least latent) expectations of the Messiah. To them John wants to say, '*Jesus* is Messiah'. (Martyn 1979: 92)

Thus, Martyn identifies a range of people and positions in John's community of readers: Christian believers, non-Christians with Messianic expectations, and even Samaritans.[9] Furthermore, in his discussion of the motivation for John's distinctive translation of the Hebrew term 'Messiah' into Greek, namely *Christ*, Martyn identifies the possibility that there were Gentiles among John's readers who did not know the Hebrew term, Messiah.[10] But the implication of Martyn's picture is that these 'others' were virtually all members of his community.

---

8   See, for example, Wayne Meeks (1972: 70), 'It could hardly be regarded as a missionary tract', to which he appends a footnote: 'Against a large number of scholars, including K. Bornhaeuser, D. Oehler, J. A. T. Robinson, W. C. van Unnik, and C. H. Dodd, I thus find myself in agreement with R. E. Brown that John's distinctive emphases are directed to crises within the believing Church rather than to conversion of non-believers'. Other scholars who identify John's readers as Christian believers include Barrett, Schnackenburg, Bultmann, Culpepper and Bauckham. For a recent argument against this wide consensus, see D. A. Carson (1987: 639–51). In response to Barrett's important lectures on John and Judaism (delivered in German in 1967), it is crucial to distinguish between the Evangelist's own Christology and the non-Jewish influences on his theology, on the one hand, and the audience he was addressing, on the other (Barrett 1975: 17). Later, Barrett makes an unwarranted jump from 'non-biblical influence' to 'a Greek, non-Jewish readership' (1975: 30). The identity of the implied audience must be determined on the basis of the audiences actually named in the Gospel and of the issues and arguments adduced, all of which are Jewish. It cannot be deduced from the intellectual background of the message the Evangelist brings.

9   Martyn makes a fascinating intimation in exploring whether there may have been Samaritan converts in John's immediate context: 'Whether in John's city there were flesh and blood Samaritans we cannot say with certainty, although it is quite possible that John 4 reflects the remarkable success of the Christian mission amongst Samaritans known to John' (Martyn 1979: 112).

10   See Martyn 1979: 92. In this discussion Martyn also states that since many Jews such as Philo did not know Hebrew, particularly in Alexandria and other Greek cities, this translation of the Hebrew term Messiah into Greek may have been needed for Jewish as

This implication makes sense in the context of an assumed audience of readers. The Fourth Gospel was probably composed to address a community some time around the end of the first century CE. Martyn has made a strong case for seeing the Fourth Gospel as the production of a community deeply involved in theological disputes about Jesus.

This picture of the Fourth Gospel is directly related to the presupposition that its medium was a manuscript read by individual readers. Reading depends upon the availability of a manuscript and upon the desire of a person to take it up and read it. This medium would significantly limit the potential audience and lead to the conclusion that an audience for this medium would most likely consist of Christians. Thus, the assumption that the medium of the Gospel was a manuscript read by individual readers limits the potential audience to a relatively few people who had both the ability and interest to read such a manuscript.

Furthermore, the implicit assumption that the medium of John was a written text for readers underlies a set of conclusions about the meaning and message of John. In this medium, the meaning of the Gospel is identified in relation to a range of doctrinal disputes that were going on within the Christian community of the late first century. The specifics of John's message vary in different scholarly accounts. But the shared assumption about the medium of John carries with it a widely shared conclusion about the Gospel's meaning and message, namely that the primary meaning and message of the Gospel was directed to internal theological debates about the identity and significance of Jesus between groups of people who shared the conviction that Jesus was the Messiah. As Martyn's study concludes, the message of the Fourth Gospel was theology of and for John's Church.

What difference would it make if the evidence that has emerged since Martyn's landmark book requires us to reconceive the original medium of the Fourth Gospel? Specifically, how would this reconception effect Martyn's description of the two-level drama?

The Medium of John

Our historical challenge in the identification of John's medium is to specify the place of the Gospel in the evolution of ancient literate culture. We now have a much clearer picture of that history than was available at the time of the development of source, form and redaction criticism.[11] Literacy was

---

well as Gentile readers. This is important because this translation is often seen as evidence that Gentiles were the primary projected audience of the Fourth Gospel.

11   The character of ancient writing and reading has been recognized for decades. A trajectory of major twentieth-century works on oral performance of classical literature can be traced from Joseph Ballogh's 1926 articles through the works of Moses Hadas

at a much earlier stage of development than was assumed in the nineteenth century when the media culture of the nineteenth century was uncritically read back into the ancient world. The assumption that ancient biblical writers were writing for an extensive network of individual readers who would read the manuscripts in silence is anachronistic. At the time of the composition and distribution of John's Gospel, no more than 10 to 15 per cent of the people in the Roman Empire were able to read and the majority of the readers were concentrated in urban areas.[12] While there was a first-century trade in books, manuscripts could only be copied by hand and were only widely possessed by the upper class. In the first century, books were normally produced and distributed as scrolls. The transition to the codex as the normal mode of book production in the Greco-Roman world took several centuries. The first codexes were notebooks and the first evidence of a codex of a literary work is the *Epigrams* of Martial in 84–86 CE (Gamble 1995: 52). Virtually all early Christian texts are codexes rather than scrolls (Gamble 1995: 49), which may have facilitated distribution. But book production and distribution was limited and nothing like a mass audience of readers was conceivable for ancient authors.

Written manuscripts such as the Gospel of John were composed for performance.[13] Manuscripts were virtually always recited, often from memory. Indeed, some degree of memorization was required in order to perform written texts because of the character of ancient writing with no division of words, punctuation of sentences, or arrangement in paragraphs.

(1954), Eric Havelock (1963), Walter Ong (1982) and William Harris (1989). In the biblical field, this recognition has been more recent: see, for example, Thomas Boomershine (1974, 1987, 1989, 1994), Werner Kelber (1983), (Adam) Gilbert L. Bartholomew (1987), Joanna Dewey (1989, 1991, 1992, 1994), Paul Achtemeier (1990), Susan Niditch (1996), Whitney Shiner (2003), David Rhoads (2004, 2006) and David Carr (2005).

12   William Harris's recent comprehensive study of ancient literacy (Harris 1989) surveys the levels of literacy from the early first millennium BCE through the period of the late Roman empire (5th–6th century CE.). While steadily acknowledging that evidence is fragmentary and varied in different areas and among different groups, the general picture that emerges is of literacy levels that never exceeded 20 to 25 per cent, and in many places and periods were as low as 5 per cent. His estimates of literacy levels in the first century are in the range of 10 to 15 per cent.

13   See Moses Hadas (Hadas 1954: 50–77) for a series of citations from ancient literature that reflect the performance of written works as the primary mode of publication. Even historical works were published by oral recitation, as is evident in Lucian's opening of his book *Herodotus* in which he tells the story of Herodotus taking the opportunity of the Olympic Games to read his work: 'He seized the moment when the gathering was at its fullest, and every city had sent the flower of its citizens; then he appeared in the temple hall, bent not on sightseeing but on bidding for an Olympic victory of his own; he recited his Histories and bewitched his hearers' (Hadas 1954: 60). For further citations in regard to ancient performance, see Shiner 2003: 11–35.

Thus, an ancient writer wrote with the assumption that the book would be performed for audiences. As Moses Hadas has written:

> Among the Greeks the regular method of publication was by public recitation, at first, significantly, by the author himself, and then by professional readers or actors, and public recitation continued to be the regular method of publication even after books and the art of reading had become common. (Hadas 1954: 50)

Books that were read in private were normally read aloud, often as a small-scale performance for a group gathered around the reader (Hadas 1954: 61). Even when reading in private, people read out loud and, in effect, performed the writing for themselves.[14]

The medium of the Gospel of John can be reconstructed in this cultural and technological context. It was composed at a relatively early stage in the development and extension of writing technology. The Gospel of John was written for performance, not for private reading in silence. The performances of the Gospel were often done by heart. A performance of the Gospel of John in its entirety provided an evening of storytelling of around three hours. It was not a particularly long story, especially in comparison to the performances of the great Homeric epics. There were many occasions for performance: small groups in homes, larger audiences in marketplaces and synagogues.

The Gospel of John was composed as a long story. It is somewhat longer than Mark, but somewhat shorter than Matthew and Luke (Matthew is 34 pages in a recent edition; Mark 21; Luke 37; John 27). A distinguishing feature of the Gospel of John as a performance is the relative importance of the speeches of Jesus. Jesus's discourses constitute more than half of the Fourth Gospel. In Mark, the speeches of Jesus are approximately 20 per cent of the story if you count all the discourses; but the two long speeches (chapters 4 and 13) are a little less than 10 per cent of the story. In Matthew and Luke, Jesus's speeches constitute somewhat more than a third of their compositions. Thus, the speeches of Jesus are a more dominant feature of the Gospel of John than in any of the other canonical Gospels.

The centrality of Jesus's speeches for John's story also has implications for the dynamics of interaction between those who performed the story and their audiences. Comparison with the dynamics of a contrasting genre, drama, may help to clarify the particular character of storytelling. In drama the action is on the stage and the characters talk to each other. The actors

---

14   The classic example of the prevalence of ancient oral reading in private is Augustine's apology for his mentor, Ambrose, who had the strange practice of reading in silence (Augustine, *Confessions*, 5.3). Augustine concludes his apologia: 'But whatever was his motive in so doing, doubtless in such a man was a good one.'

are always presenting a character and generally each actor embodies only one character in the drama. Once in a while, often at the beginning and sometimes at the end, a character will directly address the audience. But most of the time the audience is an observer of interactions that happen on the stage.

In storytelling, by contrast with drama, the performer is first and foremost him or herself and is always addressing the audience, sometimes directly and sometimes indirectly. For example, in the prologue and epilogue of the Fourth Gospel, the performer/storyteller speaks directly to the audience *as a person, not as a character in the story*. In the recital of the entire story, however, the performer speaks *as all the characters*, often in interaction with each other. But when there is a speech, especially a long speech, the storyteller usually addresses the audience directly, not as himself or herself as in the prologue and the epilogue, but *as the character who is speaking*. And the audience, in turn, is addressed not as its own self but as whatever character in the story is the object of the speech. For example, in John's story of the Last Supper, the storyteller presents Jesus addressing the audience as his disciples. It is a long speech: chapters 14–16, with 13 as the setting and 17 as Jesus's closing prayer. Thus, for at least 20 to 25 minutes, Jesus, as embodied by the performer, speaks to the audience as his disciples.

Two imaginative transformations happen in this process. The performer 'becomes' Jesus and the audience 'becomes' his disciples. That is, in the suspension of disbelief that happens in storytelling, the storyteller presents Jesus in a manner that, when done well, makes the character of Jesus 'really' there. And likewise, the audience experiences Jesus talking to them as his disciples in a manner that, when done well, induces them to 'become' Jesus's disciples. The audience is invited to occupy that role in the story, just as the storyteller is occupying the role of Jesus. At other times in the Gospel of John, such as the prologue and the concluding words of both chapters 20 and 21, the storyteller is simply a person speaking to the audience person to person. This highly nuanced dynamic of identity becomes a central dynamic of meaning in the performance of the story. In the Gospel of John, this dynamic is centred in the character of Jesus.

Therefore, a central feature of our picture of the Gospel of John is directly connected with our conclusions about the medium of the Gospel. If we imagine that the original audience of John's Gospel was an individual reader reading in silence, our analysis of the meaning of the Gospel in its original historical context is apt to be determined by our own centuries-old reading habit of objective theological and historical reflection and projecting those same habits onto the minds of the first readers. But if we imagine that the original audience of John's Gospel was a group of persons listening to a story told by a performer, a major source of meaning is the interactions between the storyteller and the listeners. There will also be a range of meanings that may have happened for different members of the audience. Some may have been alienated or bored by the story. For those listeners, the storyteller's challenge was to get them re-engaged with the story as it proceeds. Others may have been drawn to the story and its characters, but the consequences of really believing in the story's claims were frightening.

Furthermore, the meaning of the story was shaped by the identity of the various groups in the audiences to which the story was told. To whatever degree we can identify the groups to which the story was addressed, it will assist us in identifying more clearly the range of meanings that may have been evoked for those groups.

Audience Address in the Gospel of John

The structure of audience address in John may help us to hear more of the specific dynamics of the performance of the Gospel for its ancient audiences. Among the four Gospels, John is distinctive in its manner of audience address. One of those distinctive features of John's Gospel is that there are a lot of long speeches by Jesus, more than in any other Gospel. For example, in Mark there are two long speeches while Matthew and Luke both have five. In John there are eight long speeches and several shorter speeches by Jesus. Jesus's concluding address to the disciples is markedly longer than any of the speeches in the Gospel tradition (Sermon on the Mount, 108 verses; speech at Last Supper in John, 142 verses). In the following chart, I have compiled a list of the addresses to the audience in the Gospel of John. In the first column I have listed the stories that contain speeches of two or more verses. When the speeches are embedded in a longer story, I have listed the story in the first column and the actual speech in the third column as an address to the audience. In the second column I have listed the character that is being embodied by the performer, usually Jesus but also the storyteller/performer and John the Baptist. In the third column I have also listed the character that is addressed and, therefore, the person or group with which the audience is invited to identify.

Direct Address to the Audience in John

Story	Speaker	Address to the audience
Prologue (1.1-18)	Storyteller (John)	Audience
John the Baptist's testimony (1.19-34)	John the Baptist	Pharisees (1.26-7, 29-31, 32b-34)
Calling of Philip and Nathanael (1. 43-51)	Jesus	Nathanael (1.50, 51)

Cleansing of the temple (2.13-25)	Storyteller (John)	Audience (2.21-5)
Nicodemus (3.1-21)	Jesus	Nicodemus/Pharisees (3.10-21)
John the Baptist and Jesus (3.22-36)	Storyteller/John the Baptist	Disciples of John (3.27-36)
Samaritan woman (4.1-42)	Jesus	Samaritan woman/Samaritans (4.21-4)
Samaritan woman (4.1-42)	Jesus	Disciples (4.34-8)
Healing of a crippled man (5.1-47)	Jesus	The Jews who want to kill him (5.19-47)
Feeding of five thousand (6.1-71)	Jesus	The crowd (6.26-7)
Feeding of five thousand (6.1-71)	Jesus	The crowd (6.32-3)
Feeding of five thousand (6.1-71)	Jesus	The Jews (6.43-59)
Feeding of five thousand (6.1-71)	Jesus	The disciples (6.61-5)
Feeding of five thousand (6.1-71)	Jesus	The twelve (6.67, 70)
Jesus's brothers (7.6-8)	Jesus	Jesus's brothers (7.6-8)
Feast of Tabernacles (7.10-52)	Jesus	The Jews (7.16-19)
Feast of Tabernacles (7.10-52)	Jesus	The crowd (7.21-4)
Feast of Tabernacles (7.10-52)	Jesus	Some Jerusalemites (7.28-9)

Feast of Tabernacles (7.10-52)	Jesus	Police officers from chief priests and Pharisees (7.33-4)
Feast of Tabernacles (7.10-52)	Jesus	Audience (no identified addressee in story; inference is the crowd) (7.37-8)
Feast of Tabernacles (8.12-59)	Jesus	The Pharisees (8.12, 14-18)
Feast of Tabernacles (8.12-59)	Jesus	The Jews (8.23-9)
Feast of Tabernacles (8.12-59)	Jesus	The Jews who believed in him (8.31-47)
Feast of Tabernacles (8.12-59)	Jesus	The Jews (8.48-58)
Healing of the man blind (9.1–10.12)	Jesus	Pharisees (9.41–10.12)
The Temple Festival (10.22-42)	Jesus	The Jews (10.25-30)
The Temple Festival (10.22-42)	Jesus	The Jews who want to stone him (10.32-8)
Triumphal entry (12.12-50)	Jesus	Philip and Andrew (12.23-8)
Triumphal entry (12.12-50)	Jesus	The crowd in Jerusalem (12.30-6)
Triumphal entry (12.12-50)	Storyteller (John)	Audience (12.37-43)
Triumphal entry (12.12-50)	Jesus	Audience (12.44-50)
The footwashing (13.1–17.26)	Jesus	The disciples (13.12b-20)

The footwashing (13.1–17.26)	Jesus	The disciples (13.31-5)
The footwashing (13.1–17.26)	Jesus	The disciples (14.1–16.33)
The footwashing/prayer of Jesus (13.1–17.26)	Jesus	The Father/audience as observers of Jesus's prayer (17.1-26)
Purpose of book (20.30-1)	Storyteller (John)	Audience (20.30-1)
The disciple who wrote this book (21.24-5)	Storyteller (John/ 'we')	Audience (21.24-5)

This is a list of Jesus's major speeches with the characters that are addressed:

(1) Nicodemus (3.10-21)
(2) The Jews who want to kill him (5.19-47)
(3) The crowd, the Jews and the disciples after the feeding of the 5,000 (6.26-70)
(4) The crowd, the Pharisees, the Jews who believed in him and the Jews at the Feast of Tabernacles, a long speech of at least ten minutes (7.21–8.58)
(5) The Pharisees after the healing of the man born blind (9.41–10.12)
(6) The Jews at the Temple Festival (10.25-38)
(7) Philip and Andrew, the Jerusalem crowd and the audience after the triumphal entry (12.23-43)
(8) The disciples at the Last Supper, the longest speech of at least twenty minutes (13.12–16.33; 17.1-26)

Another feature of Jesus's speeches in John is that Jesus addresses the audience as a much wider range of characters than in any of the other Gospels. For example, in Matthew's Gospel, Jesus has five long speeches all of which are addressed to the audience as the crowds and/or the disciples:

The crowds with the disciples on the mountain (Matt. 5–7)
The twelve (Matt. 10.5-42)
The crowds at the sea (Matt. 13.3-52)
The disciples (Matt. 18.2-35)
The crowds and the disciples (Matt. 23.1–25.46)

The addresses to the audience in Jesus's five major speeches in Luke are similar to Matthew's. But in John the speeches are addressed to a wide range of different characters: Nicodemus, various groups of Jews, the Pharisees and the disciples. Thus, the storyteller's interactions with the audience in John are more complex than in any of the Synoptics.

Another distinctive feature of John's storytelling is that five of his stories – Nicodemus, the feeding of the 5,000, the trip to Jerusalem for the Feast of Tabernacles, the healing of the man born blind and the triumphal entry – function as introductions to long speeches that are addressed to the audience as characters in the preceding story. In these speeches, the story moves imperceptibly from a third-person description of an event to a first-person address by Jesus to the audience. An example is the story of Nicodemus (3.1-21). The storyteller tells the story of Nicodemus coming to Jesus at night, and reports their conversation. Throughout several interchanges Jesus is talking to Nicodemus in the first person, ending with this address: 'Truly I say to you, we speak of what we know and we bear witness to what we have seen but you do not receive our testimony. If I have spoken to you about earthly things and you do not believe, how will you believe if I speak to you about heavenly things?' But in the next sentences, Nicodemus fades into the background and Jesus is talking in the third person: 'And just as Moses lifted up the serpent, so also must the Son of Man be lifted up so that everyone who believes in him may have eternal life ... For God so loved the world that he gave his only son...' (3.15-16). In the performance of this speech, the probability is that the storyteller here turns from addressing an imagined Nicodemus to directly addressing the audience. But the storyteller is still speaking as Jesus. The change from first to third person is, in effect, a turn to addressing the audience directly as Nicodemus. In the telling of the story, the storyteller as Jesus now talks directly to the audience as if the audience were Nicodemus.[15] The audience has imaginatively become Nicodemus, and Jesus's speech is addressed to each member of the audience as a Pharisee who is seeking spiritual rebirth. This speech to the audience then continues through his dialogue about those who come and do not come to the light (3.21). The effect of this structure of audience address is to create a higher degree of sympathetic identification with the characters prior to the audience being addressed as those characters. This same storytelling dynamic happens in each of these five speeches.

---

15   The punctuation of different translations reflects different decisions about the narrative character of this speech. In the RSV, NIV and NAB there are no quotation marks enclosing John 3.16–21, thereby indicating the editorial conclusion that this was not part of the speech of Jesus but is a comment by the narrator. The editors of the TEV and *The Complete Gospels* place the close-quote marks after 3.13 and indicate the beginning of the narrator's comment at 3.14. The NRSV (also NEB, CEV, JB) has the more accurate punctuation of quotation marks around the entire speech (John 3.10-21), thereby indicating that all of these words were part of Jesus's speech.

The most distinctive feature of John's Gospel is the clearly marked structure of the addresses to the audience. In chapters 1–4, the audience is addressed as various groups of first-century Jews: the Pharisees (1.26-7), the Jews in the temple at Passover (2.16-19), Nicodemus/the Pharisees (3.1-21), the followers of John the Baptist (3.27-36), the Samaritans[16] (4.21-4) and the disciples (4.34-8). The longest and most engaging address to the audience in these initial episodes is Jesus's speech to Nicodemus in which the audience is addressed as Pharisees who are interested in Jesus. All of the audiences in these first four chapters of the Gospel are either positively disposed to Jesus or seeking more understanding. No audience expresses hostility, or is described either as hostile or as rejecting Jesus.

The one possible exception is Jesus's conversation with the Jews in response to his cleansing of the temple (2.18-20). The response of the Jews has traditionally been heard as hostile both to his cleansing of the temple and his invitation: 'Destroy this temple, and in three days I will raise it up.' (2.19) However, the tone of the storyteller's report of the Jews' response in the performance of this story is indicated by the storyteller's comment to the audience: 'When he was in Jerusalem during the Passover festival, many believed in his name because they saw the signs that he was doing' (2.23). That is, the storyteller describes the response of the people to Jesus's action and words as a positive response of belief. This is in continuity with the positive responses of the people in both Mark and Luke (Mark 11.18b; Luke 19.48). The tradition of this story is a positive tradition of the people's affirmation of Jesus as a prophet who, like Jeremiah, exercises appropriate authority in cleansing the temple. The probability is, therefore, that the story-teller presented the responses of the Jews to Jesus in a positive tone of inquiry and surprise rather than hostility. The fact that the storyteller extensively explains Jesus's comment to his/her audience (2.21-2) is an indication that the listeners were surprised and puzzled by Jesus's words. Thus, throughout this initial section of the Gospel, the Jews are presented as a group that is positively drawn to Jesus and the audience is addressed as Jews who are genuinely interested in Jesus.

After the story of the healing of the lame man at the pool of Bethesda (5.1-15), there is a sudden and radical change in the identity of the audience that the storyteller as Jesus addresses. Jesus's speech to the audience as the Jews following this healing story is by far the longest speech to this point in the story. It is introduced by this narrative comment: 'For this reason the Jews were seeking all the more to kill him, because he was not only breaking the

---

16   While Samaritans were not considered to be Jews in the first century, they were part of the tradition of Israel and, like Christians in a much later period, had been effectively separated from the Jewish community. The author of the Fourth Gospel clearly includes Samaritans within the parameters of his projected audience and his understanding of 'ecumenical Judaism'.

Sabbath, but was also calling God his own Father, thereby making himself equal to God' (5.18). In its context, this is a highly surprising comment. There has been no intimation earlier in the story of this degree of hostility toward Jesus. But it marks a major shift in the dynamics of audience address.

Following this radical and sudden shift, the audience is addressed as various groups of Jews who are variously drawn to Jesus and repelled by him (John 5–12). Jesus's dialogue partners in this long section of the story are torn between believing in him and not believing in him. The narrator uses the word *schisma* three times (7.43; 9.16; 10.19) to describe this division in the response of Jesus's audiences. There is constant change in the specific identity of the character to whom Jesus is speaking in these stories: for example, as Jews who want to kill him (5), as the crowd and the disciples (6), as Jews who believe in him (8.31ff.), as Pharisees and then as Jews who took up stones to stone him (10.31ff.), as Andrew and Philip (12.23-32), and frequently throughout this section as simply Jews. In this section of the Gospel (chaps 5–12), the audience is addressed as Jews who are constantly changing in their attitude and response to Jesus from total alienation to belief and everything in between.

Finally, there is another sudden change in the address to the audience with the story of Jesus's Last Supper. The climax of the speeches of Jesus to the audience is Jesus's long talk with the disciples after washing their feet (13–17). In this long speech, the audience is addressed as Jesus's disciples.

Thus, the structure of audience address in the Gospel as a whole is clearly marked and moves from Jesus addressing the audience as various groups of Jews who are drawn to him (1–4), to Jesus addressing the listeners as Jews who believe and don't believe in him (5–12), to Jesus addressing them as his disciples (13–17). In the course of hearing the whole story, therefore, the audience is invited to move in its relationship with Jesus from being Jews who are positively drawn to him (John the Baptist, Andrew/Simon Peter/Philip/Nathanael, the wedding guests in Cana, the crowd in the temple, Nicodemus, the Samaritan woman and the Samaritans), to Jews who are violently torn between belief and unbelief, to disciples who have entered into a highly intimate relationship of mutuality and love with Jesus. This structure of audience address is a distinctive feature of John's story. In the Synoptics, most of Jesus's long speeches are addressed to the audience as the crowds or the disciples. The interactions with his opponents are usually short and do not create the same depth of audience identification with the characters who are being addressed by Jesus. This is both because the audience does not have time to identify with the characters being addressed in short speeches and because the operative norms of judgement in relation to these characters are less sympathetic. For example, in Mark's conflict stories of Jesus in the temple (Mark 11–12), the storyteller as Jesus addresses the parable of the wicked tenants to the audience as the chief priests, scribes and elders. It is the longest address to the audience as Jesus's opponents in the Gospel of Mark (the other long speech in 7.6-13 addressed to the Pharisees concerns the cleanliness laws). But the dynamics of the speech do not create a high degree of identification with the Jewish authorities, who remain more emotionally distant. Both of the long speeches of Jesus in Mark are addressed to the audience as his disciples (the twelve in 4.10-32; the four in 13.5-37). *But there is nothing in the Synoptics even remotely similar to the progressive and clearly demarcated structure of audience address in John.*

Another way of describing the patterns of audience address is the frequency of each of the characters that the audience is invited to become in interaction with the storyteller and his principal character. In the 17 long (more than one verse) speeches of Jesus, the audience is addressed as 'the crowd' three times {the feeding of the five thousand (6.26-7, 32-3), the Feast of Tabernacles (7.21-4), and the triumphal entry (12.30-6)}; as 'the Jews' three times {the feeding of the 5,000 (6.43-59), the Feast of Tabernacles (7.16-19), the Temple Festival (10.25-30)}; as the Pharisees three times {explicitly at the feast of Tabernacles (8.12, 14-18) and the healing of the man born blind (9.41–10.12) and implicitly in the dialogue with Nicodemus (3.1-21)}; as the Jews who want to kill or stone him three times {the healing of the crippled man on the Sabbath (5.19-40), the Feast of Tabernacles (8.48-58) and the festival of Dedication (10.31-8)}; once as the Jews who believe in him {at the Feast of Tabernacles (8.23-47)}, and four times as the disciples {the Samaritan woman (4.32-8), the feeding of the 5,000 (6.1-14), Philip and Andrew (12.23-8), and the Last Supper/footwashing (13–17)}. Thus, there are seventeen extended speeches of Jesus to the audience as characters in the story, thirteen to a range of Jewish groups and four to the disciples. The speech to the disciples at the Last Supper is the longest and most emotionally intense speech in the Gospel (13–17). In the whole Gospel leading up to the Passion narrative, therefore, thirteen of the seventeen extended speeches of Jesus are addressed to the audience as various groups of Jews who are torn between believing and not believing. By far the most frequent interaction between the storyteller and the audience is between the character of Jesus and the audience as groups of Jews who are struggling with whether or not to believe in him.

When heard in the context of the history of Johannine interpretation, the first striking dimension of the audience address is that all of these characters are identified explicitly as Jews. The only characters who are not explicitly named as Jews are 'the crowd', 'the disciples' and the Samaritans. But 'the crowd' is clearly identified as Jews who were fed (6.24, 41) or were in Jerusalem (e.g., 11, 35). 'The disciples' are likewise identified as Jews (1.47). And the Samaritans would be Jews except for the hostility that separates the two groups. That is, there are no non-Jews who are addressed in the interactions of the storyteller and the audience. The audience is never addressed as a character other than various groups of Jews. Throughout the story, the storyteller as Jesus addresses the audience as Jews. The structure of Jesus's speeches moves from speeches to various groups of Jews who are interested in him, to Jews who are conflicted about believing in him or being hostile toward him, to his long talk with the audience as his Jewish disciples. Furthermore, the audience is never addressed as believing members of churches. Thus, in order to participate fully in the hearing of the story, the audiences of the Gospel, regardless of their actual ethnic or religious identity, must imaginatively become Jews. Furthermore, the audience is most frequently addressed as Jews who are torn between believing and not believing in Jesus.

The treatment of non-Jews in the Gospel is also significant. Other than Pilate and the Roman soldiers who divide Jesus's garments, the only non-Jews in the Gospel are the Samaritans and the Greeks who come to Philip. The audience is addressed as Samaritans in the story of the Samaritan woman. The Samaritans are treated in the Gospel as 'separated' Israelites whose conversion to belief in Jesus is presented as a kind of re-conversion and reconciliation with the Jewish religious tradition. A sign of this is Jesus's address to the audience as Samaritans (4.21-4) in which Jesus states that a time is coming when the ethnic divisions between Jews and Samaritans will be transcended into a new religious community based on a common spirit. The Greeks, on the other hand, remain anonymous, make only one request to Philip, and disappear from the story. Jesus never talks to them in the story and the audience is never addressed as Greeks. Furthermore, the Greeks' request to see Jesus is the implicit cause of Jesus's recognition that the hour of his death has come. If anything, the story of the Greeks reinforces the ethnic identification of the audience as Jews.

The inevitable question that arises from the structures of audience address is whether there is any relationship between this structure and the actual historical audiences of the Fourth Gospel. In order to understand the Gospel of John in its original medium, we need to imagine a series of storytelling events in which audiences gathered to hear the story told by a storyteller. We have only indirect evidence about the identity of those audiences. But we have direct evidence from the script of the performances about how they were addressed by the storyteller. The audiences of the Gospel of John were always spoken to *as if* they were Jews, Jews drawn to Jesus but conflicted about believing that he was the Messiah. The structure of the addresses to the audience also has an unambiguous structure in which the audience is addressed first as Jews – followers of John the Baptist, common folk, Pharisees and Samaritans – who are drawn to him and many of whom (Andrew, Simon Peter, Philip, Nathanael, many in Jerusalem, the Samaritan woman and many in her village, the father and household of the sick son in Capernaum) believe in him, then as Jews who are torn between believing in him and wanting to kill him, and finally as his disciples. Therefore, *the most natural conclusion from this data is, first of all, that the Gospel was structured for performances to audiences of Jews. Secondly, this data would indicate that the primary Jewish audiences of the Fourth Gospel were conflicted about belief in Jesus rather than being members of believing communities.*

When heard in the context of current conclusions about the audience of the Gospel, the structure of audience address does not correspond with or support the conclusion that the Gospel was addressed to John's church or to the wider circle of churches in the eastern Mediterranean as envisioned, for example, by Richard Bauckham and his collaborators (Bauckham 1998). The central section of John's story is addressed to Jews who are profoundly conflicted about Jesus and many of whom are initially strongly opposed to him. The structure of the storyteller's addresses to the audience invites the listeners to move **from** identification with those who want to kill Jesus **to** identification with those who abide in his love. This structure indicates that the audiences needed to go through a process of confrontation and change in order to hear the speeches of Jesus to his disciples at the Last Supper sympathetically. The audiences of the Gospel in its final form are not addressed as persons who already believe that Jesus is the Messiah. They are addressed as Jews who may come to believe that Jesus is the Messiah and become his followers.

This dynamic of internal conflict in the audiences of the Gospel is reflected at several points in the Gospel by the storyteller's description of the responses of Jesus's audiences. One of the techniques of audience inclusion in storytelling is to name the responses that members of the audience are having to the story as it is being told. This happens first in Jesus's speech after the feeding of the 5,000. After Jesus's statements about being the bread of life, the storyteller describes the response of the Jews: 'Then the Jews began to complain about him because he said, "I am the bread that came down from heaven." They were saying, is not this Jesus, the son of Joseph, whose father and mother we know? How can he now say, "I have come down from heaven"?' (6.41-2). A little later in the story, the storyteller reports another audience response, 'The Jews then disputed among themselves, saying, "How can this man give us his flesh to eat?"' (6.52). The storytelling function of these statements is to name the responses that people *in the storyteller's audience* are having to Jesus's words in the story.

This technique of naming the audience's response happens even more explicitly later in the story: 'When they heard these words, some in the crowd said, "This is really the prophet." Others said, "This is the Messiah." But some asked, "Surely the Messiah does not come from Galilee, does he? Has not the Scripture said the Messiah is descended from David and comes from Bethlehem, the village where David lived?" So there was a division in the crowd because of him' (7.40-4). This naming of the divisions that were happening in the audience explicitly addresses the underlying question that the audience is asking throughout the story, namely, is Jesus the Messiah? And some *in the storyteller's audience* were saying 'Yes' and others were saying 'No.' The Johannine storyteller does this again when he names the varied responses of his audience to the story of the man born blind, and of Jesus's speech to them as the Pharisees: 'Again the Jews were divided because of these words. Many of them were saying, "He has a demon and is out of his mind. Why listen to him?" Others were saying, "These are not the words of one who has a demon. Can a demon open the eyes of the blind?"' (9.41–10.18). These statements are in effect quotations of the responses of John's audiences to the dynamics of the story as it progresses.

The addresses to the audience of the Fourth Gospel indicate, therefore, that we can most appropriately imagine this story as having been performed for Diaspora Jewish communities in the cities and towns of the Hellenistic world of the Roman Empire. That Diaspora Jews may have been open to listening to the Evangelist perform his Gospel accords well with recent studies that point not to a decisive 'parting of the ways' towards the end of the first century but to continued intermingling of Jewish Jesus-believers and other Jews, as well as of Jews with pagans, at least into the fourth century (Becker and Reed 2007: 4–5, 23). Paula Fredriksen writes, 'As with contemporary Mediterranean paganism, much of ancient Jewish religious activity (dancing, singing, communal eating, processing, and – as Chrysostom mentions with some irritation – building and feasting in *sukkot*) occurred out-of-doors, inviting and accommodating the participation of interested outsiders' (Fredriksen 2007: 51). This kind of religious activity provided ample opportunities for the performance of a story such as the Fourth Gospel.

The Medium of John and Martyn's Two-level Drama

In this context, it may be possible to reconceive the implications of Martyn's two-level drama for understanding the impact of the Fourth Gospel. If the Gospel was a story performed for audiences in the late first century rather than an imagined drama, the two levels of the story's meaning were equally present. In fact, Martyn's 'two-level' hypothesis makes the interactions of the audiences and the performers of the Gospel more explicit. The dynamics Martyn defines are descriptive at two levels, the responses of Jesus's audiences in the early 30s and the responses of John's audiences in the 90s. However, this is not a 'two-level drama' in which characters in the Jesus story *represent* the people in John's setting. Instead the responses of the audiences in the stories of Jesus *are* the responses of John's audiences. To state this more specifically, as John composed his story, he anticipated that his audiences and the audiences of the others who told his story would respond in these complex ways. And the probability is that he was right about his projections. At the very least, the script of the story indicates that this was what he anticipated and built into his story. Furthermore, to return to the question of the identity of the Johannine audiences, the responses of extreme conflict about whether or not Jesus is the Messiah are not the audience responses that a storyteller would build into a story that is directed to a community of believers. These responses resonated with audiences that were wrestling with the question of Jesus's messianic identity, not those who had already answered the question affirmatively.

However, Martyn's description of the dynamics of the 'two-level drama' also enables us to identify even more specifically the people who were present in the audiences of John's story. All of the elements of John's context and the discussions that John was having with Jews in his context that Martyn has identified are descriptive of the interactions that are implicit in the performance of John's Gospel. The probability is that the participants in those discussions or their representatives were present in the audiences for whom John's Gospel was performed. Thus, at any one performance of the Gospel in a Diaspora city such as Alexandria, the audience might have included common people of the Jewish community, representatives of the Jamnia Academy, experts in midrash who wanted midrashic proofs of Jesus's identity as Messiah, Jewish Christians who believed that Jesus was the Mosaic Prophet-Messiah but not the Son of Man/Son of God, secret believers in Jesus as Messiah/Son of God who were still part of the synagogue community, believers who had been expelled from the Jewish community and were part of the local Christian community, members of the Baptist and Samaritan communities, and Jewish Christians of John's community. The identification of John's medium as performances of the story for a wide range of Jewish communities in the great cities of the Diaspora – Rome, Ephesus, Antioch and Alexandria – as well as the Jews of the re-conquered Palestine does require a significant change in our perception of the meaning of the Gospel from the imagined two-level drama in the minds of a small, sectarian community of already believing readers. But it also gives greater vitality to our understanding of the dynamic power of the Gospel when it was performed for ancient audiences. It may also provide some further clues about the phenomenal growth of the early Christian community.[17]

Another dimension of the two-level drama that appears in a different light when the Fourth Gospel is conceived as a performed story is the role of the Johannine community. Rather than being the primary intended audience of the story, the community is an implied dimension of the identity and role of the storyteller/performer. In four places in the story, the performer speaks in the first person plural, 'we', in explicit reference to the community for whom he/she speaks (1.14, 16; 3.11; 4.22; 21.24). Not surprisingly, two of those instances are in the prologue and epilogue of the story. In the prologue, the storyteller says, 'And the Word became flesh and dwelt among us and we have seen his glory … From his fullness we have all received.' The referent of 'we' is ambiguous here and can be taken to refer to humankind as well as to the community of believers. While the most natural referent is humankind, it is also clearly a reference to the community that is bearing witness to its experience and belief. In the epilogue, 'we' refers unambiguously to the

17 Rodney Stark's sociological analysis of the growth of early Christianity identifies the late-first-century Jewish Diaspora community as the most probable source of the initial growth of the nascent Christian movement (Stark 1997: 49–71).

Johannine community: 'This is the disciple who is testifying to these things and has written them, and we know that his testimony is true' (21.24). Here the storyteller presents him/herself as speaking for the community who is bearing witness to the truth of the original disciple's story. The other usage of 'we' in reference to the community occurs in Jesus's conversation with Nicodemus: 'We speak of what we know and we bear witness to what we have seen, but you do not receive our testimony' (3.11). In this instance Jesus speaks for the believing community and addresses the community represented by Nicodemus. In each of these instances, the storyteller uses 'we' to refer to the community who is speaking through this story. A further dimension of this pronoun is Jesus's use of 'we' in his conversation with the Samaritan woman: 'You worship what you do not know; we worship what we know, for salvation is from the Jews.' In this instance, the storyteller as Jesus speaks for the community of the Jews in relation to the Samaritans. In the Gospel as a whole, therefore, the storyteller addresses the audience as a representative of wider communities, three times as a representative of the Johannine community and once as a representative of the community of Jews.

Furthermore, this definition of the audience of the Gospel in no way excludes the Johannine community that Martyn identifies as the primary location of the Gospel's readers. It is highly probable that members of the Johannine community were present in the audiences of performances of the Fourth Gospel to the wider Jewish community and that there were occasions when the story was told to communities of believers. The structure of audience address indicates, however, that the audiences of the Johannine communities were addressed as Jews who were conflicted about belief in Jesus as the Messiah. The members of the believing community were invited to enter again into the process of being drawn to Jesus while struggling with the meaning of his identity and his statements. Thus, audiences of believers were undoubtedly hearers of the Fourth Gospel but they were addressed as Jews who were wrestling with Jesus and the God he embodies, not as Christians who were already confirmed in their beliefs.

What then is the message of the Fourth Gospel? At the first level, the message of the Gospel is that Jesus is the Christ, the Son of God. This message is addressed directly to each listener by the storyteller at the end of the first resurrection appearance stories as the purpose of the Gospel: 'these are written so that you may believe that Jesus is the Christ, the Son of God, and that believing you may have life in his name' (20.31). Implicit in the story is a redefinition of what the Messiah will do and be. There are also several subsidiary messages. First, there is the message that the chief priests have no authority because of their forfeiture of legitimacy in their statement 'We have no king but Caesar!' And it is worthy of note that they have lost their legitimacy according to Jewish norms of judgement. Their collaboration with the Romans is also directly connected with the denial of Jesus's legitimacy as King. A further subsidiary message implicit in the Pilate trial and the inscription on the cross (also present in Nathanael's first confession – 1.49) is that Jesus is the King of the Jews (Israel) who died for the nation and the children of God in the dispersion (11.50-2). A related message is that all of the Jews – those in Palestine and those in the Diaspora, Baptists, Pharisees, Christian Jews and Samaritans – are one community in Christ (17.21-3).

But at another level, the message of the Gospel is directly related to the medium of the Gospel. In the telling and hearing of the story, a relationship is formed between the storyteller and the audience. That relationship in turn becomes the means by which a relationship is established between Jesus and the listener. This relationship is established in the series of long speeches that are addressed to the audience by the storyteller as Jesus. Martyn's description of the role of the Paraclete suggests a still further dimension to this relationship:

> The paradox presented by Jesus' promise that his work on earth will be continued because he is going to the Father is 'solved' by his return in the person of the Paraclete. *It is, therefore, precisely the Paraclete who creates the two-level drama.* One cannot fail to be impressed by the boldness with which John re-interprets the traditional motif of the coming of the Spirit. That is especially true when we recognize that in order for the Paraclete to create the two-level drama, he must look not only like Jesus, but also like the Christian witness who is Jesus's 'double' in that drama... (Martyn 1979: 140, emphasis in original)

Rephrased as a description of storytelling, when the story is told by the Christian witness, the Paraclete is known in and through the presence of the witness who tells the story. That is, the Gospel is *a two-level story* in which the presence of both Jesus and the Paraclete are experienced in the telling of the story. Rather than happening in the imagination of the reader, the encounter of the members of the audience with the character of Jesus and the Paraclete happens in the experience of engaged listening to the story. Martyn's account of the Paraclete implies that John would state this more boldly. John would testify that in the telling of the story, it is the Paraclete who speaks in and through the Christian witness.

The two levels of the story, the 'once upon a time' level of the early 30s and the present time of the early performances of the Gospel in the 90s, are integral dimensions of the story's meaning. As Martyn writes, 'These events to which John bears witness transpire on both the *einmalig* and the contemporary levels of the drama, or they do not transpire at all' (Martyn 1979: 151). If we substitute 'story' for 'drama', we have an accurate description of the multifaceted character of the impact of John in its original medium. The performance of John's story of Jesus was for the audiences of the Gospel an experience of the 'real presence' of Christ in their time and place.

The central meaning of the Gospel was, then, the relationship that the Gospel created between the members of the audience and the character of

Jesus. The various conceptual dimensions of Jesus's identity as the Son of God, as the Son of Man, and as a messianic prophet-Messiah like Moses rather than as a Messiah like David added to the richness of the audience's experience of the character of Jesus. But these are dimensions of the relationship of the members of the audience with Jesus who is embodied by the teller of the story. It is hoped, therefore, that the richness of Martyn's insights into the dynamics of the Fourth Gospel in its original context will be deepened and enhanced by the reconception of the Gospel as a story performed for audiences.

The Reconception of the Gospel of John

This reconception of the medium of John requires, however, a sharp distinction between the meaning of the Gospel as it has been defined by the exegesis of John's story as experienced by individual readers of the Gospel manuscript, and the exegesis of the story as experienced by audiences of performances of the Gospel. Three specific dimensions of this reconception can be identified here: (1) the framework of the Gospel's meaning for audiences rather than readers; (2) the centrality of relationship as well as belief in the Gospel's message; and (3) the impossibility of the meaning of the story being anti-Jewish.

When analysed as a text read by silent readers, the primary framework of meaning is the theological ideas that happen in the minds of readers who are looking at the manuscript with their eyes. In this medium, the dominant meaning is conceptual. In the medium of print read in silence the characters of John's story tend to be perceived as standing for or representing ideas and beliefs. That is, in addition to representing the groups of persons on the contemporary level of John's community – the Jamnia loyalists, the secret believers, the believing Jews who have been expelled from Judaism – they also represent beliefs. The Jews represent unbelief, Nicodemus and his cohorts represent belief compromised by fear of excommunication, and the Samaritan woman, the man born blind, Mary and Martha, and the disciples represent belief that is in various stages of formation. That is, the characters represent various dimensions of the theological beliefs that are interacting within the story. The history of the exegesis of John's text has been primarily occupied with the identification of the interplay of those theological dynamics.

However, when the text is analysed as a script performed for audiences, the primary framework of meaning is the relationship that is established between the performer as a believing witness, Jesus as the main character and primary speaker, and the audience. The performer's goal is to establish a relationship between the audience as individual listeners and Jesus. The performer's story creates, and invites the listener into, a multifaceted relationship between Jesus and the audience. A central facet of this relationship is a long and sustained intellectual engagement in a complex, evolving argument about Jesus's actions and their significance in relation to his identity, his relationship to God, and his role in the salvation of the world. For the listeners who became engaged in this argument, part of the fascination of the Gospel was this long and complex dialogue. Following the moves of this argument was like the demands for an ancient listener who engaged with the dialogues of Plato. As with listening to Socrates, listening to Jesus required a facile and perceptive mind in order to perceive and understand what is going on in his interactions with his various Jewish dialogue partners. Thus, a dimension of the meaning of the Gospel for a sympathetic listener was the recognition that Jesus is a major thinker, a Rabbi of substance, who invites at the very least intellectual respect and at most intellectual consent. The theological complexity of the Fourth Gospel was experienced by the audiences of the story as an encounter with the mind of Jesus.

Secondly, the story creates a relationship with the character of Jesus that invites each listener to experience growing intimacy with him. If entered into fully, that relationship ends in a profound bond of love. The emotional flow of John's story begins with the initial attraction to Jesus that is established with the storyteller's opening poem celebrating the coming of the *logos*. The *logos* is given a more human face in the exuberant responses to his presence by first John the Baptist, and then Andrew, Simon, Philip and Nathanael. The wild and instant enthusiasm of the disciples reaches its pinnacle of hilarious confession in Nathanael's explosion of joy: 'Rabbi, you are the Son of God! You are the King of Israel!' These initial responses of surprised delight are deepened in the stories of his initial 'signs' at the wedding in Cana, in the cleansing of the temple, in his dialogues with Nicodemus and the Samaritan woman, and in the healing of the royal official's son. This opening section of the story has a dynamic not unlike the initial fascination of a new love relationship. Jesus is a wonderfully fascinating character who both fulfils the long-held hopes of the listeners and utterly confounds them by his unprecedented freedom.

This relationship is tested and deepened further in Jesus's long and highly conflicting debates with Jews who are torn between believing in him and being completely alienated from him. In these stories and long speeches (chapters 5–12) the dynamics of emotional distance in relation to the character of Jesus swing wildly from a high degree of sympathetic identification to total alienation in response to Jesus's incredibly provocative statements and actions. This section culminates in the raising of Lazarus and Jesus's direct invitation to the listener to believe in him (12.44-50). The relational dynamic of this section is analogous to an engagement in which a relationship is both tested and deepened by conflict.

The culmination of this growing relationship of love between the listener and the character of Jesus happens in the listener's inclusion as an actual participant in Jesus's last evening with his beloved disciples. In this dialogue (John chapters 13–17) the intimacy of a loving relationship is firmly established. The dynamics of distance in this section are consistently positive in relation to Jesus. While he continues to make enigmatic statements, the speech ends with Jesus's prayer for the audience as his disciples. This section of the story is unambiguously intimate and is analogous to the relational dynamic of a happy and fulfilling marriage. This intimate relationship is the emotional context for the vicarious engagement in the story of Jesus's suffering, death and resurrection.

The centrality of this relationship of love for the dynamic structure of the Gospel is confirmed by the concluding dialogue of Jesus with Peter by the Sea of Tiberias. The final composer of the Gospel as we have received it probably added this story to the earlier ending of Thomas's climactic wrestling between unbelief and belief and the storyteller's statement to the audience that the purpose of the story has been that 'you' would come to believe. The three-fold question to Simon Peter – 'Do you love me?' – is addressed to the listener who identifies with Peter. Ending the story with Jesus's dialogue with Peter refocuses the central issue of the Gospel from belief to love. In the end, the story's long-term meaning for many listeners will be determined to a greater degree by the listener's response to Jesus's questions about love than about issues of belief.

Finally, in the context of hearing the Gospel as a performance, the Fourth Gospel was *not* anti-Jewish.[18] It is simply impossible that a story addressed to Jewish audiences would have been anti-Jewish. The Gospel of John, like the entire corpus of the Hebrew Scriptures, reflects a broad range of Jewish belief and practice as well as major conflicts between various Jewish groups. It is engaged in a major conflict with the Pharisees of the Jamnia Academy, who were radically narrowing the definition of what it meant to be Jewish and were expelling from the Jewish community those who accepted Jesus as Messiah. But this conflict, while resulting in a catastrophic division in the house of Israel that remains in place, was an intra-Jewish conflict in which both contestants appealed to widely accepted Jewish norms and practices, specifically authentic succession to the Mosaic tradition. Such conflict is present throughout Israel's history prior to the first century of the coexistence of what later became Judaism and Christianity.

18   For the dominant position that the Fourth Gospel was anti-Jewish in its original context, see, for example, the collection of papers for the Leuven Colloquium in 2000, *Anti-Judaism and the Fourth Gospel*. Among these papers, the position of Martinus De Boer is most congruent with the conclusions of this essay: '...the peculiar Johannine use of the term "the Jews" probably emerged in a debate *not with* but *within* the synagogue (between Jews who embraced Jesus as the expected Jewish Messiah and those who did not) about Jewish identity, i.e., about whether Christian Jews could properly be regarded as genuine "disciples of Moses"' (DeBoer 2001: 279, emphasis in original).

Audience Address and the Anti-Jewish Reading of the Fourth Gospel

The dynamics of audience address may provide a window through which light may shine on a dark corner of history. If the Gospel of John was originally addressed to late-first-century Jews and was structured to appeal for belief in Jesus as the Messiah, how is it possible that it has come to be read as an anti-Jewish document? Several changes in the relationship of this story to its audiences have taken place that may shed light on this question. The first development has been that the actual audiences of the Gospel have changed in their self-definition. The audiences who hear the performances of the Fourth Gospel have become predominantly Christian. Rather than being performed for audiences of Jews in the Diaspora communities of the Roman Empire, the Gospel has been read in the liturgies of Christian churches for congregations who do not think of themselves as Jews. As a result, the references to the Jews in the Gospel have changed in their meaning from being addressed to 'us' to being descriptions of 'them'. Rather than hearing Jesus's speeches as being addressed to the various factions in 'our' community, Jesus's speeches have been heard as addressed to 'their' community. The only part of the Gospel that has been heard as addressed to 'us' is Jesus's final speech to the disciples (chapters 13–17). Thus, later audiences of the Fourth Gospel have thought of themselves as not Jews but Christians.

The character of the performances has also changed. Rather than being performed as a long story, the Gospel has been read in short fragments. As a result, the dynamic structure of audience address has been interrupted and was no longer experienced. No longer did audiences experience an intense and deepening relationship with Jesus as the main character of the story that moved from initial interest through intense conflict to intimacy and commitment. In fact, the Gospel has rarely, if ever, been heard as a whole. Other dimensions of the performances have also changed. The story came to be performed in cathedrals for large audiences rather than in smaller, more intimate settings. In that context, it has been virtually impossible to experience the character of Jesus as speaking directly to the audience in a manner that invites response and interaction. Jesus's words have been increasingly experienced as theological pronouncements rather than elements of a passionate conversation.

Furthermore, in the course of the centuries of the Christian Church, the stories of the Gospel have come to be interpreted as encoded theology. In the aftermath of Origen's systematic reinterpretation of the Bible, allegorical interpretation became the dominant hermeneutical system. As a result, the characters of the Fourth Gospel were interpreted as allegorical representatives of doctrinal positions. It was in this context that 'the Jews' came to be experienced as an allegorical character representing disbelief. As a result, the dynamics of distance in the audience's experience of the Jewish characters with whom Jesus interacted shifted from identification to alienation.

Especially in the aftermath of the mass printing of the Gospel, a primary audience of the Gospel has become readers rather than listeners. In private reading, the audience of the Gospel has shifted from communal audiences to individual readers. One result of that shift is that the Gospel text has become the object of study in which all of the parts of the document have been seen as equally indicative of the theology of the evangelist, without regard for their place in the dynamic structure of the Gospel as a whole. In this context, the Gospel was rarely read as a diachronic whole but primarily as synchronic fragments of text.

Finally, the most radical change in the medium of the Fourth Gospel has been that it moved from the world of sound into the textual world of silence. In that world, the audiences of the Gospel have no longer heard the story with their ears but have read it only with their eyes. As a result of this development, the Gospel has been deconstructed as a story told to audiences by committed performers into a series of documentary fragments read either by silent readers or by lectors who perform these short episodes for Christian congregations in an emotionally detached manner. An additional dimension of this deconstruction of the original medium is that the Gospel of John has become a source document for scientific examination of its theological and historical data by an audience of objective readers who actively resist the invitations of the story to identify with the characters and to respond to the implicit addresses to the audience as a methodological principle.

All of these changes in the dynamics of audience address in the experience of the Fourth Gospel have been factors in the reading of the Gospel as anti-Jewish. Thus, the radical change in the meaning and message of the Gospel that has happened over the last two thousand years is connected with radical changes in the medium of the Gospel. The invitation of this volume of essays is to reorient the experience and study of the Fourth Gospel to the Gospel in its original medium. Insofar as our goal is to understand and interpret the Fourth Gospel in its original historical context, it is essential to hear the story as performed for audiences that were predominantly composed of late-first-century Jews.

Chapter 7

Jesus Retold as the World's Light in Johannine Oral Prophecy

Antoinette Wire

When I had small children, a neighbour with seven of her own invited me to her storefront church down the street from our apartments. The first woman who stood to give her testimony blew me away with her story. In the midst of a harsh life she was turned around by the Holy Spirit, saw the light for herself and was baptized by fire, and Jesus took her up into the heavenly places. I was sure this must be the 'charismatic preacher' my friend had spoken of. Then a second woman stood up and spoke of her own harsh life and present victory: she also had seen the light for herself and been baptized by fire, and Jesus had lifted her up into the heavenly places. Others recounted similar stories. We had heard nothing like this at the AME church we usually attended, nor on Sunday evenings with the Puerto Rican Pentecostals. If I had 'seen the light' for myself and joined this group, maybe I could explain how that kind of language was developing among them, and what it meant. Yet these people were not isolated from the rest of us, pushing our strollers through the snowdrifts. Why did they talk so differently?

When reading the Gospels we find ourselves asking the same question about the Gospel of John. Why does this text speak so differently from the other Gospels? Jesus, elsewhere so reticent about himself, holds forth here at great length about his identity as the light of the world, the bread of life and the good shepherd, and promises another Paraclete as his successor (8.12; 9.5; 6.35; 10.11; 14.16). Where does this way of speaking come from? Traditionally scholars have sought the answer at the two ends of the Johannine tradition, from Jesus or from the writer (Dodd 1963: 185–6). I don't exclude the possibility that Jesus spoke of being the world's light, or that the writer had a vision of this in the night, but it is the people who began to tell Jesus's story this way in the more than fifty years between these two that I expect can best account for the tradition they shaped.

Three methods in recent study promise to give us the most help in understanding the generation of distinctive Fourth Gospel traditions, namely, approaching this Gospel as *relecture*, as prophecy, and as oral tradition.

Relecture

Relecture, literally 're-reading' or 'reinterpretation', was first applied to the Bible in the study of Israelite prophecy by Albert Gelin and more comprehensively by Odil Hannes Steck. Steck saw that, once prophecies were written, they inspired further prophetic interpretations of the present and future which did not replace but supplemented the earlier prophecies. The later layers were added anonymously with the understanding that the original prophet meant as much. In this way scripture prophecy in the books attributed to an Amos or an Isaiah in fact incorporated both initial prophecies as remembered and further stages of prophecy which they provoked.

This *relecture* approach has been applied to Johannine studies particularly by Jean Zumstein in his essays collected in *Kreative Erinnerung*, by Andreas Dettweiler's study of the Last Discourse (John 13.31–16.33), and by Christian Cebulj's work on the 'I am' sayings (2000: 266–88). They may well concede that their scenario of Johannine history is itself a *relecture* of twentieth-century research, with special dependence on Rudolf Bultmann's theory of redactional layers and on Raymond Brown's correction that the tradition evolved not by rejection but by incorporation of previous stages (1979: 13–24; 2003: 62–86, 281–2). That said, *relecture* theorists do clarify the traditioning process in important ways. They see multiple reworkings of tradition over time, a story interpreted by a speech, a speech by a speech, or either by a commentary, and at any point incorporating further traditional material. The reception-text that is added cannot be understood without the reference-text which it is explicating, contextualizing or amplifying. Thus the Gospel builds up within the community in a process of agglutinization in order to confirm the believers' faith in each new crisis, developing thereby a distinctive way of speaking and hearing Jesus speak. Another practitioner of *relecture*, Klaus Scholtissek, has identified a second process he calls *réécriture* (rewriting) (2000: 137–9) to name Bultmann's insight that this Gospel says the same thing over and over in changed images.

Yet I see two major limitations to the *relecture* analysis of the Fourth Gospel from a media point of view: it is conceptualized primarily as intellectual rather than prophetic, and as written rather than oral. Zumstein does say that the *relecture* process is interpreted by the Paraclete sayings (14.16-17, 25-6; 15.26-7; 16.7-15), and he even states that 'the remembering and interpreting that make possible the Johannine tradition is not an authorial act but a prophetic one' (2004: 186–7), yet he sees this work to be taking place as re-reading in what he refers to as the Johannine school. I can find no social analysis of this school in his work. Dettweiler in one sentence hints, 'Texts like John 15–16 can very well be imagined as reflections of school discussions put in writing' (1995: 52). This suggests an oral component, but it sounds like a graduate seminar and leaves unexamined assumptions in several areas:

- (1) *Who participated?* Ancient philosophical and religious schools were known for working with authoritative texts and therefore represented the at most five per cent of the population who were literate, or the less than one per cent who were highly educated (W. Harris 1989: 248–84). A Johannine school would thus be the literate crust of the community inspired to write, read and cultivate the traditions about Jesus. The large majority of believers would be passive, or at most receptive of what had already been integrated into an authoritative tradition. It seems clear that the *relecture* theorists are speaking of an intellectual activity among the literary elite of the community, not a fluid communal tradition.
- (2) *Who taught?* Early advocates of the school thesis including Culpepper (1975: 268) saw the Beloved Disciple texts (John 13.23; 20.2; 21.7, 20) as reminiscences of the group's long-standing teacher. But it has become increasingly clear that the Beloved Disciple was introduced late into the tradition, and others such as Udo Schnelle (1987: 57–9) have proposed that the Elder who wrote 2 and 3 John and is mentioned by Papias was the founder of the school and teacher of the tradition, a person not attested in the Gospel. Still others say the Spirit was the teacher and prefer to call this a 'circle' rather than a 'school', but without changing the literary assumptions about the work done and who did it.
- (3) *How was the writing carried out?* The *relecture* approach fails to address the technical problems of space, time, materials and training necessary to produce continuous revisions of this Gospel. Advocates of this theory have not tried to demonstrate that a small and marginal group would be able to muster the money to buy writing materials, the skills to read and to write, the space to store bulky texts, and the time necessary to keep rewriting their tradition.
- (4) *What was written?* The Gospel of John does not show a clear interest in reading and writing, or in any system of teaching and learning. Christian Cebulj, himself a significant *relecture* theorist, investigated in an extended essay all the terms, themes and scripture references in the Gospel that might point to a Johannine school and came up empty (2001). He sees the deep rifts between layers of tradition and the lack of any systematic biblical exegesis as signs that there was no group guarding and shaping the tradition. In Cebulj's view, any leadership that existed was charismatic and lacked the structure to hold the community together for long after the Gospel writing.

In spite of faulty literary assumptions in each of these areas, the *relecture* thesis of multiple agglutinating interpretations can help us understand the Johannine tradition. There is no doubt that the tradition was retold, and such retellings would invariably draw upon each other and incorporate elements of previous retellings. But understanding this will require a sharper focus on oral processes of traditioning. And if the speech that transmitted this tradition was not so much theological analysis as prophetic pronouncement, we should first consider how prophecy was spoken, by whom, and for what ends.

Prophecy

To avoid ambiguity, prophecy is best defined functionally and narrowly as a practice in which someone claims to transmit a message from a divine sender to designated recipients. Martti Nissinen distinguishes such prophecy in Israel very sharply from what he calls biblical prophecy that he sees in the Hebrew prophetic books constructed scribally to address past prophecies to new situations. He thinks that this literary blooming eclipses the concrete manifestation of prophecy in Israel, or at least radically marginalizes it. This raises a question that moves beyond the scope of this study, namely whether the written Gospel of John eclipses or possibly enhances the prophetic message of Jesus as it had come to be cultivated by the time of its writing.

We need an intermediate category between the practice of prophecy as the delivery of the divine voice and the prophetic books that we read, and I will call it 'inspired speech'. This is a broader concept that includes prophecy and can cover all speech that is understood to give God's guidance and support. Paul even includes miracle-working and healing as gifts of the Spirit (1 Cor. 12.8-11), but he may be conceiving these actions as works of speech, and his final argument favouring prophecy over ecstatic tongues shows that spiritual gifts were primarily taken to be speech acts (1 Cor. 14; cf. Acts 2.4; 11.44-6; 19.6). A broad understanding of inspired speech is implied in the function of the Paraclete or Spirit of Truth in the Fourth Gospel (John 14.25-6; 15.26-7; 16.7-15). Here the verbs indicate that the Spirit of Truth reminds of, testifies to or speaks for Jesus so that the past is made present through prophecy; the Spirit defends or convicts the accused in the present trials; and the Spirit teaches, guides and tells what is to come in the future. Aune's study of early Christian prophecy, and Overholt's cross-cultural work, allow for this broad conception of inspired speech without watering down the messenger prophet's key role or ignoring the indispensable, if intricate, task of finding ancient prophecy in prophetic texts.

At the risk of generalizing, what I am calling inspired speech may be characterized as follows. It may be spoken by any participant in a ritual setting. It will be largely traditional both in words and concepts. And it can be either rejected or forgotten on the one hand, or received and remembered within a prophetic tradition on the other. It could be spoken by itinerant leaders or local believers. The only study I know that attempts a detailed reconstruction of the Johannine tradition as prophecy, written fifty years ago by Alv Kragerud, traces the tradition's development to the itinerant circle of prophets also glimpsed in Revelation's 'your slaves the prophets' (Rev. 10.7; 11.18; 22.6) and in the Didache's prophets who are called false if they stay in one place for three nights (Did. 11–13). Yet it would seem that prophetic voices must be present and active for the long term to shape the development of a community's tradition, making these possible parallels insufficient evidence for restricting inspired speech to the few itinerants. A wider range of parallel texts suggests broader participation in prophecy (Wire 1990: 237–69; 2005: 171–81).

I assume that everything spoken in the ritual context is expected to be inspired – not only visions, revelations and words of Jesus received in prophecy but also the reading of Scripture and telling the stories of Jesus, praising God and pleading with God, preaching what God has done and teaching what people need to do, even interpreting what has been taught or prophetically revealed. Public witness, including self-defence and accusation, is also taken to be inspired by God – compare the Paraclete's defending and convicting with the witness from other Gospels: 'in that hour the Holy Spirit will give you what to say' (John 16.8-11; Mark 13.11; Luke 14.26; Matthew 10.19). The street and courtroom thus become ritual space, a place of witness to the Spirit's power. Certain linguistic signs help to identify the speech of messenger prophets. They may 'cry out', say 'amen, amen', or announce that they are speaking in the first person for God. What they say may also indicate prophecy: in the Jewish tradition they bless and curse, announce salvation and judgement, and speak in traditional or everyday images, using rhythmic syntax, parallelism and comparison.

Let me address two possible objections to this broad definition of inspired speech. First, could not much of the Johannine tradition be explained as memory of the prophetic words of Jesus, since prophecy is strongly traditional and this is reportedly Jesus's speech? Definitely. But we must also explain how these expressions of Jesus have such a distinctive style so that we even call one saying not in the Gospel of John 'Johannine' (Luke 10.22; Matthew 11.27). The fact that this community considers its memory of Jesus to be inspired by the Spirit of Truth could play either way. It says the historical tradition is given – and we don't doubt that this is the same man's story we hear from the other Gospels – but it is open to inspired memory and further acts of prophecy.

Then why hasn't the tradition been totally corrupted by decades of such transmission? Apparently the discernment of what is and is not true prophecy is also taken to be inspired, and operates quite conservatively. Most of the inspired speech from this half-century must not have been retained, but what was especially memorable was repeated and built upon. The form of the tradition thus became different and influenced further inspired speech. Once this live tradition was written it became what Nissinen calls 'biblical prophecy', another phenomenon entirely, shaped by scribal hands. From it Nissinen says that the practice of prophecy can be unearthed, if at all, 'only from the bowels of the biblical text' (2004: 31). He is not surprised, on concluding his catalogue of Ancient Near Eastern prophetic texts, to find that very few prophecies were written down.

A second possible objection to conceiving inspired speech broadly is endemic in biblical studies, and comes from the Enlightenment's dread of everything spiritual. The spectre of 'enthusiasmus' seems to have kept most Germans (Dautzenberg being an exception) from applying their thorough exegetical work to the subject of prophecy in the New Testament tradition. This leaves a vacuum others must fill. Only if we recognize the practice of inspired speech as an historical phenomenon can we adequately reconstruct how prophetic insight occurs and is interpreted and passed down, what perspectives it offers on reality, and where in the social spectrum it has its impact.

Oral Tradition

A final promising method is also one that continental New Testament research seems little in touch with, the study of oral tradition in ancient texts. It was revived in the mid twentieth century in Milman Parry and Albert Lord's application to Homer of the study of Yugoslavian oral songs, and is now well represented in the work of John Miles Foley, Dell Hymes and many others. It is granted that we receive the Gospel in writing, and as writers we imagine that an aggregating tradition will need writing at each stage to hold it together, hence Culpepper and the *relecture* theorists' proposal of a school for deliberating, recording and reinterpreting. But self-adapting tradition is precisely the phenomenon seen in cultures that transmit an oral tradition. Five key insights from the study of oral literature can be particularly useful in understanding the Fourth Gospel tradition.

First, oral tradition is characterized on the one hand by formulaic patterns of speech and sequences of stock episodes that give cohesion to even long pieces, and on the other hand by variability according to the particular style of the speaker and the situation of the performance. The singer of oral epics insists that everything is being sung as always, but one night it can take an hour longer because the singer is encouraged by listeners who know the tradition and are actively engaged in its telling. The narrative line and key units do not change, but repetition is not mechanical. As Foley has pointed out (2002), the Slavic singer who claims to give the song 'word for word' is speaking about words longer than ours, units of speech and narrative that are never skipped but can greatly expand or contract within a true telling of the story. Seeing the Fourth Gospel in this light can help explain how a narrative of significant length may well be remembered and recited, and at the same time subject to expansions and adaptations. Great respect for the tradition preserves what is heard and known to be old, while the importance of the tradition requires that it be adapted to challenge the present hearers. Though the end is preservation, the means can be change.

Secondly, oral literature scholars speak of this process of adapted repetition as 'composition in performance', and Gregory Nagy following Wolfgang Rösler stresses that this recomposing happens within a group rather than before a passive audience. As Nagy puts it: 'a group can perform together for each other' (1996: 83). Even if some members take on more important roles at any one time, everyone who is present is understood to be part of what is happening, and oral responses have an effect on the story. This is because the tradition is not so much informative as dramatic, a re-enactment of prototypical events and attitudes. The community is expected to identify with figures that speak and thereby confirm their common convictions.

Thirdly, whether the oral tradition is poetic or narrative, a good performance is understood to be inspired, not simply achieved by technical training. This gives the speaker the right to adopt the first-person speech of even heroic characters, and/or provide inspired interpretations of what the tradition means. The enactment can be compared to a ritual in which the spoken words have power.

Fourthly, we see in Johannine language the very characteristics identified cross-culturally by Richard Bauman as signs of the 'performance frame' indicating that a person is speaking in the oral register. He lists the following: archaic speech or other special codes, figurative language, parallelism or other foregrounded regularity, special formulae at beginnings and ends, unusual pitch, stress, rhythm or pace, and claims or disclaimers to be speaking authoritative tradition. Direct discourse, scenes with two speaking characters, and back-channelling (group participation) have been added by others to this list. Considering how much of the so-called Johannine style fits this oral register, scholars would do better to begin here rather than with school hypotheses of composition.

Fifth, oral traditions in literate cultures interact with writing in various ways. In tracking the writing of Homer, Nagy speaks of it first appearing on the margins of the performing group in partial 'transcripts' seen strictly as aids to, or records of, a performance (1992: 41–3). Only much later do these become 'scripts' of the whole work, which are still ignored by practiced speakers. Finally, as the spoken text solidifies, the writing is granted authority and becomes 'scripture', yet often with variants still entering it from the oral tradition. In the case of Homer this process of moving from 'transcripts' to 'scripts' and finally to 'scripture' stretched more than half a millennium up to the second century BCE. It is not clear if the Fourth Gospel tradition, appearing as it does later, and in a small community with lower literacy than Athens and Alexandria, could have undergone a similar but accelerated process, or if a perceived crisis precipitated putting something strictly oral into writing.

Light for a Man Born Blind

Looking now at the story of Jesus as light of the world (8.12; 9.1-41), a world that includes a man born blind, can the hypothesis of an inspired retelling of communal oral tradition help us to explain the narrative dynamics of this story? The simplest model of development might be to see that a traditional story has grown from much telling, as in rolling a snowball or reciting 'The House that Jack Built'. Yet while one telling does build on another, it is also true that what is added is likely to have traditional elements, and the starting point of the story may be adapted to fit new layers. So rather than trying to lift off each layer as an archaeologist might, it is better to see how many major different ways the story has been focused which have left their mark on the text that we read. Each telling is thus taken as the whole story, being one stage in its development or, better, one option in the teller's repertoire, with its more vivid motifs retained as the focus shifts.

In one telling of John 9 we hear a healing story reminiscent of Jesus's two-stage healing of the blind person with his spit in Mark 8.22-6. We also hear elements from the story of Elisha who blinded and gave sight, and who healed Naaman by sending him to wash in the Jordan (2 Kings 6.17-18; 5.10). The point may be that God has again raised up a prophet for the people in their distress (Deut 18.18). The disciples asking who sinned, and Jesus's correction that God's works are being demonstrated, could set this story up (John 9.2), and the man's recognition that Jesus is a prophet could cap it off (9.17).

A fuller telling of the story may have focused on the man's stubborn witness, as one group after another press him about how he was healed. Those who hear his story deliberate, and some are drawn toward becoming disciples. The man's own gradual discovery of who Jesus is, through telling others what Jesus has done and reflecting on their reactions, may also get its start in this story of his forthright witness.

A third kind of telling is triggered by information not introduced immediately, that Jesus healed the man on the Sabbath. The teller could be drawing on stories of Jesus's Sabbath healings, but the focus here is on the man's parents who fear being put out of the synagogue, and the man who disputes with the Pharisees himself being put out, after which Jesus finds the man and makes himself known to him. This is widely thought to reflect the community's historical experience of expulsion from a local synagogue (9.22; 12.42; 16.2). It could indicate a conflict between two groups of Messianic Jews in the context of Jewish monotheism. One group, a possible source of 1 John, asserts its monotheism by stressing Jesus's humanity, remaining a synagogue (2.19; 4.1-3, 20). They expel the gospel tellers who assert their strict monotheism by identifying the Messiah with God through the Jewish wisdom tradition, calling the first group blasphemers (1.1-18; 8.58; 10.33). They take the once-blind man as the model 'excommunicate' in a move that Cebulj has identified as self-stigmatizing (2000: 81–114, 160–75, 189–91).

Their story could also provoke the prophetic warning about night and day, and the assurance that Jesus is the world's light.

A fourth telling, close to what we read, sets out to answer the disciples' opening question, 'Who sinned that this man was born blind' (9.2)? The Pharisees claim to know about sin and take Jesus's healing on the Sabbath as a sign of it, while the man pleads ignorance about sin and yet knows that he was healed. On this basis the man concludes that Jesus who healed him cannot be a sinner but must be from God. He says the authorities' persistent questions show they want to be Jesus's disciples, and they say they are Moses' disciples, reflecting parallel claims for the two as sources of God's light (Petersen 1993). The story ends with Jesus saying that he came into the world for judgement – echoing the opening 'I am the light of the world' (9.5; cf. 3.19) – so that the blind might see and the seeing become blind. And to the Pharisees' 'Surely we are not blind, are we?' he responds, 'If you were blind, you would not have sin, but now you say, "We see", your sin remains' (9.40-1). This makes a remarkable teaching story, yet its telling shows neither the perspective nor the language of teachers, but demonstrates how practical knowledge reverses traditional judgements. Sin is located in the eye of the accuser.

Other tellings can also be found within the story. One appears after the writing of the Gospel when a copyist adds, 'But he said, I believe, Lord, and worshipped him. And Jesus said ...' (9.38-9a). This returns attention to the man and thus makes the account a story of conversion – and, Brown proposes, also of baptism (1966: 375–6, 380–2), whereas the Gospel normally ignores the final state of Jesus's interlocutors, such as the Samaritan and Nicodemus, in order to focus on Jesus's self-revealing words (2.23–3.21; 4.1-42).

So did the saying of Jesus, 'I am the light of the world', derive from the blind man's story being more and more fully told? We can see that this Gospel's miracle stories often issue in announcements that Jesus is 'the bread', 'the light' or 'the life', while the parables reveal him to be 'the shepherd', 'the door', 'the way' and 'the vine'. At the same time the 'shepherd' and 'door' sayings are part of Jesus's speech at the end of the once-blind man's tale when some Jews proceed to call Jesus demonic, while other Jews say, 'A demon couldn't open the eyes of the blind, could he?' (10.19-21). But I will focus my question about the history of the Johannine tradition on the 'light of the world' saying (9.5), which is integral to several possible renditions of the man's story and cannot be dismissed as of marginal significance. Whatever its origin, once a piece like this is integrated into the story it is part of the whole, both interpreting and being interpreted by the rest, and nothing is gained by trying to pop it out of the puzzle in order to get an earlier, 'more original', picture.

The situation here is further complicated by the fact that this Gospel identifies Jesus with light seven times. Light has even been called the theme of the first half of the Gospel (Popkes 2004) and is unlikely to derive strictly from telling of the blind man's healing. The whole story then becomes the whole Gospel. Jesus's claim to be the light of the world can then only be seen by reviewing all these references, looking for whatever hints can be found about the function and significance of identifying Jesus as light.

Each of these statements contrasts light and darkness in antithetical parallelism. This contrast could derive from the parable in 11.9-10, which has been attributed to the primitive Jesus tradition by C. H. Dodd (1963: 373–4): 'Are there not twelve hours in a day? Whoever walks in the day does not fall down because he sees this world's light, but whoever walks in the night falls down because the light is not in the world' (11.9-10). Jesus says this when he insists on going to see Lazarus, so the parable in its context may mean that Jesus's hour has not yet come. Looking at all the Fourth Gospel references, this parable is adapted to interpret the darkness in many different ways. In the passage just read, the danger is that you will fall, in 12.35 that you will not know where you are going, in the blind man's story that you cannot work, in 8.23 that you will not be able to walk (which in the Semitic language context means not able to live), and in 3.20 that your evil deeds will be exposed. In each case Jesus is said to offer the light that reverses this condition, exposing good deeds, preventing falling and wandering away, and allowing living and working. Use of a parable about walking in daylight so flexibly in many different contexts strikes me, not as evidence of a theological school at work, but as a way people might tell a parable in order to make sense of why they see what others do not see.

With this parable appears the repeated identification of Jesus as light. Whereas in Matthew 5.14 Jesus says to his disciples '*You* are the light of the world', in John 9.5 he says this of himself. Both may be echoing Isaiah 49.6 where God says to the servant, 'I give you as a light to the nations.' Yet in neither case is the speaker citing an authoritative text, but rather making a prophetic identification. One can almost hear the phrase being shaped as the parable about day and night is repeated: 'the light was coming into the world' (1.9); 'the light came into the world' (3.19); 'I, the light, have come into the world (12.46); 'I am the light of the world. Those who follow me will have the light of life' (8.12); and our text: 'When I am in the world, I am the light of the world' (9.5).

This does not mean that those who took up telling the blind man's story when he left off had reached for an extraneous concept about Jesus being the light in order to frame their story. Prophecies seem to have regularly accompanied, and even overwhelmed, storytelling. The Paraclete descriptions speak of two ways Jesus is remembered, the prophetic and the historical: 'The Spirit of Truth … will witness concerning me, and you are also witnesses, because you are with me from the beginning' (15.26-7). Since it is the forte of prophecy to speak, it is no surprise that storytelling often gives way to the voice of Jesus that keeps on speaking. Yet this speech survives only by being taken up into the narrative.

Many scholars already read the Fourth Gospel as *relecture*, in the sense of hearing its multiple interpretations, and many also recognize that these interpretations were understood to be inspired. But it will be difficult, and transforming, if we can learn how to read this Gospel as an oral tradition, cultivated and treasured by the speaking of a whole community. We should go back now and check Bauman's characteristics of the oral register of language – special codes, images, parallelism, and opening formulas. I can take up only one of these characteristics, that is, the claim or disclaimer to be speaking authoritative tradition. The Fourth Gospel makes this claim, and far more than do the other Gospels. Only Paul can compare, and he writes by speaking.

In at least three repeated ways the Fourth Gospel claims to be speaking authoritative tradition. There are the recurring statements of witness: 'we know what we speak and we have seen what we witness to...' (3.11, 32; 19.35). Secondly, there is the recurring story of the Beloved Disciple who knows Jesus better than Peter does (13.23; 20.2; 21.7, 20). These two ways to claim authority for this tradition do not fit very well together and may represent different voices, but the person who writes the Gospel down puts them together at the end, saying: 'This is the disciple having witnessed these things and written them, and we know that his witness is true' (21.24). Thirdly, and without any link to these two, the Spirit of Truth is presented five times as the explanatory principle and guarantor of the Gospel's truth (14.16-17, 25-6; 15.26-7; 16.7-15). Apparently we are not the first generation with questions about the reliability of this tradition. Whether we are persuaded or not – and I will trust a community before a school any day – we must concede that these three independent efforts to defend the tradition's authority are classical indicators of the oral register.

Returning to the saying at the opening of the blind man's story, 'I am the light of the world', what can we say about its history and its meaning?

In three ways it shows its roots in the life of Jesus: in his parabolic warning about the limits of daylight (John 11.9-10), in a possible challenge to his followers to be the light of the world (Matthew 5.14), and unmistakably in his practice of healing the blind (Mark 2.22-6; 10.46-52 and parallels; Luke 4.18 and 7.21; John 4.1-41). But an adequate explanation of the tradition's composition requires also the Spirit of Truth speaking as Jesus's voice when the blind man's healing is being told, redirecting all three of the above within a community facing dark times by saying: 'We must work the works of the one who sent me while it is day. Night is coming when no one can work. When I am in the world, I am the light of the world.'

Does this indicate that the challenge of the light that reveals and judges has become a consolation in Jesus's absence, when night has come and they cannot work? Then the story of a man's remarkable discovery is a memory that keeps them faithful until the light shines again. But as part of a whole Gospel whose message is not consolation in a time of delay but a challenge to know and realize the truth, something else may be meant. Three times in this passage we are asked to think about a certain question: some Pharisees say, 'How could a sinner do such signs?' The once-blind man reasons: 'If he weren't from God he could do nothing.' Other Jews say: 'A demon can't open the eyes of the blind, can he?' (9.16, 31; 10.21) Jesus's healing the blind man is taken to prove he is not what people say he is – a sinner, a man from nowhere, a man possessed – but is what he says he is, light of the world. Jesus's good work speaks for itself. The Spirit of Truth tells them so. But in a world where those who say they see are blind, the challenge is surely to be the blind man who knows he is ignorant and comes to see. A difficult step indeed for this assertive community, but necessary if they are to be included in Jesus's first-person plural, 'We must work the works of the one who sent me while it is day ... When I am in the world, I am the light of the world' (9.4-5).

Chapter 8

SCRIPTURE *TALKS* BECAUSE JESUS *TALKS*:
THE NARRATIVE RHETORIC OF PERSUADING AND CREATIVITY
IN JOHN'S USE OF SCRIPTURE[1]

Michael Labahn

The relationship between orality and written text as two distinct forms of communication in the ancient media world is of special interest with regard to the interpretation of the Gospel of John (cf. the important introduction to the problem in Dewey 2001: 487–505). On the most basic level, there are the old and oft-discussed questions regarding the Gospel's tradition and the source of inspiration for its story. Is the Gospel of John based on a direct literary relationship with the Synoptic Gospels, as the so-called 'Leuven Hypothesis' tries to show (cf. van Belle 2007: 333–6)? Or does it use, at least in part, re-narrated stories from the synoptic tradition, which came to the author of the Gospel through secondary orality (see Labahn 1999: 195f., 294; 2000: 272–5; Labahn and Lang 2004: 465–8; cf. the evaluation of my approach by Smith (2001: 195–8)?[2] Or does John use other written or oral sources that may be part of an independent line of oral transmission (e.g., Dunn 1991: 351–79)?[3] Beyond these concerns, there have been inquiries into Jesus's speeches, their role within the text, and their function regarding the reader (implied or real) of the written record, and also studies into the oral or literary character of the Fourth Gospel. It seems that Joanna Dewey is generally correct to claim that 'an understanding of the oral world in which FG was produced may help us answer ... questions about its composition

1   My thanks are extended to Tom Thatcher for his constructive comments and for checking the English in this essay, and to the editors for their invitation to contribute.
2   On the phenomenon of 'secondary orality', 'second orality' or 're-oralization' cf., e.g., Byrskog 2000: 138–44; Kirk 2007: 135–58; Uro 1993: 306, 313. The term 'secondary orality' was coined by Ong (1982).
3   An overview on different theories about a literary pre-history of the Gospel until 1999 is given in Labahn 1999: 56–76; an outline regarding the treatment of the Fourth Gospel as a written literary entity searching for its compositional technique is given by Thatcher (2007: 487–9).

history and the Johannine Jesus tradition',[4] although I am not completely convinced by all her conclusions, particularly regarding the 'oral style' of the Johannine narrative (Dewey 2007: 247, 249–51). In contrast to such a concept of 'oral style', we must take seriously a network of intratextual references built on repetition and variation which suggests a literary composition of the Gospel text, but even as a literary entity this text was used in an oral community and was probably read aloud in church gatherings (as witness cf. Justin, *1 Apol* 67: 3, cf., e.g., Hengel 2008: 69).

The present article does not aspire to solve all the complex problems relating to the interrelation of orality and writing in the media world of the Gospel of John. Rather, I will seek to shed light on several aspects of the relationship between media of communication and social authority as that relationship is portrayed *within the text* of the Fourth Gospel itself,[5] particularly with regard to Scripture.[6] Therefore, the following short essay is not a study of intertextual relationships with regard to Scripture, nor an attempt to identify specific scriptural quotations or allusions in the Fourth Gospel or to ascertain their possible textual form (of basic importance are also e.g. Hanson 1991; Menken 1996; 1997: 367–93; Obermann 1996; Schuchard 1992). Rather, I will take a narrative-critical approach to the question, treating 'Scripture' as a character[7] that acts orally and that is interrelated with other characters by the narrator, with particular attention to Scripture's relationship to the oral hero of the story (Jesus). Further, this article will focus on those passages in the Gospel of John – generally statements by characters or the narrator – in which Scripture is portrayed as a *speaking* character, and will also consider the relationship of these passages to the presentation of the oral Johannine Jesus. Particular attention will be given to instances in which

4   Joanna Dewey provides an important introduction to the problem in 'The Gospel of John in its Oral-Written Media World', in Fortna and Thatcher (eds), *Jesus in Johannine Tradition* (Louisville: WJK Press, 2001), pp. 239–52; this quote is from p. 247; cf. also Thatcher (2007), 'John's Memory Theater. The Fourth Gospel and Ancient Mnemo-Rhetoric', *CBQ: The Gospel of John in its Oral-Written Media World*, 487–505.

5   This means that the discussion will be limited to one of the 'interactions' characterizing the Fourth Gospel: 'on one hand with the Gospel itself, on the other hand, with other literary corpora', Zumstein 2008: 121.

6   In this essay, the term 'Scripture' is mainly used with reference to ἡ γραφή and its use in the Gospel of John. Historically the reference to 'Bible' or 'Scripture' in an early Christian context is a reference to the complex history and development of texts and versions; cf. in short Maier 2004: 54.

7   An important narrative study on the use of scripture in the Gospel of John is given by Lieu (2000). Lieu studied the references to Scripture by the narrator and by the actors: 'the use of scripture will be explored in the mouths of the various participants in the Johannine drama' (p. 145). She refers to Beutler (1996: 147–62) as an ancestor of her approach. Beutler's thesis is that the Fourth Evangelist is interested in 'the "fulfilment" of "scripture" as such' (p. 147) and comparable to our study focuses on the word field γράφω/γραφή. Neither Lieu nor Beutler focus on Scripture as narrative character, nor on the relationships of authority drawn from reference to written or oral media.

the Scriptures are identified in the narrative with the terms γραφή ('writing') or γράφω ('write') as an orally-acting character that 'speaks' and 'witnesses'. Following this approach, I will seek to describe (1) the model of authority attributed to written texts within the Johannine narrative world;[8] and (2) the interrelation between Scripture and Jesus as orally-acting characters. Such an approach will offer new insights on the function of the Scriptures within the Fourth Gospel's own conception of media.

Thus, this essay is an attempt to explain how Scripture functions as a 'witness' to Jesus in the Fourth Gospel and, in the narrower interests of this particular volume, how these written Scriptures act as a character that speaks to audiences within and beyond the narrative. I will explore the problem by reflecting on how John describes the nature of Scripture as written/oral media.

The Authority and Finality of Written Texts Within the Johannine Narrative World

It is a well-known fact that early Christians used quotations, allusions and other kinds of reception of the Jewish Scriptures as tools to persuade people within and outside the group's social boundaries to accept their claims (on the role of Scripture in persuading people outside the early Christian movement, cf., e.g., Menken 2003: 179–98). Reference to an ancient written text with established authority and meaning added force to the Christian understanding of the present time. Persuasion through appeal to authoritative traditions is a common feature of oral cultures, and was thus an element of ancient rhetorical theory (on the role of rhetoric and persuasion by referring to scripture cf., e.g., Stamps 2006: 9–37; Stanley 1997: 44–58; *idem* 2004). It is undisputed that ancient written texts evidence features of the oral media world, and that they became a part of that world when they were read aloud (cf., e.g., Achtemeier 1990: 3–27). In this light, it is interesting to see how the Johannine narrative relates Scripture to the written and oral worlds and how Scripture is related to the 'oral' Johannine Jesus.

---

8   In view of this special focus, the current article addresses only those passages where the Johannine Gospel directly refers to Scripture or to its character as written text. The narrator/characters refer to a written text in 1.47; 2.17; 5.46; 6.31, 45; 8.17; 10.34; 12.14, 16; 15.25 (with γράφω) and 2.22; 5.39; 10.35; 13.18; 17.12; 19.28, 36; 20.9 (with γραφή). As written text with γράφω it is also referred to the title at the cross (19.19-22: six times of 21[22] uses of the verb γράφω in the Fourth Gospel) and to the Gospel book itself (20.30, 31; 21.24, 25). Scripture is referred to with γράφω/γραφή as an active figure (talking) by the narrator/a character in 7.38, 42; 19.24, 37; of course these passages refer to Scripture as a written entity, too. This article will not consider other texts where Scripture may be quoted or to the long range of possible allusions to Scriptures; for a broad presentation of possible quotations, allusions, echoes and motifs from Old Testament cf. Hübner, Labahn and Labahn 2003.

A few examples from the Fourth Gospel will demonstrate that, within the Johannine narrative world, Scripture has authority because it is a written document that is viewed as important by the characters in the story. First of all, this authority is established by the narrator, who frequently refers to Scripture with the formula 'it is written' (ἐστιν γεγραμμένον; John 2.17; 6.31, 45; 10.34; 12.14; see also 12.16 [with ἦν]; cf. also the fulfilment formula at 13.18; 17.12; 19.24, 28, 36). In these contexts, this formula asserts that the quotation in question has meaning because it derives from a written text whose authority seems to be beyond doubt. However, the relationship between the authoritative reference text and the reception text is a dialectic one (see also below). As far as the reference text bears this authority, narrated events must relate to that text in a particular way, and in turn these events have their own meaning in bringing the authoritative written reference text to its 'fulfilment' (cf. Moloney 2005: 462).

Such an interpretation of the written reference text written as an authoritative entity is supported by the claim at John 10.35 that Scripture cannot be 'broken'. Here, Scripture as written text is taken as a fixed but still enduring and vivid entity with an indisputable authority.[9] However, as is shown in the polemical context of the larger scene in John 10.31-9 (in which Jesus defends his unity with his Father and is accused of blasphemy), the meaning of the written text is a matter of debate and struggle. Correct or incorrect understanding, as defined by the narrator's moral and religious assumptions, are therefore part of a hermeneutical process which is guided in the Johannine story by the narrator and by the words of its hero, Jesus (cf., e.g., John 20.30-1). According to the Johannine narrative strategy, one must understand the written text of Scripture in a specific manner, a manner which is not defined by simple reference to its written status *but rather by the one to whom Scripture bears witness* (cf. Labahn 2004: 198–201). There is need for a hermeneutical process that is related to the hero of the narrative, the Johannine Jesus, who leads into understanding through his teaching. There is, then, some reflection here on the basis of the authority of the Scriptures – that reflection again directs attention to Jesus but does not aim at an 'expansion' or 'completion' of Scripture and its authority (both conclusions are made by Kraus 1997: 1–23; for a critical reply to Kraus cf. Scholtissek 2003: 153–4).

The simple fact that, and the means by which, the Johannine narrative world shows knowledge of the power of and behind a written text is indicated by the passage about the *titulus* on Jesus's cross (John 19.19-22),

---

9   Lindars (1992: 375) understood οὐ δύναται λυθῆναι ἡ γραφή as Scripture 'always remains in force' which is used by Moloney (1998: 321) as translation of John 10.35. This interpretation ascribes a more active and enduring role to the written text as in the common translation used above ('not be broken'). This more active role underlines Scripture's authority and is in accordance with other instances in the Gospel of John taking the written text as an oral actor.

which ends in Pilate's famous words, 'What I have written I have written' (ὃ γέγραφα γέγραφα; v.22).[10] Here Pilate, as a Johannine character, acknowledges the finality of a written word – the aorist form γέγραφα refers to an effective, singular act[11] through which the written entity becomes an authority in its own right. Although the personal pronoun is not mentioned explicitly, the first person singular of the verb ('I have written') claims authority for the written document in relation to a certain 'I', a person behind the text who has written it down, in this case Pilate himself. The title on the cross is thus a written text that has authority and influence; for this very reason, the unbelieving Jewish authorities within the world of the narrative want to change the text, for it does not align with their (mis)understanding of Jesus. However, the text has been written by a person with authority and, as such, he cannot be compelled to change it.

Commenting on this incident, Craig Keener underscores the fact that every other Johannine use of γέγραφα in reference to a written text refers to (Holy) Scripture; Pilate, as pagan witness, recalls aspects of Scripture as a reference text within the Gospel world (cf. Keener 2003: 1138). Keener notes that the written *titulus* ironically made God's will public and that therein Pilate became 'God's unwitting agent' (see also, e.g., Dauer 1972: 200: 'tool of God' ['*Werkzeug Gottes*']), a reading that is well founded in John's rhetorical use of irony as a guide to the reader's understanding (on Johannine irony cf., e.g., Culpepper 1996: 193–207; Scholtissek 1998: 235–55). As 'unwitting agent' of God, it is not Pilate with his authority that stands behind the truth of the written *titulus*, as the characters within the narrative would assume, but rather the authority of God himself: the written title refers to the cross as the place where the Johannine Jesus becomes visible as 'the King of the Jews', turning the cross into a sort of throne (cf., e.g., Lang 1999: 218; Lincoln 2005: 475). It is necessary to understand the Johannine play with irony in order to see that God's authority stands behind the *titulus* and that the way to the cross is according to the will of Jesus's Father. The model reader will possess the necessary understanding through recollection of Jesus's words in John 12.23-7 (cf., e.g., Labahn 2007: 444, 451–5).

In summary, it could be said that the authority of Scripture as a written document is supported in the Johannine narrative world by the claims that (a) the text is based in God (= Jesus; John 12.41), and (b) it develops a certain understanding of Jesus that is not available to all characters in the story

---

10   All English translations of the Gospel of John are from the New Revised Standard Version.

11   The usually mentioned Latin and Greek parallels to Johannine ὃ γέγραφα γέγραφα that refer to 'κέκρινα' (Epictetus *Diatr.* II 15.5 and Pliny the Younger *Ep.* I 12.10; cf. Schnelle, Labahn and Lang 2001: 821) reflect only the finality of the Aorist γέγραφα as a firm intention but do not appeal to any special character of a written text within the ancient media world.

but which can potentially be obtained by the model reader, who has been provided with further information throughout the course of the narrative.

The complex interrelation between the inherent authority of the written Scripture and the necessity for hermeneutical guidance in understanding that text is underscored by the original ending of the Gospel of John. John 20.30-1 can be understood as a 'conclusion' of the Johannine narrative that provides 'an explicit formulation of the pragmatic intention that guides the *narratio*, namely calling believers to faith ... this conclusion allows readers to verify the appropriateness of their reading' (Zumstein 2008: 124). Reading John 20.30-1 in the context of the preceding narrative, the Gospel claims to be a 'book' within the Scriptures, one that must be read within a certain hermeneutical frame.[12]

> Now Jesus did many other signs in the presence of his disciples,
>> which *are* not *written* in this book
>
> Πολλὰ μὲν οὖν καὶ ἄλλα σημεῖα ἐποίησεν ὁ Ἰησοῦς ἐνώπιον τῶν μαθητῶν [αὐτοῦ],
>> ἃ οὐκ ἔστιν γεγραμμένα ἐν τῷ βιβλίῳ τούτῳ· (20.30)

> But these are written
>> so that you may come to believe
>>> that Jesus is the Messiah, the Son of God,
>> and that through believing you may have life in his name.
>
> ταῦτα δὲ γέγραπται
>> ἵνα πιστεύ[σ]ητε
>>> ὅτι Ἰησοῦς ἐστιν ὁ χριστὸς ὁ υἱὸς τοῦ θεοῦ,
>> καὶ ἵνα πιστεύοντες ζωὴν ἔχητε ἐν τῷ ὀνόματι αὐτοῦ. (20.31)

Since ἔστιν γεγραμμένα is a formula used by the narrator to identify quotations from Scripture (cf. John 2.17; 6.31, 45; 10.34; 12.14; see also 12.16 [with ἦν]), and thus to encourage the audience to accept certain claims that shape the understanding of the model reader, it should be asked whether John 20.30 claims to place the Gospel text under or over the authority of the Scriptures that later Christian tradition would call the 'Old Testament' (cf., e.g., Hengel 1989: 276–7). In my view, we must answer this question in the

---

12 This conception of a written media text is further developed in John 21.24-5, a passage which most exegetes today view as a later extension of the Gospel text. While earlier research interpreted John 21 as a foreign body, recent readings generally try to understand it in terms of Johannine '*relecture*'; cf., e.g., Zumstein 2004: 15–30 (23–4 on John 21); on '*relecture*' now *idem*, 125–7. John 21.24-5 shows that the understanding of the Gospel as a written text that deserves a certain authority developed further, either but less plausibly to make the text readable to the Church, or with regard to the needs and questions of the later Johannine community.

affirmative (cf. Scholtissek 2000: 207–26; see also Moloney 2005: 466).[13] As a βιβλίον, the narrative is placed within a category of Scripture that deserve authority and that possess a finality that could not be broken.

The presence of John 21, however, reveals that this authoritative, unbreakable text could be *relectured*. *Relecture* is not a literary method or approach but rather a hermeneutical process that accepts the truth/meaning and authority of the written text. 'If we agree that the reception text intends to deepen the reference text – or to allow a new level of reflection about the questions it has raised – then it follows that the reception text does not in any way denigrate the validity or authority of the reference text; in fact, this is precisely what it recognizes' (Zumstein 2008: 126; see also his programmatic article, Zumstein 2003: 9–37, esp. 19). Applying the principle of *relecture* to John 21, we can see with regard to the literary development of the Fourth Gospel that its first readers accepted the authority of the Gospel text as developed within the narrative. In my estimation, *relecture* is best under-stood as an element of the written media world: because the written text is accepted as authority, it is not modified by a new performance of its content and/or meaning but rather by adding a new text, the reception text (John 21), to the existing reference text. Therefore, the Gospel of John's concept of written texts and their authority, developed by repeating and varying the word group γράφω, places the Gospel itself in the same media world as the written Scripture, a status that was affirmed when the written narrative was *relectured* by its first readers in the Johannine School.

Still, the written book is not simply an entity in itself. It has a pragmatic aim: to create belief and to strengthen faith in Jesus, who is the Messiah and the Son of God – a faith that carries the soteriological promise of life in Jesus's name. Depending upon written authorities (the Scriptures) and claiming for itself the authority of a written text, the Gospel of John portrays its main character, Jesus – God's only-born son and the sole means of access to his otherwise unseen Father (cf. John 1.1-18 as programmatic goal to the post-Easter Johannine Christological hermeneutics of the Jesus narrative) – as a person who preaches and persuades people *orally* (cf., e.g., Zumstein 2004: 126).[14] Thus, the written Gospel text, claiming authority for itself

13   For Moloney 'a desire to convince readers that the biblical narrative reached its perfection in the Johannine story of Jesus's is part of the rhetoric of the Fourth Gospel' (468). Although I am grateful to be part of Moloney's argumentation I would refrain from going that far. Scripture ('Old Testament') and Written Gospel (John) have a more dialec-tical relationship directed by the Christological hermeneutic developed by the Johannine narrative.

14   I do not wish to downplay the role of Jesus's acts, especially of his miracles, which I have elsewhere shown to be an integral part of the narrative portrait of Jesus as giver of life (Labahn, *Jesus als Lebensspender*, passim). With regard to the media question, it might be possible to refer to Jesus's acts as performances and therefore to read his actions in close relation to his discourses: the acts are a form of direct address to people which

as Scripture, *narrates an orally-persuading hero whose main weapon is authoritative speech that deserves undisputed acceptance.* The authority in and behind this written text is the oral Jesus.

These brief remarks show that it is not only very difficult to place the Gospel of John, with its possible relations to tradition and other pre-texts, into the ancient oral-written media world, but also very difficult to place its own claims to authority within that media world. This is the case simply because the text refers to itself as, and establishes its authority as, 'Scripture' by portraying an oral hero. In this case, the interplay between orality and literacy seems to be a vivid and dialectical one governed by a hermeneutical aim: to create and to strengthen faith in Jesus as God's gift of eternal life.

Scripture as Character in John: Witness and Speaker

Building on the above considerations of the Fourth Gospel's location in its media environment, I will now explore ways in which the Scriptures are characterized as an orally-performing character within the 'book' (John 20.30) developing the Johannine narrative world.

The narrative setting of the first example for our consideration is the healing of a lame person. In John 5.1-9a Jesus heals a man at a pool in Jerusalem that, despite its reputation for its healing properties, had been unable to assist this individual, who had been there for thirty-eight years (a possible allusion to Deut 2.14; cf., e.g., Labahn 2007: 89–90). The indication that the healing took place on a Sabbath comes belatedly in v. 9b and is not stated in the narrative setting of v. 1 ('there was a festival of the Jews' (cf. Thatcher 1999: 53–77)).[15] The time reference, however, is of crucial importance within the argument of Chapter 5, because it leads Jesus to identify his work on a Sabbath day with God's preservation of the world on the seventh day of the week (cf., e.g., Asiedu-Peprah 2001: 77–8; Beutler 2006: 20): 'My Father is still working, and I also am working' (ὁ πατήρ μου ἕως ἄρτι ἐργάζεται κἀγὼ ἐργάζομαι; v. 17). This statement leads the Jewish opponents to the conclusion that Jesus makes himself equal to God, and for this reason they establish a plot to kill Jesus (v. 18 taking up and elaborating v. 16 by giving the verb ἐδίωκον a deadly meaning).

change their life and/or their self-understanding. Furthermore, acts and words stand in a dialectical relationship in the Fourth Gospel.

15   According to Thatcher the belated mentioning of the Sabbath represents the rhetorical technique of *unstable irony* that should prepare the readers for a 'deconstruction' and lead them into a new understanding of Jesus. Thatcher might be correct in terms of the rhetorical affect of the belated mentioning of the Sabbath. However, the Sabbath motif is more crucial for the understanding of Chapter 5 as far as it provokes the comparison of God's and Jesus's work, with the monologue at 5.19–47 developing Jesus's role of giving (eternal) life (cf., e.g., Labahn 1999: 261–3, 264).

Within this distinctive setting, Jesus elaborates on his authority in a discussion with his opponents, who are directly addressed (5.19, 20, etc.). In this monologue, Jesus refers to different witnesses who have given testimony relevant to the issue. These include John the Baptist (5.32-5), the 'works that the Father has given me to complete' (5.36), the Father himself (5.37-8), and also the Scriptures (5.39, on the different witnesses cf. Beutler 1972: 254–65). Jesus argues:

> You search the Scriptures
>> because you think
>>> that in them you have eternal life;
> and it is they that testify on my behalf
> ἐραυνᾶτε τὰς γραφάς,
>> ὅτι ὑμεῖς δοκεῖτε
>>> ἐν αὐταῖς ζωὴν αἰώνιον ἔχειν·
> καὶ ἐκεῖναί εἰσιν αἱ μαρτυροῦσαι περὶ ἐμοῦ·

Clearly, an active role of Scripture is described: a 'witness' is a person who gives a statement/proof within a certain case under debate, especially in front of a court (cf. Aristotle, *Rhetoric* 1.15, 1375a, 22–4).[16] Without doubt, this is an act of communication. The Scripture takes that role with regard to Jesus.

As witness for Jesus, Scripture is not only a character in the Fourth Gospel, like John the Baptist and the Father; it also takes an active role in a court-like situation. It speaks in advance for Jesus. The written medium, which contributes to scientific research within the text world ('you search the Scriptures'), is portrayed as an oral character that refers directly to the truth of Jesus's claim for authority. It is not a mere object for study, but rather an active entity underscoring the meaning of Jesus and 'witnessing' on his behalf in advance. As far as Jesus claims Scripture as a witness on his side, Scripture deserves a certain authority which is underscored in the text – indeed, even Jesus's opponents search Scripture for advice. Outside the text world, witnesses in court were generally viewed as figures of authority, as is evident from Cicero's assertion, 'persona autem non qualiscumque est testimoni pondus habet; ad fidem enim faciendam auctoritas quaeritur' (*Top* 73).[17] Scripture, as it is referred to by Jesus, is an authoritative character that takes an active role in 'speaking' in advance of Jesus.

---

16   This is not unparalleled within ancient argumentation; see the examples in Schnelle, Labahn and Lang 2001: 319–27; cf. especially Plato, *Gorg* 525d–e (referring to Homer with his poems as witness); see also *Rep* IV 441b; *Leg* I 630a.

17   Cf. the larger context of the paragraph: 'This sort of argumentation then which is said not to be founded on art, depends on testimony. But we call everything testimony which is deduced from any external circumstances for the purpose of implanting belief. Now it is not every one who is of sufficient weight to give valid testimony; for authority

As such it is part of the oral world and it is also part of a hermeneutical rule: Scripture has to be addressed as a witness on the side of Jesus. The authority of Scripture is accepted by the characters in the text – only its role as a witness, not its authority, is a matter of dispute here – and it is the duty of the model reader to accept its authority as a witness for Jesus and to search Scripture in a way that allows it to 'talk' in advance for Jesus. According to the pragmatics of the passage, people addressing Scripture will have to listen to the witness that it gives; if they do that, they will be able to find what they seek, eternal life.

In this interpretation, Scripture does not deserve authority as a written-media text. It has authority as an oral character (witness) that might lead, through an act of communication, to a Johannine understanding of Jesus as the one sent by God who does what he has learned from his Father so that people can gain eternal life. Within that act of communication, Scripture needs a 'partner' who accepts its authority and enters with it into a hermeneutical consent.

Another instance of Scripture as an oral actor may be found in John 7–10, a section that portrays a continuously intensifying conflict between Jesus and his adversaries, including reference to several attempts to stone (8.59; 10.31-3) or arrest (7.44f.) Jesus. Jesus addresses his inner-textual opponents frankly (ἐν παρρησίᾳ; 7.26; see Labahn 2004: 321–63) and argues in an interchange of different accusations. During this conflict, the Johannine Jesus also uses Scripture in support of his argument. Again, he refers to Scripture not only as a written text, but as a written medium that comes to his aid through an oral act of communication.

At John 7.37, the Johannine Jesus invites thirsty people to come to him. John 7.38 varies and deepens the message of that invitation by associating ἐρχέσθω πρός με ('let come them to me') with ὁ πιστεύων εἰς ἐμέ ('who believes in me') and ἐάν τις διψᾷ ('anyone who is thirsty') with πινέτω ('let drink'; on the grammatical structure and reference of John 7.37-8, cf., e.g., Schnelle 2004: 164). The reason for the promise is that from Jesus's belly (not from the believer, contra the NRSV, cf., e.g., Smith 1999: 174; see also Koester 2003: 198) there will flow rivers of living water (ποταμοὶ ἐκ τῆς κοιλίας αὐτοῦ ῥεύσουσιν ὕδατος ζῶντος), which is, according to the narrator's comment, realized by the Spirit (v. 39). The metaphorical promise takes the form of direct speech, not of a quote from written Scripture (v. 38).

> ... as the Scripture *has said* ...
> ... καθὼς εἶπεν ἡ γραφή ...

---

is requisite to make us believe things. But it is either a man's natural character or his age which invests him with authority. The authority derived from a man's natural character depends chiefly on his virtue; but on his age there are many things which confer authority; genius, power, fortune, skill, experience, necessity, and sometimes even a concourse of accidental circumstances.' (Trans. Yonge, 2009.)

Jesus describes Scripture as an active oral partner in a discussion that here again refers to himself. Inasmuch as the specific content of this 'Scripture's' statement cannot be found precisely in any Old Testament text, one may ask if the oral function of Scripture in characterizing Jesus is also a matter of creativity, in which material from the Scripture as written medium is reformulated into oral speech that is influenced by the person who is described with the metaphorical formulation. Looking at the possible OT pre-texts (Exod. 17.1-7; Ps.LXX 77.16, 20; Prov. 4.23, 5.15; Isa. 55.1, 58.11; Zech. 14.8; etc.),[18] while one may find parallels and texts that influenced the metaphor of v. 38, it cannot be overlooked that the metaphor is inspired by words and acts of Jesus that he has used to identify himself, most notably in John 4.14.[19]

> The water
>   that I will give
> will become in them a spring of water gushing up to eternal life.
> τὸ ὕδωρ
>   ὃ δώσω αὐτῷ
> γενήσεται ἐν αὐτῷ πηγὴ ὕδατος ἁλλομένου εἰς ζωὴν αἰώνιον.

It appears, then, that the question raised above may be answered in the affirmative: Scripture speaks by building variations of Jesus's words that are close to material that could be found in the written text of Scripture. It is a process of intertextual as well as intratextual creativity and communication that aims for the benefit of the addressee: the believer should come and drink to receive water that provides eternal life. The oral-acting Scripture is not simply an actor in the text but is also active with regard to the implied reader, who is in turn a model for the real reader.

Again in John 7.42, Scripture is referred to as a medium that 'speaks'. Here Scripture is an entity that is used by different groups, even by the opponents within the text. Some of these opponents raise the question:

> Has not the scripture *said*
> that the Messiah is descended from David
> and comes from Bethlehem,
>   the village where David lived?

18   Cf. Hübner, Labahn and Labahn 2003; an extensive discussion of John 7.38 is given by Menken 1996: 187–203, who refers to Ps.LXX 77.16, 20 and Zech 14.8 as the most plausible reference text; see now also Köstenberger 2007: 454.

19   On the intratextual relationship including John 6.35, cf. Maritz and van Belle, in Attridge 2006: 342–3. On the other side, e.g., Lincoln (2005: 255) stresses the difference in imagery applied in John 4.14. However, John 4 introduces Jesus with the metaphor of living water as a source of eternal life that satisfies the existential thirst for 'real' life. The purpose of πηγὴ ὕδατος for the benefited addressee of Jesus shows the quality of that water which leads her/him into everlasting life. John 7 changes the image programme because it does not focus on the addressee but rather on the source of life, Jesus.

οὐχ ἡ γραφὴ εἶπεν
ὅτι ἐκ τοῦ σπέρματος Δαυὶδ
καὶ ἀπὸ Βηθλέεμ τῆς κώμης
ὅπου ἦν Δαυὶδ
ἔρχεται ὁ χριστός;

The question refers to the Scripture in general[20] and does not aim at one single reference text. To the surprise of the reader, the basic point of the question is not rejected, nor even taken up at all; only a division among the people is mentioned, which shows the need for proper understanding. Two things seem to be known to the author of John. First, there are texts in Scripture that refer to Bethlehem as the origin of the Messiah (Mic. 5.2) and to the Messiah as offspring of the Davidic dynasty (2 Sam. 7.12-16; Ps. 89.3-4, 35-7; Isa. 9.7, 11.1; etc.; cf., e.g., Köstenberger 2007: 455); secondly, historical memory indicates that Jesus is not from Bethlehem but from Nazareth.[21] Scripture stands against historical memory; the solution for the contradiction may be found in the narrative setting. Within that setting, the model reader has more extensive information about Jesus's origin, because he/she has been led into text by the prologue (John 1.1-18), which clearly states the heavenly origin of Jesus, his identity as God, and his pre-existence with God his Father (1.1-3, 18). Thus, the reader knows that the quest for Jesus's earthly origin is of no importance; rather, the meaning of Jesus lies in his heavenly origin, so that any dialogue on Scripture and history is a misunderstanding of Jesus's true origin (cf. already 7.26-31).

Interestingly enough, according to the Gospel of John even misleading voices may be heard from Scripture that could be identified through the overall Johannine narrative and by hearing the word of the Johannine Jesus. Within the narrative context he is the one who is from God (7.33-4), who leads as God's gift (cf. 6.32b) into eternal life (7.37-8), and who is the 'light of the world' (8.12). The final orientation toward Scripture and its meaning is given by the word of Jesus and by the whole 'discourse universe' as unfolded by the Johannine narrative.

In the Gospel of John, 'Scripture' is an active figure that 'talks' and 'witnesses' about the narrative's hero, Jesus. Scripture is not just a writing

20   This is questioned by Wolter 2007: 350, who claims that the reference to ἡ γραφή always refers to a quotation from Scripture. John 7.42 shows that the concept of ἡ γραφή is a more open one – in the speeches of certain characters, Scripture becomes an oral figure that talks and does not just quote (cf. 7.38, 42).

21   On the possibility of historical knowledge behind John 7.42, cf. now Heil 2008: 114–28. Note his conclusion: 'Der vierte Evangelist zitiert diese Erwartung [sc. the Messiah will come from; ML.] im Mund der Gegner Jesu, lässt sie aber unkommentiert und ironisch stehen. ... Die Bethlehem-Tradition ist in seinen Augen gleich doppelt abwegig: Sie stimmt historisch nicht und versperrt vor allem auch die Einsicht in die eigentlich himmlische Herkunft Jesu.' On the likelihood of Johannine knowledge concerning the Bethlehem-tradition cf. Böttrich 2007: 318.

(or collection of writings) but an entity that tries itself to convince people *orally* about the true (= Johannine) identity of Jesus. Therefore, according to John, *Scripture is vivid and creative in building up new meanings and in convincing people*. It has authority because it speaks as a living witness about Jesus – as witness it bears testimony to Jesus and his meaning in line with Johannine Christological understanding. Outside that line, Scripture could speak, but it does not witness with authority, according to Johannine hermeneutics. Thus, Scripture functions as a character in the story: as a living witness, it speaks to characters in the story and to the addressees outside the story in an authoritative way, so long as it develops an understanding of Jesus that remains in line with Johannine Christology.

Scripture Talks and Jesus Talks: Who Authorizes Whom?

By definition, 'Scripture' is a written entity that, if accepted by a certain group of people, holds an authority in its own right (cf., e.g., Graham (1987: 142): 'texts that are revered as especially sacred and authoritative'). This was certainly true with regard to the place of the Jewish Scriptures within ancient Judaism and early Christianity (cf., e.g., Hengel 1989a: 249–58), even if the distinct extent of the accepted corpus was under debate within the community, as was true of some writings of Hebrew (and Greek) Scripture until the first century CE. The formula 'it is written' in the Fourth Gospel clearly indicates that the authority of this written medium was accepted within early Christianity and the Johannine world, with some adaptations (as shown above). The remainder of this discussion will further specify the authority and meaning of Scripture in the Fourth Gospel's narrative world.

Scripture as Written Authority and Argument for Jesus
According to John 2.17, after Jesus's death and resurrection the disciples remembered that he would be killed by his zeal for his Father's house in accordance with the written authority of Scripture.

> His disciples remembered that it was written: ...
> ἐμνήσθησαν οἱ μαθηταὶ αὐτοῦ ὅτι γεγραμμένον ἐστίν· ...

Scripture helps in understanding the past event after new events and after later insights were gained. This is an important point for the overall Johannine perspective on crucifixion and resurrection. With regard to John 2.17, the final meaning of the Scripture-based[22] statement that Jesus's zeal

---

22   It is not the place here to discuss the problems of the textual form of the quotation from Ps.LXX 68.10. On this question cf., e.g., Rüsen-Weinhold (2004: 292–4), who

will consume him is developed by the later narrated events of crucifixion and resurrection.[23] It is a post-Easter perspective on the narrative and its hero, Jesus, so that the voice of Jesus in the text is his voice remembered from a post-Easter Johannine interpretation (on the post-Easter hermeneutical perspective of the Gospel of John cf., e.g., Hoegen-Rohls 1996).

Here again, reference to Scripture points not to an absolute meaning of a written text or its letters, but to a hermeneutical process of *remembering* and *understanding* by memory – the post-Easter perspective of crucifixion and resurrection – that guides into a deeper meaning. The written text of the Gospel itself contributes to this process. As texts, both Scripture and Gospel are guided by the lead of another character mentioned in the Johannine narrative, the Paraclete (John 14.26: 'But the Advocate, the Holy Spirit, whom the Father will send in my name, will teach you everything [διδάξει πάντα], and remind you of all that I have said to you [ὑπομνήσει ὑμᾶς πάντα ἃ εἶπον ὑμῖν [ἐγώ]]'), who is sent after Jesus's crucifixion and resurrection and confirms the memory of Jesus in the written Gospel from the post-Easter Johannine perspective, including its understanding of Scripture.

Scripture as a written text can be used by different groups with different intentions in the Johannine narrative. There is Philip from Bethsaida, who understands Jesus as the one Moses and the prophets have written (ἔγραψεν) about (John 1.45). The Jewish opponents within the bread of life discourse in John 6 cite Scripture ('as it is written, "He gave them bread from heaven to eat"'[24]) to challenge Jesus and to underscore their own self-image as a distinguished group ('*our* ancestors ate the manna in the wilderness', v. 31). Nevertheless, their use of Scripture is not in accordance with the values of the Johannine world. Jesus shows that God is the origin of the bread from heaven and that he, Jesus, is the bread of life (vv. 35, 48) that his Father is giving right now (v. 32). In other cases again, the written text of Scripture functions in service of the identity formation of a group of Jesus's opponents

discusses the possibility that John 2.17 represents an older text form. Usually, the future form of καταφάγεται is understood as Johannine adoption referring to cross and resurrection: cf., e.g., Obermann 1996: 123.

23   Cf., e.g., Klauck, 'Geschrieben, erfüllt, vollendet: Die Schriftzitate in der Johannespassion', in Labahn, Scholtissek and Strotmann 2004: 146–7, and B. Kowalski, 'Anticipations of Jesus's Death in the Gospel of John', in Labahn 2007a: 591–608, who calls 'the quotation from Ps. 69.10 ... an anticipation of Jesus's death' (598).

24   Here again, this specific form of the quoted text cannot be found in the Old Testament. Verbal affinity with Ps. 78.24 suggests that this verse is the primary background for John 6.31-2 and the concept of the 'bread from heaven' (e.g., Menken 1996: 63–5), which is re-read in a Johannine manner in the 'bread of life' sayings. However, verbal influence from other OT manna texts (Exod. 16.4, 15; Neh. 9.15) cannot be ruled out, as is rightly observed by Daly-Denton (2004: 134). In any case, the Johannine text world may have influenced the wording or shaping of the quotation from Scripture; cf., e.g., Schnelle 2004: 138, n. 38.

(8.17: ἐν τῷ νόμῳ δὲ τῷ ὑμετέρῳ γέγραπται; 10.34: ἔστιν γεγραμμένον ἐν τῷ νόμῳ ὑμῶν; see also 15.25, which has a different structure: ἵνα πληρωθῇ ὁ λόγος ὁ ἐν τῷ νόμῳ αὐτῶν γεγραμμένος, followed by a quote introduced with ὅτι[25]). However, although the opponents claim knowledge/understanding of Scripture or of the hero behind that text (cf. esp. 9.28: ἡμεῖς δὲ τοῦ Μωϋσέως ἐσμὲν μαθηταί, with the reference to 'your law' in 10.34), it contains a truth that actually opposes their argument (as in the narrative flow of John 10) or proves the opponents to be wrong (in the context of John 8).

Such references to a written text do not claim an authority for the text that surpasses group boundaries, but rather use the text's imputed authority as a more effective argument for persuading the model reader of the truth of the text's claim. If even the text that the opponents claim to be *theirs* supports the point of the hero of the Johannine narrative, then it necessarily strongly supports *his* claim. Again, a written text in itself, or a sense of ownership of such a text, does not have any meaning on its own, for there is *a need to understand that text*. This means, within the Johannine framework, that the text must be related to the Johannine Jesus, his origin, his fate, and his benefit.

In the Fourth Gospel, Scripture is an *entity of reference*. Moses and the prophets, representing Scripture, refer in their writings to Jesus: 'We have found him [Jesus] about whom Moses in the law and also the prophets wrote' (ὃν ἔγραψεν Μωϋσῆς ἐν τῷ νόμῳ καὶ οἱ προφῆται εὑρήκαμεν, John 1.45; cf. 5.46: περὶ γὰρ ἐμοῦ [= Jesus] ἐκεῖνος ἔγραψεν [= Moses]). John 5.45-7 shows again that the positive relation to a written text does not guarantee correct understanding. The opponents accept the authority of Moses and his writings (εἰς ὃν ὑμεῖς ἠλπίκατε: 'on whom you have set your hope') but they do not accept the witness of Scripture (cf. 5.39, 46), which shows the glory of Jesus, the unity between Jesus the sent son and God his Father in giving eternal life, and also the authority of Jesus's words (5.47). As noted by Keener, '[t]he irony of being accused by a person or a document in which one trusted for vindication would not be lost on an ancient audience' (Keener 2003: 662, with ancient parallels.)

Two conclusions may be drawn on the basis of these observations. First, Scripture's authority and meaning as written text does not depend on possession of it or trust in it but rather on a right understanding of it.

25 There is again some difficulty in identifying the specific passage of scripture to which the Fourth Evangelist refers, as noted by Daly-Denton (2004: 130): 'There is no passage in the Scriptures with exactly the wording of John's "scripture".' On the reconstruction of possible pre-text(s) and their Johannine 'redaction', cf., e.g., Menken 1996: 142–5; Ps.LXX 69.5. It is again important to look at the overall Gospel text to see whether there may be intratextual influences at work on the quote from Scripture. As Daly-Denton, *ibid*, p. 131, observes, 'In the narrative setting of the quotation, five references to hatred of both Jesus and his disciples create the effect of a crescendo building up to "They hated me without a cause".'

According to the Fourth Gospel there is need for a correct – a Christological[26] – hermeneutic, so that the text comes to life. Secondly, regarding that Christological aim, Scripture comes to the same end in the oral media world as the words of Jesus (cf. Hübner 1995: 166), which are of similar authority to the Scripture (cf. Beutler 1996: 154). Thus, the opponents *in the text* attribute some kind of authority to the written Scriptures but do not share an adequate understanding of them, one that is in accordance with Scripture's authority according to the Johannine narrator. This makes it impossible for them to accept the debated authority of Jesus as the sent Son of God, despite Jesus's claims that Moses and Scripture bear witness on his behalf in his favour. Without proper understanding, the authority of a written text does not reach its potential. Here, there is also a *critique of written media* from a Johannine standpoint of communication and hermeneutical debate. The model reader following the Johannine narrative should not doubt the authority of Jesus and, therefore, she/he should be able to understand God's witness in the Scripture to Jesus as God's mighty giver of life.

In the section of the Fourth Gospel that describes the passion and death of Jesus, events in the Johannine narrative take place with the meaning that Scripture is an authority that will be 'fulfilled' (John 13.18; 17.12; 19.24, 36: ἵνα ἡ γραφὴ πληρωθῇ; John 19.24: ἵνα τελειωθῇ ἡ γραφή). It is necessary that there should be a traitor, that the clothes should not be divided, that Jesus should be thirsty on the cross, and that none of his bones should be 'broken'/ 'annulled'. In these cases, while John may have specific Scriptures in mind, it is not necessary for a specific passage to be quoted. The general reference to 'fulfilment' seems to indicate that any recently narrated event is a fulfilment of Scripture in a broader sense. It is not a specific reference text but rather God's will as expressed through the medium of those documents that must be fulfilled, and there is a hermeneutical process through which the meaning of Scriptures and the narrated events are combined and identified. It seems that according to the narrative line of thought, 'the Johannine crucifixion narrative is the fulfilment of ἡ γραφή and ὁ λόγος' (Moloney 2005: 462).

John 6.45 is a good illustration that such an understanding of God's will is to be found in Scripture, here by portraying the written text alongside an act of orality.

It is written in the prophets,
'And they shall all be *taught* by God.'

---

26   Cf. the pointed statement by Müller (2004: 158): 'Die Schrift ist sozusagen leer, indem Jesus der ist, der ihre Worte mit Inhalt füllt'. Müller refers here to the hermeneutical reflections of Menken. Perhaps the statement is a little too sharp. It is necessary to say that Scripture without understanding its witness to Jesus as God's Son is empty – and it is the narrated oral Jesus and the oral voice of Scripture who with their words bring that content into the mind of the model reader.

Everyone
> who has *heard and learned* from the Father
comes to me (emphasis added).
ἔστιν γεγραμμένον ἐν τοῖς προφήταις·
καὶ ἔσονται πάντες διδακτοὶ θεοῦ·
πᾶς
> ὁ ἀκούσας παρὰ τοῦ πατρὸς καὶ μαθὼν
ἔρχεται πρὸς ἐμε (emphasis added).

With regard to his opponents and their lack of belief, Jesus refers to the Scripture. His quote from Isa. 54.13 helps to explain how people come to Jesus: it is God's gift (cf. John 6.37, 44; see Theobald 1996: 315–41). People require the help of God to arrive at a proper understanding of Jesus, to believe in him and to come to life. Such assistance takes the form of teaching, an oral act that is defined by Jesus as hearing and learning (also oral acts) from God. God addresses those people whom he invites to come to Jesus as their teacher; the reference to Scripture is not only an attempt to name a proof-text but also to name one of the ways that God teaches people. Another way is Jesus, who lets his addressees know what he has learned from God (5.19).

If this understanding is correct, the witness to God's will in Scripture is, according to the Johannine narrative, an act of teaching on God's side and an act of hearing on people's side. The latter could best be understood as an act of understanding or, *ad malum parte*, an act of misunderstanding.

With Johannine references to Scripture, then, we are not entering a written media world, but rather a 'cosmos' of hermeneutical processes in which the written Scripture text takes on authority when it participates in the oral world by being heard and understood, or misunderstood. In the process of persuading people, Scripture only succeeds if it 'talks'. John 12.14-16 underscores this interpretation. Again, a passage of the written Scripture text is aligned with narrated events, but it is clearly shown that the combination of the text and the event to which it refers is not evident to everyone. As in John 2.22, the understanding of the relationship between event and Scripture comes only later.

His disciples did not understand these things at first;
but when Jesus was glorified,
then they remembered
> that these things had been written of him
> and had been done to him.
ταῦτα οὐκ ἔγνωσαν αὐτοῦ οἱ μαθηταὶ τὸ πρῶτον,
ἀλλ’ ὅτε ἐδοξάσθη Ἰησοῦς
τότε ἐμνήσθησαν
> ὅτι ταῦτα ἦν ἐπ’ αὐτῷ γεγραμμένα
> καὶ ταῦτα ἐποίησαν αὐτῷ (John 12.16)

There is authority in the written Scripture text that encourages readers to view the narrated Johannine event as the fulfilment of the whole of the Scriptures or of a specific passage. Although John 12.14-15 does refer to its specific reference text in Zech. LXX 9.9, which is again reworked in a Johannine manner by including parallel influences from Gen. LXX 49.11 (cf. Menken 1996: 79–97), as fulfilment, in 12.16 the written text is referred to as a general background for the interpretation. The entry of Jesus into Jerusalem, like the Messiah and King of Israel, has already been announced in the written text of Scripture. One may refer to that announcement as an expression of God's will (e.g., Schnelle 2004: 224) that comes to light in the act of Jesus, so that Jesus again is portrayed as the obedient son of his Father (cf., e.g., John 12.27).

Here again, the main point regarding the relationship between oral and written media is that the text of Scripture needs to be understood. The authoritative text realizes its meaning by being understood in relation to the deeds and words of Jesus, which are recorded in John's Gospel and which lead to belief in Jesus as the God-sent son.

The Johannine community participates in such a concept of authority for, as John 10.35 states, the Scripture cannot be 'broken' or 'annulled' (NRSV; οὐ δύναται λυθῆναι ἡ γραφή). The basic and reader-guiding function of Scripture for the Johannine community can also be determined from the frequent formula 'so that scripture might be fulfilled' (ἵνα ἡ γραφὴ πληρωθῇ), which appears in the second half of the Fourth Gospel to interpret Jesus's 'Passion' (13.18; 19.24) and his overall mission (17.12, cf. Moloney 2005: 461).

The reference to Scripture is not simply a reference to proof-texts. It is part of a hermeneutical process that is largely concerned with the actual presentation of Jesus as the hero in the Johannine narrative world. Zumstein claims a dialectical relationship between reference text and reception text (Zumstein 2008: 134). Even on the intratextual level, there is a dialectical element. The event is described as fulfilment of Scripture and participates in the authority that the narrative ascribes to the Scripture as written text. On the other hand, the narrated event is the form in which Scripture actually 'bears witness' to the Johannine Jesus, and through that witness it becomes an authoritative text. Scripture is not 'annulled' but is set in a distinct relationship with the Johannine narrative, which also proclaims its own self-authority as a written text (20.30-1).

At the point where the actors of the text or the model reader come into focus, we enter an oral perspective. Scripture 'talks' and God teaches through Scripture as Jesus does through the Johannine text, so that anyone who becomes part of the Johannine 'discourse universe' 'has heard and learned from the Father' about Jesus his son, and therefore comes to Jesus to receive ultimate life.

The 'Words' of Scripture and of Jesus: John 2.22

Going against the Synoptics, the Johannine narrator places the episode of Jesus's cleansing of the temple at the start of his public ministry. Many interpreters understand this narrative strategy as an indication that the beginning of the Johannine narrative is already referring to its end – the passion, crucifixion and resurrection of Jesus (cf., e.g., Schnelle 1996; Kowalski 1998: 176–340).

After his first and programmatic miracle of turning water into wine (John 2.1-11),[27] Jesus goes to Jerusalem for the first time at Passover to cast the merchants and money-changers out of the temple. The narrative structure of the episode moves from the 'cleansing' of the temple to a reflection on Jesus's authority to perform such a prophetic act (v. 18). Jesus replies that his opponents should 'Destroy this temple, and in three days I will raise it up.' The reply leads into typical Johannine misunderstanding: the opponents find reference in Jesus's words to the Herodian temple, although Jesus, as the narrator explicitly states, is referring to the 'temple' of his body (περὶ τοῦ ναοῦ τοῦ σώματος αὐτοῦ).

John 2.22 contains the final commentary on the cleansing of the temple, in which the omniscient narrator shows his insight into even the future thoughts of the characters in the narrative.

> After he was raised from the dead,
> his disciples remembered
>   that he had said this;
> and they believed the scripture
> and the word
>   that Jesus had spoken.

> ὅτε οὖν ἠγέρθη ἐκ νεκρῶν,
> ἐμνήσθησαν οἱ μαθηταὶ αὐτοῦ
>   ὅτι τοῦτο ἔλεγεν,
> καὶ ἐπίστευσαν τῇ γραφῇ
> καὶ τῷ λόγῳ
>   ὃν εἶπεν ὁ Ἰησοῦς.

The memory of the disciples (ἐμνήσθησαν οἱ μαθηταὶ αὐτοῦ) dates to a future (ὅτε οὖν ἠγέρθη ἐκ νεκρῶν) that lies beyond narrated time: *after Jesus was raised from the dead* they remember Jesus's words about raising the temple of his body (2.18, 21). In the horizon of this future (post-Easter) memory, the narrator portrays his characters' belief in Scripture that foreshadows Jesus rising from death, and in the word (singular) that Jesus speaks. The general perspective of the Johannine post-Easter hermeneutic is established.

It is interesting to see that the only reference to Scripture in the episode of the cleansing of the temple appears in v. 17, which refers to Ps. 69 (68).10. Ps.LXX 68.10 characterizes Jesus's action as 'zeal' (ζῆλος) for his Father's house, and in this way explains what he is actually doing. However, it also may be read as a reference to the upcoming discussion about his death, inasmuch as 'consume me' (καταφάγεταί με) might refer to the destruction of the body in death. In v. 17 Scripture talks about a zeal that destroys Jesus, while v. 19 refers to an act of killing Jesus by his opponents. But while both of these statements are consistent with events that will occur later in the Fourth Gospel, the actual reference to Scripture in v. 17 does not completely illustrate Jesus's claim in v. 19, nor the comment in v. 21. This means that the model reader is asked to understand v. 22 not as a reference to an actual, specific passage of Scripture, but rather in a more general sense.

The correct line of interpretation lies in the first part of v. 22. The narrator refers to the 'word' of Jesus, a reference to Jesus's claim in v. 19. John 20 clearly proves – and the Thomas episode is something like a proof section – that Jesus's words about raising his body are true and according to God's will, although the narrator does not refer back to 2.22 in John 20. If the word that Jesus 'had spoken' becomes true within the scope of the narrative, it also authorizes the Scripture itself. Jesus's disciples believe in the Scripture insofar as it is a text that stands alongside the words of Jesus; the Scriptures are true insofar as his words are true. Scripture, as part of the written media world, establishes its reliability to the extent that it functions in accordance with the spoken words of Jesus. The oral Jesus is thus ultimately the authority behind the written text.

The Fulfilled Scripture Speaks: John 19.24, 37

The text of John 19.24 is disputed (cf. Labahn 2007: 126–36) because the common Johannine formula ἵνα ἡ γραφὴ πληρωθῇ in its pure form is not found in all manuscripts. A number of manuscripts add ἡ λέγουσα, which is marked in the text of NA[27] in brackets as a possible but not certain element of the reconstruction of the oldest text of the Gospel of John. There is, however, no need to eliminate the description of the Scripture 'speaking' (cf. Obermann 1996: 283).[28] Two thoughts regarding the oral/written media interface are combined here. On one hand, the written text is referred to as an authoritative entity that reaches fulfilment through a narrated event. On the other hand, the line between that event and the authoritative reference text is marked by a quotation, which here is characterized as an oral act ('which says'). Scripture again takes up the role of a narrative character,

---

27   On the theory that ἀρχὴν τῶν σημείων (NRSV: 'the first of his signs') not only refers to the numbering of the signs but also portrays this event as a model for other signs, cf. Labahn 1999: 71.

28   For an alternate view see, e.g., Beutler 1998: 300.

referring to its own fulfilment by naming the relationship between God's will mentioned in the reference text and the action happening in the Johannine narrative world. Through an oral act, Scripture gives the interpretation of that event.

The same is true with regard to John 19.37. The humiliating act at the cross that leads to a flow of water and blood from Jesus's side – which refers first to the actual death of Jesus, but may also be a Johannine hint at the institution of the sacraments – finds a different interpretation in John 19.35f. The first witness, the Beloved Disciple, supports the truth of the narrator's story (19.35); the second witness, Scripture, refers to its own fulfilment (vv. 36-7). Again, a narrated event within the Johannine passion narrative is related to Scripture, which itself mentions the identity between the written texts (v. 37), including 'another scripture' (ἑτέρα γραφή), and the narrated act.

It seems that the narration of the passion story needs special support from Scripture and that Scripture is therefore used as a character, to which the possible addressees of the Gospel ascribe undisputed authority, to provide the right interpretation in 'hearing and learning' from the word of Scripture: it is according to God's will that Jesus returns to his heavenly Father through the events told in the passion narrative.

Conclusion

Without doubt, the Gospel of John is a written text, a network of repetition and variation (cf. the various approaches and interpretations in van Belle, Labahn and Maritz 2009), a text showing its self-consciousness as written entity. It is a text made for readers ready and able to understand (cf., e.g., Thyen (2005: 4): the Gospel of John is a 'Buch für Leser … die des Lesens fähig sind'), and for reading aloud again and again so that new audiences may apply to themselves the conclusions of the model reader.

Considering the semantic field of the word γράφω, one may conclude that the Johannine text shows a clear sensitivity to the distinction between oral and written in the ancient media world. It refers to written documents as texts that have a special finality and authority, and the Johannine narrative characterizes itself as belonging to that sphere of communication, demanding authority and finality. As evidenced by the process of *relecture* (particularly in John 21), it seems that early readers in the Johannine School accepted the Gospel's claims.

The same balanced approach can also be detected with regard to the Johannine use of Scripture as authority and argument in the process of persuasion within the Johannine narrative world and beyond. The Scripture is referred to as a written text, most clearly shown in those references which use the verb form γεγραμμένον. As a written authority, Scripture could and should be addressed and searched into, but to find its true (= Johannine) meaning requires a hermeneutical process that the Fourth Evangelist describes as an oral enactment. The author's creative use of Scripture is based in a mindset that interprets Scripture's voice itself as creative, persuasive, and based on Jesus, who is himself God's word (*logos*) from the beginning.

The hero of the text is the oral Johannine Jesus, and Jesus and the narrator both also refer to the Scripture as an oral actor. As written text (γραφή), Scripture is a character that speaks in the Johannine narrative world. Scripture talks, and even does so in a creative manner on the side of John's main character, Jesus. The act of conversation addresses the model reader, and in the process of reading the text it also address the real reader. As a written text, the Fourth Gospel shows a sensitivity for the meaning of oral speech as an act of communication and address that introduces a herme-neutical process by which the characters in the text, and the model reader, are led to a crisis: if he/she shares the Johannine 'discourse universe' and believes, she/he will receive eternal life; if not, he/she is already judged.

Scriptures function as a character that speaks to other characters in the story, but at the same time they speak directly to the audience of the Gospel. This would also be oral speech, though, because normally these words would be read aloud to a church gathering, so that the audience would hear the Scriptures saying these things.

If these different voices may be summarized, it must be said that according to the Johannine narrative Scripture as written text deserves authority particularly because it is a text based on God and on the pre-existent *Logos*/Jesus. Scripture is clearly part of a medium, writing, which carries a special importance and authority, based on the foregoing authority of the pre-existent *Logos*/Jesus.

PART III

JOHN IN THE MEDIUM OF MEMORY

Chapter 9

JOHN'S GOSPEL AND THE ORAL GOSPEL TRADITION

James D. G. Dunn

This paper is part of an ongoing attempt to make sense of the way in which the New Testament Gospels present the mission of Jesus. The starting point is the character of the Synoptic tradition: each of the first three Gospels tells basically the same story, but with different details, different groupings of episodes and teachings, different introductions and conclusions, and often different emphases. Yet it is clearly the same tradition, the same episodes, the same themes, and the same substantive points in the teaching. These differences, I have argued elsewhere, are not best explained on the theory of literary dependency, in terms of a process best described as copying and editing. That thesis works well for some of the material, but certainly not for the whole body of shared tradition. The better solution, I have argued, is to recognize that for most of the time between Jesus's own mission and the writing of the earliest Gospel (probably Mark) the Jesus tradition was in oral form, circulating through the early churches, transmitted to new churches, and used in regular instruction and worship in these churches (see here Dunn 2003; Dunn 2005). Specialists are largely agreed that a common feature of oral tradition is 'the same yet different': retellings of the same story or teaching, but with different details that the storyteller or teacher deemed appropriate in the act of delivery or performance. In the words of Werner Kelber, 'Variability and stability, conservatism and creativity, evanescence and unpredictability all mark the pattern of oral transmission', all contributing to the 'oral principle of "variation within the same"' (Kelber 1983: 33, 54, quoting Havelock 1963: 92, 147, 184). Or, as Alan Dundes puts the same point, '"multiple existence" and "variation" [are] the two most salient characteristics of folklore' (Dundes 1999: 18–19). What I have always found exciting about this thesis is that it explains so well why such a high proportion of the Synoptic Jesus tradition has precisely this character of stability and diversity, of the same yet different.

So far as the current volume is concerned, I should at once note three basic premises on which my thesis builds. First, Jesus made a considerable impact on his disciples, an impact that is clear from the Jesus tradition of the Gospels and that is expressed to a greater or lesser degree in the tradition itself. From the impression made by Jesus, as expressed in the first place by the Synoptic tradition, we may discern a clear outline of the mission and person who made that impact. Secondly, Jesus was remembered in somewhat diverse ways, as again expressed in 'the same yet different' character of the Synoptic tradition. The shared impact was expressed differently; the shared tradition took different forms in divergent tellings of the same material. Thirdly, the differences of impact and tradition indicate that the remembered past of Jesus was not uniform or learned or repeated in parrot-like fashion. Rather, the remembered tradition was also moulded tradition, adapted in some measure to the divergent interests of the teacher and community celebrating that memory. I should probably stress the fact that this thesis is not built primarily on interdisciplinary theories of memory, but much more directly on the character of the Synoptic Jesus tradition itself. It is because this thesis explains so well the strange character of the Jesus tradition ('the same yet different') that I find it persuasive.

   John's Gospel, however, adds a further dimension or twist to the discussion, precisely because the formula which so well describes the Synoptic tradition ('the same yet different') does not seem to fit John's Gospel in its relation to the other three New Testament Gospels – 'different', certainly, but in what sense or to what degree 'the same'? On any reckoning, the contrast between the first three canonical Gospels and the fourth is striking. It is often summed up, and can be typified, in the following terms.

The Synoptics	The Gospel of John
Matthew and Luke begin with virgin conception/birth	Begins with incarnation of pre-existence *Logos*
Jesus goes to Jerusalem only for the last week of his mission; only one Passover is mentioned	Jesus is active in Judea for a large part of his mission; mission extends over three Passovers
Jesus speaks little of himself, with nothing quite like John's 'I am' sayings	Jesus speaks much of himself, most notably in the 'I am' sayings
Jesus calls for faith in God	Jesus calls for faith in himself
The central theme of Jesus's preaching is the kingdom of God	The kingdom of God barely figures in Jesus's discourses

Jesus often speaks of forgiveness and repentance	Jesus never speaks of repentance, and speaks of forgiveness only in 20.23
Jesus typically speaks in aphorisms and parables	Jesus engages in lengthy dialogues and circuitous discussion
Jesus speaks only occasionally of eternal life	Jesus speaks regularly of eternal life[1]
Strong concern for the poor and sinners	Little concern for the poor and sinners[2]
Jesus is notable for his ministry of exorcism	No exorcisms

Older harmonizing explanations, keen to affirm that John's Gospel is as historical in its presentation as the Synoptics, tried to explain such differences in terms of the different audiences to whom Jesus spoke – the Synoptics recall Jesus's teaching to the crowds while John recalls Jesus's teaching to his disciples, etc. (cf. Dunn 1983: 314 n. 11; Anderson 2006: 61; Blomberg 2001). But as David Friedrich Strauss pointed out long ago, the style of Jesus's speech within John's own Gospel is consistent, whether Jesus is depicted as speaking to Nicodemus, or to the woman at the well, or to 'the Jews', or to his disciples (Strauss 1972: 384–6). Further, the style is very similar to that of the Johannine John the Baptist and, indeed, to that of 1 John. The inference is inescapable that the style is that of the *Evangelist* or of the Evangelist's tradition, rather than that of *Jesus* (see Anderson 1996: 58–9; Verheyden 2007).

Given this further dimension of the discussion of how Jesus was remembered by the first Christians, what are the consequences of bringing in John's Gospel for the case I have made for the character of the Synoptic tradition as oral tradition? To be more precise: if the Synoptic tradition provides

---

1   Mark 10.30 parr.; Matt. 25.46; John 3.15-16, 36; 4.14, 36; 5.24, 39; 6.27, 40, 47, 54, (68); 10.28; 12.25, 50; 17.2-3.

2   Texts like Matt. 5.3//Luke 6.20, Matt. 11.5//Luke 7.22, and Mark 10.21, 12.42-3 (all on 'the poor'), and Mark 2.15-17 parr. and Matt. 11.19//Luke 7.34 (on 'sinners') have been sufficient to indicate to most recent treatments of the historical Jesus that these were strong concerns of Jesus himself. By contrast, John 12.5-8 and 13.29, and 9.16, 24-5, 31 would never give that impression.

good evidence of the impact made by Jesus, of the speech forms in which the earliest memories of Jesus were formulated by the immediate disciples of Jesus, and of the way (the groupings, ordering and emphases) in which the Jesus tradition was used and transmitted in the earliest churches, how do we take best account of the different character of John's Gospel, and how does that different character affect the case for the oral traditional character of the Synoptics? Is John's Gospel not also the product of oral tradition? Is John's Gospel also *remembering* Jesus? Does John's Gospel indicate that the oral tradition thesis is inadequate to explain the way Jesus was remembered and the way the Jesus tradition was celebrated and passed on? The potential corollaries are of major significance for our understanding of how the Gospel tradition reached the state in which we now have it, for our understanding of the function of the Jesus tradition, and for our understanding of how and why Jesus was remembered.

The Gospel Format

First, it should be stated clearly that *the differences between John's Gospel and the Synoptic Gospels should not be exaggerated.* John's Gospel is a *Gospel* in that it shares the sense and format of the other three canonical Gospels. It recognizes that there is a story to be told, with a clear beginning, a development charting the actions and teaching of Jesus, and a climactic conclusion. Its very form defines this as 'Gospel': that John the Baptist is the beginning of the Gospel; that integral to the Gospel is the story of how Jesus both lived and taught his mission, as witnessed by his disciples; that the gospel story drives towards the culmination of Jesus's death and resurrection (see the list of narrative and structural parallels in Dunn 1999: 355–6).

The evidence suggests that it was Paul, the earliest Christian writer known to us, who baptized the noun 'gospel' (εὐαγγέλιον) into Christian vocabulary[3] and, further, made 'gospel' the term that summed up the earliest kerygmatic and catechetical tradition of the first Christians. In so doing, Paul was no doubt conscious of the wider usage of the word, particularly of the good news of the *pax Romana* established by Augustus. But it is more likely that Paul was still more conscious of the Isaianic vision of one who would 'preach the good news' (εὐαγγελίζεσθαι; see esp. Isa. 40.9; 52.7; 60.6; 61.1), a theme on which he himself drew (Rom 10.15) and which had also memorably inspired Jesus's own mission (Matt 11.5//Luke 7.22; Luke 4.16-21; cf. Luke 6.20//Matt. 5.3; see Dunn 1998: 164-9). The fact that the earliest of the four canonical Gospels (Mark) uses the same word in its opening sentence – 'The beginning of the εὐαγγέλιον of Jesus Christ'

---

3   No less than 60 of the 76 New Testament occurrences of the term appear in the Pauline letters.

(Mark 1.1) – is striking. For Mark uses it in a way which equally suggests that the term was already shifting from the *content* of what he was about to narrate to the character of the *narration* itself (see Guelich 1983: 204–16; Burridge 2004: 186–9). What Mark was writing was not simply conveying the Gospel, but was Gospel itself. Just as in Paul's usage we see εὐαγγέλιον emerging as a Christian technical term for the message preached by apostles and evangelists, so in Mark's usage we see the emergence of the idea of the Gospel as a *written document*. This also suggests that it was Mark, or the tradition on which he already drew, who framed the character of a 'Gospel', the definitive form of the Christian Gospel – as noted earlier, an account of Jesus's mission, beginning with John the Baptist and climaxing in his death and resurrection.

We should also note that it is at precisely this point that John's Gospel diverges from other documents referred to and now commonly described as 'Gospels' – the Gospel of Thomas, the Gospel of Philip, the Gospel of Judas, etc. Although these books contain what purports to be teaching of Jesus, they have none of the characteristics which attracted the title 'Gospel' (the good news of Jesus's death and resurrection) and which gave a 'Gospel' its definitive shape – a narrative account, beginning with the Baptist, within which Jesus's actions and teachings were set and which climaxed in Jesus's passion. *For all the freedom it displays in the presentation of Jesus and despite all its differences from the Synoptics, John's Gospel is far closer to them than to the apocryphal Gospels.* From all this we may deduce that John's Gospel, or the Johannine tradition on which John's Gospel is based, stood well within the mainstream of tradition, which summed up the good news of Jesus as 'Gospel' and which followed Mark's definitive expression of a written Gospel. The apocryphal Gospels, by contrast, evidence a different way in which the influence of Jesus was envisaged – a way that increasingly diverged, it would appear, from mainstream Christianity, even a mainstream broad enough to include John's Gospel.

The relevance of this to our question about the relation of John's Gospel to the oral Jesus tradition is fairly obvious. Paul's formulation of the story of Jesus as 'Gospel' belongs to the first decade or two of Christianity's existence. And the tradition on which Luke draws to formulate the preaching to the Gentile centurion Cornelius in Acts 10.34-43 already contains what was to become the Markan pattern of Gospel: beginning with John the Baptist, giving an account of Jesus's healing ministry (with a preceding reference to preaching the good news of peace), and climaxing in his death and resurrection (see Dunn 2008: #21.3c). Since Paul's formulation of the Christian message as 'Gospel' took place during the period when the Jesus tradition was still predominantly in oral form, and since the Acts 10 tradition also harks back to the period of oral tradition, we may infer that *the shaping of the Jesus tradition as 'Gospel', and in the mould that Mark provided (or indicated), was already taking place during that period when the Jesus tradition was still being told in oral form.* So long as we avoid the unjustified and misleading impression that the Jesus

tradition existed orally only in fragmentary aphoristic forms or small collec-
tions of teaching material or of stories about Jesus (a key mistake of the Jesus
Seminar; see Dunn 2003: 245–8), then it becomes entirely plausible that the
earliest tradents regularly retold the Jesus tradition conscious of the Gospel
shape of the material as a whole and often providing mini-Gospel presentations, as are still evident in the Acts 10 tradition and perhaps also in Mark
2.1–3.6, as well as in the passion narrative.[4]

In short, the Gospel-shape of John's material already attests to the
influence of the oral Jesus tradition on John's Gospel, and perhaps the
direct dependence of John's Gospel on such tradition. The grounds for these
conclusions will become clearer as we proceed.

The John the Baptist Tradition as the Beginning of the Gospel

Each of the Evangelists fills out the same Gospel framework in his own way.
As a result, the Gospels they produced provide many fascinating parallels
– fascinating just because they are parallel, versions of the same or similar
tradition, while also diverse in their detail and function. One of these
parallels is their common starting point: the John the Baptist tradition as the
beginning of the Gospel. Here I begin my closer examination of the shared
and the distinctive traditions (see also Dodd 1963: 248–78).

The shared tradition is clear:

- The mission of Jesus's immediate predecessor was characterized
  by a (once-only) baptism (Mark 1.4 parr.); he was known as 'the
  Baptizer' (ὁ βαπτίζων; Mark 6.4, 14) or 'the Baptist' (ὁ βαπτιστή
  ς; Matt. 3.; 11.11-12; Mark 6.25; 8.28; Luke 7.20, 33; 9.19; see
  further Dunn 2003: 355–7); and, he practised his mission of baptizing in the Jordan river (Mark 1.5, 9; Matt. 3.5-6, 13; Luke 3.3;
  John 1.28).
- The success of the Baptist's mission in attracting so many to be
  baptized is clearly stated or implied (Mark 1.5//Matt. 3.5; Luke
  3.21; cf. John 1.19-25; 3.25).
- Isaiah 40.3 is cited to identify the Baptist as 'the voice crying out
  in the wilderness; make straight the way of the Lord' (John 1.23;
  Mark 1.3; Matt.3.3//Luke 3.4).[5]

---

4   C. H. Dodd suggested that the transitional passages and topographical notices in
John were 'traditional data summarizing periods in the ministry of Jesus, with indications
of the places where they were spent' (1963: 243).

5   Mark gives the quotation a headline role, combined with Exod. 23.20; Luke
extends the quotation (Isa. 40.3-5), presumably to round it off with the reference to 'the
salvation of God' (Luke 3.4-6); John abbreviates Isa. 40.3 by combining the last two lines
into one (John 1.23).

- The Baptist contrasts his own status with that of the one to come – 'I am not worthy to untie the thong of his sandal' (John 1.27; Mark 1.7; Luke 3.16; Matt 3.11).[6]
- The Baptist contrasts his own mission of baptizing in water with the coming one's baptizing in Holy Spirit (John 1.26, 33; Matt. 3.11//Luke 3.16; Mark 1.8).[7]
- That Jesus was baptized by the Baptist is taken for granted, though John does not actually say so explicitly, whereas the event is described by the others (John 1.31; Mark 1.9 parr.).
- All four are clear that the central and climactic element of the encounter between the Baptist and Jesus is the descent of the Holy Spirit 'like a dove' (John 1.32-3; Mark 1.10 parr.);[8] this is the real beginning of the Gospel (cf. Acts 10.38).
- The descent of the Spirit is tied to Jesus's status as the Son of God: in the Synoptics, by the declaration of the heavenly voice which accompanied the descent of the Spirit ('You are my son, the beloved one, with you I am well pleased'; Mark 1.11 parr.); in John, by the Baptist's testimony that, because he saw the Spirit descending and remaining on Jesus, he can 'bear witness that this man is the Son of God' (John 1.34).

There can be little doubt that all four Evangelists were drawing on the same tradition: the memory of Jesus's first disciples that his mission emerged out of the successful mission of the Baptist and from what happened at the Jordan when Jesus was baptized by the Baptist – that is, with the descent of the Holy Spirit on him, confirming his status as God's Son. Almost the only part of the Baptist's teaching recalled by all four Evangelists is the contrast between his own baptizing in water and the coming one's baptizing in the Spirit, which strongly suggests that their consciousness of having been given the Spirit was

6 The variations are typical of oral retellings of the same tradition: John uses ἄξιος ('worthy') while the others use ἱκανός ('qualified/competent'); in Matthew's version, the Baptist says, 'I am not qualified/competent to *carry* his sandals'; John has singular 'sandal' while the others have the plural 'sandals'.

7 In Matthew, the Baptist baptizes with water 'for/into repentance' (3.11); Matthew and Luke have the Baptist predicting that the one to come will baptize 'in Holy Spirit *and fire*' (Matt. 3.11//Luke 3.16), whereas Mark and John have the Baptist speaking only of baptizing in Holy Spirit (Mark 1.8; John 3.33); the Synoptics predict that the one to come 'will baptize in Holy Spirit', whereas John portrays this as the coming one's defining characteristic ('the one who baptizes in the Holy Spirit'; John 3.22).

8 Mark indicates that the Spirit descended 'into' Jesus (1.10), whereas Matthew and Luke describe the Spirit descending 'upon' Jesus (Matt. 3.16//Luke 3.22) and John emphasizes that 'the Spirit descended and remained on him' (John 1.33). Mark gives the event an apocalyptic character: the heavens 'split' (σχιζομένους). Luke notes that the Spirit descended while Jesus was praying (3.21), and John has the Baptist admitting that he did not know him until the Spirit descended upon him (John 1.33).

one of the self-defining characteristics of the early Christians across the range of churches represented by the four Gospels, a claim to being the beneficiaries of the promised baptism in Spirit predicted by the Baptist. Both emphases – that Jesus's mission began with the Spirit's descent on him after he had been baptized by the Baptist, and that the first Christians experienced the Spirit directly for themselves – explain why the earliest Christians had to begin their account of the Gospel with the preaching and mission of the Baptist. We can take it for granted that this memory and this basic story were integral to the oral tradition of the first disciples and churches from the earliest days.

At the same time, an equally striking feature is the different emphases that the Evangelists have drawn from the Baptist tradition. I note the most obvious of these distinctive features.

- For the Synoptics, a central and defining feature of the Baptist's preaching and mission was his call for *repentance* (Matt. 3.2; Matt. 3.8//Luke 3.8) – indeed, his baptism was 'a baptism of repentance' (Mark 1.4; Luke 3.3; Acts 13.24; 19.4; cf. Matt. 3.11); John, by contrast, never uses the terms 'repent' or 'repentance'.
- Whereas Mark and Luke do not hesitate to describe the Baptist's baptism as a 'baptism of repentance for the forgiveness of sins' (Mark 1.4; Luke 3.3), Matthew speaks of the Baptist's baptism only as a baptism 'into repentance' (Matt. 3.11)[9] and John never uses the noun denoting 'forgiveness'.
- Both Matthew and Luke retain an account of the Baptist's strongly judgemental preaching, accounts which are so verbally similar that they could come only from a shared source, already in Greek and probably already written, usually described as Q tradition (Matt. 3.7-10, 12//Luke 3.7-9, 17). Luke also has a unique passage on the Baptist's ethical teaching (Luke 3.10-14). By contrast, Mark in contrast has no note of judgement: the 'fire' which features so strongly in the Q version (Matt. 3.10-12//Luke 3.9, 16-17) is entirely lacking in Mark, where the one to come will baptize in Holy Spirit, not in Holy Spirit and fire (Mark 1.8). This is usually explained by the fact that what was regarded as the fulfilment of the Baptist's prediction only involved an endowing with the Spirit (classically expressed in the account of the day of Pentecost; Acts 2), so there was little need to recall the fuller preaching of the Baptist.
- Matthew reflects an obvious embarrassment in some Christian circles that Jesus had undergone a baptism 'of repentance', por-

---

9   Matthew uniquely inserts the same phrase in Matt 26.28 ('This is my blood of the covenant which is poured out for many for the forgiveness of sins'), perhaps in an attempt to link (or limit) the forgiveness of sins to Jesus's sacrificial death.

traying the Baptist protesting against the request that Jesus should receive his baptism (Matt. 3.13-15). John in effect meets a similar challenge by focusing almost exclusively on the Baptist's role as a *witness* to Jesus (already signalled in John 1.6-8; see here Wink 1968: 87–106). Thus, in the Gospel of John:

o the contrast between the Baptist and Jesus is heightened (already in 1.15; also 1.30, and elaborated in 3.27-36);

o the Baptist makes a triple confession ('he confessed and did not deny it, but confessed'; 1.20) that he was not the Messiah, nor even Elijah or the prophet (1.20-1);

o the Baptist attests that Jesus is 'the Lamb of God who takes away the sin of the world' (1.29, 36), already foreshadowing Jesus's passion;

o the Baptist himself emphasizes that the main, or indeed the only, purpose of his mission is to reveal Jesus to Israel, disclosing his true status as the Son of God (1.31, 34).

It is fascinating, then, to see how the same basic tradition was and could be retold and elaborated, or curtailed, to bring out the different emphases that the Evangelists wished to highlight or, indeed, which had already become familiar in the use made of the Baptist tradition in their churches or in the tradition on which they drew. Nothing tells against this already happening during the time when the Jesus tradition was almost entirely in oral mode. To be sure, the Fourth Gospel's use of the tradition suggests that John was consciously combating what he regarded as a too high evaluation of the Baptist (a hypothesis usually traced back to Baldensperger 1898; see also e.g. Brown 1966/1970: 1.lxviii–lxx). Hence the sustained downgrading of the Johannine Baptist in relation to Jesus: he was not the light, but came only to testify to the light (John 1.6-7, 31); the Messiah always ranked before him (1.15, 30); he was not the Messiah, as he himself triply confessed (1.20; 3.28); he had to decrease while Jesus increased (3.30); he came from the earth, whereas Jesus came from above (3.31). Of course, all this comes in typical Johannine language, so we can certainly speak of the Johannine elaboration of the earlier tradition, whether that elaboration is to be traced to the Evangelist himself or to the (elaborated) traditions on which he drew. But we should also note that *the distinctive Johannine emphasis is rooted in the earlier tradition* of the Baptist speaking of the one to come possessing a far higher status than his own ('I am not worthy to untie the thong of his sandals'; Mark 1.7 parr.).

The Johannine version of the Baptist tradition is thus a good example of a tradition deeply rooted in the memory of the first disciples that was retold in different ways. All these retellings drew from the these earliest memories, some abbreviating the traditions selectively, presumably in order that the tradition might speak more meaningfully to new audiences, some elaborating the traditions, but as an elaboration of early emphases rather than as an invention and insertion of entirely new emphases. The elaboration created new material but only to reinforce the earlier emphasis, perhaps against a new, challenging evaluation of the Baptist's mission. John's version of the Baptist tradition, therefore, illustrates both the fixity of core material in the Baptist tradition and the ways in which key elements in that tradition could be developed and retold in unexpected fashion as the language and needs of the Johannine churches changed.

The Body of the Narrative

As already indicated, each of the Evangelists fills out the Gospel framework in his own way. It is easy to conclude from a superficial comparison of John's Gospel with the Synoptics that John's structure is wholly distinctive and different. In fact, however, each Evangelist draws on shared tradition in his own way to make his own points.

Mark sets out a fast-moving tale, marked by his repeated use of the historic present tense and terms like 'immediately'. He jumps straight from Jesus's anointing by the Spirit at the Jordan and his forty-day period of temptation to Jesus's entry into Galilee subsequent to the Baptist's arrest (Mark 1.14). This already suggests that Mark's intention was to focus more or less exclusively on Jesus's Galilean ministry (1.14-15), and the deliberate note that Jesus (in effect) only began his mission 'after John was arrested' (1.14) probably also indicates that he was aware that he was omitting the earlier period when Jesus's mission overlapped with the Baptist's. This was one of Mark's ways of emphasizing the difference between Jesus and the Baptist. Mark also characterizes Jesus's preaching as summed up by reference to the kingdom of God (1.14-15) and emphasizes Jesus's healing and exorcist ministries, and his role as a teacher,[10] though he does not draw on the tradition of Jesus's teaching as much as the others. The description of his Gospel as a passion narrative with an extended introduction (Kahler 1964: 80 n. 11) catches well the way Mark foreshadows the climax from early on with hints and allusions (2.20; 3.6) and with the thumping repetition of the passion predictions, which foresee the suffering and resurrection of the Son of Man (8.31; 9.3; 10.33-4). The slowness of the disciples to understand what Jesus was about is also a reminder that Jesus's mission only makes full (Gospel) sense in the light of that climax (see e.g. Schnelle 1998: 212).

Matthew and Luke both preface their accounts of Jesus's mission with birth narratives (Matt 1–2//Luke 1–2), but otherwise use the same framework for the mission itself: following Mark in focusing on Jesus's Galilean mission,

---

10   'Kingdom of God': Mark 1.15; 4.11, 26, 30; 9.1, 47; 10.14, 15, 23, 25; 12.34; 14.25. 'Teacher': Mark 4.38; 5.35; 9.17, 38; 10.17, 20, 35; 12.14, 19, 32; 13.1.

separated in time and region from the Baptist's mission (Matt 4.12; Luke 4.14); emphasizing Jesus's message as focusing on the kingdom of God;[11] describing his diverse ministry of miracles; building up to the climax of the passion narrative in Jerusalem. Matthew orders the insertion of a good deal more teaching material (Q) by presenting it in five blocks (starting with the Sermon on the Mount), probably as an echo of the five books of Moses.[12] Luke provides an elaborated version of Jesus's preaching in the synagogue of Nazareth as the 'lead story' that sets the tone for what is to follow (4.16-30) and organizes his fuller supply of Jesus tradition by setting a good deal of it in a much lengthier travel journey from Galilee to Jerusalem (9.51–19.28; see esp. Moessner 1989).

John's treatment of the main sequence of Jesus's mission, however, is quite distinctive. I focus here on four aspects: the beginning of Jesus's mission; the framing of Jesus's mission; the portrayal of Jesus's mission in the 'book of signs'; and, John's expanded emphasis on Jesus's Judean mission.

The Beginning of Jesus's Mission (John 1–3).
In presenting the opening of Jesus's mission, John seems to have been able to draw on tradition which the others had either set to one side or did not know about. He does not hesitate to include reference to a period prior to the Baptist's imprisonment (John 3.24), during which Jesus's mission overlapped with the Baptist's (John 3.22-36) and was apparently of the same character as the Baptist's (3.22-6), though John takes care to deny that Jesus himself practised baptism (4.2). This tradition almost certainly goes back to the first disciples, since it includes the detail that some of Jesus's own key disciples had earlier been the Baptist's disciples (1.35-42; see also Dodd 1963: 279–87, 302–5). Neither detail nor emphasis was likely to have been invented later, given the degree of embarrassment indicated elsewhere in the Jesus tradition over the extent to which Jesus could be counted as himself a disciple of the Baptist (note again particularly Matt. 3.14-15). Also to be noted is the fact that the emphasis on the kingdom of God has disappeared, the only echo of Synoptic-type talk of the kingdom, curiously, coming during the period of overlap with the Baptist (3.5).[13] Since for the Fourth Evangelist the Baptist was such an effective witness for Jesus, the difference between the two in style of mission did not need to be highlighted so much, or at least in the same way.

---

11   Matthew and Luke have nine references to the kingdom in common (Q), along-side a further 28 references distinctive of Matthew and 12 references distinctive of Luke.

12   A theory made more persuasive by the repeated conclusion to collected sequences of teaching, 'When Jesus finished these words' (7.28; 11.1; 13.53; 19.1; 26.1). Notably, this formula does not appear in Chapter 23.

13   Though we should not assume that the sequence of events in John 2–3 is in chronological order; see discussion below.

The outcome for our particular inquiry is that, here again, we see firm evidence of how the oral Jesus (and Baptist) tradition could be and was handled: by omitting a not unimportant aspect of the tradition in order to prevent any confusion between the two missions and to highlight the distinctiveness of Jesus's mission; or, by focusing the retold tradition to highlight the Baptist's witness-bearing function and inferior significance. The fact that the Synoptic tradition ignored or suppressed the overlap period, of course, makes it difficult for us to evaluate the Johannine tradition in the usual way (by comparing John's version with that of the Synoptics). But we can be sufficiently confident that *the Johannine tradition too goes back to the first disciples*, and indeed, in this case, *has retained a clearer memory of the overlap period than we could have deduced from the Synoptic tradition.* Any simple uniform rule that the Synoptic tradition is always more reliable than John's is immediately ruled out. John's version of the beginning of Jesus's mission is itself an example of how the memory of that overlap was handled in at least one strand of earliest Christianity.

The Frame of Jesus's Mission in John
The Synoptics frame the body of Jesus's mission in a consistent way. The first frame is provided by the temptation of Jesus and the entry into mission in Galilee (Mark 1.12-15 parr.); Luke also brings forward a filled-out version of Jesus's preaching in the synagogue of Nazareth to provide a window into the character of Jesus's mission (Luke 4.16-30). At the other end, the mission is rounded off with the entry into Jerusalem and the cleansing of the temple (Mark 11.1-17 parr.), events that point forward to the arrest and accusations against Jesus in the hearing before Caiaphas (Mark 14.53-65 parr.). The implication is clear that it was Jesus's symbolic act against the temple (11.12-14, 15-17) and what Jesus had said (or was reputed to have said) about the temple's destruction that triggered the decision to act against Jesus and contributed to the (false) accusations levelled against Jesus (Mark 14.55-8; see Dunn 2003: 769–70, 785–6).

John's Gospel, however, uses quite different framing brackets. In contrast to the Synoptics, John provides a double *opening bracket* by bringing together the temple-cleansing and the story of the wedding at Cana.

- *The marriage at Cana* (John 2.1-11) tradition was totally unknown to the Synoptics, though possibly illustrating a point made in the earlier tradition about the wedding-like character of Jesus's mission (Mark 2.18-19 parr.) by telling it as a story.[14] The symbolism is obvious: water intended for Jewish rites of purification (2.6) is

---

14   Dodd notes that Jesus is recalled as telling several parables that feature wedding feasts (he refers to Matt 22.1-14; 25.1-13; Luke 12.35-6) and suggests that 'the traditional nucleus of this *pericope* [the Cana wedding] may have been a parable' (1963: 226–7).

transformed into high-quality wine (2.10), illustrating the transformation brought by Jesus's mission, quite probably once again as a way of making the same point as Mark 2.21-2 parr.

- *The cleansing of the temple* (2.14-22) is, most probably, John's version of the tradition shared by the Synoptics, but placed by them at the *end* of Jesus's mission. It is highly unlikely that there were two such episodes in Jesus's mission, one at the beginning and the other at the end, for several reasons.

  o John's account and the Synoptic event have precisely the same character: the sellers of animals and doves are expelled from the temple precincts, and the tables of the money-changers are overturned, with some variation in detail as one would expect in an oral tradition.

  o Jesus's rebuke is different in the various accounts. In John, Jesus says, 'Stop making my Father's house a marketplace' (2.16); in Mark, 'You have made it a den of robbers' (11.17). But the effect is similar in both.

  o John has Jesus say, 'Destroy this temple, and in three days I will raise it up' (John 2.19), the very words which Mark and Matthew attribute to false testimony at Jesus's trial (Mark 14.58//Matt 26.61). It is hard to avoid the conclusion that Jesus was remembered as saying something like this, and that while the way it was turned against Jesus at his trial amounted to false witness, Jesus did in fact predict the destruction of the temple (cf. Mark 13.2 parr.) and possibly/probably also spoke about its rebuilding (whatever he meant by that; see Dunn 2003: 630–3). In which case, *John is a better witness to Jesus than the Synoptics, and shows how the oral memory of what Jesus had said was retained in the Jesus tradition, despite the way it was used against Jesus* (a similar conclusion can be drawn from Acts 6.14; see Dunn 2008: #24.2c). John's version also strengthens the probability that Jesus gave this teaching in the context of his cleansing of the temple, and that it was the combination of the two (the event and the teaching) which determined the temple authorities to take action against him.

The conclusion which follows most naturally is that John has elected to begin his account of Jesus's mission with this episode because, together with the wedding at Cana, it *foreshadowed and epitomized the effect of Jesus's mission in relation to his native Judaism.* Thus, Jesus would transform the Jewish purity ritual into new wine; he would replace the temple with his own body (John 2.21); the water he gave was far superior to the water of Jacob's well (4.12-14); as the bread of life from heaven he far transcended the bread which Moses gave (6.30-5; see further Lincoln 2005: 76–8). Similar to the way that Luke moved Jesus's preaching in the synagogue at Nazareth to the forefront of his account to indicate the character of what was to follow, John felt free (evidently) to move the climactic cleansing of the temple so as to epitomize what was to follow.[15] This may seem an overbold move, but only if we assume that the Evangelists were bound to order their material in strict chronological order, an assumption which we have no reason to make and which runs counter to too much evidence to be followed without question.[16] That there was a substantive story to be told about Jesus is clear, but as passages such as the Sermon on the Mount in Matthew 5–7, the journey to Jerusalem in Luke 9–19, and the cleansing of the temple in John 2.14-22 also clearly show, *how the individual teachings and events of the Jesus tradition were ordered within the Gospel narrative of Jesus's mission was a matter of free choice in the different tellings of the oral material.*

If John felt free to reshape the beginning of his account of Jesus's mission, he felt equally or more free in constructing the *closing bracket*, the event that sparked the decision to do away with Jesus. In the Synoptics, the symbolic 'cleansing of the temple' sets off the final spiral of opposition and leads directly to the arrest of Jesus made possible by Judas's betrayal (Mark 11.18//Luke 19.47-8; Mark 12.12 parr.; 14.1-2 parr.; Matt. 21.15-16; Mark 14.10-11 pars). John, however, provides a quite different trigger for the final move against Jesus: *the recalling of Lazarus from the dead*. The signs that Jesus had performed, climaxing in the recall of Lazarus to life, led the high priest himself to the conclusion that it was better for one man to die than for the whole nation to be destroyed (John 11.47-53, 57). John reinforces the point by narrating how famous the raising of Lazarus had become, and how threatening to the status quo the resulting support for Jesus and his message quickly became (12.9-11, 17-19).

Of this raising of Lazarus from the dead (11.1-44), none of the other Evangelists shows any awareness.[17] One could conceive that the earlier tradition set this episode aside for fear that the authorities might act against Lazarus (cf. John 12.10). But the Synoptics were written forty or more years after the event; would such a threat still be a factor after Jerusalem had been devastated and its residents widely scattered? Moreover, the Johannine presentation seems to reflect the beliefs and concerns of the later Johannine churches: the sign of Lazarus's recall to life prefiguring Jesus's own resur-

---

15   Paul Anderson is the most recent to argue that Mark's chronology for the cleansing of the temple is wrong – in his view, it is John who got the placement of the temple incident right, and thus John was correcting Mark (2006: 32, 48, 67, 71, 111, 158–61). But see John Painter's 2008 review of Anderson in *RBL*. See here also Matson 2001.

16   The words of Papias are regularly quoted on this point: Mark 'wrote accurately all that he remembered, not, indeed, in order, of the things said or done by the Lord' (Eusebius, *HE* 3.39.15).

17   The character Lazarus appears only in John (John 11.1-44; 12.1-2, 9-10, 17). The only other 'Lazarus' mentioned in the New Testament is a beggar by that name in the Lukan parable of The Rich Man and Lazarus (Luke 16.20-5).

rection (John 11.4-5, 23-7); the High Priest unwittingly confessing that Jesus died 'for the nation ... and to gather into one the dispersed children of God' (11.51-2); many of the Jews believing in Jesus (12.11); the expanding influence of Jesus being counteracted by the expulsion from the synagogue of those who believed in him (12.42); all this reflecting the high and distinctive Johannine Christology (11.4, 25-6; 12.27-36, 44-50). In all these respects, the Lazarus event provides a logical closing frame for John's understanding of Jesus's ministry.

It is hard to avoid the conclusion that John moved the account of the cleansing of the temple to the beginning of the Gospel narrative so as to provide a window through which the unfolding of Jesus's mission and revelation should be seen. Further, he did this to make room for his own version of the climax to Jesus's mission and of the events that triggered the decisive action against him.

The Book of Signs
Equally striking is the way John has structured *Jesus's mission of healing and miracles* (John 3–12), which C. H. Dodd famously designated 'the Book of Signs' (Dodd 1953). John seems to utilize a pattern whereby a characteristic miracle highlights an aspect of Jesus's mission and its significance; that significance is typically brought out by an often lengthy discourse or dialogue before or after the event. This structure is underlined by the term that John uses consistently for the miracles: 'sign',[18] a significant event that conveys a meaning far larger than the event itself. The most persistent themes related to this presentation are new life and light from darkness, both already signalled in the prologue (John 1.4-5, 7-9, 13). The pattern of sign/discourse is evident throughout the Book of Signs.

- 2.1-11: water to wine, the 'first sign' (2.11), its significance indicated by references to the 'third day' (2.1), a wedding, water of purification rites (2.6), and description as 'a sign' which 'revealed his glory' (2.11);
  - o 3.1-21: dialogue with Nicodemus on new birth (3.3-8, 15-16, 19-21);
- 4.46-54: saving a royal official's son from death, with emphasis on life (4.50-3) and description of the event as a 'second sign' (4.54), though in this case including a warning against faith based solely on signs (4.48; cf. 2.23-5);

---

18   John 2.11, 23; 3.2; 4.48, 54; 6.2, 14, 26, 30; 7.31; 9.16; 10.41; 11.47; 12.18, 37; 20.30. Despite traditions like Matt. 12.28//Luke 11.20 and Mark 3.27 parr., exorcisms apparently did not function sufficiently as 'signs' for John; see here Twelftree 2001.

o corollary to the Water of Life discourse with the Samaritan woman (4.7-26, especially 4.10, 14), and reaping the fruit for eternal life (4.35-6) already in Samaria (4.29-30, 39-43);

- 5.1-9: healing of a paralysed man, which takes a more traditional format (Jesus healing on a Sabbath);
    o 5.10-47: dialogue with 'the Jews', focusing on the Christological significance of Jesus's action on the Sabbath (a theme that reappears in 10.11-39) but also highlighting the life which is in the Son and granted by the Son (5.24-6, 40);
- 6.1-14: feeding of five thousand, attached to the walking on water (6.16-21);
    o 6.25-65: the great Bread of Life discourse (particularly 6.27, 33, 35, 40, 47, 48, 51, 53-4, 57-8, 63; rounded off by Peter's confession, 6.68);
- 9.1-7: healing of a blind man (again on the Sabbath),
    o preceded by a discussion that opens with Jesus's promise of the light of life (8.12), and leading into an extensive discourse on blindness and sight (9.8-41);
- 11.1-44: recalling Lazarus from death, the significance of which is emphasized from the beginning of the episode (11.4);
    o a discourse on eternal life despite and through death (particularly 11.23-6) prior to the miracle itself.

Aside from the distinctive sign/discourse pattern outlined above, several curiosities in the Johannine tradition are worth noting.

- No type of miracle is repeated. It is as though John has taken six characteristic miracles, perhaps even miracle types, in order to draw out the significance of each.
- For some reason, John does not include one of Jesus's most characteristic types of healing, at least according to the Synoptic tradition: exorcism. Similarly, John nowhere speaks of 'unclean spirits', and the term 'demon' is limited to accusations against Jesus (7.20; 8.48-9, 52; 10.20-1).
- The listing of the first two signs as the 'first' and the 'second' (2.11; 4.54) suggests that John may have been able to draw on a pre-existing sequence of signs, possibly already written down (see Fortna 1970; for further bibliography and critique of this theory, see Schnelle 1998: 494–6).
- The fact that John has retained the close sequence between the feeding of the five thousand and the walking on water (6.1-21; cf. Mark 6.32-52 parr.), even though the accompanying discourse develops the significance only of the former, strongly suggests that these two miracles were already so firmly attached in the various forms of the tradition that it would have raised more questions to

omit the latter than it did to retain it as the undeveloped twin (cf. Matt. 14.13-33; Mark 6.32-52; Luke, however, omitted the walking on water, 9.10-17).

* The recalling of Lazarus from death (John 11) brings to a fitting climax the theme of life out of death so prominent in the earlier discourses (new birth, water of life, renewed life, eternal life, bread of life, the light of life).

One question raised by these observations is whether John has drawn the actual miracles that he relates from his tradition, or whether he is providing a sequence of stories (a) partly drawn from common tradition (feeding of the five thousand, healing a child at a distance), (b) partly illustrating types of healing for which Jesus was famous (paralysis and blindness), and/or (c) partly expressing the rich significance of Jesus even if not actually rooted in specific historical events (water of Jewish purification turned into abundant and high-quality wine, recalling Lazarus to life). The first of these possibilities, (a) above, is intriguing, since John's account of the healing of the royal official's son is so different from the parallel in Matthew and Luke,[19] and since virtually the only significant points of agreement between John and the Synoptics on the feeding of the five thousand are the actual numbers (five thousand people; two hundred denarii; five loaves and two fishes; twelve baskets of fragments).[20] Here is *important evidence of the degree to which the same memory and tradition could be diversely retold.* The second of the possibilities, (b) above, suggests that John or his tradition had no qualms in telling the story of Jesus using *types* of his healing ministry rather than particular instances (see also Dodd 1963: 174–88; Dunn 1991: 374). The third possibility, (c) above, cannot be excluded, since it is so hard to locate both the water-into-wine miracle[21] and the recalling of Lazarus to life[22]

---

19   The possibility that the healing of the royal official's son is a variation of Matthew's and Luke's account of the healing of the centurion's boy certainly cannot be excluded (see Dodd 1963: 188–95; Dunn 2003: 212–6).

20   See also Dunn 1991: 363–5. In *Jesus Remembered*, I also point out that John's report that the crowd wanted to 'take Jesus by force to make him king' (6.15) is very plausible as recalled historical data (understandably passed over by other tradents), not least because it helps explain the oddities of Mark's account at the same point (Dunn 2003: 645–7).

21   The provision of 480 to 720 litres of wine would certainly be grotesque as a historical event, but as a symbolic parable it is very powerful.

22   If John knew one or more of the raising-from-the-dead miracles attributed to Jesus by the earlier tradition (Jairus's daughter, Mark 5.35-43 parr.; Luke 7.11-15), he presumably thought they were not climactic enough for his purposes. He may also have known the tradition that Jesus himself claimed to raise the dead (Matt 11.5//Luke 7.22). So a parabolic story of Jesus raising a dead person was hardly unjustified, especially when it could serve as such a fitting climax to his own retelling of Jesus's mission. See further the careful discussions of Dodd (1963: 228–32) and Lincoln (2005: 531–5).

within Jesus's mission, and since both so powerfully illustrate the effect of Jesus's mission. This could suggest that *John or his tradition felt free to document Jesus's mission with parabolic stories and not only actual remembered events.* Also, it would fit with John's attribution of speeches/discourses to Jesus, as will be seen below. If this is the case, it would be quite wrong and a serious misunderstanding of John and his purpose to accuse him of deception. That is to say, *the evidence of John's Gospel itself suggests that we should not assume that he saw his role as simply recalling memories of actual events of Jesus's mission, or simply reciting the earlier tradition, in the fashion of the Synoptics.* John may have concluded that to bring out the full significance of Jesus's mission he had to retell the tradition in bolder ways.

The Judean Mission
One of the most striking differences between the Synoptics and John is that, whereas the Synoptics focus on Jesus's mission in Galilee, the bulk of John's narrative focuses on Judea and Jerusalem (2.13–3.36; 5.1-47; 7.10–Chapter 20). It is not unlikely that Jesus paid more visits and spent longer time in Judea and Jerusalem than the Synoptic tradition allows (see Dunn 2003: 323–4). Several pieces of information point to this suggestion.

- The early period of overlap between the missions of the Baptist and Jesus suggests an early mission in Judea (cf. John 3).
- Luke records the discipleship of Mary and Martha (10.38-42), and though he locates them vaguely in a village passed through on the journey to Jerusalem, John is clear that the village was Bethany, close to Jerusalem (John 11.1, 18; 12.1-8);[23] John's geographical locations are generally reckoned to be evidence of firm historical roots.[24]
- That Jesus had close disciples in Jerusalem or in the near environs is suggested by the (secret?) disciples who provide the donkey for his entry into Jerusalem (Mark 11.2-3 parr.) and the availability of the room for the last supper (Mark 14.12-16 parr.).

Why did the Synoptic tradition ignore or set to one side Jesus's earlier Jerusalem visits? The fact that they deliberately excluded the overlap period with the Baptist is evidence enough that they felt free to do so. And perhaps Mark, or the tradition on which he drew, wanted to make the (final) visit to Jerusalem the climax of the Jesus story, and Matthew and Luke simply

---

23   The depiction of Martha and Mary in John 12.1-2 (Martha serving; Mary focusing attention on Jesus) echoes the similar presentation in Luke 10.39-42. On the larger account (John 12.1-8), see Dodd 1963: 162–73; Dunn 1991: 365–7.
24   See John 1.28 (Bethany across the Jordan); 3.23 (Aenon near Salim); 5.2 (pool of Bethzatha); 11.54 (a town called Ephraim).

followed him (or their main stream of tradition) in doing so. Since the leadership of the earliest Jerusalem community of believers in Messiah Jesus were all Galileans, one could understand why the tradition which they began and taught focused on the Galilean mission.

John, of course, does not ignore the Galilean mission, even though Jesus's coming and going to Galilee in the early chapters of the Fourth Gospel does read rather awkwardly (see John 2.1, 12, 13; 4.1-3, 43-6; 5.1; 6.1, 59; 7.1, 9, 10). The two miracles included in those sections are, as noted earlier, the closest to the Synoptic miracle tradition. But the likelihood grows throughout John's Gospel that John had a source for the mission of Jesus that was different from, or rather in addition to, the remembrances of Peter: the figure indicated (and obscured) by references to 'the one whom Jesus loved' (13.23; 19.26; 21.7).[25] If that disciple is also referred to in 1.35-9, then this individual would have been a good source of information on the overlap period between the Baptist's and Jesus's missions (including the recruitment of the Baptist's disciples to become followers of Jesus). Similarly if that disciple is also referred to in 18.15-16, then he had good contacts in Jerusalem (he was known to the high priest!). This suggests that this disciple could have known or cherished memories of Jesus's mission in Jerusalem on one or other of his brief visits to the capital and of episodes and contacts (like Nicodemus and Joseph of Arimathea) that the other tradents largely ignored,[26] perhaps because the Galilean tradition was more familiar and so full in itself.[27] With only John's attestation for the Judean mission, and given the freedom with which the tradition he drew upon represented the memories of Jesus's overall mission, it is difficult to draw firm conclusions. But the most likely explanation is that *John has drawn on good memories of multiple visits to Jerusalem by Jesus, even if he has treated them in his own distinctive parabolic or symbolic terms.*

25   See particularly Bauckham 2006; Bauckham 2008. Martin Hengel argues that the Fourth Evangelist had been a resident in Jerusalem, was an eyewitness of Jesus's death and a member of the earliest community, emigrated to Asia Minor in the early 60s and founded a school, where he wrote his Gospel in his old age, in which 'typical Jewish Palestinian reminiscences are combined with more Hellenistic, enthusiastic and indeed even Pauline approaches into a great synthesis [in which] the Christological doctrinal development of primitive Christianity reached its climax' (1989: 134). See also Culpepper 2000, esp. Chapter 3; Thatcher 2001a.

26   Joseph is mentioned by all the Gospels (Mark 15.43 parr.; John 19.38), but Nicodemus appears only in John (3.1-9; 7.50; 19.39).

27   Similarly with regard to any mission in Samaria (John 4), whereas the Synoptics show why such a mission might have been excluded (Matt. 10.5; Luke 9.52-4). Oscar Cullmann made much of John 4.38 at this point (1976: 47–9).

The Johannine Discourses of Jesus

So far I have concentrated primarily on the narrative tradition of John's Gospel. The other obvious area to examine is the teaching material in John. As already noted, the sayings material provides one of the most striking contrasts between John's Gospel and the Synoptics: whereas they depict Jesus as a sage who typically teaches by means of *meshalim*, aphorisms and parables, John depicts Jesus engaged in lengthy back and forth discussions in various settings.

I have already noted elsewhere that in every chapter of John's Gospel there are particular sayings or part-sayings that echo Synoptic material or form different versions of the Synoptic tradition (see Dunn 1991: 356–8; also Broadhead 2001; Tuckett 2001; Schnelle 1998: 497–8). I remain convinced that John either did not know the Synoptic Gospels, or at least did not draw his versions of these sayings from the Synoptic tradition as such.[28] Yet *the overlap with the Synoptic tradition at point after point indicates an independent awareness of the teaching that the early churches all remembered as Jesus's teaching. The lack of reworking by John at these points both allows us to recognize the parallel (the shared memory of the same teaching) and also enables us to say with confidence that John's discourses are rooted in memories of what Jesus taught during his mission, in Galilee or in Judea.*

These roots of the Johannine discourses in tradition that echoes and parallels Synoptic tradition suggest the most plausible way to understand them: they emerge out of and express the developed Christology of John and the Johannine churches, showing further reflection over some time on things Jesus said and taught in the light of the richer Christology that Jesus's resurrection and exaltation had opened up.[29] This thesis finds support in several examples (see here also Dunn 1991: 369–73 for further examples and discussion).

- The notion that entry into the kingdom depends on being born again/from above (John 3.3, 5) looks like a sharper expression of the Matthew 18.3 tradition (entry into the kingdom depends on becoming like children); these are the only kingdom references in

28   I suspect that those who conclude that John was dependent on one or other of the Synoptic Gospels (see here Smith 1984b, chaps 6 and 7; Smith 1992) are too much governed by a literary mindset, assuming that any close parallel can be (plausibly) explained only by literary dependence.

29   Tom Thatcher notes the substantial body of riddles in the Johannine dialogues. Since riddles are a widely attested oral form, he suggests that at least some of these sayings circulated orally in Johannine circles before the Fourth Gospel was written, and that some of the larger dialogues may also have circulated orally as riddling sessions (he refers particularly to John 8.12-58; see Thatcher 2001b).

John that come close to the Synoptic kingdom of God motif (see Caragounis 1991).

- John likens Jesus's presence to the presence of the bridegroom (John 3.29) as marking the difference between Jesus and the Baptist, a move that echoes Mark 2.19 parr. (See also Mark 2.21-2 parr.); I have already suggested influence from this motif on John's account of the wedding at Cana (John 2.1-11).

- The great Bread of Life discourse (John 6.26-58) is most obviously to be understood as a reflection on Jesus's words at the Last Supper (Mark 14.22-5 pars), bringing out not so much the Passover significance as the contrast with Moses and the manna of the wilderness.

- The Good Shepherd theme in John 10 most obviously takes up the memory of Jesus's use of the same imagery in his teaching (cf. Matt 18.12//Luke 15.4; Mark 6.34; Matt 10.6; 15.24; Luke 12.32).

- John's principal theme of presenting Jesus as the incarnate Word who reveals God most fully (John 1.14-18) forms a consistent theme of Jesus's discourses.

  o Jesus's repeated talk of himself as *the Son* of God as Father is an obvious elaboration of the much more limited early memory of Jesus's praying to God as 'Abba', perhaps already elaborated in the Synoptic tradition.[30]

  o Jesus's repeated talk of his having been *sent* by the Father (John 4.34; 5.24, 30, 37; 6.38-9, 44; etc.) is an obvious elaboration of the memory of Jesus's occasional self-reference in similar terms (cf. Mark 9.37 parr.; 12.6 parr.; Matt 15.24; Luke 4.18; 10.16).

  o John elaborates Jesus's talk about 'the Son of Man' by adding the thoughts of his *descent and ascent* (John 3.13; 6.62; cf. 1.51) and his *being lifted up/glorified* (3.14; 8.28; 12.23; 13.31).

  o The 'Amen, Amen' introductory formula so regularly used by John is obviously drawn from the tradition, well known in the Synoptics, of Jesus introducing a saying with 'Amen' (see Culpepper 2001).

  o The noteworthy 'I am' sayings of John's Gospel (6.35, 41, 48, 51; 8.12, 24, 28, 58; 10.7, 9, 14; 11.25; 13.19; 14.6; 15.1, 5; 18.5-8) are certainly formulations unknown to the earlier Synoptic tradition (what Evangelist could have omitted such sayings of Jesus?), but it is likely that the memory of some awe-inspiring assurances of Jesus (Mark 6.50 parr.; John 6.20) provided the stimulus for the uniquely Johannine forms.

---

30   Jeremias noted the tremendous expansion of references to God as 'Father' in the words of Jesus within the tradition – Mark 3, Q 4, special Luke 4, special Matthew 3, John 10 (1967: 30, 36).

These data strongly suggest that *many if not most of the principal themes of the Johannine discourses are the fruit of lengthy meditation on particular sayings of Jesus or of characteristic features of what he said and of how he acted*. In other words, they exemplify not simply the passing on of Jesus tradition, but the way that tradition stimulated understandings of Jesus in the light of what had happened subsequently. John himself attests to and justifies this traditioning process.

- John twice explicitly notes that Jesus's disciples did not understand what Jesus was saying or doing, but that they remembered and later understood in the light of Jesus's resurrection and glorification (2.22; 12.16; similarly 13.7; 14.20; 16.4). This makes precisely the point that the claims regarding Jesus were rooted in Jesus's own mission as illuminated by Easter. His immediate disciples already had a true knowledge of Jesus during his mission (6.69; 17.7-8), but they did not fully understand; their knowledge was still imperfect (8.28, 32; 10.6, 38; 13.28; 14.9; see also Thatcher 2005a: 82–5; Thatcher 2006: 24–32).
- To the same effect is the role that John ascribes to the Spirit/ Paraclete. During Jesus's mission 'the Spirit was not yet' – that is, presumably, not yet given (John 7.39). But when the Spirit came, he would teach Jesus's disciples everything and remind them of all that Jesus had said to them (14.26), guide them into all truth, and declare more of Jesus's truth that they were as yet unable to bear (16.12-13).[31] This is the same balance between revelation already given and received and fuller revelation still to come, a fuller revelation that makes the revelation already given clearer and enables it to be more fully grasped.[32]

In short, it is hard to doubt that *John's version of Jesus's teaching is an elaboration of aphorisms, parables, motifs and themes remembered as characteristic of Jesus's teaching as attested in the Synoptic tradition*. John's

---

31   In his review of Anderson 2006, John Painter observes that 'the historical tradition in John has been thoroughly shaped by deep theological reflection from a perspective that makes difficult the separation of the tradition from the later theological development. It is the degree to which this has happened in John that separates it from the Synoptics. That need not rule out continuity between the tradition and the interpretation, but it does not mean that the interpretation is in some sense already present in the tradition, even if it is rooted there and in some way grows out of it. The experience of the resurrection and the Spirit created Johannine interpretation that was not foreseen or foreseeable beforehand' (Painter 2008).

32   The dialectic of the Johannine conception of revelation is summed up in the word ἀναγγέλλω, which John uses three times in 16.13-15 and which can have the force of '*re-announce/re-proclaim*', but which also denotes the announcing of new information/revelation in 16.13. Arthur Dewey thus speaks of 'anticipatory memory' (2001: 65–7).

version was not pure invention, nor did it arise solely out of Easter faith; rather, it was elaboration of typical things that Jesus was remembered as saying. Unlike the later, non-canonical 'Gospels' John does not attribute the fuller insight into who Jesus was to secret teaching given to a few following Jesus's resurrection. Rather, he roots it in the Jesus tradition that he shared with other churches (who knew mainly the Synoptic tradition) and that was itself rooted in the memory of Jesus's mission. This was the truth of Jesus for John: not a pedantic repetition of Synoptic-like tradition, but the significance of that tradition brought out by the extensive discourses that John or his tradition drew out of particular features of Jesus tradition as exemplified in the Synoptic tradition. To criticize John's procedure as inadmissible is to limit the task of the Evangelist to simply recording deeds and words of Jesus during his mission. But John evidently saw his task as something more: the task of drawing out the fuller meaning of what Jesus had said (and done) by presenting that fuller understanding as the Spirit both *reminding* Jesus's disciples of what Jesus had said, and *leading them into the fuller understanding of the truth* made possible by Jesus's resurrection and ascension.

The Johannine Passion Narrative

The Johannine passion narrative shares the same structure as its Synoptic equivalents, each with its own distinctive features and characteristics, though once again John shows how varied at least some re-presentations of the final part of Jesus's mission could be.[33]

- Like the Synoptics, John begins the final phase with Jesus's last meal with his disciples (John 13). Further, like the others,
  o the meal is linked to the Passover (John 13.1);[34]
  o Jesus predicts his betrayal (John 13.18, 21; Mark 14.18 parr.), causing confusion among his disciples (John 13.22-5; Mark 14.19 parr.);
  o the account emphasizes that the traitor eats from the same dish as Jesus (John 13.26-7; Mark 14.20 parr.);

---

33   Dodd concludes his lengthy discussion of the passion narrative by saying, 'there is cumulative evidence that the Johannine version represents (subject to some measure of "writing up" by the evangelist) an independent strain of the common oral tradition, differing from the strains of tradition underlying Mark (Matthew) and Luke, though controlled by the same general *schema*' (1963: 150). See also Schnelle 1998: 500–2. For a recent attempt to reconstruct the pre-Johannine passion narrative, see Scherlitt 2007.

34   Whether the meal itself was on Passover (Mark 14.12 parr.) or on the day of preparation for the Passover (John 19.14) remains unclear. See further Dunn 2003: 771–3.

    o Peter protests his loyalty and Jesus predicts his denial ('The cock will not crow until you deny me three times'; John 13.36-8; Mark 14.29-30 parr.).
- The shared tale recalls Jesus leading his disciples to the other side of the valley (John 18.1; Mark 14.32 parr.), Judas leading the arresting troop, and Jesus's arrest after some brief resistance in which 'the slave of the high priest' had his ear cut off (John 18.2-12; Mark 14.43-7 parr.).
- There follows the hearing before the high priest Caiaphas (John 18.13-14; Mark 14.53 parr.), with some cross-examination by Caiaphas (John 18.19-21; Mark 14.60-1 parr.).
- In all Gospel accounts, Peter follows the arresting party, gains entry to the courtyard (John 18.15-16; Mark 14.54 parr.), and denies Jesus as predicted (John 18.17-18, 25-7; Mark 14.54, 66-72 parr.).
- In all four Gospels, the case is transferred to Pilate (John 18.28; Mark 15.1 parr.), who begins by asking Jesus 'Are you the king of the Jews?' (John 18.33; Mark 15.3 parr.) and eventually finds no case against him (John 18.38; most specifically Luke 23.4).
- On account of the feast, the crowd is offered the release of one prisoner, Jesus or Barabbas, and chooses Barabbas (John 18.39-40; Mark 15.6-11 parr.). To Pilate's query as to what should be done with the 'King of the Jews', the crowd call for Jesus to be crucified (John 19.5-6, 15; Mark 15.13-14 parr.). Pilate gives way and hands Jesus over to be crucified (John 19.16; Mark 15.15 parr.).
- The flogging and mockery of Jesus (crown of thorns, purple robe, and the mock acclamation 'King of the Jews') is a shared memory, though set at different points in the sequence of events (John 19.1-3; Mark 15.15-19 parr.).
- Jesus carries his own cross (John 19.17; Mark 15.21 parr.) to the place called Golgotha (John 19.17; Mark 15.22 parr.), where he is crucified with two others (John 19.18; Mark 15.24, 27 parr.). The inscription reads, 'The King of the Jews' (John 19.19; Mark 15.26 parr.). His clothes are divided among the soldiers by the casting of lots (John 19.23-5; Mark 15.24 parr.).
- Jesus asks for, or is offered, a drink and drinks, then yields up his life (John 19.28-30; Mark 15.36-7 parr.).
- Joseph of Arimathea asks Pilate for Jesus's body because it is the day of Preparation, and attends to his burial in a tomb (John 19.38-42; Mark 15.42-6 parr.).

The distinctive features of John's version of the passion are not quite as obvious as the distinctives of his earlier accounts of Jesus's ministry. Yet even here there are various indications of the shared tradition on which John drew and which he elaborated in his own way.

- Surprisingly, John does not actually describe Jesus's last supper with his disciples, though we have already noted that 'the words of institution' seem to have been the basis for the extended meditation in 6.51-9.
- The focal point of the evening is presented as Jesus washing the disciples' feet (13.1-20) – an oddity if it was part of the shared memory, since it illustrates so well what Jesus was recalled as having said earlier, that he came not to be served but to serve (Mark 10.42-5 parr.). The fact of the parallel suggests that John told the story to illustrate what that very teaching could/should involve. The parallel between John 13.16 (cf. 15.20) and Matthew 10.24// Luke 6.40 ('the slave is not above/greater than his master') points in the same direction. And the echo of Matt. 10.40//Luke 10.16 in John 13.20 ('he who receives me receives him who sent me') similarly suggests one of the roots of John's distinctive growth of tradition.
- The command to love one another (13.34-5) can presumably be seen as an extension of Jesus's more widely known teaching on love of one's neighbour (Mark 12.31 parr.).
- The most strikingly distinctive feature of the Johannine passion narrative is the extended discourse that he attributes to Jesus at the close of the shared meal (John 14–16), particularly Jesus's great prayer of intercession for his disciples (John 17). These should be seen as extended meditations on the definitive significance of Jesus's revelation and what the disciples could expect after his departure. Even in these chapters, however, there are various points at which the roots in the early memories of Jesus are sufficiently clear.[35]
  o The promises of the Paraclete Spirit (John 14.26; 15.26-7; 16.4-15) probably originated with the elsewhere-remembered assurance of Jesus that the Spirit would inspire what the disciples should say (Mark 13.11 parr.).
  o Jesus's assurance that his disciples are more than servants (John 15.14-15) echoes Jesus's teaching that whoever does the will of God is a member of his family (Mark 3.35 parr.). Likewise, the promise of effective prayer in his name (John 15.16) echoes the similar promise of Mark 11.23-4 parr.

---

35   Johannes Beutler boldly concludes 'that John 13–17 is pervaded by early Jesus tradition, mostly tradition of a synoptic character and perhaps even derived from the Synoptics themselves', though 'no single coherent discourse source can be uncovered. Rather, there has been creative use of the traditional material, forging it into a new form that expresses [the] FE's peculiar view of Jesus' (2001: 173).

o Jesus's forewarning of the world's hatred (John 15.18-25) probably grew out of the same tradition as Matthew 10.24-5, 28//
Luke 6.40; 12.4.

o Even more clearly, the warnings to expect persecution in John
16.1-4 echo several similar traditions in Mark 13.9, 12-13//
Matt.10.17-18, 21-2.

o Even Jesus's great prayer for his disciples (John 17) owes its
inspiration to the tradition of Jesus praying in the Garden of
Gethsemane (Mark 14.32-42), and though the Johannine prayer
has nothing of the angst of the Synoptic tradition, the earlier prayer of John 12.27 does share a similar troubled quality
(Mark 14.33-6 parr.), remembered also in Hebrews 5.7.

• The exchange between Jesus and Pilate (John 18.33-8; 19.9-12,
19-22) is a fascinating elaboration of the 'King of the Jews' charge,
even though it is unlike any of Jesus's other teachings on the kingdom of God.

• John includes several distinctive utterances of Jesus from the cross
(19.26-7, 28, 30), but so does Luke (23.34, 43, 46). If the Beloved
Disciple was one of John's sources, that would help to explain
John 19.26-7 (Jesus's mother being consigned to the care of the
Beloved Disciple). The concern was evidently to express the spirit
of Jesus as clearly as possible during his greatest suffering leading
to death.

• John makes a point of vouchsafing some of his distinctive testimony, notably Jesus's side being pierced and the emission of blood
and water: 'He who saw this has testified so that you also may
believe. His testimony is true and he knows that he tells the truth'
(19.35).

• John's version of the empty tomb tradition has a similar distinctiveness, though all agree on the timing of its discovery and on the
leading involvement of Mary Magdalene. Luke 24.12 also accords
with John on Peter's involvement and on his seeing the linen wrap-
pings left behind from Jesus's body.

• Similarly, John's account of Jesus's resurrection appearances looks
as though it was dependent upon another source, perhaps not
known to or not used by the Synoptic tradition; the obvious tra-
dent in this case would have been Mary Magdalene.

• The Thomas episode (John 20.24-9) reminds readers of the New
Testament of the much more extensive Thomas tradition in apocryphal writings and suggests that John was able to draw on some
or several source traditions no longer known to us.

• A final affidavit confirms that the Gospel had a first-hand source
of substantial authority: 'This is the disciple [the Beloved Disciple]
who is testifying to these things and has written them, and we
know that his testimony is true' (21.24).

The most plausible inference to draw from all this data is that *different members of the initial disciple group drew somewhat varying emphases from what was a shared stream of tradition, each with memories of the same period, events and teachings, but distinctively their own memories of individual details.*

Conclusion

John's Gospel cannot and should not be simply paralleled to the other three Gospels. Although all four Gospels can be set in parallel, as in the Aland *Synopsis*, the first three Gospels are clearly parallel in a way and to a degree that is not true of John's Gospel – that is why Matthew, Mark and Luke can be referred to collectively as 'the Synoptic Gospels'. John's Gospel is not a synoptic Gospel.

The distinctiveness of John's portrayal of Jesus should not be diminished or ignored. The older attempt to harmonize all four Gospels should be recognized as wrong-headed. John was evidently *not* attempting to do the same thing as the Synoptics. And though we should recognize that all Evangelists had theological axes to grind, *the briefest of comparisons is sufficient to show that the Synoptics were much more constrained by the forms of their tradition than John was.* The closeness of the Synoptic parallels cannot be explained otherwise. And contrariwise, it is equally impossible to make sense of John's Gospel on the assumption that he was attempting to do the same thing as the Synoptics. We should not hesitate to draw the unavoidable corollary: that *to read and interpret John's Gospel as though he had been trying to do the same as the Synoptics is to misread and misinterpret his Gospel.* This remains the challenge for those who approach John's Gospel from a conservative perspective: by so doing, they may be missing and distorting John's message! The truth of Jesus, the story of his mission and its significance, were not expressed in only one way, as though the gospel of Jesus Christ could be told only by strictly limiting the interpretation of the earliest Jesus tradition – the ways in which Jesus was remembered. For John, *the character and themes of Jesus's mission provided the basis for fuller and deeper reflection on what Jesus stood for and achieved*, yet his presentation is still the gospel of Jesus Christ.

At the same time, it is equally important to note that John clearly knew the same sort of tradition known to and used by the Synoptic Evangelists.

- He follows the same Gospel format in giving his account of Jesus's mission.
- He had access to earliest memories of close disciples of Jesus, memories that filled out parts of Jesus's mission that the other Evangelists passed over for understandable reasons (the overlap period between

the Baptist and Jesus's earlier trips into Judea and Jerusalem being probably the most obvious).

- The indications that John had good sources of tradition (Baptist tradition, the attempt to make Jesus king in Galilee, contacts in Jerusalem), of which we would not have known had John not retold them, suggests that other parts of John's Gospel are better rooted in historical tradition than we now can tell. Inasmuch as the Synoptic Evangelists also did not include all the traditional material available to them, John 21.25 speaks for all the Gospels.
- John's use of the tradition of Jesus's miracles was selective, but the types of miracle he described and which he encompassed by profound discourse and teaching were mostly familiar as types of Jesus's healing ministry.
- Again and again, the elaborate Johannine discourses and teaching give evidence of being rooted in Synoptic-like tradition, or seem to be an elaboration of particular sayings/parables of Jesus known from the Synoptic tradition.
- John evidently knew the final passion of Jesus first hand or from first-hand sources, a claim that is emphasized at 19.35 and 21.24 in particular; the Beloved Disciple and Mary Magdalene may be identified as such sources.

The most obvious way to explain and understand the distinctiveness of John's portrayal of Jesus is to suggest that John knew well the tradition that he shared with the Synoptics, and that *he wove his much more refined fabric from the same stuff as the Synoptics*. His Gospel is thus the product and expression of many years of reflection on the significance of what Jesus had taught and done, and on the significance of the revelation he had brought and constituted in his life and mission (see also Dunn 1991: 378–9). While we should not understate the distinctiveness of John's Gospel, neither should we exaggerate the difference. *John was telling the same story as the other Evangelists.* That he chose to do so by elaborating that story in its own way should be acknowledged and properly appreciated. John's Gospel should be valued for what it is, not devalued for what it is not.

In terms of the oral Jesus tradition, *John's Gospel shows just how diverse and varied the Jesus tradition could become in its various retellings.* In terms of memory, John's Gospel shows clearly the degree to which the memory of Jesus could be, and was, informed by subsequent insight and conviction, and could be shaped to portray Jesus as the Johannine author(s) or communities now saw him or wanted to present him to their contemporaries. The elaboration that John provided made his version of the Jesus tradition controversial; he sailed near the edge of what was acceptable. To speak of John's Gospel as 'the remembered Jesus' is bound to make a historian nervous, somewhat as a Shakespeare play performed in a twenty-first century setting might make Shakespearean scholars somewhat nervous. Are aspects of the play that are tightly interrelated to the historical setting of the play as given by Shakespeare lost in the twenty-first-century setting?

The facts that John retained the Gospel character and that his book was clearly rooted in the earlier oral tradition were presumably sufficient to ensure that his Gospel would be recognized as one of the four Gospels to be designated 'canonical'. At one and the same time, however, John demonstrated that for the remembered Jesus to continue to be seen as relevant to subsequent generations, the way he was remembered would have to be adaptable.

Chapter 10

MEMORY, COMMEMORATION AND HISTORY IN JOHN 2:19-22: A CRITIQUE AND APPLICATION OF SOCIAL MEMORY

Anthony Le Donne

> ...so when he was raised from the dead, his disciples remembered that he said this,
> and they believed the scripture and the saying which Jesus had spoken.
>
> (John 2.22)

Within the past three years, New Testament scholarship has shown a growing interest in the historiographical implications of a theory called Social Memory.[1] It is my hope that the adaptation of Social Memory to the concerns of historical Jesus research is a productive endeavour, one that does not simply reaffirm the same matters of consensus, argument and impasse that represent the current state of Jesus research. With this in mind, I will discuss both the virtues and the limitations of Social Memory and how this theory can best serve the interests of historical Jesus research and exegesis.[2] My critique will describe two ways in which Social Memory has been historiographically utilized with an aim to better define 'memory' and 'commemoration' as different but overlapping phenomena. Because Social Memory theorists do not often differentiate these two spheres, there is much more to be said about how they interact. It is in this way that I will offer a critique of a common shortcoming of Social Memory theory. Finally, I will suggest a particular exegetical use of Social Memory and apply it to Mark 14.56-9 and John 2.18-22.[3]

---

1   For instance, see the recently launched Society of Biblical Literature consultation *Mapping Memory* and the subsequent publication (Kirk and Thatcher 2005). For an extensive bibliography on Social Memory in biblical studies see my and Thatcher's introductory essay at the beginning of this book.
2   As I have given elsewhere (Le Donne 2007) a fuller overview of Social Memory theory, its brief history and its contemporary adherents, I will not do so here.
3   My thanks to Stephen Barton who first directed me to John 2.22 as an example of early Christian memory.

Memory as Metaphor

One hundred and sixty years before Vico's *Scienza Nuova*, François Baudouin (1520–1573) wrote this of ancient oral historians:

> I would not take the trouble to mention their barbaric ways, except that they could justly accuse us of still greater barbarism, if we refuse to study history; and we could and should learn from them to show diligence in preserving the public memory. (1561: xii)[4]

This quote is appropriate to my topic for two reasons. The most obvious is that it provides an early connection between history, orality and memory and demonstrates how these were understood to relate. But perhaps more importantly, it shows just how long the word 'memory' has been used by historiographers to refer to something other than *personal* memory. Baudouin refers to *'publicae memoriae'* to connote historical knowledge that is collectively preserved by a group of people, perhaps not preserved formally enough to be considered 'history', but preserved nonetheless. So even in seeds of modern historiography, historians have considered memory an apt metaphor for history, and (according to Baudouin) pseudo-history.

In the past twenty years, historiographers have employed this metaphor with exponential fervour. Memory has become the common denominator shared by history, orality and commemoration.[5] Many historiographers now echo Jacques Le Goff in saying that history is a process based upon the subjective reconstruction of human memory (1977: 106–10).[6] Le Goff described the relationship between history and memory in terms of mutual dependence (1977: 99). Accordingly, memories are no longer understood simply as historical data. Rather, there is a growing sentiment that the very essence of history is memory that has been socially formalized. History is now understood to be memory, *both as metaphor and in essence*.

It was not until very recently that historical Jesus research was introduced to Social Memory and its value for navigating early Christian memories. In his 2003 introduction to the Society of Biblical Literature's special session on Social Memory, Tom Thatcher described SM in this way:

---

4   Latin: 'Non dignarer illorum barbariem meminisse, nisi si nostram nobis barbariem exprobare maiorem illi possent, si simus anistoretoi, et nos ab iis discere possemus atque deberemus diligentiam conservandae publicae memoriae.'

5   No doubt, this has helped to formalize academic interest in the latter two categories.

6   Here Le Goff adapted the memory theory of Maurice Halbwachs (more on Halbwachs below). Le Goff was among the first – arguably *the* first – of those who attempted to bridge the gap between Halbwachs's original theory and historiography. Unfortunately, his work has been largely ignored by English-speaking memory theorists.

Social Memory theory is essentially concerned with the social dimensions of memory, specifically with the ways in which present social realities impact the way that groups envision and use the past. 'Memory' is taken in the broadest possible sense here to include any means by which groups attempt to preserve the past, construct the past, or evoke the past, including oral traditions, rituals, trends and styles, bodily practices and habits, and written texts.[7]

Thatcher's estimation of the connotative value of 'memory' is helpful in that it highlights that Social Memory theorists commonly employ the word as a metaphor. Much like Baudouin's reference to public memory, the value of this word lies in its ability to provide a relative image of the relationship between the construal of the past and collective identities. And yet, the use of this metaphor implies that something other than the word's denotative value is being employed.

Here Thatcher correctly defines memory in the 'broadest sense' so that it includes rituals, trends, styles, bodily practices, etc. I would also add calendars, festivals, laws, taboos and prejudices under the headings of traditions and rituals. This aptly describes the use of the word 'memory' among Social Memory theorists. However, it is also important to acknowledge that memory can be (and most often is) defined more narrowly, namely to denote personal recollection. Social Memory theorists are not only interested in commemorative rituals for anthropological and sociological reasons; they also analyse autobiographical accounts and oral traditions that took shape in relationship with living, personal memories.

Put simply, there is a difference between how people remember their relationship with their own fathers and how people 'remember' an historical patriarch from thousands of years before. I would call the first 'personal memory' (i.e. literal memory)[8] and the second 'commemoration' (i.e. memory as a metaphor). No doubt, the mnemonic process is much the same with both kinds of remembering, but there is a reason why we differentiate the genres of ancient history and autobiography: they overlap but are not synonymous. It is at this point that I turn to the central concern of this essay.

If Social Memory is to be of value to Jesus historians, it must be acknowledged that there are two ways to utilize this theory.[9] One of these deals more directly with the social constraints on personal memories, the other

---

7   I extend my gratitude to Dr Thatcher for providing the text of his introduction.

8   In a recent response to R. Bauckham, Judith C. S. Redman explores the nature of 'autobiographical memory' in psychological terms. As I see it, my conception of 'personal memory' is synonomous with 'autobiographical memory'. 'How Accurate Are Eyewitnesses?: Bauckham and the Eyewitnesses in the Light of Psychological Research', JBL 129 no. 1 (2010), pp. 177–97.

9   There are several subsets (Kirk 2005: 1–24). My concern is with the two most basic aims of SM.

deals more with the commemorative activity of communities (A. Assmann 1999: 64). The former explores the ways in which present cognitive states evoke, constrain and refract a person's perception of his or her personal past. The latter explores the ways in which group memories are formed and employed, and instruct collective identities. The remainder of this section will discussion personal memories as social phenomena. The next section will demonstrate how personal memories interact with, and become, commemorative activity.

It is important to note that social frameworks guide the process of personal memory at every level. Families, friends and communities continually stimulate, correct and add to personal memories. Moreover, the social construct of language shapes memory in a seminal way (Schudson 1995: 347). Personal memories are never constructed as individualized bits of mental content.[10] Personal memories are always given shape within external social frameworks.

However, there is no metaphor being employed in the case of personal memory. For example, when autobiographical accounts are being constructed, memory's denotative value is being used. Thus, the phenomenon of 'literal memory' should not be confused with the concept of *a priori* knowledge or pure factuality. Social Memory theorists hold that all memory (whether it is individual or collective) is an evolving process that conforms to the needs and activities of the ever-shifting present. As such, memory is always refracted though the social lenses of contemporary environments. From this historiographical vantage point, analysis of personal testimony is equally interested in what is being remembered and in who is doing the remembering.

Such analysis is valuable to historical inquiry in cases where historical events have been relayed through oral and written testimony within a generation of the events. This is a decided shift away from the tendencies of historical-positivism which seek to recover the closest approximation of the actual past. In my estimation, Social Memory provides a needed corrective to both those who hope to preserve the past devoid of interpretation, and those who lament that the past is altogether unknowable. Both approaches mistakenly think that history is something that it never can be. Rather, historians ought not to be interested in the actual past but in how the past has been remembered and mediated. That is, we can study the impacts of the past but cannot conjure the actual events to verify our historical reconstructions. Personal memories are central to the historian's task, not obstacles to be navigated around in order to attain something more objective.

---

10   This idea has a helpful parallel in the field of analytical philosophy (Burge 1998). To my knowledge, Social Memory theory has not interacted with the idea of the externalism of mental content (or anti-individualism). However, see my forthcoming work (Le Donne 2010) for a cursory application.

In order to evaluate the socially charged, mnemonic process involved in the articulation of personal memories, Social Memory theorists rely on the original ideas of French sociologist Maurice Halbwachs (Halbwachs 1992).[11] Halbwachs is now widely celebrated for his pioneering works on Social Memory. Contemporary SM theorists pay homage to him as their founding father. It is ironic then that Halbwachs himself was reluctant to use memory as a metaphor for history.[12] When Halbwachs referred to Social (and Collective) Memory he was not attempting to employ a metaphor. Instead, he intended to describe how the dividing lines that isolate an individual's memory from others' blur as they enter into social dialogue, and how social thought-constructs inform an individual's memories at the outset. It is important to realize that his central argument was that *all personal memory is social memory.*

Halbwachs made a strict distinction between memory, which was largely oral and therefore subjective, and history, which was textually organized and therefore more objective (cf. J. Assmann 1997: 42, 46–8). Halbwachs maintained that history (or tradition) is something different from memory (Weissberg 1999: 15). When he did try his hand at historiography (Halbwachs 1941), he concluded that commemorative history had very little to do with personal memories.[13] According to Halbwachs, the two were fundamentally different in nature and not merely in form. On this point, Weissberg rightly places Halbwachs within the context of nineteenth-century historical-positivism.

> Indeed, the nineteenth century was ardently 'historical', insisting upon history as a means to counter as well as to save memory. Written documents and recorded facts promised to aid a personal and often oral memory in crisis. History seemed to claim Truth and vouch for an 'objective' reality that would correct memory's seemingly subjective, unreliable stance in a world of objects. History was written and thus verifiable. It was public. Memory would be banished to the private realm; like a naughty child, it was, moreover, in need of guardianship and guidance, and often censorship as well. (1999: 11)

---

11   For an excellent adaptation of Halbwachs's ideas in contemporary memory theory, see J. Fentress and C. Wickham (1992).

12   He, much like his contemporaries, used this metaphor in a very qualified way.

13   It must be noted that Halbwachs's study on commemorative sites in the Holy Land, *La Topographie des Evangiles en Terre Sainte. Etude de mémoire collective,* was deficient in several ways, not least of which was that he had a very loose understanding of Christian origins and was largely ignorant of biblical scholarship. Also, Halbwachs chose a topic where the commemorative activity took place long after the initial perceptions and memories of the historical events; cf. Gedi and Elam (1996: 40–6). Yet it was his method of emphasizing the localization of tradition over and against the historical event that endeared him to later historiographers. See Pierre Nora (1996) for the most extensive application of this method.

In contrast, contemporary Social Memory theorists have abandoned the dichotomy between objective history and subjective memory. Most theorists are careful to point out that memory is a conflation of these spheres (J. Assmann 1995: 366; Lowenthal 1985: 210; Schwartz 1982: 396; Weissberg 1999: 10). Halbwachs's original theory described the mnemonic process in terms of 'localization'. Localization is the process through which perceptions are placed within specific mental frames of meaning (1992: 38–43). Such frames reinforce new perceptions within previously established interpretative categories (Hutton 1993: 78; J. Assmann 2000: 114). Mental images associated with the past are localized within imaginative contexts that serve to render them meaningful and intelligible (Halbwachs 1992: 53). In order for something to be remembered at all, it must be localized and reinforced within a familiar frame of meaning.

Thus memory could be thought of as an interpretative vacillation between new perceptions and previously established cognitive frameworks. Personal memory is now thought to be 'an active, constructive process, not a simple matter of retrieving information. To remember is to place a part of the past in the service of conceptions and needs of the present' (Schwartz 1982: 374). With this in mind, memory's contemporary use as a metaphor for history was bound to be reconsidered. This leads us to the (previously mentioned) second, and now more popular, application of Social Memory.

Memory and Commemoration

My essay has thus far shown the dissimilarity between memory's denotative value and its metaphorical use. For the sake of clarity and consistency, I will hereafter refer to this as the difference between *memory* and *commemoration*. Unfortunately, this is not a semantic distinction that is common to Social Memory. Memory as metaphor is most often considered the same as commemorative activity. But, in the conflation of these semantic spheres, memory's denotative value (and its importance for historiographical discussion) often goes under-appreciated. For this reason, I would contend that words like *tradition* and *commemoration* are ultimately more helpful in such discussions (cf. Gedi and Elam 1996: 30–2). Because I see value implied in the metaphor, I will use the word commemoration in the rest of this essay.

The commemorative process involves the selection, isolation and celebration of historical events or figures that are deemed significant or in some way defining of a group's collective identity. While commemoration is often thought of in terms of physical sites (e.g. statues or *Festschrifts*) and times (i.e. dates on a calendar), the act of historical writing is also a commemorative act. Alan Kirk aptly summarizes the relationship between commemorative narrative and collective identity:

[Memories of a community's origins] are shaped into a community's 'master commemorative narrative'; moreover, through recitation of its master narrative a group continually reconstitutes itself as a coherent community, and as it moves forward through its history it aligns its fresh experiences with this master narrative, as well as vice versa. (Kirk 2005: 5)[14]

Kirk's 'vice versa' warrants further explanation. It is perhaps academically intuitive to affirm the role that metanarratives play in self-identification and world view. In order to fill out this picture, it must be said that community-defining stories are subject to change alongside new perceptions and emerging ideologies.[15] Significant historical events are often reinterpreted to accommodate shifting ideologies and used to promote idealized cultural identities. That commemoration is useful to the aims and ideals of the present context is more important than its 'accurate' representation of the past (Zerubavel 1995: 7–8).

This approach to Social Memory emphasizes the role of the contemporary interpreters over that of the original perceivers of the event. As a result, analysis of commemoration tells us more about the commemorators and less about the historical events being commemorated. In addition, it is important to state that Social Memory most commonly employs commemorative analysis when a long period of time has elapsed between the initial perceptions and the commemoration, by which I mean a period measured by multiple generations.

For example, when Pierre Nora examines the ideological and political motives behind the planning of France's bicentennial celebration, his aim is to speak of an imposed national commemoration; in other words, a politically-charged and strategic commemoration (1996: 611–37). Nora is ultimately interested in the French national identity as it stands two hundred years after the revolution. Similarly, when Barry Schwartz (1982) examines the changing significance of the national monuments in Washington DC, his aim is to speak of how later generations utilized perceptions of the past. In both cases, the interest is in the *history of tradition*, and therefore the emphasis is on the commemorating communities. One is free to apply this method to commemorative activities that occur within the same generation of the event (cf. Zerubavel 1994), but in such cases the historian is obligated to fill out this picture by discussing personal testimonies (i.e. the memories of those contemporary to the event). This measuring of commemorative aims

---

14   Cf. Y. Zerubavel (1995: 4–7). It is also important to note that commemorative activity is not limited to a particular genre. Rather, it is a 'culture-formative impulse that ramifies into a wide range of artifacts, commemorative narratives, and ritual practices' (Kirk 2005: 7).

15   Each point of gravity holds the other in check during this process.

against personal memories simply returns the discussion to personal, social memory as Halbwachs originally conceived it.[16]

My point is that Social Memory's historiographical interest in commemoration should only be applied *independently* when there are no personal memories to be measured. To avoid discussion of personal memory when the commemoration has been shaped by living memories of the historical event is irresponsible. It is important for historians to know and state clearly when they are using memory as a metaphor, and when they are referring to literal memories. Indeed, failure to do so misleads the analysis. Evidence of early perception demands historiographical analysis that is appropriate to this phenomenon (Dunn 2004: 478–9). Social Memory can best provide such analysis when Halbwachs's original work on personal memory is adapted and utilized, and then supplemented with his later work on commemoration.

It is important, however, that I emphasize that the hermeneutics of commemoration begin at a very early stage in personal memory. Indeed many theorists argue that personal memory and commemoration cannot be disentangled. I agree that the two are inextricably enmeshed. What I add to this stance is that when commemorative activity exists alongside personal memory, both forms of social memory analysis should be considered as equal movements around the hermeneutical circle (Le Donne 2009: 65–92).

A suitable example of the interaction between memory and commemoration can be seen in the 2006 funeral of Coretta Scott King. She was best known for her marriage to Martin Luther King, and her funeral became a celebration of America's civil rights movement. Because the significance of her life was localized in memories of the civil rights movement, the occasion of her death was a national commemoration. Memories of Coretta Scott were filtered through this mnemonic localization. The commemorating community utilized their memories of Coretta Scott King to ideologically reinforce the ideal of racial reconciliation and social justice, virtues that have been repeatedly commemorated in the celebration of her husband.

These observations represent the interests of commemorative analysis and are important because they speak to the condition of a specific idealized American ideology in 2006. But what is equally important in this discussion is the fact that this commemorative event was composed of personal testimonies. There is no doubt that the shared memories of Coretta Scott King were refracted (Schudson 1995: 346)[17] by selection and convention so as

---

16   Again, I must point out the notable caveat that contemporary Social Memory theorists return to this discussion with historiographical interests. As discussed, this is a departure from Halbwachs's interests.

17   M. Schudson uses the phrase 'memory distortion' as it is a common term in SM. I prefer to use the word memory 'refraction' as it carries less negative connotations (Le Donne 2009: 50–2). By 'distorted' SM theorists do not mean 'false'. In this case, I apply the word refraction to the social conventions required of people attending funerals. In such contexts, one almost intuitively knows how to filter out inappropriate memories. And when one does not, the individual will be corrected by the group.

to make them appropriate for the ceremony. Thus the commemoration itself acted as a social constraint. Within this framework, the memories of King spoke to the impact of her life in the 1960s and, of course, reinforced the impact of her husband's life in the process. These memories provide a window (no doubt, tinted) on a historically significant movement of the 1960s. Thus our discussion and analysis is not limited to 2006. The memories of King's life represent an unbroken continuity between her history and her historical impact. It was this historical impact that helped to launch the ideological frameworks by which her life was eventually commemorated. In other words, she played a major part in determining how her own life would be appropriately refracted.

Within the first two generations of a historical event (or in this case, a movement) it is nearly impossible to analyse the commemoration without also analysing the initial perceptions, memories and interpretations of that event. One cannot completely isolate a historical event from its impact and the trajectory of stories set in motion thereby.[18] If a story becomes culturally significant enough to transcend its original application and is applied to a larger ideological framework, a distance is created between the story and the event. Even so, such refraction is held in check by the initial interpretations of that event. The further removed the commemoration is from the historical event, the less likely these spheres will interact. Memory theorists call this transition a 'crisis of memory'.[19] But until this crisis has completely run its course, commemorative analysis must be coupled with memory analysis.

James Dunn has recently observed that Social Memory has tended to place 'emphasis on the *creative*, rather than the *retentive* function of memory'. In his view, an overemphasis on the interpretative reinforcement (i.e. distortion) of memory weights the analysis too heavily toward 'the character of the communities which maintained the tradition' (2007: 180). Dunn's criticism suitably describes the tendencies of *commemorative* analysis but overlooks the other half of the equation. As argued here, this tendency can and should be tempered when coupled with *memory* analysis. What Dunn notices, then, is the lack of clarity provided by Social Memory theorists with regard to the use of the word 'memory'.

Because the Gospels represent a marriage between memory and commemoration, neither approach will be independently sufficient for a mnemonic

---

18   Cf. M. Moxter (2002: 78–87), who borrows from Ricoeur in his discussion of the relationship between event and story.

19   J. Assmann (1992: 11, 50–6) suggests a span of forty years for 'kommunikative Gedächtnis', or, more specifically, the period when the first generation begins to die. He juxtaposes this with 'kulturelle Gedächtnis'. Elsewhere (Assmann 2006: 30), he speaks of communicative memory in terms of a three-generation framework. M. Bockmuehl (2007) has recently suggested a 'living memory' that extends to the second generation (approximately 70 to 150 years).

analysis of the Jesus tradition. But conversely, when Social Memory is applied in both respects to the Gospels, one can expect results that shed light both on how Jesus was initially remembered, and on how these memories contributed to his commemoration in early Christianity. Over the remainder of this essay, I will apply both of the above approaches to Jesus's relationship with ideology concerning the eschatological temple.

Jesus's Temple-saying: Memory or Invention?

In the above discussion, I have borrowed from Halbwachs to speak of memory in terms of *imaginative* reinforcement; this should not be confused with wholesale *imagination*. The acknowledgment that memory is a *creative* process should not be confused with wholesale *creation*. There is, after all, a difference between an invented story and a memory-story. While the two narratives might look similar, the initial act of telling a memory-story is different. While there is likely overlap in the cognitive processes, the crucial difference is this: *Does the story have an origin in perception or invention?* In most cases, both the storyteller and the audience presuppose an answer to this question and thus the historian must attempt to answer it as well.[20]

To appeal to the role of memory in interpretation, one must first determine that there was an initial perception. This, of course, cannot be assumed with regard to the Gospels. Therefore, within Jesus research, judicious use of authenticity criteria is often required.[21] Consider the following texts:[22]

> The Jews then said to him, 'What sign do you show us as your authority for doing these things?' Jesus answered them, 'Destroy this temple, and in three days I will raise it up.' The Jews then said, 'It took forty-six years to build this temple, and you will raise it up in three days?' But he was speaking of the temple of his body. (John 2.18-21)

> For many were giving false testimony against him, but their testimony was not consistent. Some stood up and began to give false testimony against Him, saying, 'We heard him say, "I will destroy this temple made with hands, and in three days I will build another made without hands."' Not even in this respect was their testimony consistent. (Mark 14.56-9)

---

20   This is by no means the historian's only task, but it is important nonetheless. A large part of the interpretation of history is the accounting of the interpretations of the initial perceivers.

21   In my view, authenticity criteria cannot provide a window to past events; rather they help to plausibly explain certain accounts and sayings as early and widespread memories. Because of this, I use the word 'authenticity' reluctantly.

22   ἐγὼ καταλύσω τὸν ναὸν τοῦτον τὸν χειροποίητον καὶ διὰ τριῶν ἡμερῶν ἄλλον ἀχειροποίητον οἰκοδομήσω (Mark 14.58); cf. λύσατε τὸν ναὸν τοῦτον καὶ ἐν τρισὶν ἡμέραις ἐγερῶ αὐτόν (John 2.19).

In both texts, a quote of Jesus has been framed within a particular redactional interpretation. Before moving forward to mnemonic analysis, three observations are required. (1) While the quotations attributed to Jesus share a conceptual kinship, there is enough variance to suggest independent circulation (Dodd 1963: 90–1; Bultmann 1971: 126; Brown 1966: 2:120–1; Beasley-Murray 1999: 38), and therefore the criterion of multiple attestation is warranted.[23] (2) Both Evangelists seem to have included their respective quotations in reaction to a previous (perhaps embarrassing)[24] perception of Jesus. Both seem intent on counteracting a similar perception, thus providing evidence that these quotations represent a reaction to an early and widespread memory of Jesus. (3) The Evangelists are both making an interpretative move away from this memory but are moving in different directions: Mark places the purported quotation on the lips of false witnesses, while John turns the saying into a metaphor for Jesus's resurrection.

By analysing the disparate redactions concerning Jesus's words, I will suggest an approximate mnemonic sphere that gave rise to these interpretative trajectories. In this way, the issue of Jesus's temple-saying will be measured against previous and parallel mnemonic categories, and against the redactional tendencies of the Evangelists. In doing so, my analysis of mnemonic trajectories will also set an interpretative backdrop for the historical Jesus. This will require analysis of two ideologies concerning the eschatological temple, one where Jesus has been remembered as temple builder/bringer, the other where Jesus has been commemorated as metaphorical temple. I will begin with the latter.

Johannine Commemoration of Jesus as Temple Replacement

One of the central questions that commemorative analysis attempts to answer is: *What does the commemorative activity tell us about the identity of the community?* Several subsets branch forth from this central interest. For example: *How does the community want to define itself? How does the community want outsiders to perceive them? Are there competing interests within the community? Does the commemoration in question represent a shift in the community's ideology?*[25] And in the case of early Christianity, it is appropriate to speak of *ideology* in terms of *theology*.

---

23   There are, of course, other sayings in the Jesus tradition with similar content which solidify this appeal (Mark 15.29-30; Thom. 71). And if Mark 11.23; 13.1-2 were to be included as related sayings, one could also appeal to the criterion of multiple forms.

24   'All of the evangelists have to face the difficulty that Jesus did not literally fulfil the promise involved in this saying' (Brown 1966: 2:120).

25   As previously discussed, all of these questions presuppose that perceptions of the past can be utilized to serve the ideological interests of the present. Hence these questions often yield results that confirm this premise. But it will be helpful to offer a qualification

Recently, Thatcher has applied such analysis to John 2.13-22. He points out that the disciples remembered Jesus's temple-action and temple-saying in a way that 'altered' their 'initial neurological impressions' (2005a: 82–3). This seems to be the case in both verses 17 and 22. In the first instance, the disciples 'remembered' Jesus's temple action in light of Ps. 69.9. In the second instance, the disciples 'remembered [ἐμνήσθησαν[26]]' Jesus's temple-saying in light of his resurrection and Scripture. It is worth noting that in the latter case, there is no scriptural citation. Verse 22 should therefore probably be seen as a mnemonic reflection on both pericopae. So while it is the temple-saying that most interests the present study, Thatcher's assessment of verse 17 is of immediate pertinence (2005a: 83):

> John does not portray the disciples' memory of the temple incident as a simple act of recall … this memory was accompanied by the disciples' 'belief', a belief not in the veracity of their own recollections but rather in the words that Jesus had spoken on that occasion and 'the Scriptures' of the Hebrew Bible. (John 2.22)

Thatcher draws from John 7.37-9 and 20.22 to label this kind of commemoration 'pneumatic memory', and he describes it as 'a complex reconfiguration of past experience' in light of new interpretations of Scripture that had been prompted by the Holy Spirit.[27] In doing so, he argues that the Fourth Gospel was, by nature, a commemoration of how the community's religious experience interacted with their memories of Jesus.

In addition to these insights, it is crucial to point out that, in the case of John 2.18-22, Jesus's resurrection is the mnemonic centre of gravity. There are several mnemonic spheres at work in this pericope: (1) the temple, (2) 'the Jews', (3) Hebrew Scripture and (4) Jesus's resurrection. But it is the last, most dominant, category that informs the significance of the others. John 2.22 suggests that Johannine belief in the resurrection was so important for the group's collective identity that this mnemonic frame realigned previous memories of Jesus accordingly. The resurrection of Jesus became a sort of interpretative memory-grid through which the other mnemonic spheres were reshaped and given new meaning. While the first three mnemonic

on this point. There is no doubt that commemorative activity consciously manipulates perceptions of the past. Returning to the example of Coretta Scott King, funerals tend to consciously filter out negative memories of the person being commemorated. But it is also true that many ideologies undergird commemorative activity; they exist primarily on a subconscious level. Most often ideologies exist on the level of world view, and are simply taken for granted by communities. In such cases, it would be misleading to speak of commemoration in terms of 'manipulation' as this connotes conscious intention.

26   The same inflection of μιμνήσκω is used in both verses.

27   Thatcher concludes that 'because John does not view memory as a mental archive of information but rather as a complex spiritual experience, it seems unlikely that he would [write a Gospel] in order to preserve traditional material about Jesus for later review and recitation' (2005: 84–5).

categories held prominent places in the Jewish-Christian metanarrative,[28] Jesus's resurrection came to be seen as the teleological climax of Israel's salvation-history,[29] a keenly realized eschatology. It is not within the scope of this study to discuss how Johannine resurrection-belief coloured the interpretation of Scripture or 'the Jews'; I will here limit my discussion to Jesus and the temple.

That the Jerusalem temple represented the presence/glory of YHWH and the locus for Israel's worship is well known. But for the Johannine community, Christ occupied this locus. Beasley-Murray comments that, in Johannine theology, '[T]he glory of God and the presence of God are revealed in the only Son and his redemptive acts; it is in and through him that mankind experiences that presence, is transfigured by that glory, and offers a worship worthy of his name' (1999: 42). John's commemoration of Jesus's temple-saying demonstrates a theological shift from one pole to another. The divine locus, once occupied by the temple, had shifted in John's eschatological framework to the resurrected body of Jesus. The memory of Jesus's temple-saying was commemorated as such.

There is perhaps no better example in the Gospels of a discrepancy between saying and interpretation. John's interpretative shift plainly illustrates the disparity between Jesus's original preaching and later preaching about Jesus. And yet John 2.19 includes Jesus's saying all the same. There has been no attempt to place the Johannine interpretation on the lips of Jesus. E. P. Sanders rightly asserts: 'John 2.19 shows how deeply embedded in the tradition was the threat of destroying and the promise of rebuilding the temple. It was so firmly fixed that it was not dropped, but rather interpreted' (1985: 72–3). So while Thatcher (2005a: 85) is correct to say that John's Gospel was not written 'in order to preserve traditional material about Jesus for later review and recitation', such material is nonetheless evident and available for analysis. Moreover, it has been prominently displayed in this pericope. The memory has been framed by the commemoration.

Markan Commemoration of Jesus as Righteous Suffering Servant

There can be no doubt that Mark, like John, is a commemorative account. In many ways, Mark has reinterpreted memories of Jesus in light of a particular post-Easter agenda. Mark's narrative commemoration of Jesus speaks to certain concerns about his present reality, not the least of which is that the 'idea of a Messiah who is rejected by the priests and who dies on a cross is

---

28   Cf. Kirk's discussion of 'master commemorative narrative' quoted above.

29   On this point it is difficult not to echo Karl Barth (1922: 77): 'Jesus von Nazareth ist unter diesen vielen [zerstreuten Punkten der Geschichte] derjenige, an dem die übrigen in ihrer zusammenhängenden Bedeutung als Linie, als der eigentliche rote Faden der Geschichte erkannt werden.'

unimaginable. But this is what happened' (Evans 2001: 20). What is being commemorated in Mark's Passion is Jesus's supposed innocence and vindication. Jesus, much like the Righteous Sufferer of the Psalms (e.g. Psalms 22, 31, 34, 35 and 69), was innocent and accused falsely, and would eventually be vindicated by God. Joel Green writes:

> Like the Servant, Jesus (1) is God's chosen one who will complete his mission through suffering; (2) willingly submits to his divine mission; (3) is innocent; (4) maintains his silence; (5) dies 'for many'; (6) is 'handed over'; (7) is abused; (8) is 'numbered with transgressors'; (9) anticipates his vindication; and (10) is vindicated after maltreatment. (1988: 317–8)

It should be expected then that Mark's account of Jesus's trial and his time on the cross are commemorated with this agenda in mind. Pertinent to the present study is the inclusion of Jesus's temple-saying in these contexts.

> For many were giving false testimony against him, but their testimony was not consistent. Some stood up and began to give false testimony against him, saying, 'We heard him say, "I will destroy this temple made with hands, and in three days I will build another made without hands."' Not even in this respect was their testimony consistent. (Mark 14.56-9)

> Those passing by were hurling abuse at him, wagging their heads, and saying, 'Ha! You who destroy the temple and rebuild it in three days, save yourself, and come down from the cross!' (Mark 15.29-30)

Like John, Mark is uncomfortable with this perception of Jesus. However, instead of turning the quote into a metaphor, Mark employs what memory theorists call a counter-memory. This is a memory that aims to dispel, cover over or correct another popular manifestation of a memory. In an attempt to counteract this memory, Mark utilizes the quote within Green's third and seventh interpretative categories to commemorate Jesus's innocence (14.56-9) and his wrongful abuse (15.29-30). This utilization influenced the placement of the quote on the lips of Jesus's antagonists. Still, Mark is also uncomfortable with the direct denial that Jesus said as much. Notice that the 'false witnesses' are merely 'inconsistent'[30] in their testimony; there is no reframing of the saying which claims that they fabricated it. While Mark's agenda motivated him to place the saying on the lips of Jesus's antagonists, he is constrained by sayings such as Mark 11.23 and 13.1-2, which hold his agenda in check.

As with John, we see that the commemoration has not eclipsed the memories. The memories of Jesus's historical stance concerning the temple are prominently displayed, framed in the counter-memory of the commemo-

---

30   ἴσος is used in both 14.56 and 59.

rative narrative. With this in mind, our mnemonic analysis has already moved from commemorative analysis to memory analysis.

Memories of Jesus as Eschatological Temple Builder

All things considered, we can best describe Mark 14 and John 2 as commemorative lenses which refract the same memory in separate directions. Furthermore, it is highly likely that these stories represent commemorative trajectories which share the same mnemonic sphere – namely, the perception that Jesus made a claim similar to that of which he was accused by Mark's false witness in 14.58 (Dibelius 1932: 193). This does not necessarily speak to the historicity of Mark's trial narrative. It is more likely that the Evangelist has placed this on the lips of his antagonists in response to an early and widespread memory of Jesus's claim. Nonetheless, it is likely that Jesus was remembered to have made such a claim.

In order to examine how this saying might have been perceived and initially remembered by contemporaries of Jesus, it will be necessary to discuss the interpretative categories available in this context. In other words, I aim to describe the social frameworks which spurred and constrained memories of Jesus and his relationship to the Jerusalem temple.

It is not advisable to depict a single national Jewish sentiment toward the Jerusalem temple. Surely the first century alone manifested a wide spectrum of perspectives in this regard. It is, however, necessary to observe that there was a long-standing Jewish sentiment (among many) that considered the temple to have been defiled by its ministers and no longer worthy to house the presence of God. Ezek. 8–10 describes the glory of God departing from the temple for this reason. Because of this, the prophet believes that a new temple is required in order for God's glory to return (Ezek. 43.1-12). Ezekiel 40–8 is the prophet's final vision of a new and eternal heavenly temple, Jerusalem and theocracy.

Central to this portrayal is the notion that the earthly temple and its ministers had failed to mirror the temple and cultus of heaven. This is confirmed by the *Apocalypse of Weeks* which states that every generation from the exile onward has been corrupt because no one during that time was able to understand the true temple cult or heavenly matters.[31] It is upon this foundation that the *Testament of Levi* makes a similar critique of the earthly priesthood, and expects an eschatological priest to eventually come and establish a new temple from heaven. The author writes of this priest in this way: 'The heavens shall be opened, and from the temple of glory

---

31   M. O. Wise (1992: 814) points out that this should be understood within the larger indictment of 1 En. 83-90 where the Temple of Zerubbabel is criticized for being ritually impure. According to the writer, all of the bread on the altar is 'polluted and impure' (1 En. 89.72-3).

sanctification shall come upon him' (T. Levi 17.10). Granted, exegetical use of *T. Levi* to establish a Jewish interpretative trajectory is complex because this book has been substantially redacted by a Christian editor. Fortunately, 4Q541 preserves a comparatively large fragment (9, Col. 1) of *T. Levi* which confirms that the pre-Christian version expected this eschatological figure to re-establish an effective temple cult. This document expects the figure to make atonement for his generation, and enact God's commands on earth as they have been issued in heaven. The fragment does not specifically preserve the statement of 17.10 which speaks of the heavenly 'temple of glory', but 4Q541 confirms enough about this figure to take seriously the possibility that the pre-Christian version was extending the trajectory of Ezek. 40-8. What is new is the belief that the eschatological temple would be ushered in by a specific figure. This belief comes not from Ezekiel, but most likely from Zechariah.

Zechariah offers a prophecy concerning Zerubbabel: 'Behold, a man whose name is Branch, for he will branch out from where he is, and he will build the temple of YHWH' (6.12). The Targum of Zechariah interprets this messianically by inserting the title 'Messiah' in place of the name 'Branch'.[32] The belief that the Messiah would rebuild the temple is also attested in Tg. Isa 53.5. Elsewhere YHWH himself is expected to build the temple (11QTemple 29.7-10; cf. 2 Bar. 4.3). These beliefs do not necessarily contradict each other if the Messiah is seen as God's agent on earth. One could say that YHWH's metaphorical 'hands' are the literal actions of the Messiah.[33] Indeed, this metaphor is made explicit in the rabbinic interpretation of Solomon's first temple construction: 'But when He [YHWH] came to build the temple, He did it, as is done, with both of His hands, as it is said, "The sanctuary, Oh Lord, which your hands have established"' (*Mekilta* on Ex. 15.17-21). Here the rabbi is not claiming that YHWH built the temple instead of Solomon, he is merely giving the proper credit to God for Solomon's construction. In this same way, the Meturgeman(s) can envision the Messiah as the temple builder and elsewhere speak of God's 'palms' doing the work.

In summary, criticism of Israel's priesthood was a well-established voice in Hebrew Scripture. This voice was given a specific shape by Ezekiel, who depicted YHWH's presence forsaking the temple until a new temple of heaven was erected in the eschaton. This trajectory was extended to include an eschatological temple builder. Some circles, like those represented by *T. Levi* (cf. 4Q541), envisioned this figure as a priest who would minister in the temple of heaven. Other circles, like those represented by *Tg. Zech.* and *Tg. Isa.* (cf. Zech. 6.12), emphasized the role of the Davidic Messiah as the temple builder. Still others, like those represented by 11QTemple and

---

32   It is important to remember that Zechariah speaks of two anointed figures (cf. 4.14); one sprouting from David's family tree ('branch', i.e. Zerubbabel) and the other being the high priest (Joshua).

33   This is the image given in Ps. 110.2 where YHWH extends the king's sceptre.

2 Baruch, believed that YHWH himself would build the eschatological temple.

Crucial to this discussion is the eschatological character of these interpretative trajectories. These texts not only represent possible mnemonic categories, but they are also intended to project forward and provide an interpretative grid by which future realities might be measured. In the first century, some communities were more eschatologically-minded, some less. Those who were inclined to interpret contemporary events in eschatological ways were also inclined to associate specific characters, regimes, problems, victories and salvations of the past with those of the present. It is possible that fervent expectation for a new temple and a pure priesthood acted as a catalyst for dissatisfaction with the contemporary temple and temple establishment. And, of course, dissatisfaction with the first-century temple establishment called to mind such texts and thus spurred eschatological hopes. The cyclical character of mnemonic localization provides continuity between perceptions of the past and present.

With eschatological memory, this continuity has the capacity to collapse into a single historically defining moment, one where metanarratives, future hopes and present realities collapse into one climatic event. The expectations for a new temple from heaven seem to have the markings of such mnemonic categories. Commenting on Jesus's temple-saying, Wise writes that 'it is felicitous to see here a messianic declaration in which Jesus clears the way for the temple of the eschaton [...] and, presumably, a new Jerusalem' (Wise 1992: 814). Similarly, Theissen sees in the temple-saying an outworking of such eschatological hopes as well as a statement coherent with the rest of Jesus's preaching ministry. In his assessment, the saying stems from 'the desire for a temple which directly comes from God and is not woven into the net of human interests'.[34] If this is so, we may conclude that Jesus was perceived by many as the Davidic Messiah or/and the eschatological priest associated with the above mnemonic categories. In either case, Jesus's claim would have been perceived as (1) a stance of opposition to the current temple establishment, and (2) an aim to usher in the eschatological temple of heaven.

'λέγω δὲ ὑμῖν ὅτι τοῦ ἱεροῦ μεῖζόν ἐστιν ὧδε' (John 12.6).

From Memory to Commemoration

I have thus far charted three interpretative trajectories – that of (1) Mark's agenda to vindicate Jesus, (2) the FG's agenda to move Jesus to the locus of veneration in place of the fallen temple, and (3) the negative Jewish sentiments concerning the temple's purity and eschatological remedy. As Jesus was a Jew who spoke out concerning the temple, and was also a historical

---

34   G. Theissen 1976: 158. Theissen is speaking specifically of the hopes of rural Israel as opposed to the city-dwelling population.

figure who became the object of veneration for early Christianity, the sphere of his mnemonic impact must stand in relationship to these trajectories.

At first glance, the initial interpretation of Jesus's saying and the Evangelists' framing of it seem thoroughly dissimilar. Indeed, the FG's commemoration has significantly altered the force of the initial memory. While there can be no doubt that a significant theological shift has taken place between these mnemonic spheres, neither interpretation was formed in a vacuum. The two spheres are therefore connected by an interpretative trajectory (Schröter 2002: 204). As dissimilar as they might seem, John 2.18-22 stands (with at least one foot) along the same interpretative trajectory that spurred and constrained the initial perceptions of Jesus as represented by Mark 14.58-9. Following the cycle of the mnemonic process, Jesus's temple-saying, in turn, became a mnemonic vehicle which carried a particular Jewish eschatology into early Christian commemoration. Specifically, this saying mnemonically evoked the Jewish-messianic hope that YHWH's presence would be mediated purely, free from a polluted Jerusalem priesthood. At least this much can be localized within an Ezekiel (*et al*) framework.

Upon entering the Johannine SM frame, the temple-saying was commem-orated in light of the belief in Jesus's resurrection and in the reality that the Jerusalem temple had been destroyed. In the post-70 absence of the temple, the resurrected Jesus came to represent the very presence and glory of God. John's localization of the temple's significance within Jesus's resurrection was a dramatic shift from what Jesus's original audience would have remembered of this saying in a pre-Easter, pre-70 context. Still, these two mnemonic frames cannot be wholly divorced from one another as the latter owes its mnemonic heritage to the eschatological framework evoked by the historical Jesus. Jesus claimed to finally mediate God's pure presence among his people with a new temple, and John believed that Jesus accomplished this very thing in his resurrection and new life.

If indeed there is continuity between these spheres, we ought to be able to plausibly map this interpretative shift. So what evidence do we have of a middle-ground between how Jesus was initially remembered and John's commemoration? After all, it is quite an exegetical leap from eschatological temple to resurrection. By 'middle-ground' I mean a saying or story that could be exegeted along either line, i.e. a pericope that could be read in light of either mnemonic sphere.

Perhaps Matthew 12.5-6 provides evidence of such. After an appeal to David in a discussion about the Sabbath, the Matthean Jesus adds, 'Or have you not read in the Law, that on the Sabbath the priests in the temple break the Sabbath and are innocent? But I say to you that [something] greater than the temple is here.'[35] How are we to understand Jesus's meaning? From a Johannine vantage point it would seem that Jesus was claiming that his

---

35 'λέγω δὲ ὑμῖν ὅτι τοῦ ἱεροῦ μεῖζόν ἐστιν ὧδε' (John 12.6).

personal presence had trumped the significance of the temple. If this is the case, we should translate it as '*someone* greater than the temple...' On the other hand, if the saying is read from the vantage point of Ezekiel *et al*, Jesus would seem to be anticipating the imminent arrival of the eschatological temple. For the purposes of the present study, I will not attempt to answer the question of origin. What is presently important is that this saying would seem to be at home in either mnemonic sphere. I am not under the impression that the Fourth Evangelist or his community had knowledge of the saying represented by Matthew 12.5-6. But the (possible) dual character of this saying might be suggestive of John's point of departure and subsequent logic. In this way, the interpretative leap from Jesus to John can be plausibly mapped.

John's commemorative redaction was authored within a uniquely Jewish, eschatological framework. These commemorators believed that the hopes first enunciated by Ezekiel had been realized in the life of Jesus. In this respect, Jesus and John shared the same social framework.

Conclusion

In my analysis of Jesus's temple-saying, I have attempted to demonstrate that (1) commemorative analysis is most helpful to Gospel study when it is coupled with memory analysis. (2) Once the exegete has located two or more commemorative trajectories, a plausible mnemonic origin can be postulated and measured against the backdrop of the historically relevant interpretative categories. (3) The ensuing discussion about the continuity from memory to commemoration helps to complete the historical picture; by discussing the mnemonic frameworks available to Jesus's contemporaries, a fuller analysis of John's commemoration has been offered.

Finally, I would be remiss not to acknowledge the affinity of this approach with early form criticism (Kirk and Thatcher 2005: 30; Dunn 2007: 179). Essentially the premise is the same. By employing mnemonic analysis, I have distinguished primitive forms from later redaction. 'Redaction', of course, is not how the community of the FG would have thought of it. However, it is still a useful term to show the seeds of historical memories within commemorative frameworks. And on this point, I must remind myself not to become so focused on the character of the communities that I neglect the character of the tradition. I think that my approach has avoided this tendency of classic form criticism. By emphasizing the essential continuity between the remembered and the commemorated forms, I have not presented an insurmountable rift between Jesus and the early Church. Surely, memories of Jesus must stand somewhere in between, morphing with and stabilizing the commemoration as all significant memories will do.

Chapter 11

ABRAHAM AS A FIGURE OF MEMORY IN JOHN 8.31-59

Catrin H. Williams

The aim of this investigation is to analyse the Johannine depiction of
Abraham in the light of the first-century media culture from which John's
Gospel emerged, a culture in which orality and memory played decisive
roles in the composition and reception of texts. By identifying features which
indicate that John 8.31-59 was designed for oral delivery, possibly from
memory, this essay will seek to determine the extent to which the discovery
of orally-derived techniques and communicative devices within this text can
shed light on its portrayal of Abraham and on the intended impact of that
portrayal on the text's original audience, particularly with regard to the
shaping of their self-understanding as a group. It will be argued that one of
the key strategies for group demarcation identifiable within the passage is the
way in which it draws upon a selection of traditions about Abraham in order
to develop a distinctively Johannine collective memory of the patriarch. For
this purpose, the role of memory in John 8.31-59 will be investigated in the
light of recent social and cultural memory approaches, in order to address
the questions: how is Abraham remembered, and what do we learn about
those who remember him?

As in the case of other figures from Israel's past, all 11 references to the
patriarch Abraham in the Gospel of John are confined to the narrative of
Jesus's public ministry. Unlike other patriarchs or prophets, especially Moses,
whose name and deeds are recalled, sometimes incidentally, in several of the
Gospel's narratives and discourses, Abraham only comes to prominence in
one extended dialogue between Jesus and those described, at least initially, as
'the Jews who had believed in him' (8.31-59). The role played by Abraham in
the three parts of this discussion can be outlined as follows: appeal to descent
from the patriarch is made by those who reject Jesus's offer of freedom (8.31-
6), which leads to a discussion on matters relating to kinship and paternity
(8.37-47), before the scene concludes with a heated exchange about the
relationship between Abraham and Jesus (8.48-59). What is less clear is the
interrelationship of these three dialogue components, and, especially with
reference to the second, whether a connection is established within the text
between descent from Abraham and descent from God.

The text's apparent ambiguity on these issues accounts, to a large extent, for the wide divergence in the scholarly assessments of its presentation of Abraham. While all commentators agree that the enduring Johannine image of the patriarch is that of a witness to Jesus who has seen his 'day' (8.56), it has been proposed, on the basis of this and earlier statements in the passage, that Abraham, for John, proved himself to be a 'disciple of Jesus', a 'child of God' (Siker 1991: 142), and even that Jesus is implicitly depicted as 'the true descendant of Abraham' (Barrett 1978: 334, 346). Such estimations differ significantly from recent interpretations of the relationship between Abraham and Jesus in terms of contrast rather than continuity, with the result that 'the Johannine Christians view such basic figures of Jewish tradition as Abraham from the standpoint of outsiders' (Hakola 2005: 187). This variety of opinion is, of course, part and parcel of the wider debate about the 'Jewishness' of John's Gospel, how it appropriates its scriptural heritage, and the ways in which the author and first recipients try to articulate their self-definition in relation to Judaism. Attempts at examining the portrayal of Abraham in John 8 have, nevertheless, either tended to focus on some of its textual features more closely than others, or paid insufficient attention to the function of Abraham with reference to each of its three main parts (8.31-6, 37-47, 48-59). The present discussion will seek to demonstrate that considerations of memory and oral composition can provide a more viable interpretation of the depiction of the patriarch in John 8.31-59.

Given the low literacy rate in the first-century CE Mediterranean world (Harris 1989; Hezser 2001), as well as the expensive and unwieldy nature of much of its writing materials, New Testament scholars are increasingly coming to terms with the highly oral/aural environment in which written texts were produced and received. Some texts were transcripts of oral performances, while others were written with a view to their oral communication, to be read aloud in a communal setting rather than for silent consumption by a solitary reader. The recognition that written texts needed to fulfil an effective performative function for a listening audience meant that oral conventions continued to influence their composition, so that a close symbiotic relationship existed between a written text and the dynamics of its oral delivery.

The implications of the ongoing interaction between orality and textuality in what can be described as the 'residually oral' (Ong 1982: 43) or 'oral-written' (Dewey 2001) media world of the first century CE are only now beginning to be explored in Johannine studies. There is much work to be done in this area, not least investigating whether the text of John's Gospel offers clues that, as a written composition, it was designed from the outset for the purpose of oral communication and has been constructed in a way that facilitates its aural reception in a group setting. The need to engage with this particular task has been affirmed by Joanna Dewey, who claims that John, like Mark, belongs at 'the oral end of the continuum' as far as the New Testament writings are concerned (2001: 242). She notes, for example, that John contains many simple clauses and instances of present tense verbs, and, building on her earlier engagement with the work of Eric Havelock (1963: 20–35, 174, 180; cf. Dewey 1989: 34–8), she identifies a number of features in the text that are characteristic of oral media, including its many and visually concrete 'happenings' in the form of miracles, dialogues and discourses (2001: 250). Without focusing on individual passages, Dewey also offers a number of helpful guidelines on how to detect other oral traits and oral compositional techniques in the Gospel. These guidelines will, in part, assist my own exploratory attempt at identifying some of the elements in 8.31-59 that point to the author's consciousness of the oral/aural context in which the text would be used. Among these elements, as we shall see, are the use of *inclusio*, striking patterns of repetition, devices that encourage audience engagement, and the agonistic tone of the encounter between Jesus and his Jewish interlocutors.

Orality, Oral Performance, and John 8.31-59

That John 8.31-59 forms a discrete unit of communication is supported by the clear demarcation, at its end, between the reference to Jesus's departure from the temple (8.59) and the introduction to his encounter with the man blind from birth (9.1). There has, however, been much debate as to where the unit begins: do 8.30 and 8.31 belong together, denoting one group of believing Jews, or should these two verses be separated, to distinguish between two groups with differing faith responses to Jesus? Establishing 8.31 as the beginning of a new unit intended for oral performance, or at least as the sub-section of a larger unit (8.12-59) held together by Jesus's utterance of ἐγώ εἰμι, does, in fact, resolve some of the difficulties in interpreting 8.30-1 as the description of a single group. If 8.12-30 and 8.31-59 are treated as interconnected, albeit separable, units of communication, this can account for the indicators of continuity between the two sections, including the presence of οὖν at the beginning of 8.31. It can also explain the otherwise puzzling introduction in 8.31 of new references to 'Jesus' and 'the Jews who had believed in him' (πρὸς τοὺς πεπιστευκότας αὐτῷ Ἰουδαίους) immediately after the remark at the end of 8.30 that 'many believed in him' (πολλοὶ ἐπίστευσαν εἰς αὐτόν), features which point to an intended (brief) break at the end of 8.30, before resuming with the next 'performative instalment' concerning the same group of Jews in 8.31.

The fact that references to Abraham frame the dialogue between Jesus and his interlocutors (8.33, 58) is a further indicator that 8.31-59 should be treated as a separate unit. Marking boundaries with the aid of an *inclusio* has been shown to be a characteristic feature of narratives composed in an oral/aural context, often fulfilling the very practical function, as with the introduction in 8.31, of providing structural cues of internal divisions for those reading aloud from a manuscript with no line and paragraph divisions, and without punctuation or spaces between words (see Achtemeier 1990: 17–18). Repeating the same theme at the beginning and end of a passage also serves as an acoustic aid for the hearers of the performance, although, as this essay will later argue, the resumption of references to Abraham in 8.52-8 is evidently not to be assessed solely in terms of its mnemonic and structural functions.

The formulaic repetition of key words and motifs not only at both ends of, but throughout, a communicative unit is another prevalent oral narrative technique. Repetition is indispensable, both for rhetorical and mnemonic purposes, in a predominantly oral environment. As Werner Kelber has noted, without the benefit of being able to return to a written text for further reflection, 'the ear has to be attuned to live speech and must grasp it momentarily. In those circumstances, repetition is the oral substitute for the eye's privilege to revisit words' (1983: 67; cf. Ong 1977: 103–5; 1982: 39–41). To maintain that 8.31-59, like most Johannine discourses, displays a particular fondness for repetition is something of an understatement. In addition to the 11 occurrences of Abraham's name in the first (8.33), second (8.37, 39[x3], 40) and third (8.52, 53, 56, 57, 58) parts of the dialogue, other unmistakable leitmotifs include the repeated use of ποιέω (8.34, 38, 39, 40, 41, 44, 53), ἀλήθεια (8.32[x2], 40, 44[x2], 45, 46) and the clustering of references to ἐλευθερόω and its cognates in the initial part of the encounter (8.32, 33, 36[x2]). Nevertheless, the most striking case of repetition, one which undoubtedly holds together the central part of the discussion, is the use of ὁ πατήρ with three different referents: God (8.38, 41, 42, 49, 54), Abraham (8.39, 53, 56) and the devil (8.41, 44[x3]), although in one, possibly deliberately, ambiguous case (8.38b) the referent in question could be either Abraham or the devil. Repetition can extend to whole statements, as when Jesus's words are reiterated, virtually verbatim, by his interlocutors (8.32-3, 51-2). It can also take the form of variation, as when Jesus emphasizes the importance of remaining in (8.31), making a place for (8.37), hearing (8.43) and keeping (8.51, 52, 53), his λόγος.

Such patterns of repetition would certainly provide a mnemonic aid for the speaker and would help to keep the hearers on track, but the primary role of such devices must surely be to encourage the audience to be drawn in and *experience* the performance (cf. Dewey 1994: 151). All scholars of oral cultures, ancient and modern, are in agreement that live communicative events are deliberately designed to ensure interaction and involvement, due, in particular, to the actual presence of the audience. Strategies to encourage active participation in John 8.31-59 include its 'riddling sessions' (8.31-3, 38-41, 51-3, 56-8; see Thatcher 2000), since the puzzled (and puzzling) reactions of Jesus's interlocutors are intended to evoke a response from an audience prompted to search eagerly for 'the right answers' from within the text. The fact that 8.31-59 has been constructed as a highly charged, direct-speech encounter between two dialogue partners is similarly a response-inducing tactic, one that compels the audience to display empathy with Jesus, whose spoken word dominates the exchange and whose opponents are described as wanting to kill him (8.37, 40) and eventually attempt to do so (8.59).

One aspect that has, so far, received little attention in studies of the vitriolic language of John 8.31-59 is the discovery that a confrontational tone is a regularly encountered feature in narratives bearing traces of the interchange between a written text and its oral communication.

> Many, if not all, oral or residually oral cultures strike literates as extraordinarily agonistic in their verbal performance and indeed in their lifestyle. Writing fosters abstractions that disengage knowledge from the arena where human beings struggle with one another. It separates the knower from the known. By keeping knowledge embedded in the human life world, orality situates knowledge within a context of struggle. Proverbs and riddles are not used simply to store knowledge but to engage others in verbal and intellectual combat. (Ong 1982: 43–4; cf. Kelber 1983: 54–5)

Identifying the severe name-callings and 'verbal tongue-lashings' (Ong 1982: 44) in 8.31-59 as a trademark of oral-written narratives does not deny the validity of the many searches for a social and historical explanation of its harsh speech. Nevertheless, the preference for the language of contrasts, confrontation and conflict in residually oral cultures deserves a more prominent place in discussions of the background and function of the vocabulary that undoubtedly marks John 8.31-59 as one of the most controversial passages in the New Testament.

This examination of forms and techniques pointing to a conscious interplay of orality and textuality in 8.31-59 has been far from exhaustive, while discussion of certain orally conditioned devices impinging directly on its presentation of Abraham will be undertaken in a later part of this study. What has so far been proposed is that several aspects of this passage strongly suggest that it was composed for a listening rather than a reading audience, not only to enable its hearers (and speaker) to follow and remember the narrative, but also, through its rhetorical strategies, to allow them to participate in the story and to draw conclusions about the identity of Jesus, about the claims made by his dialogue partners and, as we shall see, about the status and significance of Abraham.

Social Memory and Social Frameworks

Several references have already been made in this essay to the role of memory in the first-century media world. Given that memorization, though not necessarily for the purpose of word-for-word repetition, was fundamental to the success of the delivery and reception of a text, several of the oral compositional techniques identifiable in John 8.31-59 can be viewed as facilitating recall. Nevertheless, notions of memory and remembrance, in both oral and literate cultures, cannot be defined purely in terms of the ability to store knowledge, because the multifaceted character of the processes and practices of memory should not be overlooked.

That memory is a complex phenomenon is unanimously acknowledged by social and cultural memory theorists, whose work is now gradually making an impact on biblical scholarship as it begins to use memory as an analytical category or model (see Kirk and Thatcher 2005; Stuckenbruck, Barton and Wold 2007). Building on the work of the French sociologist Maurice Halbwachs during the early decades of the twentieth century (1925; 1941; 1950), contemporary social memory studies investigate the ways in which communities and individuals interpret the past in the light of their present social realities. The emphasis in such studies lies on the social dimensions of the formation, preservation and transmission of memory. Halbwachs himself argued that memory is socially conditioned, in that groups and individuals remember the past through their reliance on 'social frameworks': 'It is in society that people normally acquire their memories. It is also in society that they recall, recognize, and localize their memories' (1992: 38). Social groups determine what is remembered and how it is remembered. Even personal memories, according to Halbwachs, only acquire meaning and coherence within social frameworks, because, when individuals remember, they do so as social beings within social contexts; the content of their recollections is determined by their interaction with others and conforms to social patterns (see 1992: 43–83; 1997: 51–96). Halbwachs therefore defined 'collective memory' as a fluid, variable and selective phenomenon relating closely to the identity of a group; it entails the construction of a shared past which is continuous with the present and, at the same time, serves to unite the group.

The pioneering nature of Halbwachs's work remains undisputed, but the fact that he offered an overly generalized description, rather than a well-defined theory, of social memory and the mechanics of its transmission (Connerton 1989: 37–9; Gedi and Elam 1996: 40) has prompted his successors to adopt a far more nuanced approach in their own explorations of memory's processes and practices. Contemporary social memory theorists readily acknowledge the significance of Halbwachs's focus on the ways in which a group's representation of the past is shaped by present concerns and experiences, but memory, it is argued, should not be categorized as 'an entirely malleable construction in the present' or, alternatively, as 'the authentic residue of the past'. Rather, it involves a 'fluid negotiation between the desires of the present and the legacies of the past' (Olick 2006: 13; cf. Olick and Robbins 1998: 128–30; Misztal 2003: 67–73). Memory can provide a conceptual framework that both mirrors the present and stands in continuity with the past (on how the past can be highly resistant to change, see Schudson 1989: 107–13). It is, in other words, a case of perpetual dialogue between the past and the present, 'at times attributing greater force to the remembered past and at times to the remembering present' (Kelber 2005: 234).

Much attention is also paid to the interconnectedness of group memory and group identity formation, especially in the work of the Egyptologist Jan Assmann, who has refined Halbwachs's category of 'collective memory' by distinguishing between 'communicative memory' and 'cultural memory'. Communicative memory is based on everyday interaction and possesses a limited temporal horizon, whereas cultural memory focuses on fixed events of the past (Assmann 1992: 48–66; 1995: 126–33), 'whose memory is maintained through cultural formation (texts, rites, monuments) and institutional communication (recitation, practice, observance)' (1995: 129; cf. Kirk 2005: 5–6). 'Cultural memory', or 'social memory' (the favoured term among Anglo-American scholars), accordingly fulfils the important function of defining the collective identity of a group; it preserves and communicates a store of knowledge that forms the basis of the group's sense of duration and uniqueness, as well as relating that knowledge to a contemporary situation through a process of reconstruction. Of particular relevance to this essay is the fact that Assmann has applied his theoretical analyses of cultural memory to what he describes as a 'mnemohistorical investigation' of the figure of 'Moses the Egyptian' (1997). As the term implies, mnemohistory is not interested in determining the historical validity of traditions relating to the past, but in focusing on the past as it is *remembered*, on events and places, and on people like Moses, in their role as 'figures of memory' ('Erinnerungsfiguren'; 1997: 8–15).

Before examining how Abraham is 'remembered' in John 8.31–59, and given social memory's focus on how the past is commemorated in the light of actual social realities, can one identify the social and historical context of the 'remembering present' reflected in John's Gospel? In other words, to what extent is it possible to recover the social frameworks within which the author and first audience operated? There is of course much debate on this issue, but, following J. Louis Martyn's 'two-level reading' of the Gospel (2003, 3rd edn), it is widely held that the three references to expulsion from the synagogue (9.22; 12.42; 16.2) provide some clues about the social and historical circumstances at the time of the Gospel's composition. Granted that we only have access to the Johannine version of events, it is difficult to accept recent attempts at interpreting the references to synagogue expulsion purely as literary devices aiming to persuade Johannine Christians to stay away from the synagogue (cf. Kimelman 1981: 234–5), or as belonging to the Gospel's 'imagined symbolic world' (Hakola 2005: 74–86). The unparalleled use of the term ἀποσυνάγωγος, as well as the intensity and extent of the bitter exchanges with 'the Jews' in some parts of the narrative, must have had some basis in actual experiences of a, probably localized, conflict between Johannine Christians and a synagogue community (see further Lincoln 2000: 268–9). Otherwise it is difficult to explain how this language could act as an effective deterrent against synagogue participation and to account for the introduction of the language into the Johannine 'symbolic universe'. Whatever factors gave rise to the situation of conflict, the Gospel in its final form responds in a variety of ways to the impact of these traumatic experiences on the Johannine Christians now separated from a group of synagogue Jews.

An even more challenging task is the attempt to move from a general description of at least some aspects of the social and historical context of John's Gospel to a more precise reconstruction of the *Sitz im Leben* of its individual scenes of confrontation. One element in 8.31-59 that has prompted scholars to try and identify some of the contours of its social setting is the reference to, and depiction of, Jesus's interaction with those designated as 'the Jews who had believed in him' (8.31). Although Jesus's discussion partners are at first described as believers, their limited faith is soon exposed after he challenges them to remain in his word (8.31); he then accuses his interlocutors of seeking to kill him (8.37, 40) and denounces them as children of the devil (8.44), which may suggest that his initial dialogue partners are subsequently subsumed under, or even replaced by, a group of unbelievers described as 'the Jews' (8.48). What therefore begins, at least superficially, as an internal dialogue is rapidly transformed into a controversy with those unquestionably proving themselves to be outsiders. A possible scenario, as many have suggested (cf. Lincoln 2000: 92, 283–5; Theobald 2004: 175–83), is that this encounter, or at least its initial parts, responds to the attitude and actions of those who, despite professing to be believers, wanted to remain within the synagogue community and, for that reason, were not prepared to confess openly a full Johannine faith in Jesus (cf. 12.42-3). It cannot be determined whether the author was addressing a situation that remained a live issue at the time the Gospel was written or one now belonging to the past, but 8.31-59 may afford some significant glimpses into how the Johannine Christians came to terms with their existence as a separate community with a distinctive identity. Some of the strategies used for shaping or asserting that identity are brought to light by analysing the ways in which Abraham, particularly within an oral performative context, is (re)constructed as a figure of memory.

Contesting a Memory of Freedom and Paternity (8.31-6, 37-47)

Memory begins to feature early in Jesus's encounter with 'the Jews who had believed in him'. Following Jesus's appeal that, by remaining in his word, they will truly reveal themselves to be his disciples and will know the truth that makes them free (8.31-2), his interlocutors indignantly respond: 'We are descendants of Abraham (σπέρμα Ἀβραάμ) and have never been slaves to anyone' (8.33). So begins a riddling session exposing starkly different perceptions of 'freedom'. Those described as believers in Jesus are depicted as immediately laying their cards on the table by stating that freedom has always been in their possession; they rule out from the outset the need to accept Jesus's offer of freedom through his revelation (ἀλήθεια). They do so by appealing to a collective, living memory that centres on the privileges associated with a key aspect of their ethnic identity, namely their physical descent from Abraham (cf. Esler 2006: 25–9). They are given a self-description (σπέρμα᾽Αβραάμ) for which the text's original audience would require no further explanation, due to its well-established role as a designation for the children of Israel (e.g., Isa. 41.8; Ps. 105.6; 3 Macc. 6.3; *Pss. Sol.* 9.9; cf. Rom. 9.7; 2 Cor. 11.22), and which, in all likelihood, many of the Gospel's first hearers would, at one time, have used to describe themselves (and, possibly, some still do). The claim to be 'the seed of Abraham' attests, above all, to the centrality of the memory of Abraham as the great ancestor of Israel who was chosen by God (Sandmel 1972: 30–95; Hansen 1989: 175–99; Esler 2003: 178–80; de Lange 2008: 98–106), a subject that underpins much of the ensuing dialogue.

More intriguing is the link established by Jesus's interlocutors between Abrahamic descent and their claim to unbroken freedom (8.33). It would be difficult for a late-first-century CE audience to accept this as a declaration of political freedom, but it could be understood as an assertion of spiritual freedom by virtue of the status of 'the seed of Abraham' as the children of the patriarch who received God's promise that Israel would become a great people (on Jewish and early Christian traditions associating Abraham with freedom, see de Lange 2008: 123–7). The emphatic and uncompromising nature of this pronouncement, together with its likely focus on spiritual rather than political realities, suggest that it operates according to what social memory theorists identify as memory's selective processes in reconstructing the past: some subjects are remembered, others are forgotten, so that the collective memory of a group is made to serve the image that it seeks to project of itself. The claim to a past uninterrupted by slavery (8.33) therefore belongs to a reconstructive feature of memory observed by Halbwachs (see 1997: 135–42) and Assmann (1992: 42–3), that is, how a group relates to its past in a way that seeks to exclude change: it looks for similarities and continuities that present the group with a durable image of its past that is recognizable at every stage: 'We have *never* been slaves to *anyone*.'

If memories involve reconstructions of the past, they often prove to be sites of contestation (cf. Olick and Robbins 1998: 126–8). According to John, Jesus's immediate response is to challenge, in reverse order, the two components of the wavering believers' collective memory: freedom and Abrahamic descent. The processes of memory contestation at work here centre on the required response to Jesus's 'word' (8.34-6, 37). The contention of his interlocutors that they have never been enslaved is rejected because, whatever its basis, those who commit sin are slaves to sin (8.34). The subsequent analogy and its application clarify that freedom from slavery to sin is only possible through knowing the truth that comes from remaining in Jesus's word: the slave, in contrast to the son, does not have a permanent place in the household (8.35), but Jesus, as Son, can indeed offer freedom

(8.36). Furthermore, the interlocutors' failure to accept Jesus's word is cited as one of the reasons why he now directly confronts the other component of their collective memory, their self-identification as 'the seed of Abraham' (8.37). Jesus does acknowledge their physical descent from the patriarch, but highlights its incompatibility with the behaviour of those whom he addresses at this point. Their desire to kill him (8.37; cf. 8.40, 44, 59) demonstrates that Jesus's word finds no place in them, and manifests their slavery to sin. Following their response, 'Abraham is our father' (8.39), the context in fact suggests a deliberate shift from the language of physical descent (σπέρμα Ἀβραάμ) to that of spiritual kinship (τέκνα τοῦ Ἀβραάμ), because to warrant the designation 'children of Abraham' they need to imitate their ancestral father by acting like him (8.39-40).

What is striking about this dialogue concerning Abrahamic lineage is that, like the earlier riddling session (8.31-6), it is expressed and structured in a way that points to it having been composed with a view to the dynamics of its oral performance and aural reception. It contains a number of what can be described as orally conditioned devices and 'shared' memories, designed to secure a listening audience's active engagement with the fast-moving encounter between Jesus and his Jewish interlocutors, particularly in the initial part of the discussion on paternity (8.37-41). One such device, as noted earlier in this essay, is the repetition of the verb ποιέω, accompanied by numerous references to the name 'Abraham' (8.37, 39[x3], 40), to highlight the priority of proper actions over physical descent. Instead of 'doing sin' (8.34: ὁ ποιῶν τὴν ἁμαρτίαν), 'the children of Abraham' should be *doing* what their father *did* (8.38, 39, 40). A related communicative technique seeks to prompt hearers of the text to search for clues that will help them answer the question: who, then, is the father of those claiming Abrahamic descent? When Jesus states, 'I declare what I have seen with the Father, and you therefore do (ποιεῖτε) what you have heard from the father' (8.38), deciding whether ποιεῖτε in this verse is intended to express appeal (imperative command) or a statement of fact (indicative) dictates whether the father in question is Abraham or, in fact, somebody else. Those addressed by Jesus take the former option, but another possibility will come more clearly into view in 8.41 with the aid of another occurrence of ποιεῖτε ('You are doing the works of your father').

As well as the repetition of key themes, the notion of commonly held memories is introduced (8.39-40) for the purpose of evoking a response and inviting interpretation, both from the characters within the text and by the audience listening to the text being read aloud. Jesus disputes the validity of his interlocutors' claims by stating, 'If you are really (ἐστε) the children of Abraham, you would be doing (ἐποιεῖτε) the works of Abraham' (on the interpretative issues arising from this mixed conditional sentence, see Hakola 2005: 189–90). The aim, at this point, is not so much to contest, but to *appeal* to their collective memory of Abraham as the ancestor whose actions and behaviour should be emulated. The role of Abraham as an exemplary progenitor is widely attested (cf. Isa. 51.2; 1 Macc. 2.52; 4 Macc. 9.21, 15.28, 16.18-20), and would undoubtedly have been a well-known theme to those steeped in the heritage of Israel. The focus, therefore, at this point is on how retrieving the past should shape present actions rather than on how present realities can transform the memory of the past. It is the kind of memory process that contemporary social memory theorists describe as one of fluid negotiation between the concerns of the present and 'the legacies of the past' (Olick 2006: 13). Furthermore, in view of the low literacy rates and the general inaccessibility of scrolls, several members of John's original audience would, almost certainly, have encountered such traditions about Abraham in an oral setting, through hearing them being performed, re-performed and reformulated as they were brought into conversation with other orally communicated traditions (cf. Horsley and Draper 1999: 140–4; Esler 2005: 152–5, 166–71).

The impact of a highly oral environment on the reception of scriptural and Jewish traditions, and on the role of collective memory in the interaction between text and audience, is a particularly pertinent issue with reference to 'the works of Abraham' (τὰ ἔργα τοῦ Ἀβραάμ) in 8.39. This concise phrase, for which there is no precise parallel, serves as a verbal signal for a wide range of deeds and attributes for which the patriarch is remembered in late Second Temple Judaism, such as his opposition to idolatry and his role as a model of righteousness, hospitality, faithfulness and receptiveness to God's word. Consequently, due to the cultural inheritance or 'memory pool' shared, in all probability, by a significant proportion of his original audience, John draws on a form of metonymic referencing firmly attested in oral compositions (cf. Horsley and Draper 1999: 160–74, 191–3, 252–4; Dewey 2001: 244–5), a mode of referencing which is intended to recall a whole network of traditional associations relating to Abraham's 'works'. Having said that, the remainder of Jesus's statement (8.40) appears to focus on one particular aspect of, or event linked to, the patriarch's works, since the opponents' attempt to kill Jesus is contrasted with the behaviour of the one whom they maintain is their father: 'This is not what Abraham did (τοῦτο Ἀβραάμ οὐκ ἐποίησεν).' John's original audience may well have been in a position to associate this highly condensed remark with a specific event. And given the widespread emphasis on hospitality as one of Abraham's most memorable virtues (cf. Josephus, *Ant.* 1.196-7; *T. Ab.* Rec. A 1.1-2, 5, 3.7-9, 4.1-6, 17.7; Rec. B 2.10, 4.10, 13.5-6), many scholars regard Abraham's reception of the three heavenly messengers by the oaks of Mamre (Gen. 18.1-8) to be the event in question (cf. Neyrey 1987: 524; Motyer 1997: 191). It would then follow that Abraham is cited to his physical descendants as an example of how they should be responding to Jesus, the heavenly messenger sent by God to reveal the truth (8.40). However, even if the veiled remark, 'This is not what Abraham did' (8.40), is intended as an allusion to the patriarch's encounter with the three messengers of God, it does not necessarily exhaust the range of 'works' to which reference is made in 8.39. In other words, the complex of traditions signalled by John as 'the works of Abraham' need not be restricted to one narrative event. Indeed, from a performative perspective, if 8.31-59 is treated as a single unit of oral communication, other 'works', or aspects of a particular 'work', may later be recalled with the aid of different cues when, as we shall see, Abraham emerges once again as a figure of memory (8.52-9).

Explicit references to Abraham cease, at least for now, but Jesus's dialogue partners are said to respond to his declaration that they are doing (ποιεῖτε) the works of their own father, by stating, 'We have one father, God himself' (8.41b). This marks an important development in the discussion of paternity in John 8. The interlocutors now trace their lineage to God, not in order to reject but to affirm their Abrahamic ancestry. It is, in fact, by virtue of their position as the descendants of Abraham (8.33, 39) that they stake their claim, in only their third, and final, brief utterance in this part of the exchange (8.31-47), to God as their father (8.41; cf. Exod. 4.22; Deut. 14.1; Jer. 31.9). This assertion of belief in the one God of Israel can be regarded, in this respect, as an unspoken expression of their pride in their Abrahamic status, particularly in view of the frequent praise of the patriarch for his rejection of idolatry (cf. *Jub.* 11.16-17, 12.2-5, 13.8-9; *Apoc. Ab.* 1-8; Josephus, *Ant.* 1.154-7). Nevertheless, Jesus declares at this point that the only decisive criterion to become 'a child of God', a designation implied rather than stated in the text, is to recognize him as the one sent by the Father: 'If God were your Father, you would love me, for I came from God' (8.42). Underlying this assertion is a denial of the notion that descent from Abraham is synonymous with descent from God; only through belief in Jesus, not because of an ethnic identity tied to Abrahamic status, can one claim God as Father. To understand how this reconfiguration 'works' within the text, it needs to be set within the wider framework of the contestation of paternity and origins in 8.37-47.

An important aspect of the relationship between collective memory and identity, as explored in social memory studies, is how a group establishes its origins or 'beginnings' (cf. Schwartz 1982: 375–6), with common ancestry often forming the 'social cement' that holds descendants together (Zerubavel 2003: 55–81). 'Membership in a group inevitably entails a common perception of when it was "born"' (Zerubavel 1993: 457). With regard to John 8.37-47, the discussion of origins, and in particular the issue of descent from God, centres on the contrast between the horizontal/temporal and vertical/spatial dimensions within which John's Gospel operates and which are given expression in two of the text's narrative levels, that is, its 'earthly' and 'cosmological' dramas (see Reinhartz 2002: 101–10; Lieu 2008: 175–8). Its earthly drama tells the story of Jesus who teaches, performs miracles, encounters opposition, is crucified, and then appears to his disciples; the cosmological drama, expressed most clearly in the prologue and in Jesus's discourses, is the story of the Son who descends from heaven, having been sent by the Father to reveal a message of truth, defeats the 'ruler of this world', and returns to his Father. Thus, on the question of origins, it will be argued that the different notions of descent from God set out in 8.37-47 are tied to different axes, the horizontal and the vertical, and indeed belong to two narrative worlds, the earthly and the cosmological dramas.

From the early stages of the dialogue Jesus's interlocutors are presented as forcefully expressing a sense of connectedness to a common ancestor. Because their self-understanding, as encapsulated in their claim to physical descent from Abraham (8.33), possesses a horizontal/temporal perspective, it is within the Johannine earthly drama, rather than the 'cosmological tale' (Reinhartz 2002: 106–9), that this claim should probably be placed (8.33). Due to their rejection of Jesus, their origins or 'beginnings' with God, which they link to their status as the children of Abraham, are denied (8.39, 42). The Johannine contestation of their collective memory then involves a recon-figuration of origins that takes the issue of paternity and descent to a wholly different plane, one that belongs firmly within the framework of the cosmo-logical narrative, as set out in the spoken word of Jesus, the heavenly revealer. In line with the vertical/spatial perspective, Jesus claims to have come from God (8.42), declaring what he has seen in the Father's presence (8.38) and the truth that he has heard from him (8.40, 46). In contrast, Jesus's interlocutors are accused of failing to accept his word (8.37, 43), of refusing to love him as the Son sent by the Father (8.42), and consequently of rejecting his offer of truth that can set them free from slavery to sin (8.31-6, 45-6). Because of their deeds, namely attempting to kill Jesus and failing to accept the truth, their origins are traced to the devil, the antagonist within the cosmological narrative, who is described as a murderer from the beginning and the father of lies (8.44-5). For this reason they cannot, according to John, claim descent from God, because, as the conclusion of this part of the dialogue makes explicit, only the one who hears the words of God, revealed through the word of his Son (8.38, 40), is 'of God' (8.47: ἐκ τοῦ θεοῦ).

From the perspective of the audience hearing this text being read aloud, there is no doubt that its language, content and structure are moulded in a way that is intended to evoke a response from them. Both the dualistic language bubbling under the surface (8.38, 41) until its eruption into an explicit either-or scenario (8.44-7), and the failure of Jesus's opponents to respond to his warning that one's origins are evident from one's actions, are designed to encourage John's audience to place themselves firmly on the side of 'true disciples' (8.31): they must believe in Jesus as God's exclusive heavenly envoy and accept his revelation in order to receive the liberating truth and in order to warrant the status of children of God (cf. 1.12-13; 11.52; and 3.3-6; 20.17). What is produced, as a result, is a distinctively Johannine memory of origins and descent from God.

The dialogical dimensions of the text come to the fore in its perpetual movement between the two very different ways of understanding origins and paternity as encapsulated in its horizontal and vertical frameworks. The oscillation between these two narrative levels not only calls for a totally different perspective on the question of origins from God, but also invites the question: where does it leave Abraham and his descendants? It must be acknowledged that, to a certain degree at least, the themes of Abrahamic and divine lineage are allowed to stand side by side in John 8. Jesus's opponents are told: if Abraham were truly their father, they would not reject Jesus; if God were truly their Father, they would believe in Jesus. But to infer from this juxtaposition that a true child of Abraham is, at the same time, a child of God (cf. Siker 1991: 134; Spaulding 2009: 147) is to make a connection on which the text is silent, because, while the cosmological drama can certainly provide a commentary on the earthly drama, it does not follow that the one can simply be superimposed upon the other (cf. Lieu 2008: 175). What is asserted is that descent from God 'begins' not with Abraham, the patriarch of the Jewish people, but with Jesus; neither physical ancestry nor continuity with the past is the necessary prerequisite to claim God as Father, to become a 'child of God' (cf. Esler 2007: 130-1). As far as the patriarch Abraham is concerned, he is remembered, within the Johannine earthly drama, as an ancestor whose behaviour should be reproduced by his physical descendants. Even a role for him within the cosmological drama is not excluded if an appeal is being made to the patriarch as one who, in contrast to his descendants, accepted the truth revealed by God's heavenly messenger. Nevertheless, at this juncture in the text the precise contours of Abraham's role as a figure of memory in 8.31-59 remain undefined.

Reconfiguring the Memory of Abraham (8.48-59)

Significant shifts occur in the final part of the exchange. All traces of the, albeit inadequate, belief displayed by Jesus's initial interlocutors have long disappeared, and the wider group, 'the Jews', overtly takes over as the voice of opposition (8.48, 52, 57). The escalation in hostility coincides with a transition from the hitherto brief responses of Jesus's dialogue partners, characterized by their defensive stance on issues relating to lineage and paternity, to their far more vocal and accusatory role as they persistently question Jesus's assertions about his own identity. While they charge Jesus with being a Samaritan and demon-possessed (8.48, 52; cf. 7.20; 10.20), in what amounts to yet another attempt within the dialogue at establishing a 'counter-memory' of origins, and then use Abraham as a screen through which to challenge Jesus (8.53, 56), his self-defence is that he does not glorify himself but the Father (8.49) who seeks his glory (8.50, 54).

Despite these marked developments in terms of tone and content, the basic pattern of exchange that initiated this encounter (8.31-3) reappears in 8.51-3. Jesus's offer of salvation, now defined as deliverance from death to those who keep his word, prompts his opponents to appeal once more to Abraham, this time with reference to his own death together with that of the prophets. As part of the dynamics of another riddle, 'the Jews' are depicted as using earthly criteria to articulate their collective memory of

Abraham, thereby displaying their total misapprehension of Jesus's offer of the gift of eternal life. Indeed, by placing the spotlight on the physical death of the patriarch, '*even* he died' (emphasis added; for this interpretation of ὅστις in 8.53, see BDF 293.2), the interlocutors' response may echo 'a piece of popular consolation in the face of death' (Motyer 1997: 203). Though Abraham was 'a man in every virtue supreme' (Josephus, *Ant.* 1.256), not even he could avoid death. Thus, according to one tradition, despite the patriarch's attempt to escape his own demise, Michael, in language strikingly similar to John 8.52, reminds Abraham that no human being, not even 'the prophets' and 'the forefathers', was able to escape the mystery of death (*T. Ab.* Rec. A 8.9). Faced with Jesus's offer of life that transcends death, the memory of Abraham's mortality prompts 'the Jews' to ask, 'Are you greater than our father Abraham?' and 'Who do you claim to be?' (8.53). After emphasizing, in response to their second question, that his unique relationship with the Father stands in stark contrast to their inability to know God (8.54-5; cf. 8.41-2), Jesus answers their first question by elucidating Abraham's position in relation to himself: 'Abraham, your father, rejoiced (ἠγαλλιάσατο) that he would see my day; he saw [it] and was glad (καὶ εἶδεν καὶ ἐχάρη)' (8.56).

This declaration, together with the climactic statement in 8.58, plays a decisive role in the Johannine clarification of Abraham's position in relation to Jesus. It also yields important insights into the strategies adopted at this point in the passage to determine how, precisely, the patriarch should be remembered. What is presented is not a totally new memory formulated from 'a blank page', but one assembled from a wealth of Jewish traditions about Abraham (see Lona 1976: 292–313; Motyer 1997: 206–8; de Lange 2008: 127–34). Abraham's rejoicing is widely attested, both with reference to all the blessings promised by God at the time of his covenant with the patriarch (cf. *Jub.* 14.21; *Apoc. Ab.* 10.15) and, more specifically, in relation to his joy (Gen. 17.17: laughter) at the gift of a son (*Jub.* 15.17; 17.2; cf. Philo, *Mut.* 154-69) and the promise of a 'holy seed' from the sons of Isaac (*Jub.* 16.17-19; 17.25-7). None of these memories of Abraham's rejoicing is accompanied by an overt reference to 'seeing' on the patriarch's part, although the association between God's covenant blessings and Abraham as the recipient of visionary experiences is well documented. Since the use of the aorist εἶδεν in 8.56 points to a particular event during Abraham's lifetime as the setting for what 'he saw', the most likely interpretative context for this vision is a variety of Jewish traditions on Genesis 15, the so-called covenant of the pieces, during which the patriarch is said to have been granted visions (cf. 15.1, 'in a vision'; 15.12, 17) of the future and of the end times. According to *4 Ezra* 3.14, Ezra says to the Most High on this occasion: 'To him [Abraham] only you revealed the end of the times, secretly by night', and in the *Apocalypse of Abraham* the patriarch is told, during his tour of heaven, that he is seeing 'what will be, and everything that will be in the last days' (24.2; cf. 9.10; 29.2; 31.1-2; *Gen. Rab.* 44.21, 22).

If widespread traditions about the patriarch's joy and visions provide the raw material for Jesus's declaration in John 8.56, they are now reconstructed, through a series of manoeuvres, to create a Christologically marked reconfiguration of the memory of Abraham. In this respect, the linking together of his 'rejoicing' and 'seeing', a fusion for which commentators have searched in vain for a parallel in Jewish tradition, attests the mosaic-like character of memory (Zelizer 1995: 224), in that fragments of the inherited past are pieced together to produce a new mnemonic framework aligned to present realities. The new reality, as set out in John 8.31-59, is belief in Jesus as the heavenly revealer of God, with the result that the reason for Abraham's joy and the object of his vision must be Jesus's day. Due to this retrospective reconstruction of the past, the new mnemonic focus of Abraham's rejoicing is neither the birth of Isaac nor, given the dialogue's repeated emphasis on Jesus's divine descent (8.36, 38, 42, 47, 49, 54-5), the promise of the 'holy seed' of Abraham (*pace* Grelot 1987: 628), but Jesus himself. For this reason he also becomes the centre point of the patriarch's visionary experiences. Admittedly, some of the Jewish traditions relating to Genesis 15 state that Abraham, on this occasion, sees the hidden things that already exist in heaven (*2 Bar.* 4.3-4; *Apoc. Ab.* 9.6, 12.10; *L.A.B.* 23.6), which could, from a Johannine perspective, have been interpreted as a vision of the pre-existent Jesus (cf. 8.58). However, because the emphasis in 8.56 is upon Abraham as having seen Jesus's 'day', it must point to a vision of the future whereby Abraham 'sees' the earthly mission of the Son.

There is no doubt that this particular memory of Abraham represents the high point of his presentation in the narrative, for what is commemorated is his role as one who was privileged to testify to Jesus's coming. Like other Johannine witnesses, Abraham's testimony is based on what he saw through divine disclosure (e.g., 1.32-4; 12.41). Indeed, Jesus turns the tables on his opponents at this juncture (*pace* Hakola 2005: 194-5, who claims that 8.51-6 centres on a *Johannine* contrast between the dead Abraham and Jesus who gives life): while they, ironically, highlight Abraham's mortality in their 'living memory' of him, Jesus declares that the patriarch, different from those claiming descent from him (8.56: 'Abraham, your father'), was able to look beyond physical death to Jesus's day and its offer of life (cf. 8.51). This declaration provides a clear example of how the Gospel's different narrative levels, the earthly and cosmological dramas, can impact on each another: as a result of a heavenly vision, experienced during his earthly life, Abraham receives a revelation of the future descent of the Son to bring salvation to the world.

From the perspective of John's original audience, searching, since the early stages of this encounter (8.31-3, 37-40), for clues regarding the significance of Abraham in relation to Jesus, the statement about his rejoicing at seeing Jesus's day now spells out what has, up to this point, been a vaguely defined role for the patriarch. In Jesus's earlier appeal to his interlocutors that they should emulate their physical ancestor, both the succinct reference to 'the works of Abraham' (8.39), with its capacity to invoke a variety of deeds and attributes, and the ambiguously phrased 'this is not what Abraham did' (8.40) create a sense of anticipation that, certainly from an oral performative perspective, is not immediately resolved but left hanging in the air. Only when Jesus himself, for the first time since 8.39-40, refers once more to Abraham (8.56) are his earlier, open-ended remarks about the patriarch elucidated for the hearers of the text: the paramount 'work' to be reproduced by the true children of Abraham is the acceptance of Jesus's true identity and mission; they should rejoice that they are seeing Jesus's day. By rejecting Jesus, this is precisely what 'the Jews' are not prepared to do.

The gulf separating Jesus and his opponents becomes more and more evident as their 'mnemonic battle' (Zerubavel 1996: 295) over Abraham intensifies and moves towards its climax. Even when told that their own ancestor joyfully received the heavenly revelation about Jesus's day, their failure to embrace anything other than what is based on earthly criteria, and their conviction that Abraham is greater than Jesus, lead them to ask how the relatively young Jesus could claim to have seen the patriarch (8.57). This question, however misconstrued, gives Jesus the opportunity to inform his antagonists that, by virtue of his true identity, their proposition is not inconceivable: 'Very truly, I say to you, before Abraham was, I AM' (8.58). Jesus's striking pronouncement provides an incontrovertible answer to earlier challenges (8.48, 52-3, 57) and, in particular, sets out forcefully his identity and status in relation to Abraham. To categorize Jesus's pronouncement as a declaration of pre-existence does not capture the full force of his appropriation of the absolute divine ἐγώ εἰμι (on its background and use in 8.58, see Williams 2000: 275–83). The use of εἰμι (rather than ἤμην) expresses Jesus's claim to a timeless, absolute form of being (cf. 1.1-3), closely aligned to what social memory theorists describe as frames that relate past, present and future, because they are frames that profess 'to reveal or describe ultimate reality rather than to offer a perspective on it' (Olick 2006: 7). As in the earlier discussion on freedom, paternity and origins (8.31-6, 37-47), this Johannine claim to reveal 'ultimate reality' articulates how Jesus's identity and mission, set firmly within the cosmological drama, transcend all earthly, horizontal categories. What, however, sets this pronouncement apart, at least as far as John 8.31-59 is concerned, is that its intersection of the horizontal and vertical axes involves a direct comparison of Jesus and Abraham, so that the time-bound form of existence (γενέσθαι) attributed to the patriarch is unequivocally contrasted with the timeless form of existence (ἐγώ εἰμι) claimed by Jesus.

For the interlocutors within the text, Jesus's concluding declaration (8.58) is a claim to superiority over Abraham and a pronouncement of divinity that amounts to blasphemy (8.59). For the hearers outside the text, it asserts that Abraham, though an authoritative witness, is in fact incomparable to the Johannine Jesus, whose identity as the definitive revelation of God is encapsulated in his ἐγώ εἰμι self-declaration.

Conclusion

Investigating John 8.31-59 from a first-century media perspective uncovers a number of its communicative strategies as it 'remembers' the patriarch Abraham. Through the extensive use of orally conditioned devices designed to secure engagement and communal interpretation in an oral/aural performative context, and by drawing on a rich reservoir of Abrahamic memories familiar, in all likelihood, to many of the original hearers, a reconstructed collective memory is established that has been shaped by the concerns and expectations of those to whom the Gospel is, at least initially, addressed. By contesting (8.33-8), appealing to (8.39-40) and reconfiguring (8.56-8) selected memories of Abraham in the light of the 'new reality' of Johannine belief in Jesus as the exclusive heavenly revealer and mediator of God's gift of salvation, this significant figure from the past emerges as a witness to Jesus, because his work *par excellence* is his joyful response upon 'seeing' Jesus's earthly mission. His affirmation of the Gospel's Christological claims therefore becomes, in Johannine terms, the only valid form of memory of Abraham.

Because the collective self-understanding of the Johannine Christians involves a significant redefinition of their memory of origins, their cohesion as a group does not depend on a shared ethnic identity originating with Abraham as the great ancestor of Israel. Different from Paul (Gal. 3.7, 29; cf. Rom. 4.1, 9.6-8), the designation 'children of Abraham' is not used by John as one of the defining identity markers of believers (cf. Theobald 2004: 158–9, 180–1), because descent from God is available exclusively through Jesus. Not only is it nowhere explicitly stated that Abraham is 'of God', probably to avoid attempts at reconnecting Abrahamic and divine descent (cf. 8.39, 41), but neither does Jesus, due to the emphasis on his divine origins, claim Abrahamic lineage for himself (cf. 8.56: 'Abraham, *your* father'). With regard to Johannine 'social frameworks', this distinctive redefinition of origins may well form a response to the claim made by a group of synagogue Jews, and even to those unwilling to confess openly their belief in Jesus, that their status as God's children is secured by virtue of their ethnic identity. Due to the lines of demarcation established in John 8.31-59 between 'earthly' and 'cosmological' perspectives on the question of origins and paternity, Abraham's significance as 'father' is greatly diminished.

And yet, though redefined, Abraham has not been deleted from the Johannine collective memory. Rather than being viewed as a figure of contrast, and from the standpoint of outsiders, his memory has been reconfigured to allow continuity with the past insofar as it speaks to the present. Since 'all beginnings contain an element of recollection' (Connerton 1989: 6), Abraham has been counted among the figures from Israel's past who have a part to play in the Johannine commemorative narrative, which, through the written text, also becomes an inscribed memory with a future.

PART IV
REFLECTIONS AND DIRECTIONS

Chapter 12

What Difference Does the Medium Make?

Barry Schwartz

Provocation and proof are the traditional means of scholarly progress. The contributors to this volume are nothing if not provocative and persuasive. This valuable collection not only assesses first-century media culture in terms of its role in the written and oral propagation of John's Gospel; its assessment generalizes to other Gospels and other first-century events as well.

Reading this volume's chapters on media culture from the standpoint of social memory theory leads me, unwittingly, to an argument about an important aspect of the development of early Christianity, namely, reaction to the delay of the Parousia. Before Jesus dies, he declares that the Kingdom of God will be established during the lifetimes of most of his contemporaries. That his prophecy fails is a challenge to the very core of first-century Christian belief. Reinterpreting Jesus's words, or rather, finding in these very words the reason for the delay, resolves the problem; but this new understanding is not based on a change in media culture. Narratives of Jesus's life and teachings change over time *within* the same oral culture, and essential aspects of these narratives remain unchanged as predominantly oral cultures convert into predominantly print cultures. There is, as I shall argue and hope to demonstrate here, a weak correspondence between changes in media culture and changes in Gospel content.

In the pages that follow, I proceed in three steps, each inspired by one or more related chapters in the present volume. First, I raise the issue of how oral traditions get started in the first place, and how memories of those who knew Jesus were transformed into a tradition that transcended the lives of the individuals who formed it. The second part of my argument asks and provides provisional answers to the question of how oral traditions, once established, are consolidated and passed across communities and generations. I focus on the lectors (whom contemporary communication scholars would call 'opinion-leaders') who conveyed to an illiterate public the written Gospels. In the third and longest phase of my argument, I defend the assumption that changes in Gospel content from Mark to John reflect changes in the way Jesus was popularly conceived in the first century. Many popular conceptions distorted the life of Jesus, as remembered by his closest contemporaries. An unambiguous account of social memory is required to identify these distortions and determine whether oral communication is more susceptible to them than is written communication. Emphasis will be placed on the two great perspectives of social memory theory, namely, the *presentist* perspective, wherein changes in the social memory are related to changes in the problems and concerns of the environment in which the past is invoked, and the *traditionalist* perspective, whose models align memory more closely to historical realities than to subsequent social developments. This third phase of discussion concludes with an explanation of why biblical studies' pre-eminent concept of social memory, namely Jan Assmann's generational *traditionsbruch*, must be supplemented in order to understand why media culture alone cannot explain the Gospels' changing content and representation. The *traditionsbruch*, as will be shown, resulted from a creedal crisis, not a media change. Knowing how Christian leaders managed the delay of the Parousia leads to a keener understanding of the role of media and memory in the rapidly changing beliefs of the first century.

How Oral Traditions Begin

The apostles probably knew most about Jesus and his ministry, but when he died, it is fair to assume that nothing was left to keep them together. 'Men who have been brought close together' to learn new ways of religious thinking, observed Maurice Halbwachs, 'may disperse afterwards into various groups ... Once separated, not one of them can reproduce the total content of the original thought' (1992: 32). This is what Halbwachs meant when he said that social memory disappears when the group changes or ceases to exist (1950 [1980]: 80). Of course, individual memories continue to exist, but unless one individual's memories supplement or support another's, no oral tradition can be established.

To supplement does not mean to duplicate. Different versions of a narrative may, in the aggregate, make for a perfectly coherent message. Edmund Leach's description of the variant expressions of myth applies to the variant stories of those who knew Jesus personally:

> Let us imagine the situation of an individual A who is trying to get a message to a friend B who is almost out of earshot, and let us suppose that communication is further hampered by various kinds of interference – noise from wind, passing cars, and so on. What will A Do? If he is sensible he will not be satisfied with shouting his message just once; he will shout it several times, and give a different wording to the message each time, supplementing his words with visual signals. At the receiving end B may likely get the meaning of each of the individual messages slightly wrong, but when he puts them together the redundancies and the mutual consistencies and inconsistencies will make it quite clear what is 'really' being said. (Leach 1970: 63–4)

The meaning of the message is not in any one of its versions but in all taken together. In the case that concerns us, let the apostles' messages to acquaintances and fellow Christians represent A and B; we then realize that each need not tell the same story in order for a fair estimate of the original reality to appear at the 'receiving end'. Nor do we need to know which shout is the original, any more than we need to know which text is original. Chris Keith's 'A Performance of the Text' is right to deny that an original Johannine text would necessarily tell a more authentic story than a later one. The first 'shout' might, indeed, be no better than the last.

Redundant oral communication is at the root of every oral tradition – not only in the first century but in all. Several examples can illustrate the point. No one knew much about Abraham Lincoln's young adulthood when he died. William Herndon, Lincoln's former law partner, located and interviewed as many former New Salem residents as he could find who had known Lincoln while he lived there in the 1830s. Because thirty-five to forty years had passed since these people last saw Lincoln, Herndon had to weed out distortions, rumours and mistakes from their testimony in order to identify its truth value. As a second case, the Works Progress Administration, seventy years after the Civil War ended, provided for interviews of African Americans born into slave families. The oral history project covered all slave-holding states during the Civil War and resulted in a vast collection titled *The Slave Narratives*, which can be found in any university library. Based on the memory of very elderly people remembering their childhood on the plantation, these narratives are in themselves imperfect sources, but the thick methodological literature that forms around them defines their contribution to our understanding of slave life. As a third example, Katsuichi Honda in 1971 interviewed survivors of the December 1937–February 1938 Nanjing Massacre. These illiterate victims could not have written their own stories, but their oral retellings, after almost forty years, were essential to reconstructing what had happened in Nanjing during the Japanese occupation. Memory thus solidifies when a collectivity tells its story, even after the passing of decades.

An obvious parallel may be drawn between the witnesses to life in New Salem, slave narratives, stories by survivors of Nanjing, and early traditions about Jesus's ministry: all are characterized by discrepancy and overlap. Before individuals spoke to any interviewer, they spoke to one another, and it was this interaction that converted overlap among individual memories into an oral tradition. When individual recollections react directly upon one another, they combine according to their own principles; they become realities which, while maintaining their dependence on individual memory, are independent of the memory of any one individual. Social memory cannot be reduced to the individual memories composing it, simply because the collective remembrance remains after these individuals disappear. Social memory is therefore something that individuals produce but do not constitute. This 'collective representation', as Emile Durkheim has named it, is what biblical scholars refer to as a 'tradition'. But we must avoid the way this volume's Introduction states the matter: it is not that 'oral recollections tend to move toward fixed and durable forms as the core of a tradition stabilizes'. This is a definition of tradition's 'surface structure'. Stable tradition is *composed* of fixed and durable forms, and these exist latently in social memory, actualized in individual beliefs about the past, just as, in de Saussure's (1987) model of linguistics, *langue* is realized in the 'surface structure' of *parole*, the spoken word. The 'thick autonomy of memory' (Casey 1987: 286), not its separate manifestations, thus defines tradition. The key point for present purposes is that no single individual, not even those who wield writing instruments, can 'silence' collective representations of the past.

How Oral Tradition Flows

The Fourth Gospel and First-Century Media Culture is inspired by Werner Kelber's groundbreaking *The Oral and the Written Gospel* (1983), which projected (then) recent discoveries about oral culture (Havelock 1963; Parry 1991; Ong 1992) to first-century Christianity. The current volume's own insights into the qualities and power of oral communication are stunning, but the project would tell us even more about orality, writing and memory if its contributors recognized the limits of Kelber's argument and widened their own intellectual scope.

The same elements of redundancy and collective representation that result in the *origin* of a tradition are at play in its *maintenance* and *transmission*. Multiple writers and speakers convey discrepant but overlapping information which, in its assemblage, is coherent to most readers and listeners. Traditions begin, subsist and change, however, under different conditions. Elihu Katz (1954) and his colleagues have established that public communication flow, which would include first-century communication about Jesus, involves two steps: first, information is disseminated; secondly, it is received by 'opinion-leaders', interpreted by them, then passed on to their associates and friends. More attuned to the media than their contemporaries, opinion-leaders are not content to learn what is happening around them; they seek to convince others of their understanding of events. Because opinion-leaders' influence is related to who they are and what and whom they know, the information they convey does more than instruct; it is a source of *social pressure* to conform to community leanings, and provides *social support* for doing so. Gospel writers therefore have *less* direct influence on individuals than do the opinion-leaders, the lectors, who bring their text to the public.

This two-step theory of communication – disssemination to opinion-leaders; interpretation and further distribution – describes the stream of first-century gospel tradition. But it is important to understand this transmission at a deeper level. It is by now common knowledge that modern mass media, in the process of transmitting information, introduced the era of 'celebrity', and today's celebrities include not only entertainers but also transmitters of secular news (syndicated writers, television 'news anchors') and sacred information ('television preachers' and clergymen). Although lectors were, for many, the only source of information about Jesus and his message, their fame, in John's time, was for the most part confined to the local communities where they lived or visited. One of the virtues of the present collection is to tell us something about these people, although, given its emphasis on orality, it fails to tell us enough.

In Jeffrey Brickle's essay, the crucial link between Gospel authors and their audiences is the lector, 'the person who reads or describes texts and scripture to illiterate congregations'. Ancient lectors and modern opinion-leaders play analogous roles. Gospel authors make their texts 'lector-friendly' with repetition, regular use of figurative language, analogy, emphasis and de-emphasis, passionate assertion and declaration, aphorism, parallelism, marking of beginnings and endings, appropriate pitch, stress, rhythm, pace, and other fixed language patterns that promote listeners' understanding and remembering. These formulaic patterns, Antoinette Wire adds, not only give coherence to texts: the performer mediating divine voices and prophetic writings is inclined toward hyperbole, or 'inspired speech'. However, prophecy, the passing of a message from a divine sender to designated recipients, often fails. Without talented lectors, text alone, even for the literate, lacks rhetorical power. Behind every written Gospel, then, are performers who bring words to life. As with musical compositions, Wire tells us, the player or singer makes a difference. The lector therefore enhances the message he conveys. Jesus appears more wondrous in the words of a gifted lector than in those of a mediocre one. But Wire understates her case. Even the Gutenberg press, the first great turning point of scribal communication, probably made printed messages available to a much smaller percentage of people than did lectors presenting the same messages orally.

Tom Thatcher's two essays enlarge Brickle's and Wire's remarks. Lectors, he contends, 'smooth' discontinuities in the text: that which is anomalous in written form, including John's Prologue, appears well-connected in oral presentation. Thatcher also identifies dual vocalizations: the lector plays the role of Jesus speaking to his contemporaries, and the role of himself speaking to his own audience. In the process speakers come to be admired, even identified with Jesus and venerated. Lectors also succeed by tailoring their remarks to specific social and political situations. In contrast to readers learning in isolation, oral performance is situated in homes, markets, synagogues and other social places, making the story of Jesus part of the lives of its listeners. Thirteen of the seventeen speeches in John, explains Tom Boomershine, were read to Jews gathered in these places. The situations in which spoken words are lodged define their meaning, but this is not to say, as Chris Keith makes clear, that the written word is trans-situational or subject to narrower interpretation than the spoken word.

This volume's essays, indeed, demonstrate lectors' dependence on text, and it is this relation that tells us most about the way people thought and felt about Jesus. Many written portrayals of Jesus during this period, it is true, reflected the people's taste; some writers shared that taste; some exploited it, dealing mainly with the features of Jesus's life that would interest their audience. Other writers, however, believed their efforts would be of no significance if they did not in some way affect as well as reflect their audiences' conceptions of Jesus. Writers explained that Jesus's life and words revealed God's plan and their fate, and for that reason the sacred story had to be accurately recorded and faithfully conveyed. For the most part, the carriers of Jesus's story, writers and lectors alike, did their best to get it right. The relationship between writer, lector and audience – between memory and society – however strong or weak, probably remained the same throughout the first century. Given this assumption, the difference between Mark's mid-century and John's late-century portrayals can be taken as an index of change in the way ordinary men and women perceived Jesus.

This premise takes us to this book's most significant shortcoming, its ambiguity on the role of memory. The stories conveyed by John's lectors, no less than Mark's, Matthew's and Luke's, were stories about the past, stories ultimately based on memories of Jesus's contemporaries. At question is the extent to which these stories were distorted with the passage of time, what parts were distorted, what motivated the distortions, and what were their social functions. Above all, were spoken distortions more or less common than written ones? Does that which makes scripture permanent also make it more likely to be true? These questions concern the changing image of Jesus in first-century Christian memory.

Two Faces of Social Memory

According to Le Donne and Thatcher's Introduction, our memory of all historical events is subject to multiple interpretations and constant redefinitions, all driven by values, ideal interests and power relations. 'Ultimately, then, social memory theorists are less concerned with the content of social memory and its potential historical value than in the ways that specific artifacts of memory (such as the Johannine writings) reflect the structure, values and identity of the groups that produced them.' This statement applies to part, but by no means the entire field, of social memory studies. I take nothing away from the authors' present work by calling this particular statement misleading, and insisting that it underestimates the value of social memory theory for historical Jesus scholarship.

This book's concluding section, 'Memory as Medium', is a continuation of Alan Kirk and Tom Thatcher's pioneering volume on *Memory, Tradition, and Text* (2005). Le Donne initiates the discussion by distinguishing individual memory, which he correctly identifies as 'literal memory', from social memory, which marks past events through such physical objects as texts and commemorative symbols – hence Le Donne's reference to social memory as a 'metaphor'. This is a correct and useful distinction, so long as we understand that social memory and individual memory perform different functions.

'Social memory' refers to the distribution throughout society of individual knowledge, belief, feeling and moral judgement of the past as well as identification with past actors and events. Only individuals, as Le Donne notes, possess the capacity to contemplate the past, but this does not mean that such capacity originates in the individual alone or can be explained solely on the basis of his or her experience. Individuals do not know the past singly; they know it with and against others situated in different groups, and through the knowledge and traditions that predecessors and contemporaries transmit to them (Halbwachs 1926; 1980 [1950]; Shils 1981).

During the last three decades, two perspectives on social memory have emerged, each of which is defined by analytical models that depict the way memory works. In the 'presentist' perspective, articulated by constructionist, postmodern, political and pragmatist models of memory, beliefs about the past are construed as hostage to present circumstances, with different elements of the past becoming more or less relevant as circumstances change. This volume's editors and most of its contributors are drawn to the presentist model. In its extreme form, presentism holds that contemporary events alone are real and that the past is construed according to its present relevance. However extreme or understated, I use the most inclusive term, 'presentist', in order to emphasize what its analytical models have in common, namely, a focus on current situations, including political, economic and ideological predicaments, as the basis of the past's perception. In this light, social memory becomes a dependent variable as the political and knowledge elites of each new generation, and in each community, forge a past compatible with their own circumstances and with minimal regard for historical truth (see, for example, Halbwachs 1926; 1980 [1950]; Coser 1992; Zerubavel 2003).

Of the three chapters in this volume's social memory section, Catrin Williams' analysis conforms most closely to the presentist model. After her reference to Halbwachs's observation on how groups determine what is remembered and forgotten, and Olick's account of memory as a conflictual reconstruction of the past, she explains how storytelling about Jesus reflected disagreements between Christians and Jews. Her case in point is John's account of Abraham. One can hardly think of a better example. John denies that descent from Abraham is descent from God. Abraham is part of Jewish beginnings, but descent from God begins with Jesus alone. Accordingly, Jesus can say, 'Before Abraham was, I am.' When asked whether he is greater than Abraham, Jesus replies, 'Abraham your father rejoiced to see my day.' John thus reconfigures Abraham to meet the claims and challenges of his potential Jewish converts and opponents.

The strength of presentist analysis is that it focuses on the situation in which events are remembered and forgotten, and this is a great strength indeed, for we cannot grasp the meaning of any event or gesture without knowing the context in which it occurs. One might borrow from Clifford Geertz (1973: 3–30) and define context-driven accounts as 'thick descriptions' of social memory. A problem arises, however, when the past becomes a captive of the present. When presentist insights, however profound, focus on the reconstructive (and deconstructive) potential of social memory research, they minimize memory's relevance to biblical studies by ignoring the ways in which the past resists revision. 'There are limits to the pasts that can be reconstructed, and there is an integrity to the past that deserves respect' (Schudson 1993: 221). Social memory scholarship, with its full range of analytical tools, promotes appreciation of this resistance and this integrity; it recognizes the conservation as well as distortion of the past.

Whereas presentism conceives the past according to a 'relevance principle', culturalism works according to a 'reality principle'. The cultural perspective on social memory manifests itself in realist and traditionalist models that define memory as an ordered system of information and symbols, activated by cultural values supplying standards and frames of reference for the present. Because values, standards and reference frames vary from one group to another and from one generation to another, cultural theory itself is inherently presentist. But if memory becomes so malleable as to be dismissive of the realities of the past, history becomes superfluous and social memory loses its survival value. Societies whose idea of history is warped are then no worse off than societies which acknowledge their history. To possess the truth is to possess no advantage.

The term 'cultural memory' is used here in the realist sense: the past is no less objective than the present and exists independently of the concepts we use to describe it. In this tradition, which broadens Jan Assmann's conception of memory, culture's roots in individual activity are recognized, but culture's 'emergence' from these roots is deemed a fact rather than an exercise in 'reification' (Berger and Luckmann 1966: 79–92). Cultural memory, then, remains stable as it is modified across generations and nations (Shils 1981: 1–62; 162–94). Cultural memory is a source of moral direction, an independent variable, a distinguishing, formative aspect of culture (see Burke 1790; Durkheim [1915] 1965; Pelikan 1984, 1985; Schudson 1989, 1992; Assmann 2006; Yerushalmi [1982] 1996). In this light, the work of memory agents and entrepreneurs (Fine 1996) account for nothing; the success of their activities is itself to be explained, and part of that explanation involves an estimate of the past *wie es eigenlich gewesen* ('as it actually happened').

Michael Labahn's 'Scripture Talks because Jesus Talks' touches on the premises of the cultural perspective by declaring that written biblical texts are inherently authoritative, not only because they are written but because they bear witness to the authority of Jesus. True, the community only *hears* the Gospel, but the ultimate authority behind the spoken word is the text; behind the text, the actuality. The written Gospel, then, does not silence orality, as Kelber and others insist. Rather, it achieves fulfilment through oral narration. Indeed, the lector gains authority by displaying to his audience the manuscript he is reciting (Shiner 2003).

Among the several contributors to this volume, James Dunn, with his emphasis on tradition remaining 'the same yet different', gives cultural memory its clearest articulation. Dunn is compelling, as long as we take his work as a point of departure rather than conclusion. W. V. O. Quine's (1998) famous statement about the under-determination of theory by facts – his belief that science is full of instances in which two or more plausible theories can be derived from the same body of data – is a version of Dunn's 'same but different' concept of tradition. Neither Dunn nor Quine means that one theory is as valid as another. Both believe that every theory, however derived, is testable, and that from these tests emerges truth.

In sum, the memory chapters in this volume demonstrate not only external conditions causing writers and lectors to misrepresent reality; they also show the past resisting revision. Memories, as the editors claim, subordinate reality to 'the structure, values and identity of the group that produced them', but this can only be affirmed if reality is known. Such knowledge need only consist of fundamental features, but the more accurate it is, the more (1) we can know whether accounts of a historical event have been distorted or accurately represented; (2) we can tell what kind of distortion is occurring; (3) we can identify accretions to and deletions from historical accounts; and (4) we can adjudicate among competing interpretations.

Reciprocally, deviations from historical reality illuminate reality itself. To take but one major example of interest to this collection: a major change from Mark to John concerns the theme of apocalypticism, and because this theme eroded from the time of Jesus's death to John's day, we may infer (not conclude) that the apocalyptic Jesus resonated more strongly among *his* contemporaries than among John's. Of course, one must always ask whether the passage of time gives society a clearer view of the kind of man Jesus had been. The answer is simple: time clarifies when it provides the opportunity to gather new, or supplement existing, evidence.

The presentist and cultural perspectives are the two great ideas of social memory scholarship. But if presentist and cultural perspectives are known, they have not been fully investigated. In particular, neither perspective gives us an adequate understanding of symbolic formulation. Much is said about memory being 'invented' or its providing a controlling 'blueprint' for experience, but we know little about how either is accomplished. The link between the causes and consequences of memory is weak because the 'connecting element, the process of symbolic formulation', as Geertz (1973: 207) would call it, is passed over. The singular contribution of this volume is to explore one of the most important of these formulations: lectors telling the story of Jesus to illiterate listeners. But how did the story of Jesus, the first written account of which appeared thirty to forty years after Jesus's death, remain plausible?

Orality, Literacy and the Real Traditionsbruch

The present volume fails to trace continuity and change from Mark to John in their respective portrayals of Jesus. Its general theme is more concerned, as Jan Assmann (2006) would put it, with the consequence of 'communicative memory' mutating into 'cultural memory' – that is to say, how the oral claims which people (including lectors) make about the past differ from what people write about the past in order to perpetuate it.

Assmann's statement resonates perfectly with the assumptions of orality scholarship, but to follow him is to take memory scholarship down the wrong path. First-century Christianity's major crisis is not the disappearance of the generation that saw and knew Jesus or the problem of committing their experience and memories to writing; rather, it is the failure of a prophecy that Joseph Ratzinger (1988: 19–45) deems the essential, although ambiguous, core of Christianity. The new Christians embraced Jesus's declaration that the kingdom of heaven was at hand, that the Son of man was about to come to earth on a cloud of glory and rid the world of evil. On this matter the present volume is almost silent, but because it was a primary concern of first-century Christian communities, the failure of Jesus's prophecy constituted a grave threat to their belief. Maurice Halbwachs had already said as much: in the early to mid first century, 'the hope for the return of Christ and the appearance of the heavenly Jerusalem had not yet been turned aside'; past and present, the old Judaism and the new Christianity, remained fused (1992 [1926]: 94). All Christian writings, canonical or apocryphal, testify to the same thing: 'we are approaching the end of things; God will have his vengeance; his Messiah will appear or reappear. There is no doubt that it was this element in Jewish thought that the Christians retained above all' (Halbwachs 1992 [1926]: 96). In Jaroslav Pelikan's more recent words, Jesus's 'teaching and preaching had as its central content "the gospel of God ... The time is fulfilled, and the Kingdom of God is at hand; repent and believe in the gospel"' (1987: 21). The generation to which Jesus, and before him John the Baptist, addressed their proclamation was, we are told, a generation 'standing on tiptoes in expectation' (Pelikan 1987: 24). In all three Synoptic Gospels, Jesus declares that his generation will not pass away before the kingdom of God is established. But then Pelikan asks a key question: 'How could, and how did, the person of Jesus retain hold on an authority whose validity had apparently depended on the announcement of the impending end of history?' (1987: 25). Many writers and lectors addressed this question, to which no Christian community anywhere could have been indifferent.

This crisis must not be exaggerated. Even Mark, whose apocalyptic warnings are most vivid, revealed that not even the angels knew when the

Parousia would arrive. Many of Jesus's statements could be used to explain the Parousia's delay (see, for example, Ratzinger 1988: 32); but if uncertainty about the Parousia's timing comforted some, the imminence of the Great Judgement was certain to almost everyone. Thus, by the second century, what might have been a fatal disconfirmation of Christianity's core belief resolved itself into a two-phase doctrine: Jesus's prophecy was reinterpreted to mean that the Kingdom of God, the eschaton, had already established itself through the Resurrection and the advent of Christianity; however, after a long continuation of earthly history, Jesus would reappear, the virtuous would then be rewarded and the sinner punished. By the turn of the second century, this formulation had replaced the earlier vision of an imminent apocalypse. But John's Gospel hardly mentions it.

Why did most first-century Christian communities accept this explanation of the Parousia's delay? Not media culture but a psychological tendency, confirmed and reconfirmed in twentieth-century psychology laboratories, provides the most credible explanation.

When Prophecy Fails, a mid-twentieth-century analysis of a doomsday cult,[1] explains how 'cognitive dissonance', occasioned by failure of the prophecy of catastrophe, actually increases the commitment of cult members and intensifies the recruiting activity of those inwardly committed to the cultic belief. If the truly faithful are in contact with and in a position to support one another, they easily and convincingly rationalize the failure, then work harder to convince others to believe as they do, which reduces, even eliminates, the dissonance of their experience. Some element of this process, as Festinger and his colleagues suggest, may well have been at play among first-century Christians.

The delay of the Parousia is important to us because it is a case study of the way tensions and doubts of early Christianity were faced and resolved through written and oral media. Media culture, however, indicates how stories, questions and doubts about Jesus were *told*, not how orality and writing led to different *conceptions* of his life and teachings. Readers and listeners, it is true, *experienced* Jesus differently, but did they *conceive* him in significantly different ways? Thatcher and Le Donne's assumption is that the unique dynamics of oral communication distort reality and render everyone less likely to apprehend it as it was – just as linguistic determinists, like Edward Sapir and Benjamin Whorf, would insist that original Aramaic meanings must be inevitably warped in the written Greek Gospels. The dilemma is clear: on the one hand, there can be no unmediated perception; on the other, mediated perception distorts reality.

The dilemma would be insoluable if the Great Divide between writing and speaking were not an exaggeration. Few scholars have outdone Alan Kirk in

---

1   Leon Festinger, Henry W. Riecken and Stanley Schatcher, *When Prophecy Fails* (Minnesota: University of Minnesota Press, 1956).

documenting the interdependency of first-century oral and scribal elements. There never has been a sphere of pure orality where an oral world view and ethos prevails. Each of the four oral Gospel traditions is set within a scriptural frame and saturated with scriptural content (Kirk 2008). Chris Keith, using as his case the adulteress's story inserted into an earlier version of the Gospel of John, expands on Kirk. He not only demonstrates that there was no 'Great Divide' between scribal and oral media cultures but also shows texts to be as malleable and responsive to extrinsic pressures, including the pressure to portray a literate Jesus, as are oral performances.

My impression builds on Keith's: first-century media were mixed unevenly (which this book emphasizes), but it was still a mixed-media culture, and the mixing process had minimal effect upon media content. Suppose the percentage and distribution of literate and illiterate people were *identical* throughout the first century. In that case, changes in the Gospels, specifically the change from an apocalyptic Jesus in Mark and Matthew to a non-apocalyptic Jesus in John (not to mention the Gospel of Thomas in the early second century) could not be attributed to media culture change. This proposition makes media culture constant by stipulation. I assume it was constant in fact: there was no significant surge in literacy during the first century. Written and oral communications, in truth, portrayed Jesus differently, but that difference was relatively trivial. The literate person reading a story of Jesus and the illiterate person (of comparable intelligence) hearing a story of Jesus formed essentially the same conceptions.

As we move toward this section's conclusion, let us again assume what many biblical scholars take for granted: that Jesus was an apocalyptic prophet. Neither oral nor written culture reveal why the apocalyptic message of Jesus was emphasized in Mark and Matthew, muted in Luke, absent in John, and opposed by Thomas. As Gospel commentary on the imminence of God's kingdom diminished, the early Christian churches – small, temporary communities founded by charismatic leaders – became large, permanent hierarchies led by an establishment of elites and oriented toward an indefinite future. Changing expectations of the Parousia, not changes in orality or scribal media, make this institutional transformation meaningful. If the end were believed imminent, permanent structures would have been superfluous.

Let us assume, further, that mid-first-century Christians had no interest in or basis for setting a date for the Parousia, but believed that the eschaton had already begun with the ministry of Jesus. In Jewish eschatology, resurrection is the eschaton's defining feature, and few Christians doubted it. But if Christians were *indifferent* to the delay of the Parousia, then we would find no steep decline in the frequency with which writers and lectors mention it as we approach the end of the first century. The decline does not reflect indifference but rather successful *explanation* of the delay. A great achievement of John's Gospel, the only Gospel to portray Jesus as a non-apocalyptic prophet, is its distinctive approach to the delay of the Parousia, one that merges future into present eschatology while retaining belief in, although scarcely mentioning, the Parousia itself. Thus, John foreshadows the Christian world's new idea of their Messiah's return.

What, at last, is to be said of John? If Jesus were actually an apocalyptic prophet, then late-first-century portrayals of him must be less valid than earlier ones. By any of the standard criteria, in fact, Mark and Matthew are more historically dependable than John. Mark's and Matthew's apocalyptic portraits pass the tests of dissimilarity, independent attestation, contextual credibility, and closeness in time to the original events (Ehrman 1999). They also pass the tests of concomitant variation (reduced emphasis on apocalypticism as the Parousia's delay lengthens). Because early Christian media culture did not change significantly during this period, it cannot account for these diminishing references to the promised kingdom.

That John's Gospel is anomalous is well known. James Dunn recognizes John's uniqueness as well as anyone, but he gives John's version of the life of Jesus the benefit of the doubt. He finds the miracles that John alone attributes to Jesus to be ways of saying something true about him: '[H]e had to retell the tradition in bolder ways.' Although Dunn's listing of the differences between John's and the Synoptic Gospels is fundamental, it is not exhaustive. One can also say that, in John, (1) Jesus is portrayed as a divinity, existing with God from the beginning; (2) Jesus himself, not his message, is the object of veneration; (3) Jesus conducts miracles to prove his own identity rather than to help his followers; (4) Jesus rarely mentions the Parousia. Perhaps the reason John wrote a Gospel – to gain the support of friends and weaken enemies – is the reason why that Gospel is the least valid source of information about the historical Jesus.

If John is an inferior source of information, does his overestimation of written communication explain why? If not, then why is the topic of orality so extraordinarily relevant to present scholarship? That question is difficult to answer on the basis of evidence. Indeed, the appeal of the orality hypothesis depends in part on its romantic as well as its evidential qualities. Werner Kelber's 'Great Divide' between orality and literacy resembles, in this regard, Pierre Nora's distinction between the *milieux de memoire* and the *lieux de memoire*. The *milieux* of which Nora speaks relate to peasant culture, 'the quintessential repository of memory'. These societies long assured the conservation and transmission of memory, smoothing the passage from past through present and future. The memory of peasant culture is 'integrated, dictatorial memory – unself-conscious, commanding, all-powerful, spontaneously actualizing ... linking the history of its ancestors to the undifferentiated time of heroes, origins, and myth'. However, memory and history are in fundamental opposition. 'Memory is life, borne by living societies founded in its name. It remains in permanent evolution, open to the dialectic of remembering and forgetting, unconscious of its successive deformations, vulnerable to manipulation and approbation, susceptible to being long dormant and periodically revived.' In contrast, history, because it is an intellectual and secular production, calls for analysis and criticism. 'At the heart of history is a critical discourse that is antithetical to spontaneous memory. History is perpetually suspicious of memory, and its true mission is to suppress and destroy it' (Nora 1989: 8–9). In Nora's work, like Kelber's, one detects a certain sympathy for the earliest forms of social memory, earmarked by the traditional elements of romanticism, including sentiment over reason, primitivism, authenticity of feeling, reaction against form, boldness, freedom and release.

'Memory is life, borne by living societies founded in its name.' This phrase captures as well as any other Nora's romantic attraction to oral culture. It might or might not capture Kelber's and Thatcher's, too. It should be stressed that Nora's *lieux de memoire* are thought to be entities whose very existence testify to the diminished relevance of the past. By contrast, orality, the culture of the *milieux de memoire*, reminds us of the living past that modernity has taken from us. Orality is the warm media culture of our family, of our friendship circles, and of our lives.

Nora's distinction, like Kelber's, between warm memory and cold history, is too fierce to capture first-century Christianity (see Thatcher 2008: 10–14, 23–4, and citations therein). In Alan Kirk's words, the 'reification of the written word distinct from its embodiment in speech, the separation of the visual and aural aspects of the text that enable us to treat print and speech differently, was not established in antiquity … Written artifacts enjoyed an essentially oral cultural life' while orality itself was rooted in writing (2008: 217). If oral tradition (the memory of peasant culture) is the means by which Scripture (the memory of elite culture) is transmitted, then there can be no *theoretical* difference between the two – which means that social experience will bend written and oral history in the same directions. Writing and orality are, and, we have good reason to believe, always have been, different codings of one and the same message.

Chapter 13

INTRODUCING MEDIA CULTURE TO JOHANNINE STUDIES: ORALITY, PERFORMANCE AND MEMORY

Gail R. O'Day

This collection of essays on media culture and Johannine studies takes as its framing presupposition that locating the Gospel of John intentionally in ancient media culture will yield fresh understandings of the development, context and reception of the Gospel. More particularly, the collection posits that explicit attention to ancient oral culture can serve as a corrective to scholarly approaches to John in particular (and the NT more generally) that take written traditions as their methodological framework and so overlook, diminish or misread the decisive influence that oral culture had on the Gospel of John. The essays demonstrate that the methodological wager of the collection was worth taking, as the interpretative yield provided by the essays is high and would not be possible without the methodological and hermeneutical framing that attention to oral media culture makes possible.

I

The Introduction by the volume's two editors, Anthony Le Donne and Tom Thatcher, makes the volume's operating presupposition explicit: 'The essays in this volume, both individually and collectively, proceed from the assumption that the Johannine Literature was a product of first-century media culture, and in turn significantly contributed to early Christian memory and identity' (see p. 3). For the editors, attention to first-century media culture involves attention to a set of overlapping issues: 'the nature of ancient oral cultures; the dynamics of ancient oral performance; and the workings of memory' (p. 3). In addition, 'the intersection of these three concerns has led to an increasing interest in aurality, particularly in the active dimension of hearing oral art/texts/traditions performed and in the hermeneutical implications of the relationship between a composer and a live listening audience' (p. 3). The essays in the volume are organized into three parts that reflect these three central issues identified by the editors: John and Oral Culture, John as Oral Performance, and John in the Medium of Memory.

This organizational decision has its strengths. The distribution of essays according to the editors' three key issues helps to show the complexity contained in the very concept of 'oral media culture'. The explicit identification of these three categories has its own pedagogical value for the volume, since the very structure of the book leads the reader into a new awareness of the multiple dimensions of oral media studies. The introduction makes this pedagogical function explicit, by providing a brief general overview of each of the three categories, including highlighting the pertinent seminal scholarly literature for each category, and then identifying how each essay fits the category to which it has been assigned.

Nonetheless, this organizational decision makes the three categories seem more distinct than they actually are. No essay in any given section holds to the editors' category distinctions. Each essay could be located in any of the book's three sections almost equally well. As the reader moves through the book, it becomes clear that each essay in the book participates in and makes contributions to all three conversations about oral culture, oral performance and memory. This essential overlap among these categories is masked to a degree by the strict divisions of the book's contents. The essays in the oral performance section, for example, make active use of scholarly literature about oral culture and memory, as well as that of oral performance, so that this reader, at least, wondered if the three categories are distinctions without real differences. The overlap of categories in the essays shows the ways in which these three areas of media studies are inevitably intertwined.

One of the challenges and strengths of the book is the way in which it attempts to introduce fresh approaches into Johannine studies, and the full range of what ancient media studies offers is restricted by structuring the book in a way that works against, rather than taking advantage of, the fluidity of methodological approaches. The essays are more effective when each of them is read as illustrating the possibilities of ancient media culture as a general framework for interpreting the Gospel of John, rather than as illustrations or applications of distinct aspects of ancient media culture studies.

II

The turn to ancient media culture studies as a fresh avenue for understanding the Gospel of John is extremely promising, because it grapples explicitly with one of the central methodological and historical paradoxes that confronts New Testament scholars. As a discipline, we study written texts because those are the only literary artifacts that we have, yet the discipline also takes as a given that these written texts had their origins in oral culture and oral traditions. This paradox means that communication medium, as well as time, separates contemporary scholars from the experience of the emerging Christian communities. The classical disciplinary canons have attempted to resolve this paradox through recourse to source, form and redaction criticisms, and have used the Synoptic Gospels as their methodological laboratory.

Each of these classic methods resolves the oral/written relationship in slightly different ways. Source criticism posits a shared oral tradition, but also assumes that shared oral tradition cannot account for the detailed agreements found across the Gospels, and so posits a literary dependence model to explain those agreements. Source criticism's focal point of inquiry is what lies behind the Gospel texts as we have them, and assumes that the production of written documents was the decisive event in the shaping and fixing of early traditions about Jesus. Form criticism also takes what lies behind the Gospel texts as its focal point of inquiry, but places its primary attention on the individual elements of oral tradition that eventually gave rise to the written Gospels. Form criticism correlates story form with the social setting that would have necessitated such a form – a controversy story to meet the needs of a situation of debate in the early church, for example. The oral forms that form criticism posits helps to tell the story of the development of early Christian communities, and can also be studied to help identify which were the 'earliest' forms of Jesus tradition and, in combination with source criticism, which were the most 'authentic'. Redaction criticism shifts the balance between oral and written towards written, with an eye toward the distinctive emphases employed by the Evangelists in creating a coherent Gospel narrative out of the oral and written sources at their disposal.

Yet in each of these classic approaches, the written Gospel form is the determinative hermeneutical lens. Oral tradition, oral traditions and the oral traditioning process are means to a written end. Oral tradition is by and large the more 'primitive' stage of the Jesus tradition, both in form and content. Attention is given to the *sitz im Leben* of these oral traditions, the community setting that necessitated distinctive forms, but the *sitz* in which the story possibly originated is the focal point, rather than the story, or the storyteller and the listeners as participants in oral culture and performance. Whether intentional or not, one by-product of each of these classic approaches to the oral/written paradox is to render the oral as a dispensable medium on the way to a written refinement.

This collection of essays builds on the work of NT scholars who were pioneers in rethinking the relationship between oral and written media in the development of the Gospels, most notably Werner Kelber, James D. G. Dunn and Joanna Dewey, who called attention to the distinctive traits of oral media which had a decisive impact on written traditions. For these scholars, oral media is more than a means to a written end. Rather, oral media shaped the very way that written forms developed, and lent an oral/aural quality to written documents and their reception by early communities. Kelber, Dewey and others suggested ways in which the balance might shift between oral and written media in assessing gospel literature, so that the two were held in hermeneutical tension, rather than always resolving the tension towards the priority of the written.

Three essays in particular, in this volume, show both the hermeneutical potential and the interpretative yield when oral and written are held in a more tensive relationship. The essays by Chris Keith, Michael Labahn and James D. G. Dunn, in very different ways, succeed not only in shifting the hermeneutical balance between oral and written media, but also in showing how the lines of difference between oral and written media are regularly overstated. At a quick glance, James D. G. Dunn's essay could be misread as subscribing to the classic conventions of form and redaction criticism, in the service of identifying the authentic kernels of Jesus tradition in the Gospel of John. Yet to read his essay this way would be to miss the genuine advance in identifying and assessing gospel traditions in Dunn's work. This essay on John continues the work in history, memory and gospel traditions that has been at the centre of Dunn's scholarly publications for over a decade (see this volume's Bibliography for details of Dunn's work in this area).

Dunn shifts the hermeneutical balance between oral and written media by changing a model of literary dependency in the Gospel traditions to a model of interlinked oral traditions that themselves show variations depending on the context of the retelling. This recognition of the role of variation in oral tradition is shared by all the authors in this volume, and makes a significant contribution to revitalizing our understanding both of oral tradition and of the vibrancy of early Christian communities. Rather than a point-to-point correspondence between form and situation, for example, this richer understanding of oral tradition, well demonstrated in the work of folklorists and other scholars of ancient oral media (see this volume's Bibliography), envisions an oral *culture* rather than simply fragmented oral traditions, a culture in which both telling and listening to stories exerted an influence on the ways by which traditions are actively remembered and passed on.

Yet what makes Dunn's work so clear and compelling is that while theories of oral culture, and especially theories of memory, support his hypothesis, he builds his portrait of oral tradition primarily on the character of the Jesus traditions themselves. Dunn helpfully characterizes that tradition as 'the same yet different'. For Dunn, the shaping question is whether the Jesus tradition in John can be explained as 'the same yet different', as the Synoptic traditions can, or if it strains this understanding of the role of tradition and memory. In this essay, and throughout his work on the role of memory and tradition, Dunn makes a compelling case that the transmission of Jesus traditions in early faith communities will be misunderstood as long as oral tradition is thought of in terms of form-critical categories. Rather, the Synoptic and Johannine traditions show that the oral transmission of Jesus traditions involved the shaping of those traditions as 'Gospel', and that shaping is equally in evidence in all the canonical Gospels.

Readers of this volume can judge the success of Dunn's careful and extensive cataloguing of Jesus traditions in John as they relate to the synoptic traditions, but I personally find his results persuasive. What distinguishes Dunn's project from many other attempts to either claim Jesus traditions in

John as 'authentic', or to reject Jesus traditions in John as close to spurious, is the high hermeneutical and theological value that Dunn places on memory and its impact. Freedom in retelling a tradition does not equate with unreliability for Dunn, but rather confirms the impact of the tradition for the tradent/reteller. Dunn works carefully through different parts of the Gospel traditions to show the ways in which John exercises freedom in appropriating the tradition to give it his distinctive emphasis, but this distinctive emphasis is nonetheless rooted in earlier traditions that all the Gospels share. His discussion of the John the Baptist traditions in this essay are a perfect example of Dunn's method at work.

I had a professor in graduate school who was adamant that the best exegetical work was that which seemed to show you the obvious; when you read a textual study, for example, if your reaction was that the exegetical observations seemed so simple that you must have known them even before you read the essay, the essay was a success. Dunn's work in this essay fits that category. In reading his handling of Jesus traditions, shaped by an almost common-sense attention to the role of individual and communal memory, Dunn reaches conclusions about the transmission of tradition that I seem to have known all along. Yet their very commonsensical articulations should not be allowed to mask the significance of their contribution. Dunn recognizes the role of retelling and memory as essential ingredients in oral tradition and in the creation and transmission of Jesus traditions, and in so doing advances a coherent theory of the role of tradition, oral and written, in all four canonical Gospels. For Dunn, John's difference in remembering and retelling the Jesus tradition may sometimes be at a magnitude higher than that found in some of the more shared retellings and rememberings in Matthew, Mark and Luke, but the same practices bind the handling of tradition in all four Gospels.

Chris Keith also shifts the balance between oral and written traditions in his chapter, and he does so by introducing questions of orality and textuality into discussions of text criticism. As Keith points out at the beginning of his essay, the overlapping issues in textual criticism, orality/textuality studies and social/cultural memory studies have not been sufficiently attended to, and the strength of this essay lies in the methodological clarity with which investigation of this overlap is conceived and executed. Keith uses the Pericope Adulterae (John 7.53-8, 11; PA) as a case study for demonstrating the performance dimensions that written traditions share with oral traditions. Although he includes a caveat that this account is an exercise in inductive reasoning that may or may not be relevant for broader theories of the Jesus tradition, this reader finished the essay persuaded that Keith's work is not only relevant, but has the potential to correct false presuppositions about the differences between oral and written traditions and cultures that dominate NT scholarship.

I will not rehearse here the details of Keith's argument, as the essay is clear in structure and lucid in argumentation. What stands out as one of the essay's contributions is that it exposes the way most NT scholars simply accept and repeat unexamined assumptions about topics as basic as the nature of scribal activity, 'original' text, and the 'Great Divide' between oral and written tradition. While constantly grounding his argument in the specific case of the PA, Keith is able to show how the dichotomy between orality and textuality (or, even, the opposition between oral and written cultures) cannot be maintained in the face of at least this piece of textual evidence. Even Dunn, Keith notes, subscribes to a theory that differentiates oral modes of transmission of tradition from written modes, when Dunn explains the fluidity in written tradition 'as if it were oral tradition'.

Keith's central point, substantiated by reference to PA, is that written texts are also performances in their own right, and that their fluidity is inherent in the nature of written texts, not a hangover from oral traditions. 'In short, the Jesus tradition emerged in a culture that was not oral *rather than* textual, but oral *and* textual' (see p. 60; emphasis in original). To quote Keith again, 'the proper contrast is not between our typographical mindset and the ancient oral mindset, but rather between our oral-written matrix and their oral-written matrix, between our appropriation of texts and their appropriation of texts' (p. 61). In the case of the PA, the insertion of this pericope at John 7.53 demonstrates both the interpolator's role as 'the audience of John's author' and his 'own role as author/storyteller who has creative control over the tradition, augmenting it for ... his own audience' (p. 62). In this way, writing is storytelling – not because it is imitating (or retaining vestiges of) oral tradition, but because such performance is intrinsic to writing.

Methodologically, Keith's essay is an advance on the understanding of the relationship between oral and written traditions found in Dunn's work, in that Keith explicitly claims the role of performance for written texts. Indeed, this element of performance in John's handling of the Jesus traditions in general seems to discomfit Dunn slightly, as he admits:

> The elaboration that John provided made his version of the Jesus tradition controversial; he sailed near the edge of what was acceptable ... The fact that John retained the Gospel character and that his book was clearly rooted in the earlier oral tradition were presumably sufficient to ensure that his Gospel would be recognized as one of the four Gospels to be designated 'canonical'. At one and the same time, however, John demonstrated that for the remembered Jesus to continue to be seen as relevant to subsequent generations, the way he was remembered would have to be adaptable. (P. 185)

Yet if one takes what Keith says about the PA and applies it to all written performance, and so to the Gospel of John's overall use of traditions, then there is no need for a 'however' in the final sentence cited above from Dunn. Rather, written tradition, like oral tradition, is always an active hermeneutical exercise, reflecting community memory and shaping community identity. There is no written text without those factors, so that the adaptability of tradition is an essential feature of cultural memory (whether realized in oral or written performance), and no transmission of Jesus traditions is possible without it. Keith convincingly uses oral media studies to show the limited use of the concept of 'original text' when it comes to the actual performance functions of written texts in early Christian communities, and his work suggests that there may be similar limited use of the concept of 'original tradition' as regards the move from oral to written traditions.

Michael Labahn's chapter provides an important conversation partner with Keith's essay. Although it is not written in direct conversation with Keith's methodological perspective and work, Labahn's account moves Keith's observations to the next level – from one passage (the PA) as a case study of the performative dimensions of oral and written traditions, to a careful study of the dynamics of oral and written performance in the Gospel of John more broadly. When read together, Keith and Labahn are models of methodological clarity and interpretative potential at the intersection of attention to oral media culture and Johannine studies.

One of the unavoidable problems in attempting to interpret written texts through the lens of oral culture is the need to explain a written text either through recourse to hypothesized oral sources, or through recourse to suppositions about what the oral performance might have been like. In many essays in this volume, for example, authors have no choice but to rely on probabilities to advance their theses: the storyteller may have made a gesture here, changed his/her intonation for effect, turned to face the audience to mark this transition, and so on. While such probabilities help to create a rich picture of what the oral transmission of the Gospel of John may have been like, and how original audiences may have heard the Gospel, there is no way to move beyond the level of probability and supposition. Keith eliminates this methodological problem by positioning the written text (rather than the hypothetical oral source) as the determinative datum for the relationship between oral and written. Labahn solves the scholarly conundrum of having to explain a written text through recourse to hypothesized oral sources by using evidences of oral culture and performance in the written artifact itself. For Labahn, as for Keith, the written text, the non-hypothetical artifact, provides methodological controls.

Labahn acknowledges the complex problems relating to 'the interrelation of orality and writing in the media world of the Gospel of John', and takes as his starting point for analysis 'the relationship between media of communication and social authority as portrayed *within the text* of the Fourth Gospel itself' (p. 136; emphasis in original). In particular, Labahn focuses on Scripture 'as a character that acts orally and that is interrelated with other characters by the narrator, with particular attention to Scripture's relationship to the oral hero of the story (Jesus)', especially with those passages where Scripture is portrayed as a speaking character (p.136). This is a conceptually creative and fruitful move because by focusing on Scripture, Labahn is able to attend simultaneously to the authority that John gives to written texts

(Scripture as γραφή), and to the interrelation of oral and written in the narrated story through the written gospel medium. Γράφω and its cognates occur more frequently in John than in any other NT text (Labahn notes the uses of γράφω in footnote 7 on p. 136, without discussing comparative frequency), and Jesus's status as oral performer is foregrounded much more in John than in the other Gospels, so Labahn's approach suggests that there may be something distinctive about the intersection and interaction of oral and written in John that makes attention to its media world hermeneutically promising. One of the significant methodological (as well as substantive) contributions of Labahn's essay is that it does not minimize the authority of the written word to advance an argument about oral culture. Labahn grapples with the inevitable dual foci of oral and written that are contained within the contours of a written document.

There is no need to rehearse the careful exegetical work that undergirds and illustrates Labahn's central theses; readers of this volume can explore Labahn's essay on their own. What Labahn's nuanced readings demonstrate is the way a seemingly simple thesis, that the interplay between orality and literacy in John is an intentional part of its rhetorical force and hermeneutical aim, can make sense of so much of the Gospel's literary and theological world. John's decisive and distinctive perspective is that the Word became flesh, and Labahn's essay suggests the myriad ways that orality and literary shape the enfleshed Word's engagement with the world (the story world, and the reader's world). Labahn's textually and hermeneutically nuanced essay compellingly shows how the written word 'talks' in John, and how the spoken word is given fresh voice through writing.

III

Each of the other essays in this book uses ancient media studies to good effect, shedding fresh light on the dynamics of the Johannine narrative, and each of them makes a contribution to understanding distinctive aspects of the Johannine literature. None of them is as methodologically suggestive as the three essays cited above, but each of them adds something significant to one's understanding of selected Johannine texts – from Boomershine's attention to the performance dimensions of John that help to shape the voice of the narrator and the reception of the audience, to Thatcher's use of oral tradition to make a case for the centrality of the John the Baptist traditions in John 1.1-18. Each essay in the volume is worth reading.

Yet I did find myself wondering at times whether the exegetical insights and yield of these essays really could be attributed primarily or even exclusively to the author's attention to ancient media culture. There is no question that attention to ancient media culture was the shaping perspective for each author, but it was not as clear that the conclusions were dependent on that perspective. For example, in several essays (e.g., Brickle on 1 John, Le Donne on John 2, Williams on John 8, and even Wire, Boomershine and Thatcher on John 1), it was not apparent what would be lost if 'written traditions' were substituted for 'oral traditions' in the shaping of the argument. At many points in these essays rhetorical patterns were identified, both for their style and their content, yet whether these patterns were a result of oral culture – and not equally at home in, or explicable by, written patterns – remains an open question for me.

The lines of demarcation and distinction between written and oral are consistently asserted by the authors, but in practice I could not always find exegetical insights that could *only* be argued on the basis of oral tradition and performance, and not on the basis of writing. Memory – and the shaping of traditions on the basis of individual and communal identity – has a decided impact on written texts as well as on oral traditions and performance, and it often seemed that what was asserted here about oral media could equally well be explained by recourse to theories of written composition.

This observation does not diminish the impact of the individual essays, or of the overall project, but underscores the complexity of trying to theorize about oral traditions and performance on the basis of written artifacts. This is especially true with the Gospel of John, where intentionality about communication is so intrinsic to the content that is communicated. Several of the authors highlight John 2.22 and 12.16, where the act of remembering is an essential part of the Gospel message, as well as 20.30-31 and 21.24, where the writing of traditions is given decisive theological valence. The Gospel of John does not allow the interpreter to ignore questions about the mode of communication. This volume as a collection makes an important contribution to Johannine studies because it moves the issue of the mode of communication to the centre of the conversation, but some of these contributions may overstate the heuristic value of ancient media as providing a unique perspective on the Gospel, its contents and its composition.

To repeat one of Keith's central methodological presuppositions, the interpretative disjunction is not so much between an oral matrix and a written matrix in the Gospel of John, or between an oral interpretive culture and our 'literate' interpretative culture, but from 'our oral-written matrix and their oral-written matrix'. Navigating those two matrices is the challenge and possibility that all of these essays place before the Johannine interpreter.

IV

In closing, this rich collection of essays leads me to ask about some possible future directions for the engagement of Johannine literature with ancient media culture.

First: *Would attention to the liturgical context in which New Testament literature was often heard bring fresh perspectives to the use of oral media studies in studying John?* The essays in this volume tend to focus on storytelling as a self-contained art and event (one reads in some essays about 'an evening of storytelling', for example), a posited context that assumes both that the Gospel of John was always read/told all in one sitting, and that the reason for a storytelling gathering was simply to hear the story of the Gospel of John. Yet there is significant NT evidence (e.g. Rev. 1.3) that the primary setting for oral performance was liturgical and not mainly entertainment. In addition, the evidence of lectionary use in synagogue worship suggests that the story would not necessarily have been recited (or read) in a single setting, but could be told sequentially across several weeks or months.

Evidence of the preaching practices in the synagogues and in early Christian gatherings (see, e.g., Luke 4.16-30, Acts, as well as the evidence of targums) suggests that these liturgical performances too, and not just classical rhetoricians and ancient storytellers, may be a helpful comparative point for thinking about ancient media culture. Wire's is the one essay in this volume that takes a ritual setting as a starting point for her reflections on oral culture, and it seems that this is an area ripe for further study from the perspective of ancient media culture. For the Gospel of John in particular, in which almost all of Jesus's oral performances are set on Jewish feast days, the intersection of orality and liturgy could be a quite significant area of study.

Secondly: *Could attention to ancient media culture provide an important bridge between questions of composition and reception of the Gospel of John?* Keith's essay points in this direction, when he names the interpolator of PA as both audience and author, and attention to the performative dimensions of both oral and written traditions seems worth pursuing as a fresh approach to the reception history of John. The written commentary tradition was created in response to the Fourth Gospel. Heracleon's commentary is his written response to the Gospel, but – perhaps of even more interest with regard to performance culture and memory theory – this commentary is extant only in the remembering of it in Irenaeus and Origen. Their written responses themselves take on a performative dimension, as they are both audience and author for Johannine interpretation. In addition, John also gave rise to sustained series of oral interpretative performances in the early Church (e.g., the sermon series of Chrysostom and Augustine). Both of these intersections of oral and written may contain clues to how oral traditions, oral performance and written texts functioned in early Christian communities which were transmitting the Jesus traditions.

Third: *As suggested above, can attention to ancient media culture generate a new set of questions for Johannine studies?* The introduction to the volume identifies 'four well-worn channels of Johannine research': 'the Fourth Gospel's historical value (or lack thereof); the sources of the Johannine tradition and possible relationships between that tradition and the Synoptic trajectory; the compositional development of the text ... and the potentials inherent in reading the Gospel as a self-contained narrative whole' (p. 1). The editors note that each of these research approaches, while insightful, have tended to neglect the 'media culture in which the Johannine Christians lived and in which Johannine literature was produced' (p. 1). The essays in this volume correct that neglect, by engaging ancient media culture directly, but to a great extent these four channels of research remain the questions that dominate the volume, with questions of the historical Jesus and the reliability of Johannine traditions always lurking in the background. Many of the essays posit that attention to ancient media can provide fuller answers to – or refine – conventional questions of Johannine scholarship.

Yet, as Keith and Labahn – to single out two essays – suggest, there are also new questions that derive more from the intrinsic nature of ancient media culture. Can ancient media studies suggest new questions, which may not only reframe old answers, but open new territory for investigation? Helping Johannine scholars identify and understand the new questions that a fresh angle of vision can make possible would be a lasting contribution of this promising field.

BIBLIOGRAPHY

Achtemeier, Paul J., 'Omne Verbum Sonat: The New Testament and the Oral Environment of Late Western Antiquity', *JBL* 109 (1990), pp. 3–27.

Aland, Kurt, 'Glosse, Interpolation, Redaktion und Komposition in der Sicht der neutestamentlichen Textkritik', in *Apophoreta: Festschrift für Ernst Haenchen*, W. Eltester and F. H. Kettler (eds), BZNW 30 (Berlin: Alfred Töpelmann, 1964), pp. 7–31.

Aland, Kurt and Barbara Aland, *The Text of the New Testament: An Introduction to the Critical Editions and to the Theory and Practice of Modern Textual Criticism*, trans. Erroll F. Rhodes. 2nd edn (Grand Rapids, MI: Eerdmans, 1989).

Aldrete, Gregory S., *Gestures and Acclamations in Ancient Rome*. Ancient History and Society (Baltimore, MD: The Johns Hopkins University Press, 1999).

Alexander, Loveday, 'Ancient Book Production and the Circulation of the Gospels', in *The Gospels for All Christians: Rethinking the Gospel Audiences*, Richard Bauckham (ed.) (Edinburgh: T&T Clark, 1998), pp. 71–111.

Anderson, John L., *An Exegetical Summary of 1, 2, and 3 John* (Dallas, TX: Summer Institute of Linguistics, 1992).

Anderson, Paul N., *The Christology of the Fourth Gospel: Its Unity and Disunity in the Light of John 6* (Valley Forge, PA: Trinity Press International, 1996).

———, *The Fourth Gospel and the Quest for Jesus: Modern Foundations Reconsidered*. LNTS (London: T&T Clark, 2006).

Aristotle, *Aristotle on Memory*, trans. W. S. Hett. LCL (Cambridge: Harvard University Press, 1954).

———, *Topica*, trans. E. S. Forster. LCL (Cambridge: Harvard University Press, 1960).

Asiedu-Peprah, Martin, *Johannine Sabbath Conflicts as Juridical Controversy*. WUNT (Tübingen: Mohr Siebeck, 2001).

Assmann, Aleida, *Zeit und Tradition: Kulturelle Strategien der Dauer*. Beiträge zur Geschichtskultur (Cologne, Weimar and Vienna: Böhlau, 1999).

Assmann, Jan, *Das kulturelle Gedächtnis: Schrift, Erinnerung und politische Identität in frühen Hochkulturen* (Munich: C. H. Beck, 1992).

———, 'Collective Memory and Cultural Identity', *New German Critique* 65 (1995a), pp. 125–33.

———, 'Ancient Egyptian Antijudaism: A Case of Distorted Memory', in *Memory Distortion: How Minds, Brains, and Societies Reconstruct the Past*, Daniel L. Schachter (ed.) (Cambridge: Harvard University Press, 1995b), pp. 365–78.

———, *Moses the Egyptian: The Memory of Egypt in Western Monotheism* (Cambridge, MA: Harvard University Press, 1997).

———, 'Form as a Mnemonic Device: Cultural Texts and Cultural Memory', in *Performing the Gospel: Orality, Memory, and Mark*, Richard A. Horsley, Jonathan A. Draper and John Miles Foley (eds) (Minneapolis, MN: Augsburg Fortress, 2006a).

———, *Religion and Cultural Memory: Ten Studies*, trans. Rodney Livingstone. Cultural Memory in the Present series (Stanford, CA: Stanford University Press, 2006b).

Attridge, Harold W., 'The Cubist Principle in Johannine Imagery: John and the Reading of Images in Contemporary Platonism', in *Imagery in the Gospel of John. Terms, Forms, Themes, and Theology of Johannine Figurative Language*, ed. Jörg Frey and Jan van der Watt. WUNT (Tübingen: Mohr Siebeck, 2006).

Augustine, *The Works of St. Augustine: A Translation for the Twenty-first Century*, trans. Maria Boulding (Hyde Park, NY: New City Press, 1997).

Aune, David E., *Prophecy in Early Christianity and the Ancient Mediterranean World* (Grand Rapids, MI: Eerdmans, 1983).

———, *The New Testament in Its Literary Environment*. Library of Early Christianity 8 (Philadelphia: Westminster, 1987).

Bagnall, Roger S., *Reading Papyri, Writing Ancient History*. Approaching the Ancient World series (New York: Routledge, 1995).

Baldensperger, Wilhelm, *Der Prolog des vierten Evangeliums: sein pole-misch-apologetischer Zweck* (Tübingen: Mohr, 1898).

Balogh, József, '"Voces Paginarum": Beiträge zur Geschichte des lauten Lesens und Schreibens', *Phil* 82 (1926), pp. 84–109, 202–40.

Barr, David L., 'The Apocalypse of John as Oral Enactment', *Int* 40 (1986), pp. 243–56.

Barrett, C. K. 1971. *The Gospel of John and Judaism*, trans. D. Moody Smith (Philadelphia: Fortress Press, 1971).

———, 'John and the Synoptic Gospels', *ExpTim* 85 (1974), pp. 228–33.

———, *The Gospel According to St John: An Introduction with Commentary and Notes on the Greek Text*. 2nd edn (London: SPCK, 1978).

Barth, Karl, *Der Römerbrief* (Zürich: Theologischer Verlag, 1922).

Bartholomew, Gilbert L., 'Feed My Lambs: John 21.15-19 as Oral Gospel', in *Orality, Aurality and the Biblical Narrative*, ed. Lou

H. Silberman. *Semeia* 39 (Atlanta: Society of Biblical Literature, 1987), pp. 69–96.

Bauckham, Richard, ed., *The Gospels for All Christians: Rethinking the Gospel Audiences* (Edinburgh: T&T Clark, 1998).

———, *Jesus and the Eyewitnesses: The Gospels as Eyewitness Testimony* (Grand Rapids, MI: Eerdmans, 2006).

———, 'The Fourth Gospel as the Testimony of the Beloved Disciple', in *The Gospel of John and Christian Theology*, ed. Richard Bauckham and Carl Mosser (Grand Rapids, MI: Eerdmans, 2008), pp. 120–39.

Baudouin, François, *De Institutionae historiae universae: libri II: et ejus cum jurisprudencia conjunctione* (Paris: A. Wechelum, 1561).

Baugh, Steven M., *A First John Reader: Intermediate Greek Reading Notes and Grammar* (Phillipsburg, NJ: P&R, 1999).

Bauman, Richard, *Verbal Art as Performance* (Rowley, MA: Newbury, 1977).

Beare, J. I. and G. R. T. Ross, *The Works of Aristotle*, ed. W. D. Ross (Oxford: Clarendon Press, 1975).

Beasley-Murray, George R., *John*. 2nd edn. WBC (Nashville: Thomas Nelson, 1999).

Beaton, Richard C., 'How Matthew Writes', in *The Written Gospel* ed. Markus Bockmuehl and Donald A. Hagner (Cambridge: Cambridge University Press, 2005), pp. 116–34.

Berger, Peter and Thomas Luckmann, *The Social Construction of Reality: A Treatise in the Sociology of Knowledge* (Garden City, NY: Doubleday, 1966).

Beutler, Johannes, *Martyria. Traditionsgeschichtliche Untersuchungen zum Zeugnisthema bei Johannes*. Frankfurter theologische Studien 10 (Frankfurt: Knecht, 1972).

———, 'The Use of "Scripture" in the Gospel of John', in *Exploring the Gospel of John. In Honor of D. Moody Smith*, ed. R. Alan Culpepper and C. Clifton Black (Louisville, KY: Westminster John Knox Press, 1996), pp. 147–62.

———, 'Der Gebrauch von "Schrift" im Johannesevangelium', in *Studien zu den johanneischen Schriften*. SBAB (Stuttgart: Katholisches Bibelwerk, 1998), pp. 295–315.

———, 'Synoptic Jesus Tradition in the Johannine Farewell Discourse', in *Jesus in Johannine Tradition*, ed. Robert T. Fortna and Tom Thatcher (Louisville, KY: Westminster John Knox, 2001), pp. 165–73.

———, *Judaism and the Jews in the Gospel of John*. SubBi 30 (Rome: Editrice Pontificio Istituto Biblico, 2006).

Black, C. Clifton, 'The First, Second, and Third Letters of John: Introduction, Commentary and Reflections', in vol. 12 of *NIB*, ed. Leander Keck (Nashville, TN: Abingdon, 1998), pp. 363–469.

Blomberg, Craig L., 'The Historical Reliability of John', in *Jesus in Johannine Tradition*, ed. Robert T. Fortna and Tom Thatcher (Louisville, KY: Westminster John Knox, 2001), pp. 71–82.

Bockmuehl, Marcus, 'New Testament *Wirkungsgeschichte* and the Early Christian Appeal to Living Memory', in *Memory in the Bible and Antiquity*, ed. Loren T. Stuckenbruck, Stephen C. Barton and Benjamin G. Wold (Tübingen: Mohr Siebeck, 2007), pp. 341–68.

Boegehold, Alan L., *When a Gesture Was Expected: A Selection of Examples from Archaic and Classical Greek Literature* (Princeton, NJ: Princeton University Press, 1999).

Boomershine, Thomas E., 'Peter's Denial as Polemic or Confession: The Implication of Media Theory for Biblical Hermeneutics', in *Orality, Aurality and the Biblical Narrative*, ed. Lou H. Silberman. *Semeia* 39 (Atlanta: Society of Biblical Literature, 1987), pp. 47–68.

———, *Story Journey: An Invitation to the Gospels as Storytelling* (Nashville, TN: Abingdon Press, 1988).

———, 'Biblical Megatrends: Toward the Paradigm for the Interpretation of the Bible in the Electronic Age', in *SBL 1989 Seminar Papers*, ed. Kent Richards (Atlanta: Scholars Press, 1989), pp. 144–57.

———, 'Jesus of Nazareth and the Watershed of Ancient Orality and Literacy', in *Orality and Textuality in Early Christian Literature*, ed. Joanna Dewey. *Semeia* 65 (Atlanta: Society of Biblical Literature, 1994), pp. 7–36.

Borgman, Paul C., *The Way according to Luke: Hearing the Whole Story of Luke–Acts* (Grand Rapids, MI: Eerdmans, 2006).

Böttrich, Christfried, 'Was kann aus Nazaret Gutes kommen? Galiläa im Spiegel der Jesusüberlieferung und bei Josephus', in *Josephus und das Neue Testament. Wechselseitige Wahrnehmungen. II. Internationales Symposium zum? Corpus Judaeo-Hellenisticum, Mai 2006, Greifswald*, ed. Christfried Böttrich and Jens Herzer. WUNT (Tübingen: Mohr Siebeck, 2007), pp. 295–333.

Brant, Jo-Ann A., *Dialogue and Drama: Elements of Greek Tragedy in the Fourth Gospel* (Peabody, MA: Hendrickson, 2004).

Brickle, Jeff, 'Aural Design and Coherence in the Prologue of First John'. PhD thesis, Concordia Seminary, St Louis, 2001.

Broadhead, Edwin K., 'The Fourth Gospel and the Synoptic Sayings Source', in *Jesus in Johannine Tradition*, ed. Robert T. Fortna and Tom Thatcher (Louisville, KY: Westminster John Knox, 2001), pp. 291–301.

Brodie, Thomas, *The Quest for the Origin of John's Gospel: A Source-oriented Approach* (New York, NY: Oxford University Press, 1993).

Brooke, Alan E., *The Johannine Epistles*. ICC (Edinburgh: T&T Clark, 1912).

Brown, Raymond E., *The Gospel According to John*. 2 vols. AB (Garden City, NY: Doubleday, 1966/70).

————, *The Community of the Beloved Disciple: The Life, Loves, and Hates of an Individual Church in New Testament Times* (New York, NY: Paulist, 1979).

————, *The Epistles of John*. AB (Garden City, NY: Doubleday, 1982).

————, *An Introduction to the Gospel of John*, ed. Francis J. Moloney. ABRL (New York, NY: Doubleday, 2003).

Bryan, Christopher, *A Preface to Mark: Notes on the Gospel in Its Literary and Cultural Settings* (New York, NY: Oxford University Press, 1993).

Bultmann, Rudolf, *The Gospel of John: A Commentary*, trans. G. R. Beasley-Murray, R. W. N. Hoare and J. K. Riches (Philadelphia: Westminster, 1971).

————, *The Johannine Epistles*, trans. R. Philip O'Hara, Lane C. McGaughty and Robert W. Funk. Hermeneia (Philadelphia, PA: Fortress, 1973).

Burge, Gary M., 'A Specific Problem in the New Testament Text and Canon: The Woman Caught in Adultery (John 7.53–8.11)', *JETS* 27 (1984), pp. 141–8.

————, 'John, Letters of', in *DLNT*, ed. Ralph P. Martin and Peter H. Davids (Downers Grove, IL: InterVarsity, 1997), pp. 587–99.

Burke, Edmund, *Reflections on the Revolution in France* (Buffalo, NY: Prometheus Books, 1961).

Burrell, Barbara, 'Reading, Hearing, and Looking at Ephesos', in *Ancient Literacies: The Culture of Reading in Greece and Rome*, ed. William A. Johnson and Holt N. Parker (Oxford: Oxford University Press, 2009), pp. 69–95.

Burridge, Richard A., *What are the Gospels? A Comparison with Graeco-Roman Biography*. 2nd edn (Grand Rapids, MI: Eerdmans, 2004).

Byrskog, Samuel, *Story as History – History as Story: The Gospel Tradition in the Context of Ancient Oral History* (Boston, MA: Brill, 2002).

Campbell, B. G., *Performing and Processing the Aeneid*. Berkeley Insights in Linguistics and Semiotics 48 (New York: Peter Lang, 2001).

Caragounis, Chrys C., 'The Kingdom of God: Common and Distinct Elements Between John and the Synoptics', in *Jesus in Johannine Tradition*, ed. Robert T. Fortna and Tom Thatcher (Louisville, KY: Westminster John Knox, 2001), pp. 125–34.

————, *The Development of Greek and the New Testament: Morphology, Syntax, Phonology, and Textual Transmission*. WUNT (Grand Rapids, MI: Baker, 2006).

Carr, David M. 2005, *Writing on the Tablet of the Heart: Origins of Scripture and Literature* (New York, NY: Oxford University Press, 2005).

Carruthers, Mary J., *The Book of Memory: A Study of Memory in Medieval Culture*. 2nd edn (Cambridge: Cambridge University Press, 2008).

Carson, D. A., *The Gospel According to John* (Grand Rapids, MI: Eerdmans, 1991).

———, 'The Purpose of the Fourth Gospel: John 20.31 Reconsidered', *JBL* 106 (1995), pp. 639–51.

Casey, Edward S., *Remembering: A Phenomenological Study*. 2nd edn (Bloomington, IN: Indiana University Press, 1987).

Cebulj, Christian, *Ich bin es: Studien zur Identitätsbildung im Johannesevangelium*. SSB (Stuttgart: Katholisches Bibelwerk, 2000).

———, 'Johannesevangelium und Johannesbriefe', in *Schulen im Neuen Testament? Zur Stellung des Urchristentums in der Bildungswelt seiner Zeit*, ed. Thomas Schmeller. HBS (Freiburg: Herder, 2001), pp. 254–342, 349–51.

Childs, Brevard S., *The New Testament as Canon: An Introduction* (Philadelphia: Fortress, 1985).

Cicero. *Ad Herennium*, trans. Harry Caplan. LCL (Cambridge: Harvard University Press, 1954).

———, *De Oratore*, trans. E. W. Sutton and H. Rackham. LCL (Cambridge: Harvard University Press, 1959).

———, *De Inventione*, trans. H. M. Hubbell. LCL (Cambridge: Harvard University Press, 1960a).

———, *De Partitione Oratoria*, trans. H. Rackham. LCL (Cambridge: Harvard University Press, 1960b).

Clark, W. P., 'Ancient Reading', *CJ* 26 (1930–31), pp. 698–700.

Connerton, Paul, *How Societies Remember* (Cambridge: Cambridge University Press, 1989).

Cullmann, Oscar, *The Johannine Circle: Its Place in Judaism, Among the Disciples of Jesus, and in Early Christianity*, trans. John Bowden (London: SCM, 1976).

Culpepper, R. Alan, *The Johannine School: An Evaluation of the Johannine-School Hypothesis Based on an Investigation of the Nature of Ancient Schools*. SBLDS (Missoula, MT: Scholars Press, 1975).

———, *Anatomy of the Fourth Gospel: A Study in Literary Design* (Philadelphia: Fortress, 1983).

———, 'Reading Johannine Irony', in *Exploring the Gospel of John. In Honor of D. Moody Smith*, ed. C. Clifton Black and R. Alan Culpepper (Louisville, KY: Westminster John Knox, 1996), pp. 193–207.

———, *The Gospel and Letters of John*. Interpreting Biblical Texts (Nashville, TN: Abingdon, 1998).

———, *John: The Son of Zebedee, The Life of a Legend* (Edinburgh: T&T Clark, 2000).

———, 'The Origin of the "Amen, Amen" Sayings in the Gospel of John', in *Jesus in Johannine Tradition*, ed. Robert T. Fortna and

Tom Thatcher (Louisville, KY: Westminster John Knox, 2001), pp. 253–62.

Daly-Denton, M., 'The Psalms in John's Gospel', in *The Psalms in the New Testament*, ed. Stephen Moyise and M. J. J. Menken (New York, NY: Continuum, 2004), pp. 119–37.

Dauer, Anton, *Die Passionsgeschichte im Johannesevangelium. Eine traditionsgeschichtliche und theologische Untersuchung zu Joh 18. 1-19, 30*. StANT (München: Kösel, 1972).

Dautzenberg, Gerhard, *Urchristliche Prophetie: Ihre Erforschung ihre Voraussetzungen im Judentum und ihre Struktur im ersten Korintherbrief* (Stuttgart: W. Kohlhammer, 1975).

Davis, Casey W., *Oral Biblical Criticism: The Influence of the Principles of Orality on the Literary Structure of Paul's Epistle to the Philippians*. JSNTSupp (Sheffield: Sheffield Academic Press, 1999).

De Boer, M. C., 'The Depiction of "the Jews" in John's Gospel: Matters of Behavior and Identity', in *Anti-Judaism and the Fourth Gospel*, ed. Riemund Bieringer, Didier Pollefeyt and Frederique Vandecasteele-Vanneuville (Assen: Royal Van Gorcum, 2001), pp. 260–80.

De Lange, Tineke, *Abraham in John 8.31-59: His Significance in the Conflict Between Johannine Christianity and its Jewish Environment* (Amsterdam: Amphora Books, 2008).

Dean, Margaret E., 'The Grammar of Sound in Greek Texts: Toward a Method for Mapping the Echoes of Speech in Writing', *ABR* 44 (1996), pp. 53–70.

———, 'Textured Criticism', *JSNT* 70 (1998), pp. 79–91.

Dettweiler, Andreas, *Die Gegenwart des Erhöhten: Eine exegetische Studie zu den johanneischen Abschiedsreden (Joh 13.31–16.33) unter besonderer Berücksichtigung ihres Relecture-Characters* (Göttingen: Vandenhoeck & Ruprecht, 1995).

Dewey, Arthur J., 'The Eyewitness of History: Visionary Consciousness in the Fourth Gospel', in *Jesus in Johannine Tradition*, ed. Robert T. Fortna and Tom Thatcher (Louisville, KY: Westminster John Knox, 2001), pp. 59–70.

Dewey, Joanna, 'Oral Methods of Structuring Narrative in Mark', *Int* 53 (1989), 32–44.

———, 'Mark as Interwoven Tapestry: Forecasts and Echoes for a Listening Audience', *CBQ* 53 (1991), pp. 221–36.

———, 'Mark as Aural Narrative: Structures as Clues to Understanding', *STRev* 36 (1992), pp. 45–56.

———, 'Textuality in an Oral Culture: A Survey of the Pauline Tradition', in *Orality and Textuality in Early Christian Literature*, ed. Joanna Dewey. Semeia 65 (Atlanta: Society of Biblical Literature, 1994a), pp. 37–65).

———, 'The Gospel of Mark as an Oral-Aural Event: Implications for Interpretation', in *The New Literary Criticism and the*

New Testament, ed. Elizabeth Struthers Malbon and Edgar V. McKnight. JSNTSupp (Sheffield: Sheffield Academic Press, 1994b), pp. 145–63.

———, 'The Gospel of John in Its Oral-Written Media World', in *Jesus in Johannine Tradition*, ed. Robert T. Fortna and Tom Thatcher (Louisville, KY: Westminster John Knox, 2001), pp. 239–52.

Dibelius, Martin, *From Tradition to Gospel* (London: Ivor Nicholson and Watson, 1934).

Dodd, Charles H., *The Johannine Epistles* (London: Hodder and Stoughton, 1946).

———, *The Interpretation of the Fourth Gospel* (Cambridge: Cambridge University Press, 1953).

———, *Historical Tradition in the Fourth Gospel* (Cambridge: University Press, 1963).

Dudrey, Russ, '1 John and the Public Reading of Scripture', *Stone Campbell Journal* 6 (2003a), pp. 235–55.

Dundes, Alan, *Holy Writ as Oral Lit: The Bible as Folklore* (Lanham, MD: Rowman & Littlefield, 1999).

Dunn, James D. G., 'Let John be John', in *Das Evangelium und die Evangelien*, ed. Peter Stuhlmacher. WUNT (Tübingen: Mohr Siebeck, 1983).

———, 'John and the Oral Gospel Tradition', in *Jesus and the Oral Gospel Tradition*, ed. Henry Wansbrough. JSNTSupp (Sheffield: JSOT Press, 1991), pp. 352–79.

———, *The Theology of Paul the Apostle* (Grand Rapids, MI: Eerdmans, 1998).

———, 'Altering the Default Setting: Re-envisaging the Early Transmission of the Jesus Tradition', in *A New Perspective on Jesus: What the Quest for the Historical Jesus Missed* (London: SPCK, 2003a), pp. 79–125.

———, *Christianity in the Making, Vol. 1: Jesus Remembered* (Grand Rapids, MI: Eerdmans, 2003b).

———, 'History, Memory and Eyewitnesses', *JSNT* 4 (2004), pp. 84–145.

———, *A New Perspective on Jesus: What the Quest for the Historical Jesus Missed* (London: SPCK, 2005a).

———, 'Q^1 as Oral Tradition', in *The Written Gospel*, ed. Markus Bockmuehl and Donald A. Hagner (Cambridge: Cambridge University Press, 2005b), pp. 45–69.

———, 'Social Memory and the Oral Jesus Tradition', in *Memory and Remembrance in the Bible and Antiquity*, ed. Loren Stuckenbruck, Stephen Barton and Benjamin Wold (Tübingen: Mohr Siebeck, 2007).

Durkheim, Emile, *The Elementary Forms of the Religious Life* (New York: The Free Press, 1965).

———, 'Individual and Collective Representations', in *Emile Durkheim:*

Sociology and Philosophy, ed. J. G. Peristiany (New York, NY: The Free Press, 1974), pp. 1–34.

Ehrman, Bart D., *The Orthodox Corruption of Scripture: The Effect of Early Christological Controversies on the Text of the New Testament* (New York, NY: Oxford University Press, 1963).

———, *Jesus: Apocalyptic Prophet of the New Millennium* (New York: Oxford University Press, 1999).

Epp, Eldon Jay, *The Theological Tendency of Codex Bezae Cantabrigiensis in Acts*. SNTSMS (Cambridge: Cambridge University Press, 1966).

———, 'The Multivalence of the Term "Original Text" in New Testament Textual Criticism', *HTR* 92 (1999), pp. 245–81.

———, 'Issues in the Interrelation of New Testament Textual Criticism and Canon', in *The Canon Debate*, ed. Lee McDonald and James A. Sanders (Peabody, MA: Hendrickson, 2002), pp. 485–515.

———, 'It's All about Variants: A Variant-Conscious Approach to New Testament Textual Criticism', *HTR* 100 (2007), pp. 275–308.

Esler, Philip F., *Conflict and Identity in Romans: The Social Setting of Paul's Letter* (Minneapolis, MN: Fortress, 2003).

———, 'Collective Memory and Hebrews 11: Outlining a New Investigative Framework', in *Memory, Tradition, and Text: Uses of the Past in Early Christianity*, ed. Alan Kirk and Tom Thatcher. Semeia Studies (Atlanta: Society of Biblical Literature, 2005), pp. 151–71.

———, 'Paul's Contestation of Israel's (Ethnic) Memory of Abraham in Galatians 3', *BTB* 36 (2006), pp. 23–34.

———, 'From *Ioudaioi* to Children of God: The Development of a Non-Ethnic Group Identity in the Gospel of John', in *In Other Words: Essays on Social Science Methods and the New Testament in Honor of Jerome H. Neyrey*, ed. Anselm C. Hagedorn, Zeba Crook and E. Stewart. The Social World of Biblical Antiquity series (Sheffield: Sheffield Phoenix, 2007), pp. 106–37.

Evans, Craig A., *Mark 8.27–16.20*. WBC (Nashville: Thomas Nelson, 2001).

Farber, Barry, *How to Learn Any Language Quickly, Easily, Enjoyably, and on Your Own* (New York, NY: Citadel, 1991).

Fentress, James and Chris Wickham, *Social Memory* (Oxford: Blackwell, 1992).

Festinger, Leon, Henry W. Riecken and Stanley Schachter, *When Prophecy Fails* (Minneapolis: University of Minnesota Press, 1956).

Fine, Gary A., 'Reputational Entrepreneurs and the Memory of Incompetence', *American Journal of Sociology* 101 (1996), pp. 1169–93.

Foley, John Miles, *The Theory of Oral Composition: History and Methodology* (Bloomington: Indiana University Press, 1988).

———, *How to Read an Oral Poem* (Chicago: University of Illinois Press, 2005).

Fortenbaugh, William W., *Aristotle on Emotion*. 2nd edn (London: Duckworth, 2002).

Fortna, Robert T., *The Gospel of Signs: A Reconstruction of the Narrative Source Underlying the Fourth Gospel*. SNTSMS (Cambridge: Cambridge University Press, 1970).

Fortna, Robert, T. and Tom Thatcher, eds, *Jesus in Johannine Tradition* (Louisville, KY: Westminster John Knox, 2001).

Gamble, Harry Y., *Books and Readers in the Early Church: A History of Early Christian Texts* (New Haven, CT: Yale University Press, 1995).

———, 'Literacy and Book Culture', in *Dictionary of New Testament Background*, ed. Craig A. Evans and Stanley E. Porter (Downers Grove, IL: InterVarsity Press, 2000), pp. 644–8.

Gavrilov, Alexander K., 'Techniques of Reading in Classical Antiquity', *CQ* 47 (1997), pp. 56–73.

Gedi, Noa and Yigael Elam, 'Collective Memory – What Is It?', *History and Memory* 8 (1996), pp. 30–50.

Geertz, Clifford, 'Ideology as a Cultural System', in *The Interpretation of Cultures: Selected Essays* (New York, NY: Basic Books, 1973), pp. 193–233.

Gelin, Albert, 'La question des "relectures" bibliques a L'intérieur d'une tradition vivante', in *Sacra Pagina: Miscellanea Biblica Congressus Internationalis Catholici de Re Biblica*, Vol. 1, ed. J. Coppens, A. Descamps and E. Massaux (Gembloux: Éditions J. Duculot, 1959), pp. 303–15.

Gench, Frances Taylor, *Back to the Well: Women's Encounters with Jesus in the Gospels* (Louisville, KY: Westminster John Knox, 2004).

Gerhardsson, Birger, *Memory and Manuscript: Oral Tradition and Written Transmission in Rabbinic Judaism and Early Christianity* (Lund: C. W. K. Gleerup, 1961).

Gilfillan Upton, Bridget, *Hearing Mark's Endings: Listening to Ancient Popular Texts through Speech Act Theory*. BIS (Leiden: Brill, 2006).

Gilliard, Frank D., 'More Silent Reading in Antiquity: *Non Omne Verbum Sonabat*', *JBL* 112 (1993), pp. 689–96.

Goodspeed, Edgar J., *A History of Early Christian Literature* (Chicago, IL: University of Chicago Press, 1942).

———, *Problems of New Testament Translation* (Chicago, IL: University of Chicago Press, 1945).

Graf, Fritz, 'Gestures and Conventions: The Gestures of Roman Actors and Orators', in *A Cultural History of Gesture: From Antiquity to the Present Day*, ed. Jan Bremmer and Herman Roodenburg (Ithaca, NY: Cornell University Press, 1992), pp. 36–58.

Graham, William A., *Beyond the Written Word: Oral Aspects of Scripture in the History of Religion* (Cambridge: Cambridge University Press, 1987a).

———, 'Scripture', in *ER* Vol 13, ed. Mircea Eliade (New York, NY: Macmillan, 1987b).

Green, Joel B., *The Death of Jesus: Tradition and Interpretation in the Passion Narrative*. WUNT (Tübingen: Mohr Siebeck, 1988).

Greenlee, J. Harold, *Introduction to New Testament Textual Criticism*. Rev. edn (Peabody, MA: Hendrickson, 1995).

Grelot, Pierre, 'Jean 8.56 et Jubilés 16.16-29', *RevQ* 13 (1987), pp. 621–8.

Griffith, Terry, *Keep Yourselves from Idols: A New Look at 1 John*. JSNTSupp (Sheffield: Sheffield Academic Press, 2002).

Guelich, Robert A., 'The Gospel Genre', in *Das Evangelium und die Evangelien*, ed. Peter Stuhlmacher. WUNT (Tübingen: Mohr Siebeck, 1983), pp. 183–219.

Hadas, Moses, *Ancilla to Classical Reading* (New York, NY: Columbia University Press, 1954).

Hakola, Raimo, *Identity Matters: John, the Jews and Jewishness*. NovTSup (Leiden: Brill, 2005).

Halbwachs, Maurice, *Les Cadres sociaux de la mémoire* (Paris: F. Alcan, 1925).

———, *La Topographie légendaire des évangiles en terre sainte: Étude de mémoire collective* (Paris: Presses Universitaires de France, 1941).

———, *La Mémoire collective* (Paris: Éditions Albin Michel, 1950/80).

———, *On Collective Memory*, ed. Lewis A. Coser (Chicago, IL: The University of Chicago Press, 1992).

Halverson, John, 'Oral and Written Gospel: A Critique of Werner Kelber', *NTS* 40 (1994), pp. 180–95.

Hansen, G. Walter, *Abraham in Galatians: Epistolary and Rhetorical Contexts*. JSNTSS (Sheffield: JSOT Press, 1989).

Hanson, A. T., *The Prophetic Gospel. A Study of John and the Old Testament* (Edinburgh: T&T Clark, 1991).

Harris, Max, *Theatre and Incarnation* (Grand Rapids, MI: Eerdmans, 1990).

Harris, William V., *Ancient Literacy* (Cambridge, MA: Harvard University Press, 1989).

Harvey, John D., *Listening to the Text: Oral Patterning in Paul's Letters*. Evangelical Theological Society Studies (Grand Rapids, MI: Baker, 1998).

Havelock, Eric A., *Preface to Plato* (Cambridge, MA: Harvard University Press, 1963).

Hearon, Holly E., 'The Implications of Orality for Studies of the Biblical Text', in *Performing the Gospel: Orality, Memory, and Mark*, ed. Richard A. Horsley, Jonathan A. Draper and John Miles Foley (Minneapolis, MN: Fortress, 2006), pp. 3–20.

Heil, C., 'Jesus aus Nazaret oder Betlehem? Historische Tradition und ironischer Stil im Johannesevangelium', in *Im Geist und in der Wahrheit. Studien zum Johannesevangelium und zur Offenbarung des Johannes sowie andere Beiträge. FSM. Hasitschka SJ zum 65. Geburtstag*, ed. Konrad Huber and Boris Repschinski. NTA (Münster: Aschendorff, 2008), 109–30.

Hendrickson, George L., 'Ancient Reading', *CJ* 25 (1929–30), pp. 182–96.

Hengel, Martin, *The Johannine Question* trans. John Bowden (London: SCM, 1989).

———, 'Die Schriftauslegung des 4. Evangeliums auf dem Hintergrund der urchristlichen Exegese', *JBTh* 4 (1989a), pp. 249–88.

———, *Die vier Evangelien und das eine Evangelium von Jesus Christus. Studien zu ihrer Sammlung und Entstehung*. WUNT (Tübingen: Mohr Siebeck, 2008).

Hezser, Catherine, *Jewish Literacy in Roman Palestine*. TSAJ (Tübingen: Mohr Siebeck, 2001).

Hoegen-Rohls, Christina, *Der nachösterliche Johannes. Die Abschiedsreden als hermeneutischer Schlüssel zum vierten Evangelium*. WUNT (Tübingen: Mohr-Siebeck, 1996).

Horsley, Richard A., 'Oral Tradition in New Testament Studies', *Oral Tradition* 18 (2003), pp. 34–6.

———, 'Prominent Patterns in the Social Memory of Jesus and Friends', in *Memory, Tradition, and Text: Uses of the Past in Early Christianity*, ed. Alan Kirk and Tom Thatcher. Semeia Studies (Atlanta: Society of Biblical Literature, 2005), pp. 57–78.

Horsley, Richard A. and Jonathan Draper, *Whoever Hears You Hears Me: Prophets, Performance, and Tradition in Q* (Harrisburg, PA: Trinity Press International, 1999).

Horsley, Richard A., Jonathan A. Draper and John Miles Foley, eds, *Performing the Gospel: Orality, Memory, and Mark* (Minneapolis, MN: Fortress, 2006).

Houlden, James L., *A Commentary on the Johannine Epistles*. Harper's New Testament Commentaries (New York, NY: Harper & Row, 1973).

Hübner, Hans, *Biblische Theologie des Neuen Testaments 3. Hebräerbrief, Evangelien und Offenbarung, Epilegomena* (Göttingen: Vandenhoeck & Ruprecht, 1995).

Hübner, Hans, Antje Labahn and Michael Labahn, *Vetus Testamentum in Novo. Vol. I.2: Evangelium secundum Iohannem* (Göttingen: Vandenhoeck & Ruprecht, 2003).

Hurtado, Larry W., 'Greco-Roman Textuality and the Gospel of Mark: A Critical Assessment of Werner Kelber's *The Oral and the Written Gospel*', *BBR* 7 (1997), pp. 91–106.

——, *The Earliest Christian Artifacts: Manuscripts and Christian Origins* (Grand Rapids, MI: Eerdmans, 2006).

Hutton, Patrick, *History as an Art of Memory* (Hanover and London: University Press of New England, 1993).

Hymes, Dell, '*In vain I tried to tell you'*: *Essays in Native American Ethnopoetics* (Philadelphia: University of Pennsylvania Press, 1981).

Jaffee, Martin S., *Torah in the Mouth: Writing and Oral Tradition in Palestinian Judaism, 200 BCE–400 CE* (Oxford: Oxford University Press, 2001).

Jenkinson, E. J., *The Unwritten Sayings of Jesus* (London: Epworth Press, 1925).

Jeremias, Joachim, *The Prayers of Jesus*. SBT (London: SCM, 1967).

Johnson, William A., 'Toward a Sociology of Reading in Classical Antiquity', *AJP* 121 (2001), pp. 593–627.

Kahler, Martin, *The So-called Historical Jesus and the Historic Biblical Christ*, ed. and trans. Carl Braaten (Philadelphia, PA: Fortress, 1896, repr. 1964).

Kannaday, Wayne C., *Apologetic Discourse and the Scribal Tradition: Evidence of the Influence of Apologetic Interests on the Text of the Canonical Gospels*. SBLTCS (Atlanta: Society of Biblical Literature, 2004).

Katz, Elihu, 'The Two-Step Flow of Communication: An Up-To-Date Report on an Hypothesis', *Public Opinion Quarterly* 21 (1957), pp. 61–78.

Katz, Elihu and Paul Lazarsfeld, *Personal Influence: The Part Played by People in the Flow of Mass Communications* (Glencoe, IL: The Free Press, 1955).

Keener, Craig S., *The IVP Bible Background Commentary: New Testament* (Downers Grove, IL: InterVarsity, 1993).

——, *The Gospel of John: A Commentary*. 2 vols (Peabody, MA: Hendrickson, 2003).

Keith, Chris, 'The Role of the Cross in the Composition of the Markan Crucifixion Narrative', *Stone Campbell Journal* 9 (2006), pp. 61–75.

——, 'Recent and Previous Research on the *Pericope Adulterae* (John 7.53–8.11)', *CurBS* 6 (2008), pp. 377–404.

——, *The* Pericope Adulterae, *the Gospel of John, and the Literacy of Jesus*. New Testament Tools, Studies, and Documents (Leiden: Brill, 2009).

Kelber, Werner H., *The Oral and the Written Gospel: The Hermeneutics of Speaking and Writing in the Synoptic Tradition, Mark, Paul, and Q* (Bloomington: Indiana University Press, 1983).

——, 'The Works of Memory: Christian Origins as Mnemohistory – A Response', in *Memory, Tradition, and Text: Uses of the Past in Early Christianity*, ed. Alan Kirk and Tom Thatcher. Semeia Studies (Atlanta: Society of Biblical Literature, 2005), pp. 221–48.

Kelhoffer, James A., *Miracle and Mission: The Authentication of Missionaries and Their Message in the Longer Ending of Mark*. WUNT (Tübingen: Mohr Siebeck, 1999).

Kennedy, George A., *New Testament Interpretation through Rhetorical Criticism. Studies in Religion* (Chapel Hill: The University of North Carolina Press, 1984).

Kimelman, Reuven, '*Birkat Ha-Minim* and the Lack of Evidence for an Anti-Christian Jewish Prayer in Late Antiquity', in *Jewish and Christian Self-Definition Volume Two: Aspects of Judaism in the Graeco-Roman Period*, ed. E. P. Sanders (London: SCM, 1981), 226–44.

Kirk, Alan, 'Tradition and Memory in the Gospel of Peter', in *Das Evangelium nach Petrus. Text, Kontexte, Intertexte*, ed. Thomas J. Kraus and Tobias Nicklas. TU (Berlin: de Gruyter, 2007), pp. 135–59.

———, 'Manuscript Tradition as a *Tertium Quid*: Orality and Memory in Scribal Practices', in *Jesus, the Voice, and the Text: Beyond the Oral and the Written Gospel*, ed. Tom Thatcher. (Waco, TX: Baylor University Press, 2008), pp. 215–34.

Kirk, Alan and Tom Thatcher, eds, *Memory, Tradition, and Text: Uses of the Past in Early Christianity*. Semeia Studies. (Atlanta: Society of Biblical Literature, 2005).

Knowles, Michael, 'Reading Matthew: The Gospel as Oral Performance', in *Reading the Gospels Today*, ed. Stanley Porter (Grand Rapids, MI: Eerdmans, 2004), pp. 56–77.

Knuuttila, Simo, *Emotions in Ancient and Medieval Philosophy* (Oxford: Oxford University Press, 2004).

Koester, Craig R., *Symbolism in the Fourth Gospel. Meaning, Mystery, Community*. 2nd edn (Minneapolis, MN: Fortress, 2003).

Konstan, David, *The Emotions of the Ancient Greeks: Studies in Aristotle and Greek Literature*. Robson Classical Lectures (Toronto: University of Toronto Press, 2006).

Köstenberger, Andreas J., *John*. Baker Exegetical Commentary on the New Testament (Grand Rapids, MI: Baker Academic, 2004).

———, 'John', in *Commentary on the New Testament Use of the Old Testament*, ed. G. K. Beale and D. A. Carson (Grand Rapids, MI: Baker Academic, 2007), pp. 415–512.

Kowalski, Beate, 'Anticipations of Jesus' Death in the Gospel of John', in *The Death of Jesus in the Fourth Gospel*, ed. Gilbert van Belle. BETL (Leuven: Peeters, 1998), pp. 591–608.

Kragerud, Alv, *Der Lieblingsjünger im Johannesevangelium: Ein exegetischer Versuch* (Oslo: Osloer Universitätsverlag, 1959).

Kraus, Wolfgang, 'Johannes und das Alte Testament. Überlegungen zum Umgang mit der Schrift im Johannesevangelium im Horizont Biblischer Theologie', *ZNW* 88 (1997), pp. 1–23.

Kruse, Colin G., *The Letters of John*. The Pillar New Testament Commentary (Grand Rapids, MI: Eerdmans, 2000).

Kysar, Robert, *I, II, III John*. ACNT (Minneapolis, MN: Augsburg, 1986).

Labahn, Michael, *Jesus als Lebensspender. Untersuchungen zu einer Geschichte der johanneischen Tradition anhand ihrer Wundergeschichten*. BZNW (Berlin: de Gruyter, 1999).

———, *Offenbarung in Zeichen und Wort. Untersuchungen zur Vorgeschichte von Joh 6.1-25a und seiner Rezeption in der Brotrede*. WUNT (Tübingen: Mohr Siebeck, 2000).

———, 'Die παρρησία des Gottessohnes im Johannesevangelium: Theologische Hermeneutik und philosophisches Selbstverständnis', in *Kontexte des Johannesevangeliums: Das vierte Evangelium in religions- und traditionsgeschichtlicher Perspektive*, ed. Jörg Frey and Udo Schnelle. WUNT (Tübingen: Mohr Siebeck, 2004), pp. 321–63.

———, 'Bedeutung und Frucht des Todes Jesu im Spiegel des johanneischen Erzählaufbaus', in *The Death of Jesus in the Fourth Gospel*, ed. Gilbert van Belle. BETL (Leuven: Peeters, 2007a), pp. 431–56.

———, 'Deuteronomy in John', in *Deuteronomy in the New Testament*, ed. M. J. J. Menken and Stephen Moyise (London: T&T Clark, 2007b), pp. 82–96.

———, '"Verlassen" oder "Vollendet". Ps. 22 in der "Johannespassion" zwischen Intratextualität und Intertextualität', in *Ps. 22 und die Passionsgeschichten der Evangelien*, ed. Dieter Sänger. BThSt (Neukirchen-Vluyn: Neukirchener Verlag, 2007c), pp. 111–53.

Labahn, Michael and Manfred Lang, 'Johannes und die Synoptiker. Positionen und Impulse seit 1990', in *Kontexte des Johannesevangeliums: Das vierte Evangelium in religions- und traditionsgeschichtlicher Perspektive*, ed. Jörg Frey and Udo Schnelle. WUNT (Tübingen: Mohr Siebeck, 2004), pp. 443–515.

Labahn, Michael, Kurt Scholtissek and Angelica Strotmann, eds, *Israel und seine Heilstraditionen im Johannesevangelium. Festgabe für Johannes Beutler SJ zum 70. Geburtstag* (Paderborn: Schöningh, 2003).

Lang, Manfred, *Johannes und die Synoptiker. Eine redaktionsgeschichtliche Analyse von Joh 18–20 vor dem markinischen und lukanischen Hintergrund*. FRLANT (Göttingen: Vandehoeck & Ruprecht, 1999).

Le Donne, Anthony, 'Theological Memory Distortion in the Jesus Tradition: A Study in Social Memory Theory', in *Memory and Remembrance in the Bible and Antiquity*, ed. Stephen Barton,

Loren Stuckenbruck and Benjamin Wold. WUNT (Tübingen: Mohr Siebeck, 2007), pp. 163–77.

Le Goff, Jacques, *History and Memory* (New York, NY: Columbia University Press, 1996).

Leach, Edmund, *Claude Levi-Strauss*. Modern Masters series (New York, NY: Penguin Books, 1976).

Lenz, Tony M., *Orality and Literacy in Hellenic Greece* (Carbondale: Southern Illinois University Press, 1989).

Lewis, Naphtali, Yigael Yadin and Jonas C. Greenfield, eds, *The Documents from the Bar Kokhba Period in the Cave of Letters: Greek Papyri*. JDS (Jerusalem: Israel Exploration Society, 1989).

Lieu, Judith, *The Second and Third Epistles of John*. Studies of the New Testament and Its World (Edinburgh: T&T Clark, 1896).

———, *The Theology of the Johannine Epistles*. New Testament Theology (Cambridge: Cambridge University Press, 1991).

———, 'Narrative Analysis and Scripture in John', in *The Old Testament in the New Testament. Essays in Honour of J. L. North*, ed. Stephen Moyise. JSNTS (Sheffield: Sheffield Academic Press, 2000), pp. 144–63.

———, 'Anti-Judaism, the Jews, and the Worlds of the Fourth Gospel', in *The Gospel of John and Christian Theology*, ed. Richard Bauckham and Carl Mosser (Grand Rapids, MI: Eerdmans, 2008a), pp. 168–82.

———, *I, II, & III John: A Commentary*. NTL. (Louisville, KY: Westminster John Knox, 2008b).

Lincoln, Andrew T., *Truth on Trial: The Lawsuit Motif in the Fourth Gospel* (Peabody, MA: Hendrickson, 2000).

———, *The Gospel according to St John*. BNTC. (London: Continuum, 2005).

Lindars, Barnabas, *The Gospel of John*. NCB (London: Oliphants, 1972).

Lona, H. E., *Abraham in Johannes 8: Ein Beitrag zur Methodenfrage*. Europäische Hochschulschriften (Frankfurt: Peter Lang, 1976).

Longenecker, Bruce W., *Rhetoric at the Boundaries: The Art and Theology of New Testament Chain-Link Transitions* (Waco, TX: Baylor University Press, 2005).

Lorayne, Harry, *How to Develop a Super Power Memory* (New York, NY: F. Fell, 1957).

Lord, Albert B., *The Singer of Tales*. 2nd edn with CD-ROM disk, ed. Stephen Mitchell and Gregory Nagy (Cambridge, MA: Harvard University Press, 1968).

Lowenthal, David, *The Past is a Foreign Country* (Cambridge: Cambridge University Press, 1985).

Maier, Johann, 'Schriftrezeption im jüdischen Umfeld des Johannesevangeliums', in *Israel und seine Heilstraditionen im*

Johannesevangelium. Festgabe für Johannes Beutler SJ zum 70. Geburtstag, ed. Michael Labahn, Kurt Scholtissek and Angelica Strotmann (Paderborn: Schöningh, 2004), pp. 54–88.

Malbon, Elizabeth Struthers, 'Echoes and Foreshadowings in Mark 4–8: Reading and Rereading', *JBL* 112 (1993), pp. 211–30.

Malherbe, Abraham J., *Moral Exhortation, A Greco-Roman Sourcebook*. Library of Early Christianity (Philadelphia, PA: Westminster, 1986).

Marshall, C. W., 'Postscript on Silent Reading', *CQ* 47 (1997), pp. 74–6.

Martyn, J. Louis, *History and Theology in the Fourth Gospel*. 3rd edn (Louisville, KY: Westminster John Knox, 1979).

Matson, Mark A, 'The Temple Incident: An Integral Element in the Fourth Gospel's Narrative', in *Jesus in Johannine Tradition*, ed. Robert T. Fortna and Tom Thatcher (Louisville, KY: Westminster John Knox, 2001), pp. 145–53.

Meeks, Wayne, 'The Man from Heaven in Johannine Sectarianism', *JBL* 91 (1972), pp. 44–72.

Menken, M. J. J., *Old Testament Quotations in the Fourth Gospel. Studies in Textual Form*. CBET (Kampen: Pharos, 1996).

———, 'The Use of the Septuagint in three Quotations in John. Jn 10.34; 12.38; 19.24', in *The Scriptures in the Gospels*, ed. Christopher M. Tuckett. BETL (Leuven: Peeters, 1997), pp. 367–93.

———, 'Fulfilment of Scripture as a Propaganda Tool in Early Christianity', in *Persuasion and Dissuasion in Early Christianity, Ancient Judaism, and Hellenism*, ed. Pieter W. van der Horst and M. J. J. Menken. CBET (Leuven: Peeters, 2003), pp. 179–98.

Metzger, Bruce M., *A Textual Commentary on the Greek New Testament*. 2nd edn (New York, NY: United Bible Society, 1975).

Millard, Alan, *Reading and Writing in the Time of Jesus* (Sheffield: Sheffield Academic Press, 2001).

Minear, Paul S., 'Writing on the Ground: The Puzzle in John 8.1-11', *HBT* 13 (1991), pp. 23–37.

Misztal, Barbara A., *Theories of Social Remembering* (Philadelphia: Open University Press, 2003).

Mitchell, Margaret M., 'New Testament Envoys in the Context of Greco-Roman Diplomatic and Epistolary Conventions: The Example of Timothy and Titus', *JBL* 111 (1992), pp. 641–2.

Moessner, David P., *Lord of the Banquet: The Literary and Theological Significance of the Lukan Travel Narrative* (Minneapolis, MN: Fortress, 1989).

Moloney, Francis J., *John*. SP (Collegeville, MN: Liturgical Press, 1998).

———, 'The Gospel of John as Scripture', *CBQ* 67 (2005), pp. 454–68.

Morris, Leon, *The Gospel According to John*. NICNT (Grand Rapids, MI: Eerdmans, 1971).

Motyer, Steohen, *Your Father the Devil? A New Approach to John and 'the Jews'* (Carlisle: Paternoster Press, 1997).

Moxter, Michael, 2002. 'Erzählung und Ereignis: Über den Spielraum historischer Repräsentation', in *Der historische Jesus: Tendenzen und Perspektiven der gegenwärtigen Forschung*, ed. Jens Schröter and Ralph Brucher. BZNW (Berlin: de Gruyter, 2002), pp. 67–88.

Müller, M., 'Schriftbeweis oder Vollendung? Das Johannesevangelium und das Alte Testament', in *Bekenntnis und Erinnerung. FS H.-F. Weiß*, ed. Klaus-Michael Bull and Eckart Reinmuth. Rostocker Theologische Studien 16 (Münster: LIT Verlag, 2004), pp. 151–71.

Murphy O'Connor, Jerome, *St Paul's Ephesus: Texts and Archaeology* (Collegeville, MN: Liturgical, 2008).

Nagy, Gregory, 'Homeric questions', *TAPA* 122 (1992), pp. 17–60.

———, *Poetry as performance: Homer and Beyond* (Cambridge: Cambridge University Press, 1996).

Neirynck, Frans, 'John and the Synoptics', in *L'Èvangile de Jean: Sources, Rédaction, Théologie*, ed. Marinus de Jonge. BETL (Leuven: Leuven University Press, 1997).

Neufeld, Dietmar, *Reconceiving Texts as Speech Acts: An Analysis of I John*. BIS (Leiden: Brill, 1994).

Neyrey, Jerome H., 'Jesus the Judge: Forensic Process in John 8.21-59', *Bib* 68 (1987), pp. 509–41.

Niditch, Susan, *Oral World and Written Word* (Louisville, KY: Westminster John Knox, 1996).

Nissinen, Martti, 'What is Prophecy? An Ancient Near Eastern Perspective', in *Inspired Speech: Prophecy in the Ancient Near East. Essays in Honor of Herbert B. Huffmon*, ed. John Kaltner and Louis Stalman (London: T&T Clark, 2004), pp. 17–37.

Nora, Pierre, 'Between Memory and History: Les Lieux de mémoire', *Representations* 26 (1989), pp. 7–25.

———, *Realms of Memory: Rethinking the French Past*, ed. Lawrence D. Kritzman (New York, NY: Columbia Press, 1996).

Obermann, Andreas, *Die christologische Erfüllung der Schrift im Johannesevangelium. Eine Untersuchung zur johanneischen Hermeneutik anhand der Schriftzitate*. WUNT (Tübingen: Mohr Siebeck, 1996).

Olick, Jeffrey K, 'Products, Processes, and Practices: A Non-Reificatory Approach to Collective Memory', *BTB* 36 (2006), pp. 5–14.

Olick, Jeffrey K., and J. Robbins, 'Social Memory Studies: From "Collective Memory" to the Historical Sociology of Mnemonic Practices', *Annual Review of Sociology* 24 (1998), pp. 105–40.

Ong, Walter J., *Interfaces of the Word: Studies in the Evolution of Consciousness and Culture* (Ithaca, NY: Cornell University Press, 1977).

————, *The Presence of the Word: Some Prolegomena for Cultural and Religious History* (New Haven, CT: Yale University Press, 1981).

————, *Orality and Literacy: The Technologizing of the Word* (New York, NY: Methuen, 1982).

Overholt, Thomas W., *Prophecy in Cross-Cultural Perspective*. Sources for Biblical Study 17 (Atlanta: Scholars Press, 1986).

————, *Channels of Prophecy: The Social Dynamics of Prophetic Activity* (Minneapolis, MN: Fortress, 1989).

Packard, David W., 'Sound-Patterns in Homer', *TAPA* 104 (1974), pp. 239–60.

Painter, John, *The Quest for the Messiah: The History, Literature, and Theology of the Johannine Community*. 2nd edn (Nashville, TN: Abingdon, 1993).

————, *1, 2, and 3 John*. SP (Collegeville, MN: Liturgical, 2002).

————, Review of Paul N. Anderson, *The Fourth Gospel and the Quest for Jesus: Modern Foundations Reconsidered* (2006). *Review of Biblical Literature* (3 May 2008), http://www.bookreviews.org/bookdetail.asp?TitleId=5879.

Parker, David C., *The Living Text of the Gospels* (Cambridge: Cambridge University Press, 1997).

Parry, Milman, *The Making of Homeric Verse: Collected Papers of Milman Parry*, ed. Adam Parry (Oxford: Clarendon Press, 1987).

Parunak, H. Van Dyke, 'Oral Typesetting: Some Uses of Biblical Structure', *Bib* 62 (1981), pp. 153–68.

Pelikan, Jaroslav, *Jesus Through the Centuries: His Place in the History of Culture* (New York: Harper & Row, 1985).

Perkins, Pheme, *The Johannine Epistles*. New Testament Message 21 (Wilmington, DE: Michael Glazier, 1979).

Petersen, Norman R., *The Gospel of John and the Sociology of Light: Language and Characterization in the Fourth Gospel* (Valley Forge, PA: Trinity Press International, 1993).

Petersen, William L., 'What Text Can New Testament Textual Criticism Ultimately Reach?', in *New Testament Textual Criticism, Exegesis, and Early Church History: A Discussion of Methods*, ed. Barbara Aland and Joël Delobel (Kampen: Kok Pharos, 1994).

Plato, *Philebus*, trans. Harold North Fowler. LCL (Cambridge: Harvard University Press, 1925).

————, *Theaetetus*, trans. Harold North Fowler. LCL (Cambridge: Harvard University Press, 1952).

———— *Timaeus*, trans. R. G. Bury. LCL (Cambridge: Harvard University Press, 1961).

Pliny, *Natural History*, trans. H. Rackham. LCL (Cambridge: Harvard University Press, 1947).

Plotinus, *Enneads*, trans. A. H. Armstrong. LCL (Cambridge: Harvard University Press, 1984).

Popkes, Enno Edzard, '"Ich bin das Licht" – Erwägungen zur Verhältnisbestimmung des Thomasevangeliums und der johanneischen Schriften anhand der Lichtmetaphorik', in *Kontexte des Johannesevangeliums: das vierte Evangelium im religions- und tradiтionsgeschichtlicher Perspektive*, ed. Jörg Frey und Udo Schnelle. WUNT (Tübingen: Mohr Siebeck, 2004), pp. 641–74.

Quine, W. V. O., 'Two Dogmas of Empiricism', in *Philosophy of Science: The Central Issues*, ed. Martin Curd and J. A. Cover (New York, NY: W. W. Norton, 1998), pp. 288–301.

Quintillian, *Institutio Oratoria*, trans. Donald A. Russell. LCL (Cambridge: Harvard University Press, 2001).

Rahner, J., 'Er aber sprach vom Tempel seines Leibes', in *Jesus von Nazaret als Ort der Offenbarung Gottes im vierten Evangelium*. BBB (Bodenheim: Philo, 1998).

Ratzinger, Joseph, *Eschatology: Death and Eternal Life* (Washington, DC: Catholic University of America Press, 1988).

Reed, Christopher, 'Dazzlers: Ancients Reborn in Bright Array', *Harvard Magazine* 110 (2007), pp. 32–5.

Reinhartz, A., 'The Gospel of John: How "the Jews" Became Part of the Plot', in *Jesus, Judaism and Christian Anti-Judaism: Reading the New Testament after the Holocaust*, ed. Paula Fredriksen and Adele Reinhartz (Louisville, KY: Westminster John Knox, 2002), pp. 99–116.

———, 'John and Judaism: A Response to Burton Visotsky', in *Life in Abundance: Studies of John's Gospel in Tribute to Raymond E. Brown*, ed. John R. Donahue (Collegeville, MN: Liturgical Press, 2005), pp. 108–16.

Rensberger, David, *1 John, 2 John, 3 John*. ANTC (Nashville: Abingdon, 1997).

———, 'Conflict and Community in the Johannine Letters', *Int* 60 (2006), pp. 278–91.

Rhoads, David, *Reading Mark, Engaging the Gospel* (Minneapolis, MN: Fortress Press, 2004).

———, 'Performance Criticism, Part I and II', *BTB* 36 (2006), pp. 118–33, 164–84.

Richards, E. Randolph, *Paul and First-Century Letter Writing: Secretaries, Composition and Collection* (Downers Grove, IL: InterVarsity, 2004).

Rius-Camps, Josep, 'The Pericope of the Adulteress Reconsidered: The Nomadic Misfortunes of a Bold Pericope', *NTS* 53 (2007), pp. 379–405.

Robinson, Maurice A., 'Preliminary Observations Regarding the *Pericope Adulterae* Based upon Fresh Collations of Nearly All Continuous-Text Manuscripts and All Lectionary Manuscripts Containing the Passage', *Filología Neutestamentaria* 13 (2000), pp. 35–59.

Rösler, Wolfgang, *Dichter und Gruppe: Eine Untersuchung zu den Bedingungen und zur historischer Funktion früher griechischer Lyrik am Beispiel Alkaios.* Theorie und Geschichte der Literatur und der schönen Künste, Texte und Abhandlungen (Munich: W. Fink, 1980).

Ross, J. M., 'Floating Words: Their Significance for Textual Criticism', *NTS* 38 (1992), pp. 153–6.

Rubin, David C., *Memory in Oral Traditions: The Cognitive Psychology of Epic, Ballads, and Counting-out Rhymes* (New York, NY: Oxford University Press, 1995).

Rüsen-Weinhold, Ulrich, *Der Septuagintapsalter im Neuen Testament. Eine textgeschichtliche Untersuchung* (Neukirchen-Vluyn: Neukirchener Verlag, 2004).

Saenger, Paul, *Space Between Words: The Origins of Silent Reading.* Reading Medieval Culture (Stanford, CA: Stanford University Press, 1997).

Sanders, E. P., *Jesus and Judaism* (London: SCM, 1985).

Sandmel, Samuel, *Philo's Place in Judaism: A Study of Conceptions of Abraham in Jewish Literature* (New York: KTAV, 1972).

de Saussure, Ferdinand, *Course in General Linguistics*, ed. Charles Bally and Albert Sechehaye, trans. Roy Harris (LaSalle, IL: Open Court, 1986).

Scherlitt, Frank, *Der vorjohanneische Passionsbericht: Eine historisch-kritische und theologische Untersuchung zu Joh 2,13-22; 11,47-14,31 und 18,1-20, 29.* BZNW (Berlin: de Gruyter, 2007).

Schilling, Frederick A., 'The Story of Jesus and the Adulteress', *AThR* 37 (1955), pp. 91–106.

Schnackenburg, Rudolf, *The Johannine Epistles: Introduction and Commentary*, trans. Reginald Fuller and Isle Fuller (New York, NY: Crossroad, 1992).

Schnelle, Udo, *Antidoketische Christologie im Johannesevangelium: Eine Untersuchung zur Stellung des vierten Evangeliums in der johanneischen Schule.* FRLANT (Göttingen: Vandenhoeck & Ruprecht, 1987).

——, 'Die Tempelreinigung und die Christologie des Johannesevangeliums', *NTS* 42 (1996), pp. 359–73.

——, *The History and Theology of the New Testament Writings*, trans. M. Eugene Boring (London: SCM, 1998).

——, *Das Evangelium nach Johannes.* 3rd edn. ThHK (Leipzig: Evangelische Verlagsanstalt, 2004).

Schnelle, Udo, Michael Labahn and Manfred Lang, *Neuer Wettstein: Texte zum Neuen Testament aus Griechentum und Hellenismus. Bd. I/2: Texte zum Johannesevangelium* (Berlin: de Gruyter, 2001).

Scholtissek, Kurt, 'Ironie und Rollenwechsel im Johannesevangelium', *ZNW* 89 (1998), pp. 235–55.

———, *In ihm sein und bleiben: die Sprache der Immanenz in den johan-neischen Schriften*. HBS 21 (Freiburg: Herder, 2000).

———, '"Die unauflösbare Schrift" (Joh 10.35). Zur Auslegung und Theologie der Schrift Israels im Johannesevangelium', in *Das Johannesevangelium - Mitte oder Rand des Kanons? Neue Standortbestimmungen Quaestiones disputatae*, ed. Theodor Söding (Freiburg: Herder, 2003), pp. 146–77.

Schröter, Jens, 'Von der Historizität der Evangelien: Ein Beitrag zur gegen-wärtigen Diskussion um den historischen Jesus', in *Der historische Jesus: Tendenzen und Perspektiven der gegenwärtigen Forschung*, ed. Jens Schröter and Ralph Brucher. BZNW (Berlin: De Gruyter, 2002), 163–212.

———, 'Jesus and the Canon: The Early Jesus Traditions in the Context of the Origins of the New Testament Canon', in *Performing the Gospel: Orality, Memory, and Mark*, ed. Richard A. Horsley, Jonathan A. Draper and John Miles Foley (Minneapolis, MN: Fortress, 2006), pp. 104–22.

Schuchard, Bruce, *Scripture within Scripture. The Interrelationship of Form and Function in the Explicit Old Testament Citations in the Gospels of John*. SBLDS (Atlanta: Scholars Press, 1992).

Schudson, Michael, 'The Present in the Past Versus the Past in the Present', *Communication* 11 (1989), pp. 105–13.

———, *Watergate in American Memory: How We Remember, Forget, and Reconstruct the Past* (New York, NY: Basic Books, 1992).

———, 'Dynamics of Distortion in Collective Memory', in *Memory Distortion*, ed. Daniel Schachter (Cambridge, MA: Harvard University Press, 1995), 346–64.

Schutz, Alfred, *Alfred Schutz: On Phenomenology and Social Relations*, ed. Helmut R. Wagner (Chicago, IL: University of Chicago Press, 1970).

Schwartz, Barry, 'The Social Context of Commemoration: A Study in Collective Memory', *Social Forces* 61 (1982), pp. 374–402.

Scott, Bernard Brandon and Margaret E. Dean, 'A Sound Map of the Sermon on the Mount', in *SBL 1993 Seminar Papers*, ed. Eugene H. Lovering Jr (Atlanta: Scholars Press, 1993), 672–725.

Segovia, Fernando F., ed., *What Is John? Vol. 1: Readers and Readings of the Fourth Gospel* (Atlanta: Scholars Press, 1966).

Shiell, William D., *Reading Acts: The Lector and the Early Christian Audience*. BIS (Leiden: Brill, 2004).

Shils, Edward A., *Tradition* (Chicago, IL: University of Chicago Press, 1981).

Shiner, Whitney, *Proclaiming the Gospel: First-Century Performance of Mark* (Harrisburg, PA: Trinity Press International, 2003).

———, 'Memory Technology and the Composition of Mark', in *Performing the Gospel: Orality, Memory, and Mark*, ed. Richard A. Horsley,

Jonathan A. Draper and John Miles Foley (Minneapolis, MN: Fortress, 2006), 147–65.

———, 'Oral Performance in the New Testament World', in *The Bible in Ancient and Modern Media: Story and Performance*, ed. Holly E. Hearon and Philip Ruge-Jones. Biblical Performance Criticism (Eugene, OR: Wipf and Stock, 2009), pp. 49–63.

Siker, Jeffrey S., *Disinheriting the Jews: Abraham in Early Christian Controversy* (Louisville, KY: Westminster John Knox, 1991).

Simonides, *Lyra Graeca*, trans. J. Edmonds. LCL (Cambridge, MA: Harvard University Press, 1967).

Slusser, Michael, 'Reading Silently in Antiquity', *JBL* 111 (1992), pp. 499.

Small, Jocelyn P., *Wax Tablets of the Mind: Cognitive Studies of Memory and Literacy in Classical Antiquity* (New York, NY: Routledge, 1997).

Smalley, Stephen S., *1, 2, 3 John*. WBC (Waco, TX: Word, 1984).

———, *The Revelation to John: A Commentary on the Greek Text of the Apocalypse* (Downers Grove, IL: InterVarsity, 2005).

Smith, D. Moody, 'The Setting and Shape of a Johannine Narrative Source', in *Johannine Christianity: Essays on Its Setting, Sources, and Theology* (Columbia, SC: University of South Carolina Press, 1984a).

———, *Johannine Christianity: Essays on Its Setting, Sources, and Theology* (Columbia, SC: University of South Carolina Press, 1984b).

———, *John Among the Gospels: The Relationship in Twentieth-century Research* (Minneapolis, MN: Fortress, 1992).

———, *John*. ANTC (Nashville, TN, 1999).

———, *John Among the Gospels. The Relationship in Twentieth Century Research*. 2nd edn (Columbia, SC: University of South Carolina Press, 2001).

Snyder, H. Gregory, *Teachers and Texts in the Ancient World: Philosophers, Jews and Christians*. Religion in the First Christian Centuries series (New York, NY: Routledge, 2000).

Sorabji, Richard, *Aristotle on Memory* (Providence, RI: Brown University Press, 1972).

———, *Emotion and Peace of Mind: From Stoic Agitation to Christian Temptation* (Oxford: Oxford University Press, 2000).

Spaulding, Mary B., *Commemorative Identities: Jewish Social Memory and the Johannine Feast of Booths*. LNTS. (London: T&T Clark, 2009).

Stamps, Dennis L., 'The Use of the Old Testament in the New Testament as Rhetorical Device: A Methodological Proposal', in *Hearing the Old Testament in the New Testament*, ed. Stanley E. Porter. McMaster New Testament Studies. (Grand Rapids, MI: Eerdmans, 2006), pp. 9–37.

Stanford, William B., 'Greek Views on Euphony', *Hermathena* 61 (1943), pp. 3–20.

———, *The Sound of Greek: Studies in the Greek Theory and Practice of Euphony.* Sather Classical Lectures (Berkeley, CA: University of California Press, 1967).

Stanley, Christopher D., 'The Rhetoric of Quotations: An Essay on Method', in *Early Christian Interpretation of the Scriptures of Israel. Investigations and Proposals*, ed. Craig A. Evans and James A. Sanders. JSNTSup (Sheffield: JSOT Press, 1997), pp. 44–58.

———, *Arguing with Scripture. The Rhetoric of Quotations in the Letters of Paul* (New York: T&T Clark, 2004).

Stanton, Graham N., *Jesus and Gospel* (Cambridge: Cambridge University Press, 2004).

Stark, Rodney, *The Rise of Christianity: How the Obscure, Marginal Jesus Movement Became the Dominant Religious Force in the Western World in a Few Centuries* (San Francisco: HarperCollins, 1997).

Starr, Raymond J., 'Reading Aloud: *Lectores* and Roman Reading', *CJ* 86 (1991), 337–43.

Steck, Odel Hannes, 'Prophetische Prophetenauslegung', in *Wahrheit der Schrift-Wahrheit der Auslegung: Eine Zürcher Vorlesungsreihe zu Gerhard Ebelings 80. Geburtstag am 6 Juli*, ed. Hans Friedrich Geisser (Zürich: Theologischer Verlag, 1992), pp. 198–244.

Strauss, David Friedrich, *The Life of Christ Critically Examined*, ed. Peter C. Hodgson, trans. George Eliot (Philadelphia: Fortress, 1846, rpt 1972).

Strecker, Georg, *The Johannine Letters: A Commentary on 1, 2, and 3 John.* Hermeneia (Minneapolis, MN: Fortress, 1996).

Stuckenbruck, Loren T., David C. Barton and Benjamin Wold, eds, *Memory in the Bible and Antiquity.* WUNT (Tübingen: Mohr Siebeck, 2007).

Taylor, Vincent, *The Formation of the Gospel Tradition.* 2nd edn (London: Macmillan and Co., 1935).

Thatcher, Tom, 'The Sabbath Trick: Unstable Irony in the Fourth Gospel', *JSNT* 76 (1999), pp. 53–77.

———, *The Riddles of Jesus in John: A Study in Tradition and Folklore.* SBLMS (Atlanta: Society of Biblical Literature, 2000).

———, 'Why John Wrote a Gospel: Memory and History in an Early Christian Community', in *Memory, Tradition, and Text: Uses of the Past in Early Christianity*, ed. Alan Kirk and Tom Thatcher. Semeia Studies (Atlanta: Society of Biblical Literature, 2005a), pp. 79–97.

———, '1 John', in *Hebrews–Revelation*. Vol. 13 of *The Expositor's Bible Commentary*, Rev. edn, ed. Tremper Longman III and David E. Garland (Grand Rapids, MI: Zondervan, 2005b), pp. 413–505.

———, *Why John Wrote a Gospel: Jesus–Memory–History* (Louisville, KY: Westminster John Knox, 2006).

———, 'John's Memory Theater. The Fourth Gospel and Ancient Mnemo-Rhetoric', *CBQ* (2007), pp. 487–505.

————, ed., 'Beyond Texts and Traditions: Werner Kelber's Media History of Christian Origins', in *Jesus, the Voice and the Text: Beyond the Oral and the Written Gospel*, ed. Tom Thatcher (Waco, TX: Baylor University Press, 2008), pp. 1–26.

————, 'Riddles, Repetitions, and the Literary Unity of the Johannine Discourses', in *Repetitions and Variations in the Fourth Gospel. Style, Text, Interpretation*, ed. Gilbert van Belle, Michael Labahn and Pertrus Maritz. BETL (Leuven: Peeters, 2009).

Theissen, Gerd, 'Die Tempelweissagung Jesu', *TZ* 32 (1976), p. 144–58.

Theobald, Michael, 'Gezogen von Gottes Liebe (Joh 6.44f.). Beobachtungen zur Überlieferung eines johanneischen "Herrenworts"', in *Schrift und Tradition. FS Josef Ernst*, ed. Knut Backhaus and Franz Georg Untergassmair (Paderborn: F. Schöningh, 1996), pp. 315–41.

Thomas, John Christopher, 'The Order of the Composition of the Johannine Epistles', *NovT* 37 (1995), pp. 68–75.

————, 'The Literary Structure of 1 John', *NovT* 40 (1998), pp. 369–81.

Thomas, Keith, 'Introduction', in *A Cultural History of Gesture: From Antiquity to the Present Day*, ed. Jan Bremmer and Herman Roodenburg (Ithaca, NY: Cornell University Press, 1992), pp. 1–14.

Thomas, Rosalind, *Literacy and Orality in Ancient Greece* (Cambridge: Cambridge University Press, 1992).

Thyen, Hartwig, *Das Johannesevangelium*. HNT (Tübingen: Mohr Siebeck, 2005).

Tompkins, Jane P., ed., *Reader-Response Criticism: From Formalism to Post-Structuralism* (Baltimore, MD: The Johns Hopkins University Press, 1980).

Trebilco, Paul, *The Early Christians in Ephesus from Paul to Ignatius* (Grand Rapids, MI: Eerdmans, 2008).

Tuckett, Christopher M., 'The Fourth Gospel and Q', in *Jesus in Johannine Tradition*, ed. Robert T. Fortna and Tom Thatcher (Louisville, KY: Westminster John Knox, 2001), pp. 281–90.

Twelftree, Graham H., 'Exorcisms in the Fourth Gospel and the Synoptics', in *Jesus in Johannine Tradition*, ed. Robert T. Fortna and Tom Thatcher (Louisville, KY: Westminster John Knox, 2001), pp. 135–43.

Uro, Risto, '"Secondary Orality" in the Gospel of Thomas?' *Forum* 9 (1993), 305–29.

Vaganay, Léon and Christian-Bernard Amphoux, *An Introduction to New Testament Textual Criticism*, trans. Jenny Heimerdinger (Cambridge: Cambridge University Press, 1991).

van Belle, Gilbert, 'Tradition, Exegetical Formation, and the Leuven Hypothesis', in *What We Have Heard From the Beginning: The Past, Present, and Future of Johannine Studies*, ed. Tom Thatcher (Waco, TX: Baylor University Press, 2007), pp. 325–7.

van Belle, Gilbert, Michael Labahn and Petrus Martiza, eds, *Repetitions and Variations in the Fourth Gospel. Style, Text, Interpretation.* BETL (Leuven: Peeters, 2009).

van Lopik, T., 'Once Again: Floating Words, Their Significance for Textual Criticism', *NTS* 41 (1995), pp. 286–91.

Vansina, Jan, *Oral Tradition as History* (Oxford: James Currey, 1985).

Verheyden, Jack, 'The De-Johannification of Jesus: The Revisionist Contribution of Some Nineteenth-Century German Scholarship', in *John, Jesus, and History Vol. 1: Critical Appraisals of Critical Views*, ed. Paul N. Anderson, Felix Just and Tom Thatcher. SBLSymS (Atlanta: SBL, 2007), pp. 109–20.

Visotzky, Burton L., 'Methodological Considerations in the Study of John's Interaction with First-Century Judaism', in *Life in Abundance: Studies of John's Gospel in Tribute to Raymond E. Brown*, ed. John R. Donahue (Collegeville, MN: Liturgical Press, 2005), pp. 91–107.

von Campenhausen, Hans Freiherr, 'Zur Perikope von der Ehebrecherin (Joh 7.53–8.11)', *ZNW* 68 (1977), pp. 164–75.

Ward, Richard F., 'Pauline Voice and Presence as Strategic Communication', in *Orality and Textuality in Early Christian Literature*, ed. Joanna Dewey. Semeia 65 (Atlanta: Society of Biblical Literature, 1994), pp. 95–107.

Watson, Duane F., 'A Rhetorical Analysis of 2 John according to Greco-Roman Convention', *NTS* 35 (1989a), pp. 104–30.

——, 'A Rhetorical Analysis of 3 John: A Study in Epistolary Rhetoric', *CBQ* 51 (1989b), pp. 479–501.

——, 'Amplification Techniques in 1 John: The Interaction of Rhetorical Style and Invention', *JSNT* 51 (1993), pp. 99–123.

Wead, David W., *The Literary Devices in John's Gospel* (Basel: Friedrich Reinhart, 1970).

Webb, Stephen H., *The Divine Voice: Christian Proclamation and the Theology of Sound* (Grand Rapids, MI: Brazos, 2004).

Weissberg, Liliane, 'Introduction', in *Cultural Memory and the Construction of Identity*, ed. Dan Ben-Amos and L. Weissberg (Detroit, MI: Wayne State, 1999), pp. 7–26.

Welborn, Laurence L., 'Paul's Appeal to the Emotions in 2 Corinthians 1.1–2.13; 7.5-16', *JSNT* 82 (2001), pp. 31–60.

Williams, Catrin H., *I am He: The Interpretation of 'Anî Hû' in Jewish and Early Christian Literature.* WUNT (Tübingen: Mohr Siebeck, 2000).

Winger, Thomas M., 'The Spoken Word: What's Up with Orality?' *Concordia Journal* 29 (2003), pp. 133–51.

Wink, Walter, *John the Baptist in the Gospel Tradition.* SNTSMS (Cambridge: Cambridge University Press, 1968).

Wire, Antoinette, *The Corinthian Women Prophets: A Reconstruction through Paul's Rhetoric* (Minneapolis, MN: Fortress Press, 1990).

——, 'Who said, "I am the way, the truth and the life. No one comes to the Father but by me" (John 14.6)? A Debate between Church and Academy', in *From Biblical Interpretation to Human Transformation: Reopening the Past to Actualize New Possibilities for the Future. Essays Honoring Herman C. Waetjen*, ed. Douglas R. McGaughey and Cornelia Cyss Crocker (Salem, OR: Chora Strangers, 2002), pp. 171–81.

Wise, Michael, 'Temple', in *Dictionary of Jesus and the Gospels*, ed. Joel Green, Scot McKnight and I. Howard Marshall (Downer's Grove, IL: InterVarsity, 1992), pp. 810–16.

Witherington III, Ben, 'Sacred Texts in an Oral Culture: How Did They Function?' *BAR* 33 (2007), pp. 28, 82.

Wolter, Michael, 'Schriftkenntnis. Anmerkungen zu Joh 20.9', in *Fragmentarisches Wörterbuch. Beiträge zur biblischen Exegese und christlichen Theologie. Horst Balz zum 70. Geburtstag*, ed. Kerstin Schiffner, Klaus Wengst and Werner Zager (Stuttgart: Kohlhammer, 2007), pp. 343–52.

Wright, N. T., *The Contemporary Quest for Jesus* (Minneapolis, MN: Fortress Press, 2002).

Yaghjian, Lucretia B., 'Ancient Reading', in *The Social Sciences and New Testament Interpretation*, ed. Richard Rohrbaugh (Peabody, MA: Hendrickson, 1996), pp. 206–30.

Yates, Frances A., *The Art of Memory* (Chicago, IL: University of Chicago Press, 1996).

Yerushalmi, Josef, *Zakhor: Jewish History and Jewish Memory* (Seattle: University of Washington Press, 1996).

Yonge, C. D., http://classicpersuasion.org/pw/cicero/cicero-topics.htm (accessed 23 March 2009).

Zelizer, Barbie, 'Reading the Past Against the Grain: The Shape of Memory Studies', *Critical Studies in Mass Media* 12 (1995), pp. 214–39.

Zerubavel, Eviatar, 'In the Beginning: Notes on the Social Construction of Historical Discontinuity', *Sociological Inquiry* 63 (1993), pp. 457–59.

——, 'Social Memories: Steps to a Sociology of the Past', *Qualitative Sociology* 19 (1996), pp. 283–99.

——, *Time Maps: Collective Memory and the Social Shape of the Past* (Chicago, IL: Chicago University Press, 2003).

Zerubavel, Yael, 'The Historical, the Legendary and the Incredible: Invented Tradition and Collective Memory in Israel', in *Commemorations: The Politics of National Identity*, ed. John R. Gillis (Princeton, NJ: Princeton University Press, 1994), pp. 105–25.

————, *Recovered Roots: Collective Memory and the Making of Israeli National Tradition* (Chicago, IL: University of Chicago Press, 1995).

Zumstein, Jean, 'Der Prozess der Relecture in der johanneischen Literatur', in *Kreative Erinnerung. Relecture und Auslegung im Johannesevangelium*. 2nd edn. AThANT (Zürich: Theologischer Verlag, 2004), pp. 15–30.

————, 'Intratextuality and Intertextuality in the Gospel of John', in *Anatomies of Narrative Criticism. The Past, Present, and Futures of the Fourth Gospel as Literature*, ed. Tom Thatcher and Stephen D. Moore. SBLRBS (Atlanta: Society of Biblical Literature, 2008), pp. 121–35.

INDEX

Note: citations noted here may appear in main body text or in footnotes on the respective pages indicated.

Achtemeier, Paul   3, 16, 17, 19, 54, 58,
        75, 99, 135, 208
Aldrete, Gregory S.   22, 23, 26
Anderson, Paul N.   22, 74, 159, 170, 178
apocalyptic   163, 233–4, 235–7
apocryphal Gospels   60, 161, 182, 234
Aristotle   76, 77–80, 85, 141
Assmann, Aleida   2, 49
Assmann, Jan   2, 7, 49, 63–5, 67–8,
        189–91, 194, 211, 215,
        226, 232, 234
audience   11, 16, 22, 39–46, 68,
        76, 82, 83, 85–91, 127,
        153–4, 159, 165, 195,
        205–9, 213–17, 220, 233,
        239, 244–6
    direct address to   96–102, 103–
        20, 135, 138, 154
    live audience   2, 11, 4–7, 17–20,
        24, 26–7, 43–4, 46, 57–8,
        63–7, 89, 92–4, 100–2,
        209, 214–15, 239, 245,
        248
    original audience   4, 29–30,
        41–2, 45, 86–7, 101, 147,
        203, 205, 211, 213, 215,
        221, 245
    response to performance   5–6,
        26–7, 39–40, 57–8, 62–7,
        100–2, 106, 127, 206–8,
        215, 217, 229–30, 246
Aune, David E.   14, 124

baptism   129, 162, 164–5, 167
Barrett, C. K.   29, 34, 74, 89, 97, 206
Bauckham, Richard   16, 25, 56, 58, 97,
        111, 175, 188
Beutler, Johannes   134, 140, 141, 148,
        152, 181
Boomershine, Thomas E.   6, 92, 99, 229,
        246, 247
Brown, Raymond   11–12, 14–15, 16,
        20, 22, 31, 35, 56, 74,
        86, 89, 95, 96, 97, 122,
        129, 165, 196
Bultmann, Rudolf   3, 24, 42, 74, 89, 97,
        122, 196
Burge, Gary M.   20, 52, 56, 189
Byrskog, Samuel   3, 24, 133

Caragounis, Chrys C.   21, 177
Carson, D. A.   30, 86, 89, 97
Cebulj, Christian   122, 123, 128
chiasm   24, 31, 33, 42
Christology   12, 20, 37, 88, 97, 147,
        171, 176
Cicero   76–7, 78–84, 91, 141
collective memory   see memory,
        collective
commemoration   2, 8, 68, 186–90,
        191–5, 196–200, 203–5,
        211, 220
    narrative commemoration   68,
        191–2, 198, 222, 231
composition   1, 3–6, 11, 12, 14–21,
        24–5, 29–30, 34, 36–47,
        63, 74–5, 79–80, 83, 84,
        87, 90, 91, 99, 127, 131,
        133–4, 205–6, 211, 215,
        229, 247–8
    compositional dynamics   30, 39,
        42
    as 'free-standing'   39, 42
    and reading   see reading,
        composition
    as revision   17, 29, 38, 42, 74, 89
    and technique   74, 86, 88, 89,
        133, 209
composition history   1, 4, 29, 133–4, 248
constructionism   see memory, and pre-
        sentism
Culpepper, R. Alan   14, 29, 31, 33, 36,
        74, 97, 123, 126, 137,
        175, 177

Dean, Margaret E. 19, 21, 167, 174

Dewey, Joanna 3, 6, 17, 19–20, 24, 99, 133–4, 206–7, 208, 215, 241

Dodd, C. H. 22, 97, 121, 130, 160, 162, 167–8, 171, 173–4, 179, 196

drama 11, 22, 36, 94–6, 100–1, 127, 134, 216–18, 220
  'John as two–level' 94–5, 98, 112–13, 115, 211

Draper, Jonathan A. 49, 215

Dunn, James 2, 3–4, 8, 25, 53–5, 57–62, 65, 66, 133, 157, 159–62, 168, 169, 173, 174, 176, 179, 184, 193, 194, 204, 233, 237, 241–3

Durkheim, Emile 227–8, 232

early Christianity 41, 60–1, 69, 113, 145, 195–6, 203, 225, 235

Ehrman, Bart D. 62, 67, 237

Epp, Eldon Jay 53–4

Esler, Philip 213, 215, 218

exegesis 12, 19, 28, 116, 123, 186

false teachers 12, 15, 24, 125, 168, 169, 195, 196, 199, 200

Foley, John Miles 4, 17, 49, 126

Gamble, Harry 2, 6, 16–18, 49, 54, 65, 67, 99

Gerhardsson, Berger 3

gesture 5, 18, 22–4, 26, 232, 245

Goodspeed, Edgar J. 51

Graham, William A. 17, 147

Halbwachs, Maurice 7, 13, 49, 187, 190–1, 193, 195, 210–11, 213, 226, 231, 234

Harris, William 3, 15, 22, 75, 99, 123, 208

Hearon, Holly 6, 18, 49, 56–7

Hengel, Martin 134, 138, 145, 175

history 1–4, 8, 12–14, 68, 85, 90, 95, 98, 109, 116, 118–19, 122, 129, 131, 144, 151, 186–92, 194, 195, 198, 213, 227, 234, 235, 242
  composition history *see* composition history
  as fluid 56, 74
  manuscript history 3
  and memory 187–92, 232, 238–9

Holy Spirit 4, 6, 13, 85, 121, 125, 146, 163–4, 197

Horsley, Richard 2, 16, 24, 49, 54, 93, 215

Hurtado, Larry W. 54, 55, 61, 67

illiteracy 60, 63

illiterate 2–3, 15–17, 43, 59–61, 75, 225, 227, 229, 233, 236

inclusio 46, 207

Jesus 1–8, 12–13, 21, 29–31, 34, 36, 41, 46, 51–4, 56–9, 60–6, 68–9, 73–5, 85–91, 93–8, 100–19, 121–5, 128–32, 133–54, 157–85, 186–8, 195–200, 202–5, 205–9, 212–22, 225–37, 241–6, 248–9
  'the historical Jesus' 2–3, 8, 37, 53, 75, 85–6, 90, 130, 159, 186–8, 196, 203, 230, 237, 249
  identity of 6, 30, 47, 51–2, 98, 112–16, 117, 121, 129, 143–5, 209, 221, 237
  Johannine Jesus 1, 7, 51, 56, 134–7, 142, 144, 147, 150, 154, 161, 181, 183–4, 204, 212, 221–2, 249
  literacy of 5, 51, 236
  memories about 13, 56, 86–7, 125, 146, 163, 169, 176, 177, 179, 184, 196, 198, 200, 230
  speeches/discourses of 100–1, 114, 117–19, 125, 133, 139, 142–4, 146, 152, 169, 174, 176–9, 181, 207–9, 213–18, 234–5

Jewish Scriptures 7, 54, 67–8, 85, 111, 118, 122, 123, 125, 133–54, 186, 197–8, 201, 229–30, 232, 238, 245
  and Abraham 8, 205–9, 211–12, 212–22, 231
  authority of 136–40, 142, 145, 147–50, 152, 154
  and David 111, 116, 143–4, 201, 202, 204
  Gospels as 140
  and Mosaic law 27, 44, 46, 51–2, 61, 63, 95, 109, 118, 147, 204
  and Moses 44–6, 51–2, 94, 106, 116, 118, 129, 146–7, 148, 167, 169, 177, 205, 211
  and Torah 51, 59

'Jews, the' 51, 85, 87–8, 93–4, 96,
103–5, 107, 109, 111,
113–16, 118–19, 137,
140, 159, 171–2, 180,
182, 195, 197–8, 205,
207, 211–12, 218–19, 221
John the Baptist 4, 29–30, 33, 36–8,
41–4, 46–8, 89, 102–3,
107–8, 110, 117, 141,
159–162, 234, 243, 246

Keener, Craig S. 16, 139, 149
Keith, Chris 2, 5, 49–50, 53–4, 60, 63,
68, 227, 229, 236, 242–5,
247, 248–9
Kelber, Werner 3, 16, 18, 20, 30, 39–41,
47, 49, 53–8, 61, 63–6,
75, 99, 157, 208–10, 228,
233, 237–8, 241
Kirk, Alan 24, 49, 66, 133, 186, 188,
191–2, 198, 204, 210–11,
230, 235–6, 238
Köstenberger, Andreas J. 86, 143–4

Labahn, Michael 7, 133, 135–7, 139–43,
146, 151–3, 232, 242,
245–6, 249
language patterns 20, 229
lector 16, 18, 22–6, 120, 225,
228–30, 234–5, 236
Lieu, Judith 12, 14–15, 136, 218, 220
Lincoln, Andrew T. 139, 143, 169, 173,
211–12
literacy 5, 49, 51, 82–3, 140, 206,
229, 246, 247
    and dictation 16–17
    high degree of modern 2, 53,
98–9
    and knowledge 51, 213–14
    low degree of ancient 16, 59–60,
63, 75, 98–9, 123, 127,
210, 219, 238–9,
Logos 35, 37–9, 41–2, 46, 117,
154, 158

manuscripts 2–5, 44, 50, 52–4, 67–8,
98–9, 116, 154, 207, 233
Martyn, J. Louis 74, 94–8, 112–16, 211
memorization 2, 16, 24–5, 66, 82–3, 99,
209
memory 1–4, 6–8, 11, 16, 27–8,
56, 60, 75–91, 131, 134,
144, 168–9, 173–81,
186–200, 202–5, 206–7,
239–40, 247–8
    cognitive approaches to 13,
78–80, 84
    collective memory *see also*

memory, social memory
3, 4, 8, 13, 65–6, 158,
176–7, 180–1, 183–4,
187, 190–5, 205, 209–22,
227, 244
    counter-memory 13, 199–200,
218
    group memory 8, 66–9, 125,
146, 151, 160, 163–5,
168, 173, 175–6, 180–1,
183–4, 187, 191, 210–11,
214, 227, 244
    and history *see* history, and
memory
    and identity 1, 4, 7–8, 13, 65–9,
191–2, 211, 213–14, 216–
17, 222, 239, 244, 247
    individual/personal memory
24–5, 77–85, 99, 175,
187–94, 210, 225–7
    and presentism 231–3
    realist model of memory 232
    refraction of memory 189,
193–4, 200,
    social memory *see also*
memory, collective
memory 2, 7–8, 13, 49,
184, 186, 187–93, 209–
17, 221, 225–8, 230–4,
237–8, 242–5, 248
    and rhetoric 24–5, 41, 44, 73,
78–84, 91, 99, 205, 208,
230
    and visual aids 6, 75–9, 82,
86–7, 90–1
memory theatre 6, 76, 80, 83, 87–8, 90
Menken, M. J. J. 134–5, 143, 146–8,
150
mnemonic(s) 25, 188–9, 191, 193–4,
196–8, 200, 202–4, 208,
220–1
mnemotechnique 78–9, 82–4, 87, 90
Moloney, Francis J. 136, 139, 148, 150

Nagy, Gregory 127
narration 87, 89, 154, 161, 233
Nora, Pierre 7, 190, 192, 237–8

Ong, Walter 57, 60, 99, 133, 206,
208–9, 228
oral communication 1, 4, 15, 39, 41,
134, 206, 209, 215–16,
226–8, 235–6
oral culture 1–4, 25, 59–60, 135,
208–9, 225, 228, 238–42,
245–8
oral historians 3, 187
oral performance 1, 4, 16, 18, 22, 36,

39, 41, 43–4, 54, 57–9,
62, 66–7, 79–80, 83, 89,
91, 93, 98, 100–1, 106,
113, 126–7, 130–40, 157,
206–9, 212, 214–15,
221–2, 236, 239–41,
243–5, 247–8

oral tradition   2–5, 49, 54–9, 61, 64–6,
68, 121, 126–8, 131,
157, 159–61, 164, 169,
179, 185, 188, 225–8,
238, 240–4, 246–8
and aurality   1, 4–5, 18–22, 25,
28, 44, 46, 206–7, 214,
238, 239, 241
and discourse   13–14, 39
and history   3, 13, 227, 238
and transmission   66, 133, 157,
242, 245

orality   27, 49, 53–60, 63–6, 69,
75, 133–4, 140, 148, 206–
7, 209, 228–30, 233–8,
243, 245–6, 248
and aurality   11, 19, 27
'original form'   5, 30, 40, 52–3

performance   1–2, 4–7, 22–4, 39–44,
56–9, 66–9, 79, 89, 106–
7, 110, 112–16, 118–20,
151, 170, 184, 214–16,
221–2, 229, 231
fluidity of   39–42, 61–4, 241
and memory   1, 6, 11, 16, 27–8,
76, 78, 81–4, 87, 91,
241–2
oral performance   *see* oral performance
and text   16–19, 56–9, 62–4, 66,
92–3, 99–102, 116, 127,
139, 208, 227, 244–8

Plato   76–9, 82, 117, 141
presentism   *see* memory, presentism
Prologue (John 1:1-18)   11, 20–2, 25,
29–31, 33–9, 41–8, 90,
101–2, 113, 144, 171,
216, 229
prophecy (early Christian)   121–2, 124–6,
130, 201, 225, 229, 234–5

Quintillian   73, 76, 79–85, 91

reader (model/implied)   58, 64, 137–8,
142–4, 147–8, 150, 152–4
reading   1, 15–20, 29–30, 33–4,
37–44, 50–5, 57–64, 76,
84–6, 88–90, 97–101,
113–16, 121–5, 128–31,
133, 137–40, 146, 175,

180, 182–3, 203–4, 209,
211, 217, 225, 228, 235–
6, 239–40, 242–3, 245–6
and composition   5, 17, 53–4,
57–60, 63–4, 66, 74–5,
82, 128, 131
'mirror reading'   12
private/silent reading   6, 17, 22,
85, 92–3, 98–101, 116,
206
public reading   2, 5–6, 16, 17–
20, 22–7, 43–4, 46–7, 58,
60, 66–8, 93, 94–6, 100,
119–20, 134–5, 206–7,
214, 217, 229, 235–6,
248

Reinhartz, Adele   95, 216–17
Rensberger, David   20, 22
rhetoric   3, 6, 12–15, 21–4, 26,
56, 60, 74, 76, 77–80,
82, 84–5, 87, 133–5,
137, 139–41, 208–9, 229,
246–8
Rhoads, David   18, 93, 99
Richards, E. Randolph   16–17

Schnackenburg, Rudolf   14, 37–8, 89, 97
Schnelle, Udo   123, 137, 141–2, 146,
150–1, 166, 172, 176,
179
Scholtissek, Kurt   122, 136–7, 139, 146
Schröter, Jens   53, 60, 62, 203
Schudson, Michael   7, 189, 193, 210, 232
Schwartz, Barry   2, 7, 191–2, 216, 225
scribes   4, 16–18, 51–2, 54, 56,
61, 67, 75, 108
Shiner, Whitney   6, 16–17, 19, 24–7, 99,
233
signs (miracles of Jesus)   76, 83, 87–8,
90, 107, 117, 123, 125,
127, 131, 138, 151, 167,
170–2
Smalley, Stephen S.   22, 27
Smith, D. Moody   31, 74, 133, 142, 176
social memory   *see* memory, social
Sorabji, Richard   26, 77, 78–9
sound mapping (soundscape)   19, 45, 47
source criticism   40, 88, 241
Stanford, William B.   17, 19
Stanley, Christopher D.   137

textuality   2, 4–5, 11, 17, 23–4, 27,
37, 49, 52–67, 69, 75,
120, 134, 143–4, 145,
147, 150, 190, 206, 209,
243–4, 246
and copying   2, 41, 129, 157
and fixed texts   2

textualization 54–5, 64–5
Thatcher, Tom 1–2, 4, 6–7, 11–16, 29, 47, 49, 55–6, 59, 66, 73, 89, 135–6, 140, 175–6, 178, 186–8, 197–8, 204, 208, 210, 229–31, 235, 238–9, 246
Thomas, John Christopher 15, 24
tradition 3, 6, 13–15, 35, 41, 49–50, 55, 107, 110, 118, 122, 124–6, 128, 131, 138, 140, 157, 160–7, 170, 175, 183, 190–2, 194, 198, 205, 208, 211, 213, 215, 219, 231–3
    Jesus tradition 2–5, 8, 49–51, 53, 54, 57–8, 60–2, 64–6, 69, 107, 130, 133, 157–62, 165, 167, 170, 179, 181, 183–4, 195, 196, 227, 241–5, 248
    Johannine tradition 1, 5, 12, 50, 54, 121–5, 129, 161, 163–5, 168, 172, 174, 248–9
    oral tradition *see* oral tradition
    synoptic tradition 133, 157–9, 168, 172, 174–9, 182, 184, 242
    textual tradition 2, 44, 50, 53–6, 58, 61, 64, 66
    transmission of 21, 25, 60, 65–6, 68, 122–3, 241–4
    written tradition 2, 5, 49, 54, 56–7, 59, 62, 64–6, 68, 239, 241, 243–5, 247–8

Watson, Duane F. 14–15
wax (metaphor for memory) 59, 77, 79, 81–2
Wire, Antoinette 6, 121, 125, 229, 247, 248
writing 1, 4, 6, 8, 22, 24, 28, 35, 49, 51–2, 60–1, 64–6, 74–80, 84–5, 87, 98, 122–3, 126–7, 129, 133–4, 157, 179, 191, 234–5
    and authority 2–3, 7, 11–12, 77, 90, 114, 127, 135–54, 161, 190, 232–3
    and dictation 2, 16–17, 19, 89, 131, 227–8
    fluidity of 54–8, 243–5
    and knowledge 208–9
    for oral delivery 2, 17, 19–20, 25, 58, 66, 82–3, 89, 92–3, 99–100, 135, 142, 206, 223–4, 228–30, 238, 241–2, 246–7
    from oral material 4, 20, 31, 55, 58, 75, 89, 122, 162, 170
    and prophecy 124–6
    purpose of 12–16, 67, 198

Zerubavel, Eviatar 7, 216, 221, 231
Zerubavel, Yael 7, 68, 192
Zumstein, Jean 74, 122, 134, 138–9, 150